DOMESDAY

The Inquest and the Bo

DOMESDAY
The Inquest and the Book

DAVID ROFFE

OXFORD
UNIVERSITY PRESS

OXFORD
UNIVERSITY PRESS

Great Clarendon Street, Oxford OX2 6DP

Oxford University Press is a department of the University of Oxford.
It furthers the University's objective of excellence in research, scholarship,
and education by publishing worldwide in

Oxford New York

Auckland Bangkok Buenos Aires Cape Town Chennai
Dar es Salaam Delhi Hong Kong Istanbul Karachi Kolkata
Kuala Lumpur Madrid Melbourne Mexico City Mumbai Nairobi
São Paulo Shanghai Singapore Taipei Tokyo Toronto

and an associated company in Berlin

Oxford is a registered trade mark of Oxford University Press
in the UK and in certain other countries

Published in the United States
by Oxford University Press Inc., New York

© David Roffe 2000

First published 2000

First published in paperback 2002

British Library Cataloguing in Publication Data

Data available

Library of Congress Cataloging in Publication Data

Roffe, David.
Domesday : the inquest and the book / David Roffe.
Includes bibliographical references and index.
1. Domesday book. 2. Great Britain—History—Norman period, 1066–1154. 3. Real
property—England—History—To 1500. 4. Land tenure—England—History—To 1500. 5.
England—Economic conditions—1066–1485. 6. Manuscripts, Medieval—England. I.
Title.
DA190.D7 R64 2000 942.02—dc21 99–056324
ISBN 0–19–820847–2 (hbk)
ISBN 0–19–925725–6 (pbk)

1 3 5 7 9 10 8 6 4 2

Typeset by Graphicraft Limited, Hong Kong
Printed in Great Britain
on acid-free paper by
Biddles Ltd,
Guildford and King's Lynn

For CHRISTINE,
JOSCHKA, *and* THEO

Preface

EVERYONE HAS HEARD of Domesday Book. In the English-speaking world of today it may not be so sharply perceived as, say, Magna Carta, the Bill of Rights, or the Declaration of Independence. Nevertheless, it exists as a subliminal presence at the beginning of our common history. Mark Twain made good use of this fact, to considerable comic effect, in *Huckleberry Finn*.

My, you ought to have seen old Henry VIII when he was in bloom. He was a blossom. He used to marry a new wife every day, and chop off her head next morning. And he would do it just as indifferent as if he was ordering up eggs. 'Fetch up Nell Gwynn,' he says. They fetch her up. Next morning 'Chop off her head!' And they chop it off. 'Fetch up Jane Shore,' he says; and up she comes. Next morning, 'Chop off her head'— and they chop it off. 'Ring up Fair Rosamun.' Fair Rosamun answers the bell. Next morning, 'Chop off her head!' And he made every one of them tell him a tale every night; and he kept that up until he had hogged a thousand and one tales that way, and then he put them in a book, and called it Domesday Book—which was a good name and stated the case. (Chapter 23)

Twain's understanding of the origins of Domesday Book might be eccentric, but there can be no doubt that it struck a chord in his readership. Why this should be generally so is a complex story. There is clearly much to be said for a good name; 'Domesday Book' is as striking as the Tibetan Book of the Dead (or, come to that, H. P. Lovecraft's Necronomicon), and such a sonorous title is bound to guarantee some degree of celebrity. But this begs the question: how did Domesday Book come to merit its name?

It does not seem to have been founded in any defining ideology, for authorities of one sort or another have done little to bring the work into a sharp focus. It has always been perceived as a document of the first import-ance, but the very fact prevented the emergence of any consensus as to its significance. In the later medieval and post-medieval periods it was used by polemicists as a stick to beat their opponents with, and in the modern world it has become the subject of often equally acrimonious academic debate. Agreement has never persisted long enough to find its way into school text-books (or analysis has been too technical to warrant inclusion).

Far from taking a lead, on the contrary, politicians and historians have followed. The best explanation for the persistence of Domesday Book in the popular mind seems to lie in the survival of a genuine folk tradition. It received its name by the acclaim of the people rather than by the calculation of any government bureaucrat, and the continuous use of the document kept alive and fuelled a mystique that has resonated into the modern period. This enthusiasm is absent from sources contemporary with the Domesday inquest, but nevertheless developed at an early period. So it is that many of its themes have been taken as integral to the authentic history of the source. From the twelfth century Domesday Book has had a life of its own that has divorced it from the circumstances that engendered it.

This is, of course, a problem with any celebrated source—the traditions of a department of state can be as misleading in this respect as common prejudice—and in the last hundred years historians have rejected some of the more florid interpretations that Domesday has had to bear. But one element of what can be called the Domesday myth has survived to colour and determine analysis of the procedures and purpose of the Domesday enterprise. There remains an all-but universal conviction that the compilation of Domesday Book was the aim of the inquest recorded in the 1086 annal of the Anglo-Saxon Chronicle. This perception draws upon, and perpetuates, a misunderstanding of the nature of the inquest as an instrument of government.

The inquest is best known from the processes of the common law that developed in the late twelfth century. Here the verdict of a sworn jury was used as an instrument of peacekeeping, dispute resolution, and administration. It is exemplified *par excellence* in the tightly structured procedures of the eyre in which oral testimony was proved against written record. Here the procedure informed a bureaucratic process, and thus it is that which has been seen as an appropriate model for a Domesday inquest in which the objective was always the production of Domesday Book. The upshot has been that almost all studies of the purpose of Domesday have concentrated on the making of Great Domesday Book (GDB) and Little Domesday Book (LDB) on the assumption that, just as the verdict in the eyre was central to the pleas that ensued from the processes of policing, so the minutiae of data collection in the Domesday inquest were directly relevant to William's aims in late 1085.

Hence, for over a century now debate has centred on the supposed dichotomies of geographically and seigneurially arranged precursors of Domesday Book, of geld and service, and of public and private. All of this has become the commonplace of academic discourse. And yet if there is one feature that characterizes the results of all this research it is the signal failure of historians to produce a coherent explanation of the Domesday process; the Domesday data have consistently refused to be squeezed into the straitjacket of a neat schema.

It is argued here that this dislocation between the common ground of Domesday studies and the ability to explain is a direct function of anachronisms in the analysis. The historiography of Domesday bristles with common law concepts. The first task here has been to rescue the inquest from the uses to which it was put from the late twelfth century as a conscious tool of royal power. In essence the device was evidentiary rather than executive and in the context of a countrywide inquest, of which Domesday was an example, was

a truly investigative procedure that was employed to ascertain facts where record
was incomplete or unavailable or the mechanisms of local government were
untrustworthy. It had developed in pre-Conquest England as both the cause
and effect of the introduction of geld and was the principal forum in which
the common interests of the king and the free men of the shire were negotiated. So the device continued to function into the reign of Edward I until it
was to be superseded by parliaments.

The inquest, then, was no bureaucratic process. Its normal outcome was
not a recognition, but a verdict constituting agreed fact that informed future
action. It was an open-ended process in which, by definition, the end was
not predicated on the beginning. The immediate implication of this formulation is an unsettling one for the historian. Verdicts informed but did not determine decisions. Put more starkly, they were only contingently related to the
purpose of an inquest and its outcome. Domesday Book can no more embody
the whole business of the inquiry than any other document drawn up in the
Domesday process.

It is this that is the starting-point of a re-examination of the Domesday
texts and the processes that produced them. The analysis makes no assumptions about the integrity of the enterprise; the Domesday inquest is un-
coupled from the making of Domesday Book. For many, the conclusions will
be surprising, for some, heretical. Evidence will be presented to demonstrate that
Domesday Book, both LDB and GDB, was unrelated to the concerns which
launched the inquest in 1085. It seems to have been compiled, probably under
the supervision of Rannulf Flambard, from the records of the inquest after
1089 and is best interpreted as a response to the revolt, and consequent tenurial
chaos, of 1088. The Domesday inquest, by contrast, is emphatically concerned
with the exemption of demesne from the geld, and its findings were the basis
on which the king negotiated a reimposition of taxation in return for a
redefinition of personal service. The Domesday inquest was about both the
geld and knight service.

Far from being mutually exclusive, 'public' and 'feudal' dues can now be
seen to be complementary. The fact highlights a wider theme, the mutuality
and reciprocity of Anglo-Norman political and social interchange. The current consensus suggests that the Domesday inquest and Domesday Book were
the function of executive fiat (albeit with tasty carrots dangled in front of the
tenants-in-chief in the form of confirmation of honours to ensure co-operation).
This, of course, is a perception that embodies several agendas. Military and
administrative energy were defining ingredients of *Normanitas* as perceived by
contemporary Normans. But at the time the concept was used, perhaps consciously, to ideological ends; to the English, *Normanitas* was simply spoliation.
And it has continued so to be used. Normanists used to conceive of a people
come to cleanse and invigorate a corrupt realm, while Saxonists saw the imposition of a harsh tyranny over a free nation. These are categories to which no

historian would now own in public. Nevertheless, the notion of the all-embracing Domesday process still panders to an enduring Norman self-image.

It is a notion that has not gone unchallenged in recent years; the administrative efficiency of the Anglo-Norman polity has come into question in a number of areas. This study suggests that the Domesday inquest is hardly testimony to Norman omnicompetence. Most national inquests in the post-Conquest period were a response to crisis of one sort or another. In 1085, as historians have increasingly stressed in recent years, it seems to have focused on the problems created by an imminent invasion and the billeting of mercenaries recruited to counter it, and, as in the pre-Conquest period and subsequently, the inquest established a body of accepted fact on which an agreed course of action could be decided. William the Conqueror was in no position to dictate to his subjects. The Domesday inquest attests a king working with his barons and the community of the shire to a common end, albeit with an eye to striking as hard a bargain as he could.

It is probably only in the production of Domesday Book itself that the mechanical hand of the bureaucrat can be detected. With the development of the Domesday myth, of course, the document took on the well-documented public life of its own. But like subsequent abbreviations of inquest records, there is nothing to suggest that it was not compiled solely for the convenience of central government. The earliest references to the source call it 'the king's book', 'the book of the Exchequer', or simply 'the book of Winchester', and, significantly, the earliest copies in non-royal archives are of a relatively late date. This was no public record. It was, rather, a land register that was compiled and used for specifically administrative purposes.

The Domesday inquest and Domesday Book are, then, witnesses to two very different processes of society and government. The one, providing the grounds on which a political relationship was defined at a time of crisis and change, was truly communal. The other, although equally prompted by crisis, was merely an administrative aid. The Domesday processes identified in this study are irreducibly manifold, and as such conform more readily to the realities of eleventh-century politics and society than the monolithic schemas of contemporary orthodoxy.

Acknowledgements

IT IS NOW almost twenty-five years since I first opened Domesday Book and
wondered what it was all about. If the present volume goes any way to providing an answer to that most fundamental of questions, it will in large part
be due to the many scholars who have taught, inspired, and corrected me in
the intervening period. First, I owe a debt of gratitude to Professor Geoffrey
Martin who, as supervisor, oversaw my first tentative steps towards an understanding. Subsequently, as an editor and friend, he has been unfailingly generous with his encouragement, advice, and expertise. Likewise, I am indebted
to Professor Henry Loyn. His acute criticism has often checked my enthusi-
asms and pointed my researches into more productive directions. Above
all, I am grateful to Christine Mahany who, as director of the Stamford
Archaeological Research Committee, first gave me free rein and provided
me with the resources to pursue my academic interests. To all three I offer
my thanks.

My debts to the scholarship of others are equally extensive. There has been
no time since the publication of the text by Abraham Farley in 1783 when
Domesday Book was not the subject of lively debate, but the 900th anniver-
sary of the Battle of Hastings, and then of the Domesday inquest itself, have
seen a veritable explosion in interest. The outcome has been an unprecedented
number of significant publications in the last twenty years or so. Particularly
influential have been the work of Professor Robin Fleming, Dr Sally Harvey,
Professor Sir James Holt, Dr Katherine Keats-Rohan, Dr Christopher Lewis,
Dr John Palmer, Dr Ann Williams, Patrick Wormald, and the numerous con-
tributors to the Alecto County Edition of Domesday Book; all have inspired
me, if not always to agree with them, then at least to direct my thoughts to
the problems they raise. My debts to the many others who have contributed
to the Domesday debate will be apparent from the text.

The specific stimulus for the writing of this volume came out of a wider
study of the inquest as an instrument of government. In 1992 the Sheffield
Hundred Rolls Project was set up, under the direction of Professor Edmund
King and the present writer, with the financial assistance of the Leverhulme
Trust, to analyse, edit, and publish rolls from a series of late-thirteenth-
century inquests. The Domesday inquest was never conceived as an integral
part of the project, but it became clear from the early results that a major
re-evaluation of the Domesday texts was warranted. Throughout, reference
has been made to the research and thanks are therefore due, in the first place,
to the Leverhulme Trust without whom it would not have been undertaken,

and then to my colleagues Professor Edmund King and Dr Leonard Scales for their help and encouragement.

Although I have been known to seek out a volume in the middle of the night to settle a nagging doubt, Domesday Book and its related texts are not exactly bedtime reading. Neither are monographs on Domesday. It is, then, to Dr Katherine Keats-Rohan that I am the more grateful, for reading this book, not once but twice, in draft and commenting upon it. To her I owe the correction of many errors of fact, interpretation, and expression; this book is the better for all of her efforts. Similarly, I am indebted to Dr John Moore for reading early drafts of Chapters 6, 7, and 8 and for his comments thereon; I am no economic historian, and I am grateful to him for ensuring that my method was sound (or soundish) and my reading up to date. Dr Elizabeth Hallam-Smith kindly read the completed typescript. I am grateful to her for various incisive comments, but, above all, for her encouragement and enthusiasm for this reassessment of the Domesday process.

For much of the period of writing I was unavoidably confined to home, and so it is that I am grateful to several scholars for references and the discussion of various points by telephone, letter, and e-mail. Dr William Aird generously availed me of his deep knowledge of matters northern and in particular provided me with a possible reference to Rannulf Flambard in Durham before 1099; Dr Trevor Foulds drew my attention to the Basset cartulary with its rather inexpert transcript of Domesday material; Laurence Keen kindly provided me with information on the early Shaftesbury survey. I am especially grateful to Dr Ann Williams, who answered numerous queries in areas where I have no expertise, and to Dr Shaun Tyas, who willingly read out long passages from volumes in his extensive library at the drop of a hat. Many of the broader themes touched upon in this volume were first aired in the Friday Seminar at Sheffield; I owe a debt of gratitude to all those who participated, but in particular thanks are due to by Dr William Aird, Dr Timothy Cooper, Professor Edmund King, and Dr Leonard Scales, who, often unconsciously, helped me to define key concepts through their comments and criticisms. It remains true that all errors of omission, commission, or stupidity are entirely my own responsibility.

Thanks are due to the publishers of the *English Historical Review* and *Anglo-Norman Studies* for permission to print extracts from three of my articles on Domesday. This book was seen through the press with dispatch by Ruth Parr, Dorothy McLean, and Michael Watson, and I am grateful to them for making the experience a pleasurable one.

Finally, I have to thank my family. My wife Christine has steadfastly encouraged me throughout the writing, and my sons Joschka and Theo have displayed such forbearance as was in their capacity when faced with an often occupied and preoccupied father. To them is this book dedicated.

Contents

List of Tables   xv

Abbreviations   xvi

1. THE MYSTIQUE OF THE BOOK   1
   Domesday Book and Historical Writings   7
   Domesday Studies   10

2. DOMESDAY AND TITLE TO LAND   17
   The Norman Settlement   19
   Sokeright and Title to Land   28
   Domesday Book and Right to Land   46

3. THE INQUEST AND GOVERNMENT   49
   Recognition and Presentment   50
   The Origins of the Inquest in England   54
   The Domesday Inquest   67

4. THE DOMESDAY TEXTS   71
   Great Domesday Book   72
   Little Domesday Book   89
   The Liber Exoniensis   94
   The Inquisitio Comitatus Cantabrigiensis   98
   The Inquisitio Eliensis and Bath A   100
   The Crowland Domesday   101
   Schedules and Other Domesday Texts   106

5. THE COLLECTION OF DATA   113
   Forums and Organization   117
   The Royal Fisc and the *Inquisitio Geldi*   128
   The Estates of the Tenants-in-Chief   140

6. COMMISSIONERS AND THE LIMITS OF
   THEIR COMMISSION   147
   The Ploughland   149
   The Resolution of Disputes   165

7. CIRCUIT REPORTS   169
   The *Breves Regis* and the Geld Schedules   171
   Circuit Reports   172
   The Summaries   180
   Disputes   183

8. THE WRITING OF GREAT DOMESDAY BOOK   186
   Format and Content   187
   Diplomatic and the Order of Writing   191
   The Great Domesday Book Scribe and the Manor in
       the North   211
   The Great Domesday Book Scribe and the Manor in
       the South and West   216
   Great Domesday Book and Little Domesday Book   220

9. THE DOMESDAY INQUEST AND
   DOMESDAY BOOK   224
   The Domesday Inquest and Domesday Book   227
   The Royal Fisc and the Income of the Crown   230
   The Lord's Demesne and the Geld   234
   The Making of Domesday Book   242

10. AFTERWORD   249

Bibliography   252

Index   265

List of Tables

2.1. Groups of manors in the Lincolnshire breves of Walter de Aincurt and Peterborough Abbey — 26

2.2. King's thegns and holders of bookland in Leicestershire in 1066 as indicated by the *tenuit* formula — 38–9

2.3. Values in LDB, Bury C, and the Kalendar of Abbot Samson — 41

3.1. Five-hide units in Normancross Hundred, Huntingdonshire — 61

4.1. The opening folios of the Yorkshire Domesday — 77

4.2. The order of entries in the Cambridgeshire breves — 79

4.3. The order of vills in Longstow Hundred, Cambridgeshire — 80

4.4. The composition of the Huntingdonshire, Yorkshire, and Lincolnshire *clamores* — 84

4.5. Groups of manors in the count of Mortain's Yorkshire breve — 87

4.6. The scribes of LDB — 90–1

4.7. Entry forms in LDB — 92

4.8. The contents of Exon — 95

4.9. Domesday schedules — 107

5.1. Domesday circuits — 124

5.2. Cross-enrolment within circuits — 126

5.3. The *Roteland* Domesday — 129

5.4. Order of vills in the Yorkshire Summary account of the hundred of Howden — 137

6.1. Burton Abbey's overstocked manors and inland in 1114 — 156

6.2. Twelve-carucate hundreds in Nottinghamshire — 161

7.1. GDB account of the Isle of Axholme, Lincolnshire — 175

8.1. Ruling patterns in GDB — 192–3

8.2. GDB formulas — 196–7

8.3. Distribution of forms in the Yorkshire Domesday — 198–9

8.4. Distribution of sokeland forms in the Yorkshire and Lincolnshire folios — 200–201

8.5. The compilation of Circuit VI — 202

8.6. The compilation of Circuit III — 205

Abbreviations

Abingdon A	D. C. Douglas, 'Some Early Surveys from the Abbey of Abingdon', *EHR* 44 (1929), 623.
Abingdon B	—— 623–5.
ASC	*The Anglo-Saxon Chronicle: A Revised Translation*, ed. D. Whitelock, D. C. Douglas, and S. I. Tucker, 2nd edn. (London, 1963).
Attenborough	*The Laws of the Earliest English Kings*, ed. F. L. Attenborough (Cambridge, 1922).
Bath A	*Two Chartularies of the Priory of St Peter at Bath*, ed. W. Hunt, Somerset Record Society, 7 (1893), 67–8.
Bath B	—— 35–6.
Braybrooke Cartulary	G. H. Fowler, 'An Early Cambridgeshire Feodary', *EHR* 46 (1931), 422–3.
Burton B	J. F. R. Walmsley, 'Another Domesday Text', *Medieval Studies*, 39 (1977), 116.
Bury A	*Feudal Documents from the Abbey of Bury St Edmunds*, ed. D. C. Douglas (London, 1932), 1–15.
Bury B	—— 15–24.
Bury C	—— 25–44.
Crowland DB	*Rerum Anglicarum Scriptores Veteres*, ed. W. Fulman (Oxford, 1684), i. 80–2.
DB Beds.	*Domesday Book: Bedfordshire*, ed. J. Morris (Chichester, 1977).
DB Berks.	*Domesday Book: Berkshire*, ed. P. Morgan (Chichester, 1979).
DB Bucks.	*Domesday Book: Buckinghamshire*, ed. J. Morris (Chichester, 1978).
DB Cambs.	*Domesday Book: Cambridgeshire*, ed. A. Rumble (Chichester, 1981).
DB Cheshire	*Domesday Book: Cheshire*, ed. P. Morgan (Chichester, 1978).
DB Cornwall	*Domesday Book: Cornwall*, eds. C. and F. Thorn (Chichester, 1979).
DB Derby.	*Domesday Book: Derbyshire*, ed. P. Morgan (Chichester, 1978).
DB Devon	*Domesday Book: Devon*, eds. C. and F. Thorn (Chichester, 1985).
DB Dorset	*Domesday Book: Dorset*, eds. C. and F. Thorn (Chichester, 1983).
DB Essex	*Domesday Book: Essex*, ed. A. Rumble (Chichester, 1983).

DB Gloucs.	*Domesday Book: Gloucestershire*, ed. J. S. Moore (Chichester, 1982).
DB Hants.	*Domesday Book: Hampshire*, ed. J. Mumby (Chichester, 1982).
DB Hereford.	*Domesday Book: Herefordshire*, eds. F. and C. Thorn (Chichester, 1983).
DB Herts.	*Domesday Book: Hertfordshire*, ed. J. Morris (Chichester, 1976).
DB Hunts.	*Domesday Book: Huntingdonshire*, ed. S. Harvey (Chichester, 1975).
DB Kent	*Domesday Book: Kent*, ed. P. Morgan (Chichester, 1983).
DB Leics.	*Domesday Book: Leicestershire*, ed. P. Morgan (Chichester, 1979).
DB Lincs.	*Domesday Book: Lincolnshire*, ed. P. Morgan and C. Thorn (Chichester, 1986).
DB Middlesex	*Domesday Book: Middlesex*, ed. J. Morris (Chichester, 1975).
DB Norfolk	*Domesday Book: Norfolk*, ed. P. Brown (Chichester, 1984).
DB Northants.	*Domesday Book: Northamptonshire*, eds. F. and C. Thorn (Chichester, 1979).
DB Notts.	*Domesday Book: Nottinghamshire*, ed. J. Morris (Chichester, 1977).
DB Oxon.	*Domesday Book: Oxfordshire*, ed. J. Morris (Chichester, 1978).
DB Rutland	*Domesday Book: Rutland*, ed. F. Thorn (Chichester, 1980).
DB Salop	*Domesday Book: Shropshire*, eds. F. and C. Thorn (Chichester, 1986).
DB Somerset	*Domesday Book: Somerset*, eds. C. and F. Thorn (Chichester, 1980).
DB Staffs	*Domesday Book: Staffordshire*, ed. J. Morris (Chichester, 1976).
DB Suffolk	*Domesday Book: Suffolk*, ed. A. Rumble (Chichester, 1986).
DB Surrey	*Domesday Book: Surrey*, ed. J. Morris (Chichester, 1975).
DB Sussex	*Domesday Book: Sussex*, ed. J. Morris (Chichester, 1976).
DB Warks.	*Domesday Book: Warwickshire*, ed. J. Morris (Chichester, 1976).
DB Wilts.	*Domesday Book: Wiltshire*, eds. C. and F. Thorn (Chichester, 1979).
DB Worcs.	*Domesday Book: Worcestershire*, eds. F. and C. Thorn (Chichester, 1982).
DB Yorks.	*Domesday Book: Yorkshire*, eds. M. L. Faull and M. Stinson (Chichester, 1986).

Descriptio Terrarum D. R. Roffe, 'The Descriptio Terrarum of Peterborough Abbey', *Historical Research*, 65 (1992), 15–16.

Domesday Monachorum A *The Domesday Monachorum of Christ Church Canterbury*, ed. D. C. Douglas (London, 1944), 80–1.

Domesday Monachorum B —— 81–98.

Domesday Monachorum D —— 98–9.

Domesday Monachorum E —— 99–104.

EHD *English Historical Documents.*

EHR *English Historical Review.*

Ely A *Inquisitio Comitatus Cantabrigiensis*, ed. N. E. S. A. Hamilton (London, 1876), 168–73.

Ely B —— 174–5.

Ely C —— 175–83.

Ely D —— 184–9.

Evesham A P. H. Sawyer, 'Evesham A, a Domesday Text', *Miscellany 1*, Worcestershire Historical Society (1960), 22–36.

Evesham F London, British Library, Cotton MS Vespasian B xxiv, fo. 11^r.

Evesham K —— fos. 57^r–62^r.

Evesham M —— fos. 62^r–63^v.

Evesham P London, British Library, Harleian MS 3763, fo. 71^v.

Evesham Q —— fo. 82^r.

Excerpta *An Eleventh-Century Inquisition of St Augustine's, Canterbury*, ed. A. Ballard, Records of the Social and Economic History of England, 4 (London, 1920), 1–33.

Exon *Libri Censualis, vocati Domesday Book, Additamenta ex Codic. Antiquiss. Exon Domesday; Inquisitio Eliensis; Liber Winton; Boldon Book*, ed. H. Ellis (London, 1816).

GDB *Great Domesday*, ed. R. W. H. Erskine (London, 1986).

ICC *Inquisitio Comitatus Cantabrigiensis*, ed. N. E. S. A. Hamilton (London, 1876), 1–96.

IE —— 97–167.

Kentish Assessment List R. S. Hoyt, 'A Pre-Domesday Kentish Assessment List', in *A Medieval Miscellany for Doris Mary Stenton*, eds. P. M. Barnes and C. F. Slade, Pipe Roll Society, NS 36 (1960), 199–202.

LDB *Domesday Book; seu Liber Censualis Willelmi Primi*, ii (London, 1783).

Orderic Vitalis *The Ecclesiastical History of Orderic Vitalis*, ed. M. Chibnall, 6 vols. (Oxford, 1969–80).

PRO Public Record Office, London.

Robertson *The Laws of the Kings of England from Edmund to Henry I*, ed. A. J. Robertson (Cambridge, 1925).

S	P. H. Sawyer, *Anglo-Saxon Charters: An Annotated List and Bibliography*, Royal Historical Society Guides and Handbooks, 8 (1968).
TRE	*Tempore Regis Edwardi*, 'in the time of King Edward', i.e. 1066 or before.
TRW	*Tempore Regis Willelmi*, 'in the time of King William', i.e. between 1066 and 1086.
VCH	*Victoria History of the Counties of England.*
Worcester A	*Hemingi Chartularium Ecclesiae Wigornensis*, ed. T. Hearne (Oxford, 1723), 83–4.
Worcester B	―― 298–313.

The Mystique of the Book

ON CHRISTMAS DAY 1085 William, duke of Normandy and conqueror and king of England, had much thought and deep discussion with his council at Gloucester about England:

how it was occupied or with what sort of people. Then he sent his men over all England into every shire and had them find out how many hundred hides there were in the shire, or what land and cattle the king himself had in the country, or what dues he ought to have in twelve months from the shire. Also he had a record made of how much land his archbishops had, and his bishops and his abbots and his earls—and though I relate it at too great length—what or how much everyone had who was occupying land in England, in land or cattle, and how much money it was worth. So very narrowly did he have it investigated, that there was no single hide nor virgate of land, nor indeed (it is a shame to relate but it seemed no shame for him to do) one ox nor one cow nor one pig which was there left out, and not put down in his record; and all these records were brought to him afterwards.[1]

So wrote the English author of the E version of the Anglo-Saxon Chronicle about what is now known as the Domesday survey or inquest.

Remarkably for the period, there survives from the process a mass of documentation of one sort or another.[2] The Liber Exoniensis of Exeter Cathedral (hereafter referred to as Exon) preserves a contemporary record of the evidence presented in the south-western shires, and the Inquisitio Comitatus Cantabrigiensis (ICC) is a twelfth-century copy of a compilation of the data collected in Cambridgeshire. Various other snippets of information from similar stages in the inquiry are also known, but by far the most substantial survival is the two volumes of Domesday Book itself preserved in the Public Record Office in London. Volume one, known as Great Domesday Book (GDB), is an abbreviation of records of the inquest. Its 382 closely written folios (that is, 764 pages) contain an account of the whole of England south of the Tees, except for the

---

[1] *ASC* 161–2. In addition to folio numbers and columns of the MSS, references to the Domesday text are made to the Phillimore edition throughout since the numbering of entries facilitates precise identification. Place-names and personal names are usually given in the form there recorded. There are, however, some deviations since usage is by no means consistent throughout the edition. Moreover, the Feilitzenization of some forms in the later volumes has been reversed so that old friends remain familiar. Hereweard, for example, has reverted to the more usual Hereward. I have generally preferred my own translations. The Alecto and Ordnance Survey facsimiles and the MSS themselves have been consulted for all paleographical matters.

[2] See abbreviations, pp. xvi–xix.

three counties of Norfolk, Suffolk, and Essex, and of those parts of Wales that had been conquered by the Normans by 1086. Volume two, Little Domesday Book (LDB) is somewhat more expansive, containing a description of the three missing East Anglian counties in its 450 folios.

The scope of the enterprise is impressive and it duly impressed and appalled the annalist in equal measure. By the strict standards of evidence he must be deemed guilty of hyperbole. The number of oxen and kine recorded in the extant Domesday corpus would be hardly enough to keep a minute proportion of the population of late-eleventh-century England in shoes, and the number of pigs noted (notional or otherwise), although large, would make bacon for breakfast a rare treat for king and peasant alike. Nevertheless, the annalist's exaggeration is fully justified in the cause of literary effect.[3] As a record of a realm the Domesday inquest was unprecedented in England and probably unparalleled in medieval Europe. For every county there is an account, manor by manor and tenement by tenement, of the lands of the king, his ministers and almsmen, bishops and clerics, and every tenant-in-chief in various degrees of detail, along with an assessment of the tax liability of each unit, its economic and social resources, and its value. The statistics are impressive: thirty-three counties described in full; 25,000 personal names of those holding in 1066, some 19,500 of lords and tenants in 1086;[4] innumerable place-names relating to over 13,000 settlements; 270,000 unnamed inhabitants of various degrees of freedom; 81,000 plough teams; 2,061 churches; 6,082 mills; and much, much more.[5] As the annalist hints, there is something almost indecent in the extent and depth of the information that William demanded and received.

The Anglo-Saxon Chronicle preserves an English and, strictly speaking, an ecclesiastical view of the survey. But the author, probably writing within a year of the events he describes,[6] was not alone in his wonderment at the process. An account of the survey by Robert Losinga, bishop of Hereford, exhibits more measured tones but nevertheless manages to convey a sense of extraordinary events.

[In the] twentieth year of his reign by order of William, king of the English, there was made a survey [*descriptio*] of the whole of England; of the lands in each of the counties; of the possessions of each of the magnates, their lands, their manors [*mansionibus*], their men both bond and free, living in cottages or with their own houses and lands; of ploughs, horses, and other animals; of the services and payments due from all the men in the whole land. Other investigators followed the first and were sent to counties that they did not know, and where they themselves were unknown,

[3] Darby, *Domesday England*, 172–4. (For full details of works cited in the notes, see Bibliography.)
[4] Keats-Rohan, *Domesday People*, 15.
[5] Darby, *Domesday England*, 336–71, providing a handy summary of statistics.
[6] Clark, *The Peterborough Chronicle*, p. xxi.

to check the first description and to denounce any wrongdoers to the king. And the land was vexed with much violence arising from the collection of the king's taxes.[7]

Unless the last sentence is intended as a comment on the process (which might suggest a perhaps anachronistic socialist sensibility), Robert's account is neutral. But, as a senior Norman cleric and tenant-in-chief, it is likely that he was consulted at Gloucester and it must therefore be supposed that he had assented to the enterprise. Indeed, co-operation by magnates is illustrated by a third notice of the inquest, a letter written by Lanfranc, archbishop of Canterbury, sometime in the course of the survey, to a royal official identified as 'S':

Lanfranc, an unworthy bishop, greets his dear and loyal friend S. and sends him his blessing. I am most grateful for your thoughtfulness and goodwill, in that from the outset of our acquaintance you have assured me of your friendship and whenever the occasion offered you have always been ready to prove it in practice. Now once more I pray and beseech you—though you have no need of so many prayers—to act as effectively on our behalf in the present business as the opportunity to do so is given you from on high. I confirm that in those counties in which you have been assigned the duty of making an inquest I have no demesne land; all the lands of our church in those parts are entirely given over to providing food for the monks. The brother who is bringing you this letter has told me a great deal in your favour, too much to be set out here in the brief limits of a letter. May almighty God, whose memory nothing escapes, recompense you according to his knowledge many times over and be your vigilant helper at all times to defend you from every evil machination.[8]

LDB preserves a record of what use 'S' made of this information.

The reception of the inquest by the commonality of English and Anglo-Norman society was less sanguine. The impact of the survey was clearly widespread; the surviving documentation attests the participation of all levels of society, from the humblest peasant to the closest allies of the king, in hundreds of records of their presentments provided in manor courts, village assemblies, and hundred and shire courts. Such a great enterprise cannot have failed to impress on the populace the momentousness of the undertaking, and it was evidently a momentousness that inspired suspicion. Echoing the restrained outrage of the 1085 annal, Robert of Hereford's note hints at popular agitation, for he would have us believe that the vexation of the country by taxation was a direct function of the inquest. It was this, the inquest and its consequences, that was the focus of the contemporary accounts, and contemporary popular judgement would seem to have been generally adverse.

[7] Stevenson, 'A Contemporary Description of the Domesday Survey', 74. This passage is echoed in a copy of Marianus' History probably from Worcester (BL Cotton MS, Nero C v). It reads: 'William, king of the English, ordered all of the possessions of the whole of England to be described, in fields, in men, in all animals, in all manors from the greatest to the smallest, and in all payments which could be rendered from the land of all. And the land was vexed with much violence proceeding therefrom.' See, Stevenson, 'A Contemporary Description of the Domesday Survey', 77.

[8] *Letters of Lanfranc*, no. 56; Barlow, 'Domesday Book: A Letter of Lanfranc', 289.

That judgement and its focus was soon to change. Probably throughout the Middle Ages, and certainly into the thirteenth century, the documentation of the inquest survived and was used by government; many early references to the survey may have been to this material.[9] But popular perception soon fixed on Domesday Book itself. The first explicit notice of the work is a reference to the *liber regius* in an authentic writ probably of 1099–1101.[10] Writing was still in progress (or was yet to start) in the early years of the reign of William Rufus,[11] and it seems clear that 'the writings' that the annalist asserts were taken to the king must have been the inquest records. Domesday Book was relatively late on the scene, but it was soon to command an approbation that the records from which it was compiled had never commanded. The transformation in opinion is largely invisible, but was probably fostered by continual use in one form or another. How commonly Domesday Book was consulted in the course of routine administration in the aftermath of the survey is unknown. There are a number of writs that appear to refer to the work in the early twelfth century. In the 1120s, for example, Henry I ordered that services be restored to the lands of Ely 'which my Winchester charter shows to have been sworn to its fee'.[12] But, judging from the clean state of the manuscript, it was relatively little used throughout the Middle Ages— copies or breviates were probably preferred, a number of which survive. Nevertheless, throughout the period it did travel around the country with the Exchequer,[13] and, moreover, most tenants-in-chief of any substance seem, latterly at least, to have had copies of the description of their own lands made, *inter alia*, for record purposes. For fifty or so years after 1086 Domesday Book must in one way or another have continually impinged on the consciousness of local communities.

Familiarity fostered recognition. By the early twelfth century Domesday Book had become the purpose of the Domesday inquest in the mind of a Worcester annalist. Paraphrasing the 1085 annal of the Anglo-Saxon Chronicle, he subtly changes its import with an explicit reference to the volume:

A.D. 1086. William, king of the English, sent through all the provinces of England, and caused it to be inquired how many hides were held in the whole of England, and how much the king had in lands and cattle and livestock in each province, and what customary dues each year. This he caused to be done in respect of the lands and dues both of all the churches and of all his barons. He inquired what these were worth, and how much they then rendered, and how much they were able to render in the time of King Edward. And so thoroughly was all this carried out that there did not remain in the whole of England a single hide or a virgate of land or an ox

---

9 See below, pp. 242–3.
10 Galbraith, 'Royal Charters to Winchester', 389.
11 Lewis, 'The Earldom of Surrey and the Date of Domesday Book', 327–36.
12 *Regesta Regum*, ii, no. 1500. For others, see ibid., nos. 236, 373, 386a, 468, 976, 1000, 1488, 1515.
13 *Dialogus de Scaccario*, 62–3; Hallam, *Domesday Book Through Nine Centuries*, 34.

or a cow or a pig which was not written in that return [*in breviatione illa*]. And all the writings of all these things were brought back to the king. And the king ordered that all should be written in one volume [*volumen*], and that that volume should be placed in his Treasury at Winchester and kept there.[14]

Probably at much the same time Domesday Book began to assume its reputation as an authority unparalleled in this worldly realm. It is variously referred to in official records as 'the king's book', 'the book of the Exchequer', or 'the book of Winchester'.[15] But *c.*1179 Richard fitz Neal wrote in the Dialogue of the Exchequer that the survey was commonly known by the native English as Domesday, that is, the Day of Judgement:

for as the sentence of that strict and terrible last account cannot be evaded by any skilful subterfuge, so when this book is appealed to on those matters which it contains, its sentence cannot be quashed or set aside with impunity. That is why we have called the book 'the Book of Judgement,' not because it contains decisions on various difficult points, but because its decisions, like those of the Last Judgement, are unalterable.[16]

From the mid-thirteenth century 'the book called Domesday' became the official name for the document.[17] But already by the late twelfth century the transformation from notorious Domesday inquest to famous Domesday Book was complete.

The stage was set for the birth of a mystique that has survived to the present day. By the time that fitz Neal wrote, Domesday Book was largely irrelevant to the government of England; its data were outdated and its format was not conducive to revision for use as a working record. It was, paradoxically, this obsolescence that fostered its mystique. Domesday Book not only documented the roots of post-Conquest English society, but did so in a form that had become especially evocative. By the early twelfth century the codex was not the normal repository of record. Anglo-Norman governance was characterized by the employment of rolls. The book was redolent of more solemn writings, notably scripture. It would seem, then, that the apocalyptic referent of the survey's popular name was not entirely a function of whimsy. And it was a symbolism that was clearly not lost on the early twelfth-century Worcester annalist; it would no doubt be fanciful to see in his assertion that William ordered Domesday Book to be written and placed in the Treasury an echo of the practice of placing a book on an altar when a solemn gift was made,[18] but he clearly perceived of an appropriate place for such a special artefact.

Domesday became an icon precisely because it was a book, and, like scripture, its mystique was enhanced by limited access. The very concept of a

[14] *EHD* ii. 853. [15] Galbraith, *Domesday Book*, 103–4.
[16] *Dialogus de Scaccario*, 64. [17] Hallam, *Domesday Book Through Nine Centuries*, 34.
[18] Clanchy, *From Memory to Written Record*, 204–5.

public document was probably meaningless until the fourteenth century: it was only in 1372 that the principle of copying documents for legal use, whether the evidence went for the king or against him, was accepted.[19] Even then, as the oldest and most treasured public document, Domesday Book was hedged about with restrictions on its use. Some early transcriptions, such as that preserved in the Historia Croylandensis,[20] may suggest some browsing. But from the late thirteenth century it was one of the records that was in the charge of two clerks or deputies of the chamberlain in the Receipt of the Exchequer, and they had the responsibility for making searches and copying extracts, for which, from 1279, they were entitled to charge.[21] From the 1470s exemplifications were made in Carolingian minuscule to reflect the authority and no doubt dignity of the text, a custom only otherwise found in the copying of final concords where a twelfth-century hand was employed. These arrangement remained in place, with little modification, until 1826.[22] It was, to be fair, as difficult consulting any other record. Nevertheless, the effect was to place a premium on the data.

As such Domesday Book attained extraordinary talismanic status in the Middle Ages. It was the fount of all wisdom for the perplexed: in the Ragman inquiry of 1274/5 a number of juries suggested that the commissioners might search Domesday to resolve problems of ancient status and standing.[23] It was the hope of the oppressed: countless villeins paid for exemplification of entries in Domesday to demonstrate a privileged status as tenants of royal demesne.[24] It was the ultimate protection of the endowed: lords and communities appealed to the survey to protect and enforce their title to land and liberties.[25] Appeal to the source might be more in belief in its legendary powers than knowledge of its contents. Litigants frequently sought corroboration of the line of boundaries, the details of service, or the nuances of status where Domesday was quite irrelevant. But only in the determination of ancient demesne, with its corollaries of higher taxes for the crown and less burdensome services for villeins, was its evidence clear-cut and effective. Nevertheless, despite the repeated frustration of expectation, Domesday Book retained its aura of consummate authority into the modern period. It continued to be cited in court cases well into the nineteenth century, although cases dropped off markedly after the abolition of fines and recoveries in ancient demesne in 1833. The document still remains a legal public record; in 1969 a judge sitting in Liverpool Crown Court cited it in a case which was brought to decide whether a motor car

[19] *Rotuli Parliamentorum*, ii. 314.
[20] Roffe, 'The Historia Croylandensis: A Plea for Reassessment', 93–108.
[21] Hallam, *Domesday Book Through Nine Centuries*, 56–7.   [22] Ibid. 57.
[23] See e.g. *Rotuli Hundredorum*, i. 354a.
[24] Hallam, *Domesday Book Through Nine Centuries*, 54, 199–209.
[25] Ibid. 199–209.

registration book was a public document. In 1958 it was used to verify the right to a market in Taunton in a dispute over rating and methods of valuation.[26]

Citation in court is now, of course, a quaint rarity. But Domesday Book retains its authority in popular consciousness as the ultimate imprimatur of heritage. Before immigration from the Commonwealth in the 1950s, there was scarcely a single Englishman who was not a lineal descendant of landholders named in Domesday Book, and yet there is a subtle social cachet in claiming to be able to point to a particular William, a Richard, or a Roger as an ancestor. Anthony Trollope made much of the comic possibilities of such pretensions in *The Small House at Allington*:

'I think something of my family, I can assure you, Adolphus, and so does my husband,' [said Lady Amelia de Courcy].

'A very great deal,' said Mr Gazebee.

'So do I of mine,' said Crosbie. 'That's natural to all of us. One of my ancestors came over with William the Conqueror. I think he was one of the assistant cooks in the king's tent.'

'A cook!' said young de Courcy.

'Yes, my boy, a cook. That was the way most of our old families were made noble. They were cooks, or butlers to the kings—or sometimes something worse.'

'But your family isn't noble?

'No, I'll tell you how that was. The king wanted this cook to poison half-a-dozen of his officers who wished to have a way of their own; but the cook said, "No, my Lord King; I am a cook, not an executioner." So they sent him into the scullery, and when they called all the other servants barons and lords, they only called him Cookey. They've changed the name to Crosbie since that, by degrees.'[27]

Where family has not provided, the estate agent can oblige. What greater recommendation can there be for a house than the confident assertion that 'it appears in the Domesday Book',[28] or, in the face of incontrovertible evidence of modern construction, that the local community to which it has so recently become an adornment has the distinction of being mentioned in the same? Domesday Book may be used to ground a rudderless society in a certain past in the face of an unsure future, but it is still a guarantee of authenticity in its own right.

Domesday Book and Historical Writings

As an icon of national identity and, for some, a touchstone of liberty, Domesday Book is paralleled by Magna Carta and the Bill of Rights. Its mystique, however,

---

[26] Ibid. 174.   [27] Trollope, *The Small House at Allington*, 324.

[28] The use of the definite article here is a sure sign of a layman. The initiated always omit it, a distinction that even the Bible does not share (although Magna Carta does). How conscious are historians that the usage is an implicit acceptance and promotion of the mystique?

has been far more pervasive and nowhere more so than in historiography.
Perhaps reflecting perceptions of the relative importance of the inquest, up
to the early twelfth century passages from Domesday Book do not seem to
have been copied. Early cartularies like those of Peterborough and Worcester,
compiled between 1086 and 1130, preferred documents from the inquest.[29]
Although it is now impossible to prove the point, the survival of so much documentation from this stage of the Domesday process may be entirely owed to
early copyists. Thereafter, it was Domesday Book that mesmerized adminis-
trators and historians alike. Tenants-in-chief and religious houses appeared
to have wanted copies of the entries relating to their land as a matter of course;
a Domesday section is a common feature of medieval cartularies after the
mid-twelfth century.[30] Concern with title was probably never far from their
minds. But at the same time there was also a desire to record the information for its own sake because Domesday Book embodied a decisive stage in
the history of their family or community. A cartulary of the Basset family of
Weldon in Northamptonshire illustrates this concern.[31] It contains the Domesday account of the main Basset estates in Nottinghamshire and Derbyshire,
but none can be proved therefrom to have been held by the family in 1086.
Indeed, the incompetent transcription and the muddling of settlements (notably
Car Colston with Colston Basset, the later *caput* of the fee) would have made
the document unusable in a court of law. Its only purpose can have been
historical. This perception of Domesday as a point of departure in English
history is, needless to say, by and large justified. For the vast majority of
families, communities, and settlements it provides the first datum of a history.

The fact has fuelled a wider ideology. From an early period Domesday Book
was perceived as a turning-point in English history. For the author of the E
version of the Anglo-Saxon Chronicle history was primarily about chaps, and,
as a cleric, he was alive to the wider significance of their actions within the
world. So it was that he took the opportunity of a pitiful account of the famine
in 1087 to comment on the virtues of men. Chief among these was, of course,
the king himself and his closest advisors.

[29] London, Society of Antiquaries, MS 60, the Black Book of Peterborough; *Hemingi Chartularium*.
Claims have been made that sections of Heming's cartulary were extracted from GDB (*DB Worcs.*,
Appendix V). For a detailed discussion of these texts, see below, pp. 106–12. Only one copy of the
privileges of Oswaldslow Hundred is identical with the entry at the beginning of the bishop of
Worcester's Worcestershire breve (GDB 172c: *DB Worcs.*, 2,1; App. V, Worcs. F). It must be remembered, however, that the bishop's breve appears not to have been compiled by the GDB scribe but
to have been copied from a cathedral source. See below, pp. 143, 208. Worcester D, a schedule of
geld liability of 28 tenants-in-chief in Worcestershire, exhibits the same order of fees as GDB, but is
clearly not directly derived from it since it contains information on exemptions that is not found there
(*DB Worcs.*, Worcs. D). For the Bath Cartulary, see below p. 101.

[30] Hallam, *Domesday Book Through Nine Centuries*, 53. There has been no systematic listing of
Domesday extracts in medieval cartularies. It is, of course, impossible to determine when Domesday
Book passages were first copied in the later compilations.

[31] Northampton Record Office, ZB 347. I am grateful to Dr Trevor Foulds for drawing my attention to this source.

But such things happen because of the people's sins, in that they will not love God and righteousness. So it was in those days, there was little righteousness in this country in anyone, except in monks alone where they behaved well. The king and the chief men loved gain much and over-much—gold and silver—and did not care how sinfully it was obtained provided it came to them. The king sold his land on very hard terms—as hard as he could. Then came somebody else, and offered more than the other had given, and the king let it go to the man who had offered more. Then came the third, and offered still more, and the king gave it into the hands of the man who offered him most of all, and did not care how sinfully the reeves had got it from poor men, nor how many unlawful things they did. But the more just laws were talked about, the more unlawful things were done. They imposed unjust tolls and did many other injustices which are hard to reckon up.[32]

This passage anticipates the obituary of William that the annalist appended to the same annal following the king's death in Normandy on 9 September 1087. According to him, William was wise and powerful, a stern and violent man who respected God but was merciless to those who opposed his will. Good and bad were mixed with an energy that at once inspired in the annalist admiration and fear. His sentiments could as easily refer to the Norman Conquest.

How the Domesday inquest fitted into his perceptions of William's reign is not made explicit; he notes it merely as a species of adroit political intrigue. Echoing the wonderment expressed in the 1085 annal he comments: 'He ruled over England, and by his cunning it was so investigated that there was not one hide of land in England that he did not know who owned it, and what it was worth, and then set it down in his record.'[33] But the context suggests a wider understanding. He goes on to assert that: 'Wales was in his power, and he built castles there, and he entirely controlled that race. In the same way, he also subdued Scotland to himself, because of his great strength. The land of Normandy was his by natural inheritance, and he ruled over the county called Maine; and if he could have lived two years more, he would have conquered Ireland by his prudence and without any weapons.'[34] It would seem that the annalist saw the Domesday inquest as a means by which England had been brought to submit to William's will.

This was a theme that, projected onto Domesday Book, was to be developed in the later Middle Ages and subsequently. The generation following the Domesday inquest was as circumspect as the annalist. The E chronicle's 1085 account of the Domesday inquest was widely copied in the twelfth century and later.[35] Robert of Hereford's version was also influential. Appended to a shortened copy of the Universal History of Marianus Scotus, it was to find its way to Worcester where Robert's interpretation was to influence a number of historians into the next century.[36] In the 1120s Henry of Huntingdon

[32] *ASC* 162–3.   [33] *ASC* 164.   [34] *ASC* 164.   [35] See e.g. *EHD* ii. 853.
[36] Hallam, *Domesday Book Through Nine Centuries*, 35–6.

combined elements of both, and this composite version was to inform numerous other works into the thirteenth century.[37] In the later twelfth century, however, wider inferences were being drawn, apparently fostered by the shift in interest from the Domesday inquest to Domesday Book itself, with all of its semi-sacral connotations. Writing in the Dialogue of the Exchequer, Richard fitz Neal perceived a high political programme in the survey:—

> Domesday Book . . . is the inseparable companion in the Treasury of the royal seal. The reason for its compilation was told to me by Henry, bishop of Winchester, as follows. When the famous William 'the Conqueror' of England, the Bishop's near kinsman, had brought under his sway the farthest limits of the island, and had tamed the minds of the rebels by awful examples, to prevent error from having free course in the future, he decided to bring the conquered people under the rule of written law. So, setting out before him the English laws in their threefold versions, namely Mercian law, Dane law, and Wessex law, he repudiated some of them, approved others and added those Norman laws from overseas which seemed to him most effective in preserving the peace. Lastly, to give the finishing touch to all this forethought, after taking counsel he sent his most skilful councillors in circuit throughout the realm. By these a careful survey of the whole country was made, of its woods, its pastures and meadows, as well of arable land, and was set down in common language and drawn up into a book; in order, that is, that every man may be content with his own rights, and not encroach unpunished on those of others.[38]

The theme was further developed by Matthew Paris in the mid-thirteenth century. For him Domesday Book was equally the aim of the Domesday inquest and it was here that 'the manifest oppression of England began'.[39] It was a sentiment that was to inform political thought into the modern period; it was the common currency of the Levellers in the Civil War and it coloured the debate between Whigs and Tories in the eighteenth and nineteenth centuries.[40]

Domesday Studies

Domesday Book is no longer the subject of political discourse. Resonances of the debate, however, have persisted in scholarly discussions, and to the present day awe of the document itself has continued to influence interpretation. The last hundred years has seen the growth of a veritable cottage industry in which the study of the Domesday text has developed into an arcane speciality in its own right. As in any discipline, debates and controversies have arisen, but certain basic assumptions have been all but universally accepted. The undoubted authority that Domesday Book enjoyed from its completion has fostered the idea that it was conceived with a single-mindedness of purpose

---

[37] *Henrici Archdiaconi Huntendunepsis Historia Anglorum*, 207.
[38] *Dialogus de Scaccario*, 62–3.
[39] *Matthei Parisienis Historia Anglorum*, iii. 172.
[40] Hallam, *Domesday Book Through Nine Centuries*, 37, 132–4.

and seen through to completion by the exercise of royal will: Domesday Book was the aim of the Domesday inquest, the product of a strong government with a mission.

Implicit in this perception is the assumption that the process was essentially executive and bureaucratic. So it is that the model adopted, consciously or unconsciously, for the procedure of the inquest has been the well-documented processes of the common law. Bureaucratic procedures there are exemplified by the conduct of the eyre. As in the Domesday inquest, the verdict of the sworn jury was central to the process. In reply to the articles of the eyre the hundred jurors presented the matters that had come before them since the last eyre and provided information on such other concerns as from time to time the justices decreed. Their evidence was checked against the records of local government and pleas ensued. Finally, the jury made a recognition and the justices then pronounced judgement.[41] The process is a fully integrated one. The jury's role was subordinate to the aim of the whole enterprise, and its presentments, in both form and content, reflected that aim; it initiated a process of indictment that led to resolution.

The model is an appropriate one where Domesday Book is seen as the aim of the Domesday inquest. It is, moreover, one that is of supreme convenience. Contemporary sources are silent on the purpose of the whole enterprise and here is a method of recovering that purpose. As the engine of an integrated process, the presentments of the Domesday jurors and the returns that are made from them must embody what the inquest, and by extension Domesday Book, was about. Thus it is that all critical study of Domesday has been founded on the content of the Domesday verdicts and the form of the texts that record them. The Bible, here as an expression of divine will, is perhaps the only other text in the world that has been subject to such a detailed analysis of its composition and precursors to the end of uncovering its purpose.

These, the terms of the debate, were effectively set by John Horace Round. Up to the late nineteenth century analysis of the survey was largely confined to antiquarian studies of Domesday Book. Round changed all that. His was a penetrating analytical mind honed to a fine acuity through acrimonious debate in the otherwise gentlemanly world of medieval genealogy. Bringing it to bear upon the purpose and procedures of the Domesday inquest and Domesday Book, he produced a brilliantly incisive examination of the survey in a series of essays published in 1895 in a volume entitled *Feudal England*.[42] His starting-point was not Domesday Book, but ICC, a geographically arranged precursor of the GDB account of Cambridgeshire. The hundredal structure of the

---

[41] Bolland, *The General Eyre*, 48–54; Crook, *Records of the General Eyre*, 30–4. For the imperceptible blurring of the inquest and the business of the eyre, see Cam, *Studies in the Hundred Rolls*, 15, 30, 127–38 and id., *Hundred Rolls*, 39–46. She traces the articles of the inquest of 1274/5 to the articles of the eyre and presupposes a similar procedure.

[42] Round, *Feudal England*, 1–146.

document provided a seemingly incontrovertible explanation for the common hundredal sequences of entries in the seigneurial *breves* of GDB, and the conclusion was self-evident: 'the original returns' of the inquiry were compiled vill by vill and hundred by hundred, only to be subsequently rearranged in the feudal form of Domesday.

The analysis was immediately accepted at the time and still remains impressive. Round himself was never explicit as to what he understood to be the function of Domesday Book. What was undeniable was that the inquest was a fiscal matter. It was left to Maitland, writing in the following year, to draw out the implications of the argument. Every item of data in Domesday Book, from assessment through ploughlands, demesne ploughs, population, and resources to value, was germane to geld assessment: 'Domesday Book is no register of title, no register of all those rights and facts which constitute the system of landholdership. One great purpose seems to mould both its form and its substance; it is a geld book.'[43] For him, Domesday Book was a geld list and the purpose of the inquiry was to reassess liability.

Round introduced the term 'return' into the debate and, with the endorsement of Maitland, the quest of every student of Domesday since has been to elucidate the form of these so-called satellites.[44] Round's method has never been questioned. The analysis was a powerful one and, although details of the argument were rejected, even his identification of 'the key to Domesday' remained unchallenged for almost fifty years. It was, however, to be attacked with devastating effect by Galbraith in 1942 and more fully in 1961.[45] Galbraith was quick to point out that the tenurial arrangement of Domesday Book was hardly conducive to its use in the collection of a geographically based tax. Starting with the seigneurially arranged Exon, a series of documents that are precursors of the Domesday account of the south-western counties, he argued that the feudal form of Domesday Book was intended from the very conception of the inquiry on Christmas Day at Gloucester in 1085, and that the text was compiled through a series of recensions that distilled a mass of seigneurially arranged material ordered by geographical lists of estates into the required form. The purpose of Domesday Book was no less than a feudal register of the new Norman order.

The all-important fact about Domesday is that it is our earliest public record, carefully preserved by the officers of the king's household for more than eight centuries, and so to be found today at the Public Record Office, Chancery Lane, where it can be seen in the Museum. There must be some good reason to explain this lone survivor of the Conqueror's no doubt considerable archives. And it is not far to seek; for, in striking contrast with later official surveys, the prudent Norman clerks at

[43] Maitland, *Domesday Book and Beyond*, 25.
[44] For a summary of work up to 1085, see Clarke, 'Domesday Satellites.' For subsequent additions to the menagerie, see Roffe, 'Yorkshire Summary' and 'Historia Croylandensis'.
[45] Galbraith, 'Making of Domesday Book' and *Making of Domesday Book*.

Winchester, subordinating completeness to practical utility, deliberately jettisoned more than half the information gathered by the king's *legati*, commissioners or justices, compressing the mass of statistics into a single volume, albeit a large one. It was, in short, a forward-looking handy summary, made to last. And so it proved, having served ever since as the blueprint of the new society created after 1066.[46]

In the aftermath of the tenurial revolution that the Conquest had seen, William the Conqueror had inaugurated military tenures, and Domesday Book was to act as both a guide to the Norman settlement and an administrative instrument for the management of the new dues to which the king had become entitled.

Galbraith had done little to explain the form of ICC; the lameness of his discussion of the document is as resounding as Round's silence on Exon.[47] Nevertheless, his analysis is now generally preferred to the Round thesis. Scholars have discussed the merits of various 'satellites' to elucidate different stages in the process,[48] but the only significant modification has been to propose a role for pre-existing documentation. Dr Sally Harvey has argued that seigneurially arranged documents were routinely used in the course of shrieval administration and it was they that informed the procedure of the Domesday inquest and determined the form of Domesday Book.[49] However, the link that Galbraith proposed between Domesday Book and the Norman Conquest and settlement has been further elaborated. Professor Hyams has argued that title was the central concern of the inquest. He postulated that right to land could be established either by producing a writ or evidence of the delivery of the land of an *antecessor*, that is, a pre-Conquest holder of land whose estates had been granted *en masse* to a Norman successor, likening the procedure to the late-thirteenth-century *Quo Warranto* proceedings where title was either established by charter or immemorial usage.[50] The case has been even more eloquently formulated by Professor Sir James Holt. In an article published in 1987 he argued that Domesday Book cannot be understood without consideration of the Oath of Salisbury which was sworn on 1 August 1086. The event is recorded in the Anglo-Saxon Chronicle: 'Then [King William] travelled about so as to come to Salisbury at Lammas; and there his councillors came to him, and all the people occupying land who were of any account over all England, no matter whose vassals they might be; and they all submitted to him and became his vassals, and swore oaths of allegiance to him, that they would be loyal to him against all other men.'[51] The event has long been seen as a crucial moment in the development of English government,

---

[46] Galbraith, *Domesday Book*, 18–19.
[47] Galbraith, *Making of Domesday Book*, 123–35. Galbraith is not at his most lucid in this passage.
[48] See e.g. Sawyer, 'Original Returns', 'Evesham A'.
[49] Harvey, 'Domesday Book and its Predecessors'.
[50] Hyams, ' "No Register of Title": The Domesday Inquest and Land Adjudication', 135–6.
[51] *ASC* 162.

when the king established the principle of liege lordship regardless of feudal bonds. But Holt further asks the pertinent question: what did they do homage for? The answer, he contends, is the lands recorded in Domesday Book and he concludes: 'Domesday Book seems to embody a hard-headed deal. William got a survey of his own and his tenants' resources; he was strengthened in the exercise of his feudal rights. His tenants got a record of their tenure, in effect a confirmation of their enfeoffment. In short, as regards the tenant-in-chief, Domesday Book was a vast land book which put a final seal on the Norman occupation.'[52] Domesday Book afforded secure title to what had been precariously held. It is almost as if it is a continuation of the Bayeux Tapestry by other means.

This view has recently been endorsed by Professor Robin Fleming in her study of the legal content of Domesday Book.[53] However, it has not met with universal acceptance. In parallel with the 'Norman order' school there has developed what can be termed a neo-fiscal view. Harvey has recognized that Domesday Book is about the transfer and possession of land, but asserts that its principal aim was to introduce a new fiscal rating to replace the geld. For her the reign of William was a period of increasing financial embarrassment for government as exemption from the geld compromised the king's ability to raise taxation. The immediate occasion of the Domesday inquest was the prospect of imminent invasion in 1085 and William's need to raise cash to pay mercenaries, and its aim was to record the resources and value of estates to the end of assessing ploughlands, a fiscal measure to replace the existing assessments in hides, carucates, and sulungs.

A coherent assembly of the evidence accumulated suggests the following picture. In or following the military crisis of 1084–5, William started a reappraisal of fiscal liability in the south-west. It seems to have been unsuccessful. It was certainly short-lived: further abbreviations of DB by the Exchequer omitted it altogether and preserved the 1066 rating in them. William had in 1084 already extorted a huge geld of 6s on the hide which was not completely collected, so there was little possibility of increasing the levy on the existing rating. Moreover, on that rating many of the wealthiest lands lay untapped and exempt. It seems likely that the abortive attempt at reappraisal formed a motive for the searching enquiry into assets and possibilities (and by inference into exemptions and their validity) called Domesday Book, with the ploughland representing a completely new assessment . . .[54]

Domesday Book was primarily a tax book.[55]

This view in its turn has been rejected. Harvey has maintained that the routine fiscal documents of local government that were used in the making

---

[52] Holt, '1086', 56.

[53] Fleming, 'Oral Testimony and the Domesday Inquest', 101–22; Fleming, *Domesday Book and the Law*.

[54] Harvey, 'Taxation and the Ploughland in Domesday Book', 103.

[55] Ibid. 86–103; Harvey, 'Taxation and the Economy', 249–64.

of Domesday Book were already seigneurially arranged and implies that the seigneurial form of Domesday Book perpetuated this practice. Dr Nicholas Higham, however, has objected that Domesday Book is hardly an adequate record for the collection of taxation and avers that there is no sign of a reassessment after the inquest; the geld continued to be collected on the basis of the Domesday assessments into the twelfth century. Rather, he sees the process as a concession to the lesser baronage and the rear vassals. Again, the crisis of 1085 was the context. William's mercenaries had been billeted on the baronage, but the burden must have been distributed according to geld assessment and this would have favoured the king and greater barons to the detriment of the rest of feudal society.

If [Domesday Book] was not directed at the distribution of geld, it follows that it was concerned with the billeting which had been imposed during 1085, in which case Domesday Book was a novel solution to a novel imposition. It created a register capable of a fairer allocation of this burden than had been possible using existing geld lists, by including the near geld-free *terra regis* and all those estates of the great vassals that enjoyed beneficial hidation. This was perhaps the only major concession which William could make, given his urgent need of renewed taxation and the necessity of billeting mercenaries over what must have seemed an indefinite period. By commissioning the Domesday Book, William was conceding an equality of misery to his baronage and agreeing to shoulder an equivalent share of that misery himself. The new system was demonstrably fairer than the geld lists as a basis for the quartering of troops.[56]

Domesday Book as quartermaster's manual.

The range of interpretation is considerable, and yet all, from Round's interpreter, Maitland, to Higham, share a common assumption that Domesday Book was the aim of the Domesday inquest and that the process was an executive and bureaucratic one. Holt's analysis, it is true, has the merit of introducing a communal element into the equation. He has rightly recognized that whatever the king wished to achieve, the inquiry could only command the co-operation of tenant-in-chief and peasant alike by recognizing their sensibilities and addressing their concerns. Fleming has gone further; for her the Domesday inquest was a drama in which the Norman settlement was re-enacted, and its conflicts resolved, in the theatre of the local courts by and on behalf of local communities.[57] Nevertheless, both Holt and Fleming still understand that the business of the inquiry, and of its record Domesday Book, was the confirmation of title by the king. None of the hypotheses has commended itself unreservedly to a wider audience.[58] The Norman-order school has failed convincingly to explain why it was felt necessary to initiate the inquest

---

[56] Higham, 'Domesday Survey', 17–18.
[57] Fleming, *Domesday Book and the Law*, 11–35.
[58] For the latest review, see Kapelle, 'Domesday Book: F. W. Maitland and his Successors', 620–40.

in 1085, some nineteen years after the Conquest, while the exponents of neo-fiscalism cannot point to any tangible change in the fiscal system. The Domesday data have consistently refused to be squeezed into the straitjacket of a single schema.

It is the contention of the present study that this failure is a function of the identification of the Domesday process with Domesday Book. A twelfth-century perception consequent to the development of the mystique around the work, the notion has encouraged the adoption of common law procedures to explain the processes of the inquest and its aftermath. The immediate focus of the enterprise was the inquest itself, and this was no executive process.

2

Domesday and Title to Land

EXECUTIVE PROCESSES COME in many different forms, but none is entirely bureaucratic. Some accounts of the workings of royal government in Angevin England give the impression of a smoothly running engine which only rarely missed a stroke and then was quickly adjusted by an omnipresent ministering justice. But the most cursory reading of court procedures reveals a reality of muddle, misunderstanding, and incompetence. As *The Good Soldier Švejk* illustrates, even the most powerful commissar cannot command absolute authority over his subjects.

[The interrogator] gave Švejk a bloodthirsty look and said:
'Take that idiotic expression off your face.'
'I can't help it,' replied Švejk solemnly. 'I was discharged from the army for idiocy and officially certified by a special commission as an idiot. I'm an official idiot.' . . .
'What you're accused of and you've committed proves you've got all your wits about you.'
And now he began to enumerate to Švejk a whole series of different crimes, beginning with high treason and ending with abuse of his majesty and members of the Imperial Family. . . .
'What do you say to that?' the gentleman with features of bestial cruelty asked triumphantly.
'There's a lot of it,' Švejk replied innocently. 'You can have too much of a good thing.'
'So there you are, then, you admit it's true?'
'I admit everything. You've got to be strict. Without strictness no one would ever get anywhere. When I was in the army . . .' . . .
'Whom are you in contact with?'
'My charwoman, your honour.'
'And you don't have any friends in political circles here?'
'Yes, I do, your honour. I subscribe to the afternoon edition of *Národní Politika*— "The Bitch." '
'Get out!' the gentleman with the bestial appearance roared at Švejk.
As they were leading him out of the office, Švejk said:
'Good night, your honour.[1]

To a greater or lesser degree all executive processes depend on co-operation. They are, nevertheless, all characterized by the administration of laws, decrees, or decisions of government or other competent authorities. The ultimate test

---

[1] Hašek, *The Good Soldier Švejk and his Fortunes in the World War*, 20–1.

of an executive process must be whether it decides (or attempts to decide) anything. The Domesday inquest can be put to that test.

In strictly fiscal terms nothing came out of the process. Harvey has claimed that the ploughland figures were a new assessment to replace the geld, but her analysis has not commanded universal acceptance: the statement that 'there is land for so many ploughs' is still often best interpreted at face value.[2] This, of course, does not mean that problems of interpretation do not remain, but the possibilities are wider than has been allowed. An element of artificiality in a data set, a key element in Harvey's argument, does not necessarily point to a fiscal system. Estimates, for example, may be round sums and yet their referents are still the real world. In these terms, the absence of any reference to the Domesday ploughlands in later records begins to look significant. Charters from the reign of William Rufus still employ the Domesday hidation, and reassessments in liability (albeit small in number) were firmly based upon it, while early twelfth-century surveys, both royal and private, betray not a hint of any other cadastre. Two alternative conclusions present themselves. Either the reassessment was a massive administrative mistake and was immediately abandoned, or the ploughland figures are to be differently interpreted. It is this latter, the more simple, that recommends itself.[3]

The determination of right is a more exacting test. In one way or another the various accounts of the supposedly executive process that was the Domesday inquest have devolved upon title to land. The question is, of course, central to the 'Norman order' view, and, although more peripheral to the argument, it is implicit in the fiscal analyses. Within the terms of these approaches what must be viewed as a concern with rights to land is ubiquitous in the Domesday corpus. The vast majority of verdicts recorded in the texts comment on the legality of tenure and standard forms are to all appearances related to title. The repeated appeal to conditions *tempore regis Edwardi*, for example, 'in the time of King Edward', or the more precise and dramatic *die qua rex Edwardus vivus et mortuus est*, 'the day on which King Edward was alive and dead', the datum at the earliest stage of the inquiry, is apparently intended to document a political and tenurial revolution.

Appearances are deceptive. Title was not an issue, for it was a matter which had largely been settled. In recent years it has become increasingly apparent that the Norman Conquest was marked by a greater degree of legal continuity than was formerly appreciated.[4] Some historians have attempted to interpret post-Conquest expressions of legitimacy in these terms as a political fiction concocted as propaganda for the Norman regime.[5] In reality, however,

---

[2] Harvey, 'Taxation and the Ploughland in Domesday Book', 86–103; Harvey, 'Taxation and the Economy', 249–64.

[3] See below, pp. 149–65.

[4] See Williams, *The English and the Norman Conquest*, for the most recent review.

[5] Garnet, review, 1236–7.

the concepts that such expressions embody can be seen to have had a profound effect on the settlement after 1066. Title to land in 1086 was already established and was founded in English law. Any confirmation of title would inevitably presuppose a determination of right. Demonstrably neither the Domesday inquest nor Domesday Book disposed of land.

The Norman Settlement

The chronology of the Norman settlement was protracted. Those thegns who fought against William at the Battle of Hastings on 14 October 1066 probably forfeited their lands *ipso facto*. Domesday Book itself is remarkably reticent —there is only a handful of references to the battle[6]—but the lands of those thegns who were killed were probably allocated to William's supporters soon after the coronation on Christmas Day 1066. A writ directed to the abbot of Bury St Edmund's *c.*1067 demanded the lands of thegns who had fought against William at Hastings for the king's own use,[7] and in 1086 the abbot of Bury St Edmund's had to concede that he had no right to land in Shelfanger in Norfolk because the pre-Conquest tenant had been at Hastings.[8] After such initial forfeitures grants were made and estates appropriated as the conquest and settlement progressed. Initially, land was redeemed by English thegns and religious houses on the payment of indemnities when they made their submission to King William; until 1068 much of the personnel of English government was retained.[9] Direct rule, and the forfeiture of English estates *en masse*, was only instituted with successive revolts, starting with that in the West Country in that year.[10] Much of southern and midland England must have come under tight Norman control by 1071 when the rebellion in the fenland was suppressed. The northern shires were also harried in 1069 and 1070, but the redistribution of estates was more protracted. Alan of Brittany's lands in the North Riding of Yorkshire were probably not acquired until the early 1080s.[11]

Some honours appear to have been created at one point in time, or at least by a single transaction. Geoffrey de Mandeville, for example, probably received all the lands of Asgar the staller in Bedfordshire, Berkshire, Buckinghamshire, Cambridgeshire, Essex, Hertfordshire, Middlesex, Norfolk, Oxfordshire, Suffolk, Surrey, and Warwickshire in or about 1067 and it was that interest that formed the bulk of his fee in 1086.[12] Others came into being piecemeal as land became available and the tenant-in-chief was favoured. Thus,

---

[6] GDB 60c, 50a, 208a: *DB Berks.*, 21,13; *DB Hants.*, 69,16; *DB Hunts.*, D7; LDB, 275b, 409b, 449a: *DB Norfolk*, 66,41; *DB Suffolk*, 31,50.76,20.

[7] *Feudal Documents*, 47.   [8] LDB 275b: *DB Norfolk*, 66,41.

[9] Williams, *English and the Norman Conquest*, 7–23.   [10] Ibid. 24–70.

[11] Kapelle, *The Norman Conquest of the North*, 44–5.

[12] In that year he was portreeve of London, an office apparently held by Asgar (Round, *Geoffrey de Mandeville*, 37; Fleming, *Kings and Lords in Conquest England*, 171).

Henry de Ferrers acquired his estates in at least three different grants or series of grants. Lands in Berkshire held by Godric the sheriff, who died in battle, possibly at Hastings, were probably received in late 1066 or early 1067; those of Bondi the staller in Berkshire, Buckinghamshire, Essex, and Oxfordshire followed between 1068 and 1070, and Siward Barn's estates in Berkshire, Derbyshire, Essex, Gloucestershire, Lincolnshire, Nottinghamshire, and Warwickshire c.1070.[13] The date and circumstances of transfer of other fees, notably numerous manors in Appletree Wapentake in Derbyshire and the adjacent area of Staffordshire, is largely undocumented.[14]

By 1086 the vast majority of estates had passed to new lords; only pre-Conquest religious houses and a handful of English lords retained their lands in chief. The Norman settlement was all but complete. Honours had by no means attained their final form, but the main outline of post-Conquest tenure had been established and, by and large, subsequent changes were determined by the framework that is evident in Domesday Book. No source outlines how this settlement was effected. Nevertheless, several mechanisms are apparent. First, there was a process which has been termed 'antecession'.[15] Like Geoffrey de Mandeville, tenants-in-chief were granted the lands of a single pre-Conquest holder of land and they thereby succeeded to all the interests and obligations of this their predecessor. The principle is explicit in the Bedfordshire folios. Robert d'Oilly held half a hide in Thurleigh in succession to a king's thegn called Wulfgeat, but his title was challenged by the men of Eudo the steward through their lord's predecessor, apparently here Wulfmer of Eaton, 'all of whose lands King William bestowed upon him'.[16] Elsewhere it is seldom so baldly stated. The mechanism, however, also informed the conduct of disputes. Short of a royal writ to the contrary, it would seem that a tenant-in-chief could make no better case for the tenure of land than that his predecessor had held it in 1066.

Secondly, estates were granted individually. Here and there throughout Domesday Book there are references to writs and charters whereby the king conveyed the title to a manor to a tenant-in-chief. In many cases only the named place was transferred, but often it is clear that the name stands for an estate centre and that a whole complex of lands might be assigned by it. In a charter pre-dating Domesday Book King William notified the sheriff of Lincolnshire and all the sheriffs in the diocese of Lincoln that he had moved the see of Dorchester to Lincoln, where he had given land with all customary dues on which to build a church, and to this church he had given the two manors of Welton and Sleaford with their appurtenances as well as confirming the earlier grants of Leighton Bromswold and Wooburn made

[13] Holt, '1086', 58 n, citing Golob, 'The Ferrers Earls of Derby: A Study of the Honour of Tutbury 1066–1279'.

[14] The twenty-four TRE holders of land in Appletree Wapentake were probably under-tenants of Siward Barn (Roffe, 'Introduction to the Derbyshire Domesday', 10–11).

[15] Fleming, *Kings and Lords in Conquest England*, 180.   [16] GDB 215b: *DB Beds.*, 28,1.

by Earl Waltheof and himself.[17] Welton here would seem to have included sokeland in Burton by Lincoln,[18] while Sleaford may have been even more extensive. The grant certainly included extensive sokeland in seven vills in the wapentake of Aswardhurn in Lincolnshire. It may also have included an extensive group of estates in Lincolnshire, Leicestershire, and Rutland which the bishop of Lincoln held in 1086 in succession to Bardi, the pre-conquest lord of Sleaford.[19]

Thirdly, land was apparently granted to individuals on a geographical basis regardless of pre-Conquest tenure.[20] In Sussex the rapes of Arundel, Hastings, Lewes, and Pevensey were granted in 1067 to Roger of Montgomery, Humphrey de Tilleul, William de Warenne, and Robert of Mortain as castleries on the continental model to guard the south coast. The fifth rape of Bramber was in existence by 1084. Similarly, Herefordshire was granted to William fitz Osbern in 1069, Cheshire to Gerbod the Fleming and then to Earl Hugh of Avranches in 1069–70, and Shropshire to Roger of Montgomery at about the same date, to create a strong Norman presence in the Welsh Marches. Cornwall was likewise given to Robert of Mortain to hold the West Country. There may have been a comparable plan to grant Kent to Odo of Bayeux, and elsewhere strategic areas seem to have been conferred on a single tenant-in-chief. Drogo de Beuvrière held Holderness and Count Alan of Brittany what became known as Richmondshire in the North Riding of Yorkshire. In all cases, the tenant-in-chief had title to the estates of all pre-Conquest holders of land except those of the church.

Fourthly, newcomers married English heiresses. The Breton Geoffrey de la Guerche had title to much of the lands of Leofwin and his son Leofric in* Leicestershire, Lincolnshire, Northamptonshire, and Nottinghamshire through marriage to Leofwin's daughter and heir Ælfgifu;[21] the Fleming Walter de Douai came into possession of Uffculme in Devon by marriage to an English woman, Eadgytha, widow of Hemming;[22] Richard Iuvenis married the widow of Alfwine, sheriff of Gloucestershire, and succeeded to his estates in Gloucestershire;[23] and Robert d'Oilly was given Alditha, daughter of the rich English thegn Wigot of Wallingford, in marriage, and thereby acquired a large holding in and around Oxfordshire.[24]

Fifthly, land was acquired by officials through the exercise of their office. Sheriffs were undoubtedly in the best position to profit in this way. Eustace, sheriff of Huntingdon, is an egregious and well-documented example. In 1086 he held ninety-four hides and half a virgate of land in Cambridgeshire, Huntingdonshire, and Northamptonshire, title to over ten hides of which was

[17] *Registrum Antiquissimum of Lincoln*, i. 2–3.   [18] GDB 344a: *DB Lincs.*, 7,9.
[19] GDB 230a, 344c–d, 221a–b: *DB Leics.*, 3,11; *DB Lincs.*, 7,38–43; 45–50; *DB Northants.*, 5,1–4.
[20] Fleming, *Kings and Lords in Conquest England*, 145–8.
[21] *Charters of the Honour of Mowbray*, pp. xx–xxi.   [22] *Chartulary of Glastonbury*, i. 126–8.
[23] GDB 167b: *DB Gloucs.*, 34,8; Williams, 'Introduction to the Gloucestershire Domesday', 35.
[24] *English Register of Oseney Abbey*, 6.

challenged. Sokeland of the king's in Orton, Catworth, Swineshead, Gidding, Winwick, Thurning, Luddington, and Old Weston had probably come into his hands by virtue of his management of the royal estates of Huntingdonshire.[25] Land in Isham, by contrast, was taken from Ramsey Abbey by force,[26] and he probably came into possession of lands in Sawtry, Botolph Bridge, Hargrave, Gidding, Grafham, Waresley, and Hail Weston through similar acts of predation.[27] Elsewhere, sheriffs acquired land that was forfeit or failed to deliver estates that had been demised to others.[28]

Sixthly, and finally, land was simply taken by powerful local lords as the opportunity arose. Throughout Domesday there are references to land illegally taken by tenants-in-chief. In the majority of counties the information is confined to the claims for restitution by the injured lord which appear in the accounts of the tenements concerned. In some counties such accounts were collected together seemingly for further action. Thus, in LDB there is a section entitled *invasiones super regem* appended to the end of the accounts of the three counties of Essex, Norfolk, and Suffolk. Similarly, the Exon Domesday contains a list of illegally held lands entitled *terre occupate*. Additionally, there survive for Huntingdonshire, Lincolnshire, and Yorkshire in GDB records of pleas that resulted from such claims.

None of these mechanisms of land transfer is necessarily mutually exclusive. As has been seen, transfer by writ could as easily convey a number of estates as one. Less obvious is the interrelation of antecession and geographical grants. Gerbod the Fleming was obviously granted territorial rights throughout Cheshire, but it is far from clear that these were entirely novel. They did not amount to palatine jurisdiction, a purely thirteenth-century concept, but were more akin to those of a pre-Conquest earldom. Hugh of Avranches, Gerbod's successor, owed fifty-five and a half hides of his ninety hides of demesne in the county to Earl Edwin in 1086. Gerbod probably succeeded to the rights of the pre-Conquest earl.[29] There are indications, moreover, that estates were distributed to tenants on the basis of antecession. Seven of the earl's barons seem to have derived their lands from the estates of a single pre-Conquest predecessor.[30] Similarly, it is not entirely clear that the Sussex rapes were a post-Conquest innovation.[31]

---

[25] GDB 206a–b: *DB Hunts.*, 19,7;11–12;15–20.   [26] GDB 228a: *DB Northants.*, 55,1.

[27] GDB 206a–c: *DB Hunts.*, 19,1;9;13;22;26–7.

[28] Abels, 'Sheriffs, Lord Seeking, and the Norman Settlement of the South-East Midlands', 19–50.

[29] Thacker and Sawyer, 'Domesday Survey', 305.

[30] Ibid. 306–7. Fleming doubts the extent of the earl's liberty (*Kings and Lords in Conquest England*, 147 n.), but the suggested mechanism is not very different from the king's control over the land between Ribble and Mersey which is explicit in GDB (GDB 269c–279b: *DB Cheshire*, R). It is significant that there is no recorded TRE holder of sake and soke, an indicator of bookland. For the apparently lowly status of most of the English, see Lewis, 'Introduction to the Cheshire Domesday', 16, and for an attempt to reconstruct patterns of tenure and patronage, Higham, 'Patterns of Patronage and Power', 1–13.

[31] See Thorn, 'Hundreds and Wapentakes', *Sussex Domesday*, 29–33, for the most recent discussion, along with a bibliography of the various arguments.

Further, it is often difficult always to determine the processes in any particular honour from Domesday Book alone since there were many changes
between 1066 and 1086. Sales, exchanges, mortgages, marriages, forfeitures,
and plain restructuring of estates changed original arrangements.[32] Nevertheless, it seems clear that most estates were transferred by legal means. Locally,
predation could be of some importance; religious houses especially stood
to lose a significant proportion of their income to private entrepreneurship.
However, the church was a special case. On the one hand, it was more
vulnerable to oppression, and on the other, the survival of documentation in
ecclesiastical archives has tended to exaggerate the impact of illegal seizures
of land. The abbey of Ely is a case in point. Before the Conquest many of
its estates had been let to laymen for a life or series of lives, and after 1066
many of these were permanently lost. The manors held by Archbishop
Stigand in Snailwell and Wood Ditton passed to the king and later to the
baronies of Percy and Camois; the land in High Easter acquired by Asgar
the staller passed into the honour of Geoffrey de Mandeville; the manors
held by Toki in Trumpington and Weston Colville were incorporated into
the honours of Skipton and Warenne respectively.[33] But supping with the devil
had always been a dangerous strategy; buying support with gifts of loanland
ran the concomitant risk of permanent loss of land as much before the Conquest
as after. The majority of Ely's claims, though, concerned rights over free men
and sokemen, and here they were as likely to be predatory as preyed upon.
The services of many free men were taken away from them simply on the
grounds of pre-Conquest commendation or, more often, mere opportunity.
Hardwin of Scales and Picot the sheriff, for example, took many of Ely's
Cambridgeshire men in this way. Conversely, the abbey itself made claim to
land on the basis of soke or commendation alone against the same Picot in
Rampton, Lolworth, Madingley, Oakington, Impington, Waterbeach, and
Cottenham.[34]

Claims of this kind add colour to the otherwise tedious litany of statistics
in the Domesday texts. It is, then, not surprising that some historians have
seen in them the reality of a Norman settlement in which self-help was the
norm.[35] But Domesday hardly warrants such a conclusion. Despite the prominence, both textual and historiographical, of claims, they are very much
the exception in the Domesday corpus. Of the many thousands of entries in
Domesday Book, there are only 1,199 claims of all kinds, representing a tiny
proportion of the land of England.[36] The record of disputes is, of course, uneven.

---

[32] Stenton, *Anglo-Saxon England*, 628–9.   [33] Miller, *Abbey and Bishopric of Ely*, 66 n.
[34] GDB 201a–c: *DB Cambs.*, 32,31–3;35;36;39;40; *ICC* 175–6.
[35] See e.g. Fleming, *Kings and Lords in Conquest England*, 183–214 and id. *Domesday Book and the Law*,
68–85.
[36] Dr Keats-Rohan's *Continental Origins of English Landowners* database provides a total of 29,694 entries
in GDB and LDB. The calculation of the number of disputes has been inclusive; the total embraces
all the *clamores*, *invasiones*, and *terre occupate* cases, and additional suits identified by Wormald in his
main list and two of his subsidiary lists, that is, 'king's pleas' and miscellaneous ('Domesday

Of the 339 cases collected by Patrick Wormald (of disputes between subjects in which a resolution was reached), no less than 55 per cent occur in the Yorkshire, Lincolnshire, and Huntingdonshire sections, another 20 per cent are found in LDB account of Norfolk, Suffolk, and Essex, and 9 per cent in Bedfordshire and Cambridgeshire, with the remainder thinly spread throughout the rest of the country.[37] Nevertheless, even in Lincolnshire, where the most disputes occur, claims were made to 148 parcels of land assessed at 266 carucates, much of it sokeland, out of the 1,655 described with a total assessment of 4,316 carucates.[38] Title to only 6 per cent of land in the county was in question in 1086. By and large, it would seem that demesne estates had been transferred, by writ or deliverer, to use the repeated phrase of Domesday Book, in licit ways or at least by means that had become acceptable. Further, right to appurtenant land was generally also well understood, albeit more open to challenge. Inland always belonged to the holder of the manorial *caput*, and sokeland usually owed service to a single manorial centre. The principles of sanctioned transfer were apparently widely shared and uncontroversial.

This is the reality throughout much of Domesday Book. Some invasions were apparently naked and opportunistic aggression on well defined interests, but they remained the exception. Title to demesne estates was rarely at issue; the overwhelming majority of cases concern the greyer area of variously dependent sokelands of divers kinds. Typically, disputes devolved upon the exact relationship between predecessors and the many kinds of interest from which they derived their income: rights to simple soke and commendation are most often cited as grounds for tenure otherwise deemed as unwarranted. If free enterprise had been a significant element in the Norman settlement, the designated successors of the victims kept remarkably quiet about it.

Of the four legal means of land transfer, two were clearly of limited importance. The role of intermarriage in the Norman settlement was probably far greater than is apparent from extant documentation, but enough is known of the family backgrounds of most tenants-in-chief to make it clear that it was a mechanism of land transfer of minimal importance on a national scale. The known examples are confined to lower-status families, and then mostly of non-Norman provenance, and it seems clear that the Norman aristocracy did not countenance the practice.[39] Likewise, the grant of individual estates by

Lawsuits', 79–94, 98–102). No attempt has been made to correlate the 'duplicates' of GDB and Exon. The total is, of course, of causes; a greater number of parcels of land were involved. The calculation of the number of hides in dispute is best left to a computer, but in terms of entries the total represents less than 7 percent of the land of England.

[37] Wormald, 'Domesday Lawsuits', 65, 95.
[38] Roffe, 'Hundreds and Wapentakes', 35. Claims to soke alone have been excluded.
[39] Keats-Rohan, *Domesday People*, 28.

charter was no doubt more extensive than the few references in Domesday Book and the extant charters would give us to understand. Again, however, it is difficult to believe that it can ever have been a significant means by which a large number of estates were transferred. If generally applied, the process would suggest something like the Domesday inquest itself and the survival of a large number of charters.

Until recently, antecession has been seen as the main mechanism of the Norman settlement. Stenton has formulated the principle most succinctly:

From first to last [King William] insisted on the principle that every Frenchman to whom he gave an Englishman's estate should hold it with all the rights, and subject to all the obligations, that had been attached to it at the beginning of 1066. It was with this principle in their minds that the commissioners who carried out the Domesday Survey approached the innumerable pleas raised in their investigations. For most of them it provided an immediate solution. The best reply that a lord could make to a claim upon his property was the production of sworn evidence that the land or the rights in dispute had belonged to his *antecessor* on the day when King Edward was alive and dead.[40]

The strict principles of succession and inheritance were adhered to throughout. There was, however, no simple re-creation of pre-Conquest patterns of tenure. As a rule tenants-in-chief were given the lands of many lords, the actual distribution being determined by local military needs. Thus, castleries like Dudley, Tutbury, and Tickhill were created by the painstaking grant of the lands of individuals. The process was as momentous as the Domesday inquest itself, and for Stenton it constituted a tenurial revolution. By 1086 four or five thousand English lords had been replaced by a few hundred tenants-in-chief.

There lies at the heart of this analysis the assumption that all of those who are named as holding land in 1066 or before were, in a legal sense, *antecessores*. It is clear from Domesday Book, however, that this was not always the case. The term *antecessor* is relatively rare. It is normally found only in the account of lands in dispute and the identity of the predecessor is sometimes provided by jurors of hundred or shire. Whether the information was collected as a matter of course is unclear, but it was evidently superfluous to the purpose of Domesday Book itself. Nevertheless, it is evident that it was used in a specialist sense. Of the 184 occurrences of the term *antecessor* in Domesday Book in which full details are given, in a handful of cases it does not refer to the named individual to whom the land is ascribed in the body of the entry. To take but one example, a certain Godwine is recorded as the pre-Conquest holder of sokeland of the Lincolnshire manor of Welbourn in Ingoldsby, but in the Lincolnshire *clamores* Robert Malet is said to have had title to it through his predecessor Atsurr, who can be identified as Atsurr

---

[40] Stenton, *Anglo-Saxon England*, 626.

TABLE 2.1. *Groups of manors in the Lincolnshire breves of Walter de Aincurt and Peterborough Abbey*

Lord 1086	Lord and Tenant 1066	Division and Wapentake
Walter de Aincurt	1. Thorir, Siward, Alwig	K30,24,21/
	2. Arnketil, Hemingr, Godric Leofric, Siward	K21,26,23/
	3. Healfdene, his two brothers	K23
Peterborough Abbey	1. Peterborough Abbey	LWR14/,K20/,21/,28,H31,K24 (addition to the text)
	2. Alnoth, Rolf, Hereward, Alnoth	LWR14,17,19,K20,21,20 (?add)

Notes: LWR = Lindsey West Riding, K = Kesteven, H = Holland. Obliques indicate spaces in the text and the numbers refer to wapentakes by their position in the common Lincolnshire sequence. *Source*: D. R. Roffe, 'Hundreds and Wapentakes', in A. Williams and G. H. Martin (eds.), *The Lincolnshire Domesday* (London, 1992), 7, 37.

son of Svala, the holder of sake and soke in Lincolnshire and lord of the manor of Bradmore in Nottinghamshire.[41] A tenant-in-chief was not always expressly granted the land of the person named in the text. Title, it would seem, was often derived from an overlord.

The existence, and something of the structure, of these lordships was first identified in the Domesday account of the northern shires.[42] In Lincolnshire and Yorkshire the composition of breves is sometimes directly related to pre-Conquest tenure. Each predecessor, typically said to enjoy sake and soke, toll and team, is accorded a separate section of the text along with the estates of those who were associated with him. The account of Walter de Aincurt's Lincolnshire lands is typical. Two blank lines define three sections which are distinguished by separate wapentake sequences (Table 2.1). In the first, Thorir held with sake and soke, while Siward and Alwig, apparently holding in parage, would appear to have been tenants since Alwig still held from Walter in 1086. In section two Hemingr similarly held with sake and soke with Godric, Arnketill, Siward, and Leofric as tenants, and section three was devoted to the lands of Halfdan and his brothers. The Lincolnshire breve of the abbot of Peterborough is similarly divided, distinguishing the pre-Conquest demesne lands of the abbey from those given by Abbot Brand's family which had been held by their tenants. In Yorkshire, the breve of the count of Mortain has been purposively divided into a number of tenurial groups, although their identity is less apparent.[43]

[41] GDB 337a, 368b, 377b, 280c, 291d: *DB Lincs.*, T5. 58,3. CK35; *DB Notts.*, S5, 25,1.
[42] Roffe, 'Norman Tenants-in-Chiefs and their Pre-Conquest Predecessors in Nottinghamshire', 3–7.
[43] Roffe, 'Yorkshire Summary', 252.

This perception was developed by Professor Peter Sawyer. He discovered similar vestiges of overlordship throughout the country, but his analysis concentrated on those parts of Domesday Book in which detailed information is given on pre-Conquest bonds of lordship. In the accounts of the eastern counties almost every entry records in one way or another the lord of each holder of land; in Cambridgeshire, Hertfordshire, Bedfordshire, Buckinghamshire, and Middlesex each man is said to be the man of whomsoever he owed his dues to, while in Norfolk, Suffolk, and Essex rights to commendation are noted. Sawyer points out that land of lord and men frequently passed to the same tenant-in-chief. Count Alan of Brittany, for example, succeeded to all but one of the demesne estates of Edeva the Fair in Cambridgeshire, along with 165 hides of land worth £150 held by over 120 of her men and women. Only fifteen parcels of land held by her tenants, amounting to a mere seven hides, passed to other tenants-in-chief. The majority of tenants were free to take their lands to whomsoever they pleased, but the dues that they conferred on their lord, as expressed by soke and customs, were usually enough to ensure that a Norman successor could successfully make claim to their lands. Sawyer asserts that, although the Norman Conquest saw much disruption and the creation of new fees, the settlement followed the lines of pre-Conquest lordship. He concludes that 'the changes in tenurial structure after the Norman Conquest were less than revolutionary'.[44]

This conclusion has in its turn been roundly dismissed by Professor Robin Fleming. She accepts that antecession was a mechanism of land transmission, but avers that the number of references to pre-Conquest overlordship in Domesday Book is small and insufficient to argue for continuity; no English overlords are explicitly named in Domesday's folios for Cheshire, Derbyshire, Huntingdonshire, Leicestershire, Nottinghamshire, Somerset, and Wiltshire, and less than twelve are found in Devon, Dorset, Lincolnshire, Northamptonshire, Oxfordshire, Shropshire, Staffordshire, Surrey, Warwickshire, and Yorkshire.[45] Further, a computer-aided analysis of lordship in the eastern counties, as indicated by explicit notice of commendation in GDB and LDB, reveals that bonds of lordship were usually not respected in the post-Conquest period. In Hertfordshire between a third and a half of assessed land in the shire belonging to men of identifiable pre-Conquest lords could not be found in the honours of their lord's successors or were not dispersed in any discernible pattern. The proportion for Cambridgeshire is 25 per cent, Buckinghamshire 20 per cent, Bedfordshire 15 per cent, and Middlesex 12 per cent. In the light of the large amount of royal, comital, and ecclesiastical land, these statistics represent an enormous amount of disruption to pre-Conquest patterns of lordship. Antecession was of limited importance. It appears to have been employed in the earliest stages of the Norman settlement and was confined to the demesne estates of English lords. Geographical distribution was a

---

[44] Sawyer, 'Tenurial Revolution', 85.   [45] Fleming, *Kings and Lords in Conquest England*, 114.

far more significant mechanism. In Nottinghamshire, Derbyshire, parts of Lincolnshire, Kent, Sussex, and Yorkshire land distribution echoed the divisions of shire, hundred, and wapentake more closely than pre-Conquest lordship. In Derbyshire, for example, it is clear that Henry de Ferrers received all of the land that had not been disposed of by antecession in the wapentake of Appletree. Similarly, William Peverel acquired surplus land in the south of Nottinghamshire in the wapentakes of Rushcliffe and Broxtow, while in the north of the county in Bassetlaw, Oswaldbeck, and Lythe lands, often of the same men, were conveyed to Roger de Bully. Fleming concludes that by any standards the Norman settlement saw a massive reorganization of land of unprecedented proportions.

Sokeright and Title to Land

Stenton's analysis of the Norman settlement and these, its two critiques, have set the terms of the debate. All three miss the point.[46] Although they ostensibly concern themselves with the continuity of tenure between 1066 and 1086, in fact they address the mechanisms of land transfer from English lord to Norman tenant-in-chief to the exclusion of tenurial relationships. To prove that an honour was composed of lands held by a single English overlord does not preclude a tenurial revolution, if nebulous bonds of soke and commendation within the estate were replaced by enfeoffment for military service. Likewise, changes in lordship do not necessarily imply a revolution in landholding. In the early eleventh century there were considerable upheavals in patterns of tenure in the aftermath of Cnut's conquest of England, but, although new forms emerged, there was no wholesale abandonment of traditional tenurial relationships.[47] The problem of continuity, then, cannot be resolved by simply looking at title, but must be examined in legal and tenurial terms.

To start with, it is not surprising that the settlement took little account of commendation. To the Norman mind it probably seemed natural that a lord, or his successor, should be entitled to the land of his men, and indeed many a tenant-in-chief claimed land on that basis.[48] It is clear, however, that in itself the relationship usually did not confer rights over land. Time and again throughout the East Midland folios of Domesday Book pre-Conquest tenants are said to have been the men of such and such a lord, but they 'were free to go with their land', or 'they could grant or sell their land'. In East Anglia pre-Conquest

---

[46] The following is taken from 'From Thegnage to Baronage', 160–173, with some revision and additions.

[47] Mack, 'Changing Thegns', 375–87.

[48] See e.g. the numerous examples in the three *invasiones* sections of LDB (LDB 99a–103b, 273b–280a, 447b–449b: *DB Essex*, 90; *DB Norfolk*, 66; *DB Suffolk*, 76).

holders are variously described as free men, or lords are said to have 'only commendation over them'. Elsewhere in Domesday Book, as is clear from parallel passages in Exon, the equivalent formula used was '*x* held freely [*libere*]'. Wherever the relationship was advanced as justification for tenure of land in 1086, the plea was rejected. Thus, in the *invasiones* sections attached to the accounts of Norfolk, Suffolk, and Essex in LDB the most frequently expressed opinon of juries was that the aggressor's predecessor had only the commendation of the men whose land had been appropriated. Mere commendation was never sufficient reason for seisin in 1086.

This was a reality of tenure in England of long standing. Commendation had always been a lordship of a circumscribed kind. In Domesday Book it is explicitly associated with protection in several passages. Augi, who held land in Easton in Bedfordshire, was commended by King William to Ralph Taillebois that he should protect him as long as he lived;[49] a free man in Tiscott in Hertfordshire turned to Wigot of Wallingford for protection.[50] Such protection seems to have included surety in court. Robert son of Wymarc, for example, was brought into the hundred when Brungar his man was accused of stealing horses.[51] It is thus clear that lordship of this type can be equated with that embodied in the *hlaford* of the late tenth- and eleventh-century English law codes. Up to *c.*950 surety for the maintenance of the peace largely devolved upon the kin, but thereafter it was invested in lordship.[52] Unruly kins had long posed a challenge to order that peace gilds had failed to check. The new provisions effectively neutralized recalcitrant families, for henceforward every free man was required to have a lord (*hlaford*) who would vouch for his good behaviour. In return the lord was invested with the warrantee's wergeld, but otherwise typically received only small monetary payments in recognition of his superiority.[53] Lordship of this kind was a public matter; it was declared in the hundred or shire court and could not be repudiated

---

[49] GDB 211d: *DB Beds.*, 17,5.   [50] GDB 137d: *DB Herts.*, 19,1.

[51] LDB 401b–402a: *DB Suffolk*, 27,7.

[52] Robertson, III Edmund 7, I Æthelred 1.5, I Æthelred 1.7, II Cnut 30.3b. Lords stood surety for their men in the reign of Athelstan (III Athelstan 7), but the context is probably the household. Abels (*Lordship*, 257) has argued that the *landhlaford* also provided surety, but the two texts he cites do not support his case. Attenborough, III Athelstan 7, does not mention land, but simply asserts that every man should hold his men in pledge. Robertson, III Edmund 7, reads 'Et omnis homo creditabiles faciat homines suos et omnes qui in pace et terra sua sunt', and it seems unlikely that the relative clause qualifies the *homines suos* (so, Robertson, p. 15, but see also p. 299 where she recognizes the possibility). Rather, it refers to another group, namely demesne tenants; they can be identified with those who could not recede and did not have freedom of commendation of Domesday Book. Cf. those in the household (Robertson, I Æthelred 1.10, II Cnut 31). In reality, however, a lord must usually have been a booklord as well as a liege lord.

[53] Typically, where explicit, monetary renders were the regular services owed (GDB 141d: *DB Herts.*, 37,10;12), but the fact is usually only apparent from the sharing of *commendatio* by a number of lords (LDB 182b, 187b: *DB Norfolk*, 9,111; 196). The close association of commendation with foldsoke in East Anglia emphasizes the judicial element, and one case in Suffolk illustrates the role of lords in legal proceedings which ensued (LDB 401b–402a: *DB Suffolk*, 27,7).

without raising suspicion of criminality.[54] Tithings were introduced at much the same time,[55] and it is thus clear that the commendation of Domesday Book was in effect the free man's counterpart of frankpledge. Lordship of this type was effectively limited to the lifetime of each of the parties; numerous English free men had to find new lords after the death or outlawry of their *hlaford*.[56] It could, therefore, never have formed a basis for the Norman settlement.

Post-Conquest perceptions of commendation, then, attest continuity of legal forms. Such continuity is also apparent in another species of lordship that is not examined by either Sawyer or Fleming. It was a lordship that was exercised over free men and their land, and as such had a direct impact on the Norman setlement. *Soca*, soke, has usually been understood as a relatively loose bond between lord and man; beyond the forfeitures and the receipt of amercements, 'the king's two pennies', it conferred no interest in land itself.[57] However, it is clear that the term was not confined to this specific meaning. In itself soke appears to have articulated nothing more than a relationship in which customary dues were rendered; it could refer to a whole host of dues from the render of a quitrent from an acre of land on the one hand, to the regalian rights of the king in the shire on the other.[58] As such it was often annoyingly vague in the eleventh century: the North Riding of Lindsey declared that Count Alan's predecessor had the soke of Eirikr's land in Tealby, but they knew not of what kind.[59]

Such a comment is enough to inspire despair. Nevertheless, an important and widespread use of the term soke is apparent in Domesday Book. In a large number of sokeland entries in the north, and their equivalent in the rest of the country, the soke *qua* jurisdiction of an estate, hereafter designated as *soca*, was held by one lord, but the land itself was in the tenure of another. The interest that the latter, the landlord, enjoyed was articulated by the word *terra*, 'land', or *consuetudines*, 'customs', and, consistently contrasted with *soca*, it referred to actual tenure both before and after the Conquest.[60] Nigel Fossard, for example, held five parcels of land in Yorkshire in succession to three named individuals, but the *soca* belonged to Conisbrough which was held by Earl Harold in 1066, and in Feltwell in Norfolk the abbot of Ely has thirty-four sokemen with all customs TRE (*Tempore Regis Edwardi*, 'in the time of King Edward, that is, 1066 or before) and six free men with *soca* and commendation only.[61]

[54] Attenborough, II Edward 7, II Athelstan 22, 22.1, 22.2, III Athelstan 4; Robertson, III Edgar 7.3, II Cnut 57, 77. But cf. Attenborough, Alfred 37.

[55] See below, pp. 55–6.

[56] See e.g. GDB 211d: *DB Beds.*, 17,5; LDB 310b–311a: *DB Suffolk*, 6,79.

[57] Stenton, *Types of Manorial Structure*, 1–55.   [58] Joy, 'Sokeright', 70–7.

[59] GDB 276a: *DB Lincs.*, CN, 18.

[60] Stephenson, 'Commendation and Related Problems in Domesday Book', 305–9; Kristensen, 'Danelaw Institutions and Danish Society in the Viking Age', 74–85; Demarest, '*Consuetudo Regis*', 161–79.

[61] GDB 373d: *DB Yorks.*, CW11–14; LDB 213b: *DB Norfolk*, 15,7.

The nature of the dues is not explicit in the Domesday text. Nevertheless, it is clear at the outset that despite the use of the term *terra* it did not normally amount to freehold. Some sokemen were not able to alienate their land without the lord's permission, and their lands were incorporated into a manor. Most ecclesiastical land was apparently of this type, and the Ely records show that the dependent estates were held in thegnage.[62] The form was by no means confined to the church—Edeva the Fair held the manor of Cherry Hinton in Cambridgeshire with thegnages in Fulbourn, Teversham, and probably many other vills in the vicinity of the estate centre[63]—and such lands were considered to be part of the lord's demesne. The sokeman's tenure was essentially ministerial; he may well have had some presumptive right to inheritance, but his continued seisin was at the will of his lord.[64] By far the majority of sokemen and free men, though, seem to have had freedom of alienation, for, although men of a superior, they were free to grant or sell their land without the permission of their lord or were free to go with it to another lord. The frequent record of the assessment of land of this kind indicates that the tenants paid their own geld and performed the duties that were required of law-worthy men of the hundred and shire: carriage and escort duties are widely reported in the Cambridgeshire and Hertfordshire folios of GDB and later evidence suggests that they owed suit of court to the wapentake in the north.[65] Typically, their land was held by partible inheritance, and it would seem that it was entailed within the family.[66]

The lord who had right to *terra* did not have rights *in* land but *over* land. Both pre- and post-Conquest charter evidence and twelfth-century estate surveys demonstrate that a number of renders was involved. The foundation charter of Blyth Priory and the Liber Eliensis and other Ely sources indicate that labour services like ploughing, sowing, haymaking, reaping, and repair of the lord's hall and mill were owed.[67] More importantly, there was a financial tribute and/or a render in kind. It was this due that constituted the essence of the customs, and it was of considerable value.[68] Three thegns held East Burnham in Buckinghamshire, for example, and could sell, but they paid 5 *oras* (6s 8d) to the church of Staines in customs.[69] In the soke of Oswaldbeck

---

[62] ICC 193–4.   [63] GDB 193d: *DB Cambs.*, 14, 1–4.

[64] Round, *Feudal England*, 25–34. The class is probably represented by the *geneat* in the Rectitudines Singularum Personarum, an early-eleventh-century treatise on estate management, in which his duties are described as riding, carrying, repairing the lord's hall and fences, and the like (*Die Gesetze*, i. 444–53; Vinogradoff, *English Society in the Eleventh Century*, 69–72). Abels, (*Lordship*, 133, 153) equates the *geneat* with the *liberi homines* and sokemen of East Anglia who performed riding service. However, the Rectitudines appears to be an account of a demesne estate, and the class is therefore closer to the radknights of the south-west. Indeed, post-Conquest versions of the document translate *geneat* as *villanus*.

[65] Roffe, 'Thegnage to Barony', 157–8.

[66] In the West Country tenure *pariter* or *in paragio* and *libere* were apparently synonymous (Welldon Finn, *Liber Exoniensis*, 71–2, 82–93).

[67] Stenton, *Types of Manorial Structure*, 22–8, 92–4.

[68] Ibid. 33–7.   [69] GDB 145d: *DB Bucks.*, 7,2.

in Nottinghamshire it seems to have accounted for the monetary issues of the land, for the twenty shillings in customs that twenty-two sokemen in Leverton rendered in 1066 seem to represent the value that is appended to all the other parcels of land in the soke.[70] In origin, the payment was almost certainly a commuted food rent or farm. A probably authentic late tenth- or early eleventh-century grant of land to Ramsey Abbey in Hickling and Kinoulton in Nottinghamshire specifies a heavy render in kind, but at the time of Domesday there is no suggestion of anything other than a money rent.[71]

In aggregate these dues were considerable, and, supplemented by even heavier dues from villagers, it is unlikely that they could be unilaterally withdrawn. Thus, in the hundred of Oswaldslow in Worcestershire the men of the church of Worcester could not keep back *consuetudines* except by the will of the bishop, and it is clear that in the Danelaw the freedom of the sokeman was similarly circumscribed.[72] *Terra*, then, as opposed to *soca qua* jurisdiction, evidently constituted the essential identity of the manor. The right of lords may well have been confined to precisely this interest. The archbishop of York, for example, probably did not enjoy the rights of jurisdiction over the manor of Laneham in Nottinghamshire until it was granted to him by a writ of 1060 × 1065; nevertheless, he still derived a profit from his soke *qua* land.[73] But *soca* and *terra* were by no means always held by different lords, and there is a considerable body of evidence to demonstrate that their liberties were then known as *soca et saca*.

With specifically jurisdictional referents, sake and soke is normally held to be synonymous with *soca*.[74] It is, however, with but few exceptions, consistently contrasted with simple jurisdiction in GDB.[75] Of Alfred's claim to two bovates

---

[70] GDB 281c: *DB Notts.*, 1,32.

[71] S1493; GDB 289a: *DB Notts.*, 11,30–1; Stenton, *Types of Manorial Structure*, 37–8.

[72] GDB 172c: *DB Worcs.*, 2,1. The freedom of sokemen has been exaggerated. Some at least of the twelfth-century charters adduced as evidence of an independent peasantry were subsequently confirmed by their lords, suggesting that they were not such free agents as supposed. See e.g. Stenton, *Free Peasantry of the Northern Danelaw* and *Documents Illustrative of the Social and Economic History of the Danelaw*, where no. 118 of the one is confirmed by the lord in no. 538 of the other. Moreover, their services were akin to those of the dependent thegnlands of Ely Abbey (Stephenson, 'Commendation and Related Matters', 308 n).

[73] *Anglo-Saxon Writs*, no. 119.

[74] Maitland, *Domesday Book and Beyond*, 84; Stenton, 'Introduction', pp. xxxvii, xxxix.

[75] There are apparently two exceptions in the Lincolnshire folios (GDB 375c, 376c: *DB Lincs.*, CS28.CW15). In both cases a Norman tenant-in-chief claimed soke over land even though his predecessor had enjoyed sake and soke in the estate. It was on the basis of these two solitary entries that Stenton postulated the identity of sake and soke with soke ('Introduction', p. xxxvii). As they stand, both are highly exceptional and cannot easily be reconciled with usage elsewhere in the north. However, it may be supposed that there was some unrecorded transaction which conferred rights to land between 1066 and 1086, or that the scribe was simply in error. Given the similarity of the terms, and the fact that the compiler must have had in front of him far more information concerning the liberties than appears in the text, confusion would not be surprising. Indeed, it can sometimes be directly observed. In a Lincolnshire *clamores* entry relating to Osbournby the curious term *soca et soca* appears (GDB 377c: *DB Lincs.*, CK53). However, it is clearly *soca* alone which is intended, for the liberty entitled

in Huttoft in Lincolnshire, for example, the South Riding of Lindsey declared that 'he ought to have one with sake and soke and the other is his in like wise, but Earl Hugh has the *soca* in Greetham'.[76] This dichotomy is reflected in the near contemporary Instituta Cnuti (1095–1150) where 'the king's thegn who has his soc' of the Laws of Cnut is glossed as *liberalis hominis qui consuetudines suas habet*.[77] But the distinction was clearly not a post-Conquest innovation, for in 1086 it was scrupulously observed in the determination of title. Thus, for example, Guy de Craon sued for six bovates of land in Gosberton in Lincolnshire which had been held by Æthelstan his predecessor, but he was unsuccessful in his suit because Ralph the staller, Count Alan's predecessor, had had sake and soke over the land.[78] Sake and soke clearly expressed the concept of full rights—*terra* and *soca*—as opposed to the limited dues conferred by the latter. Its application to title is therefore comprehensible: in precluding all claims on land, including the king's two pennies, the term is indicative of and synonymous with tenure by book.[79]

The status is recognized in the pre-Conquest law codes. From the reign of Athelstan, if not before, fines and forfeitures incurred in the breach of the peace were reserved to soke lords who presumably enjoyed the other issues of sokeland and the free men who held it.[80] Inalienable and concrete, such bookright is consistently contrasted with the rights conferred by commendation. Thus, in II Edgar 3.1 it is stated that if a man did not pay his tithes, regardless of whether he was a king's man or a thegn's, his forfeitures were to be divided between the bishop and the landlord, while in I Æthelred 1.5, 9 it is provided that if a man was found guilty his wergeld went to his lord, but if he escaped it went to the lord, that is landlord, who was entitled to his fines. Where *hlaford*, lord, refers to the commendation lord, *landhlaford* or *landrica*, landlord, is used of the holder of bookland.[81]

Ralph Pagenel to a horse from the land when he went to war. Such rights are always expressed in terms of *soca* (see e.g. GDB 357c: *DB Lincs.*, 26,45). Likewise, the statement that Countess Godiva had sake and soke over Newark Wapentake in Nottinghamshire is not only illogical but patently untrue, since Peterborough Abbey had the same liberties in Collingham within the same wapentake (GDB 280c: *DB Notts.*, S5). Cf GDB 11d: *DB Kent*, 6,1.

[76] GDB 375b: *DB Lincs.*, CS16.   [77] *Die Gesetze*, i. 359; Reid, 'Barony and Thanage', 172.

[78] GDB 348c, 377d: *DB Lincs.*, 12,76.CK69.

[79] The equation is explicit in the Laws of Cnut and the Leges Henrici, for it is stated in both that bookland was forfeited to the king alone (Roberston, II Cnut 13.1; *Leges Henrici*, c. 12). In two of the bishop of Worcester's demesne estates in Worcestershire sake and soke was 'rendered' (GDB 173a, 173d: *DB Worcs.*, 2,21;67), that is, the dues that *soca* and *terra* involved were rendered by tenants to their lord. In East Anglia sake and soke specifically refers to jurisdiction, but is almost always coupled with *consuetudines*.

[80] Attenborough, VI Athelstan 1.1; Robertson, I Edgar 2.1, III Edgar 7.1, I Æthelred 3.1, II Æthelred 3.2–3, II Cnut 25.1. Cf. Attenborough, Alfred 3.

[81] Robertson, II Edgar 3.1, I Æthelred 1.7, III Æthelred 4.1. *Landhlaford* and *landrica* occur in the context of fines and forfeitures and therefore must refer to the booklord (Attenborough, VI Athelstan 1.1; Robertson, I Edgar 2.1, III Edgar 7.1, I Æthelred 3.1, II Æthelred 3.2–3, II Cnut 25.1).

In the GDB accounts of Kent, Lincolnshire, Derbyshire, Nottinghamshire, and Yorkshire the holders of sake and soke, toll and team are listed.[82] The extent of their lands can therefore be readily determined. Some king's thegns, like Æthelstan, held vast tracts, but many seem to have had only modest holdings. However, it is nevertheless apparent that their bookland was far more extensive than GDB indicates. Harold, Fiacc, and Atsurr son of Svala had sake and soke in Lincolnshire, as did Ulf Fenisc and Countess Ælfeva in Nottinghamshire and Derbyshire, and yet their names do not appear in the body of the text.[83] Their lands were evidently held by tenants; as has already been seen, a Godwine held Atsurr's land. The relationship, however, was not one of mere jurisdiction: several other references demonstrate that *terra* was also reserved. Siward, for example, held the manor of Scrivelsby in Lincolnshire with inland in Coningsby and Wilksby, and sokeland in Mareham-on-the-Hill, but Aki his lord retained the soke in his estate of Thornton and apparently also enjoyed residual rights in the land since he conferred title to the manor on Robert the bursar.[84] Likewise, Count Alan had title to *terra* in Billingborough in Lincolnshire not by right of Karli the tenant but Ralph the staller, who had sake and soke.[85]

Elsewhere sake and soke is only coincidentally noticed. Nevertheless, others who enjoyed the liberty can be identified by the forms of GDB and LDB. The record of free tenure or commendation seems to have been directly related to sokeright. By indicating that a lord's right was limited to surety and the dues that that entailed, the implication is that the more substantial rights that conferred title were reserved. A notice of freedom to go with land and the like is in effect a record of subordination to a booklord. Conversely, the assertion that a TRE tenant simply held (*tenuit*) implies that the land was unencumbered. This form is associated with all those who are named as predecessors and as holding sake and soke, and seems to be a pointer to a king's thegn.[86] At best the form will only identify his demesne estates, but patterns of tenure often hint at more extensive interests. In Leicestershire, for example, distinct groups of estates have one, and only one, individual who is identified as a book lord in this way.[87] It seems clear, then, that the king's thegn normally enjoyed full rights over large groups of dependent manors that was other than *soca*.

In return for these privileges he owed what amounted to personal services to the king. The king's thegn seems to have been summoned to the fyrd in person and was in some wise responsible for the discharge of the military service assessed on the estate, for in the Worcestershire folios it is stated that:

---

[82] GDB 1c, 337a, 280c, 298c: *DB Kent*, D25; *DB Lincs.*, T5; *DB Notts.*, S5; *DB Yorks*, C36.
[83] GDB 337a, 280c: *DB Lincs.*, T5; *DB Notts.*, S5.
[84] GDB 363c, 375c: *DB Lincs.*, 38,3–7; CS34. The tenure of *soca* alone did not confer title.
[85] GDB 348a, 377c: *DB Lincs.*, 12,55.CK51.   [86] Roffe, 'Great Bowden and its Soke', 111.
[87] Ibid. 115.

When the king marches against the enemy, if anyone when summoned by his pro-clamation has stayed behind, if he is a free man so that he has sake and soke and can go with his land where he would, he is in the king's mercy for all of his land. But if a free man of any other lord has stayed away from the enemy and his lord has taken another man in his place, the man who was called up will pay 40s to his lord. But if no one at all has gone in his place, he will give 40s himself to his lord, and the lord himself will pay as many shillings to the king.[88]

Tewkesbury in Gloucestershire, along with dependent lands and manors that could not be withdrawn from the head manor, is specifically said to have been quit of royal service except for the service of its lord, Beorhtric son of Ælfgar.[89] As Dr Abels has argued, bookland was a precarious tenure in this respect, but otherwise it was hereditary and its lord had free disposal of it.[90] Nevertheless, in terms of the service due, the estate was probably indivisible. Thus, in Lincolnshire, for example, Sighvatr, Fenkel, Alnoth, and Asketill had divided their father Godwine's booklands between them 'share and share alike', but they held in parage as far as service towards the king was concerned.[91] In recognition of the special relationship, and the services that he owed in respect thereof, the king's thegn paid a relief to the king in person on inher-itance.[92] In Berkshire it consisted of military equipment: 'At his death a thegn or a household man-at-arms of the king sent to the king as a relief all his arms and one horse with a saddle, and one without a saddle; but if he had dogs or hawks they were presented to the king to accept if he wished.'[93] Elsewhere customs varied, but were of a similar kind.[94]

The relationship between these estates and post-Conquest honours can be directly observed. Almost without exception, predecessors can be shown generally to have enjoyed sake and soke where evidence is available. Indeed, it may have been assumed generally that title was derived from a king's thegn, for in LDB there is reference to an *antecessor ejus cum soca et saca*.[95] Further, it is evident that it was not just their demesne estates to which they gave title in 1086. The repeated plea in the West Country that one manor did not belong to another indicates that groups of estates were normally transferred *en bloc*, and patterns of pre-Conquest land tenure that are apparent in post-Con-quest fees illustrate that the process was general.[96] As Fleming argues, it is possible that the widely scattered lands of the same individual that pass to a number of tenants-in-chiefs may point to grants in a locality without regard

---

[88] GDB 172a: *DB Worcs.*, C5. Cf GDB 56c: *DB Berks.*, B10.
[89] GDB 163c–d: *DB Gloucs.*, 1,24–46. The manor may have been even more extensive, for Beorhtric held various other estates in the county.
[90] Abels, 'Bookland and Fyrd Service', 1–18; Abels, *Lordship and Military Obligation*, 116–31.
[91] GDB 375c–d, 376a: *DB Lincs.*, CS38; CN30.
[92] GDB 1b: *DB Kent*, D17. Those who had sake and soke paid their relief to the king along with, perhaps exceptionally, those who held allods.
[93] GDB 56c: *DB Berks.*, B10.   [94] Abels, *Lordship and Military Obligation*, 265–6.
[95] LDB 245a: *DB Norfolk*, 28,1.   [96] Exon, 457 ff.

to tenure.[97] But it is usually closely grouped parcels of land which are so divided. In a handful of adjoining vills in south Kesteven, for example, Osfram's estates in Dowsby, Keisby, Southorpe, and Avethorpe passed to Guy de Craon and Alfred of Lincoln, while Osfram himself retained Kirkby Underwood as a tenant of the same Alfred of Lincoln and further manors in Dowsby, Keisby, and Little Lavington as a king's thegn.[98] Such distributions are ubiquitous and can hardly indicate locality as the criterion of transfer, and individual grants would presuppose a survey equally as comprehensive as Domesday Book itself. Rather, the pattern must attest pre-existing relationships.

It seems likely, then, that the grant of a manor by right of a predecessor conferred title to all those manors that were dependent upon it. Henry de Ferrers, for example, probably claimed his lands in Derbyshire through the tenure of Ednaston, Doveridge, and Brailsford where he enjoyed sake and soke.[99] Notices of capital manors in the south and south-west, such as Northwick in Worcestershire and Deerhurst in Gloucestershire, hint at the pre-eminence of other estate centres, while the persistent references in Exon, and the more occasional ones in LDB, to a predecessort's 'honour [*honor*]' suggest that the mechanism was general.[100] The process was apparently widely understood, and exceptions may well be consistently and carefully noted. Thus, in Thurstan son of Rolf's fee in Somerset various small estates are said to have been added to the lands of Alfwold, and it can be concluded that the manors which are ascribed to other tenants without comment were held from this his predecessor, and in Suffolk it is noted that land did not belong to the honour of Geoffrey de Mandeville's predecessor Asgar (*non est de honore Ansgari*).[101] Elsewhere, as in Willoughby in the Marsh in Lincolnshire, and Fenton and Clarborough in Nottinghamshire, it is just laconically stated that the land was held with sake and soke and presumably therefore had a pre-Conquest identity distinct from that of the bulk of the fee.[102]

With such minor exceptions, it follows that many honours had decidedly pre-Conquest characteristics. Indeed, throughout the north there is a marked tendency for the demesne manors of king's thegns to remain in the hands of tenants-in-chief and over three-quarters of honourial courts in the later Middle Ages met in manors which were held with sake and soke, toll and team in 1066. The pre-Conquest identity of the groups of estates which owed service to them is most apparent where the presence of an overlord is explicit. Gilbert

[97] Fleming, 'Domesday Book and the Tenurial Revolution', 96–9; Fleming, *Kings and Lords in Conquest England*, 139–44.

[98] GDB 358c, 367b, 368a–b, 370c, 371a: *DB Lincs.*, 27,55–6.57; 12; 41,45,57.67,23;68,21–2.

[99] GDB 280c: *DB Notts.*, S5.

[100] GDB 173c, 166b: *DB Worcs.*, 2,55; *DB Gloucs.*, 19,1; Exon, 210–23; GDB 104c–105b: *DB Devon*, 15,11;15–22,29–31;47–52; LDB 393a, 395b: *DB Suffolk*, 25,52;75.

[101] GDB 97c–d: *DB Somerset*, 36, 2;7; LDB 412b: *DB Suffolk*, 32,19.

[102] GDB 355b, 286c, 287a: *DB Lincs.*, 24,59; *DB Notts.*, 9,113;128. Many small parcels of bookland like this may have been held by tenants-in-chief simply because no one else claimed them.

de Gant, for example, succeeded to the lands of Ulf Fenisc and the manors which were ascribed to others were held from this predecessor. In the Leicestershire folios this is the norm, for it appears that it is only the predecessor who is regularly named in the text. Where the tenant is noticed, however, as is the norm elsewhere, the English identity of the fee is less obvious. The honour of Tickhill a case in point. Roger de Bully succeeded to the lands of at least a hundred named individuals in north Nottinghamshire and southern Yorkshire, and his fee has every appearance of a post-Conquest castlery.[103] However, pre-Conquest overlordship apparently underlies the form of the Domesday account, for the honour was endowed with impressive privileges of an apparently early form. *Tolenea*, throughtoll, was reserved to Tickhill in Yorkshire from before 1088 when part of the banlieu was granted to the priory of Blyth in Nottinghamshire on its foundation, and tithes were owed from much of the honour to the royal free chapel of Tickhill from at least 1148.[104] Both liberties hint at the importance of Tickhill and Blyth as royal or comital centres before the Conquest—indeed, Earl Edwin had a hall at nearby Laughton-en-le-Morthen in Yorkshire[105]—and a detailed examination of the GDB account adds weight to the argument. Roger's lands in the wapentake of Oswaldbeck in Nottinghamshire, for example, are situated in the same vills as the royal soke of Oswaldbeck, and a local jury in the thirteenth century maintained that the king had formerly held the whole complex.[106] No firm conclusions can be drawn from such tantalizing detail, but it can be suggested that part, probably even most, of Roger's honour was derived from the interests of the pre-Conquest earl.

Many honours of this kind may have encompassed quite ancient groups of estates. Ralph fitz Hubert, for example, seems to have been heir to a large number of the early eleventh-century estates of Wulfric Spot through his predecessors Leofric and Leofnoth,[107] while William Peverel's Nottinghamshire estates seem to have held by the earl's thegns before the Conquest.[108] It cannot be concluded from this, however, that each honour had a single pre-Conquest identity. Sawyer assumes, or leaves the reader to assume, that such is in fact the case.[109] But in reality there were often significant changes. First, it is clear that some tenants-in-chief had more than one predecessor. Walter de Aincurt, with three predecessors, is a case in point that has already been cited. Others are explicit in the text: Asgar the staller and Haldane are named

---

[103] Stenton, *First Century of English Feudalism*, 62; Fleming, *Kings and Lords in Conquest England*, 148.

[104] Stenton, *Types of Manorial Structure*, 92–3; *Registrum Antiqusissimum of Lincoln*, i. 62, 211; *Calendar of Documents . . . France*, nos. 61, 62; Denton, *English Royal Free Chapels*, 115. For a full discussion of the institution, see Roffe, 'Nottinghamshire', 185–90.

[105] GDB 319a: *DB Yorks.*, 10W1.   [106] *Rotuli Hundredorum*, ii. 300b–301a.

[107] GDB 272a–c: *DB Derby.*, 10; Sawyer, *Charters of Burton Abbey*, 53–6.

[108] Roffe, 'From Thegnage to Barony', 173–4; Roffe, 'The Anglo-Saxon Town and the Norman Conquest', 35–6.

[109] Sawyer, '1066–1086'.

as predecessors of Geoffrey de Mandeville,[110] Withgar, Finn, and Ælmar of
Richard son of Count Gilbert,[111] Ælfric Kemp and Lisois (here a post-
Conquest predecessor) of Eudo son of Hubert,[112] and Edric and Durand of
Robert Malet.[113] Secondly, all of the estates of the same predecessor throughout the country did not always pass to the same tenant-in-chief. Pre-Conquest
tenurial relationships were often responsible. Beorhtric son of Ælfgar, for
example, was a king's thegn, but he appears to have held land from the bishop
of Worcester in Barley and Bushley in Worcestershire, and the estates were
retained by the church after the Conquest.[114] As in the twelfth century, political influence and support were bought by the grant of land to important local
personages.[115] However, what can be perceived as thegn's demesne and the
tenanted (as opposed to commended) estates through the record of sake and
soke or the use of the *tenuit* formula usually seem to have passed to a single
tenant-in-chief, at least on a local basis. The tendency is clearest in counties
like Leicestershire, where TRE holders of land are predominantly predecessors (Table 2.2), but it is evidenced throughout the country.[116]

Some of the more extensive pre-Conquest estates may on occasion have
been divided. Beorhtric son of Ælfgar's demesnes in Cornwall, Devon, Dorset,
Gloucestershire, Wiltshire, and Worcestershire, for example, passed to some

TABLE 2.2. *King's thegns and holders of bookland in Leicestershire in 1066 as
indicated by the* tenuit *formula*

Thegn TRE	TRW Successor
Aelfeva, Countess	Aelfeva, Countess
Aelmer*	Robert the bursar
Algar*	Judith, Countess
Alnoth	Hugh, Earl
Alnoth*	Robert de Bucy
Alwin Buxton	Hugh de Grandmesnil
Alwin*	Hugh de Grandmesnil
Arkell*	York, archbishop of
Arkell, Osmund, Oslac*	York, archbishop of
Aubrey, Earl	Aubrey, Earl
Auti, Ernwy*	Hugh, Earl
Baldwin, Alwin	Hugh de Grandmesnil

[110] LDB 314b–315a, 411a: *DB Suffolk*, 6,112.32,1.
[111] LDB 348b–349a, 351b–352a, 440b, 447b–448a: *DB Suffolk*, 8,35;59.67,1.76,1–7; GDB 35b: *DB Surrey*, 19,28.
[112] LDB 378a, 403a: *DB Suffolk*, 16,41.28,2. [113] LDB 304a–b, 4225a: *DB Suffolk*, 6,3.39,12.
[114] GDB 173b: *DB Worcs.*, 2,30;37; Williams, 'Introduction to the Worcestershire Domesday,' 23.
[115] Harvey, 'Knight and Knight's Fee', 6–7.
[116] A list of king's thegns and the demesne lands that they held in 1066 is in preparation by the writer.

TABLE 2.2. (cont'd)

Thegn TRE	TRW Successor
Bardi	Lincoln, bishop of
Brictmer, Ulf	Meulan, count of
Edith, Queen	Hugh de Grandmesnil
Edith, Queen	King
Edwin Alfrith	Robert the bursar
Godiva, Countess	Godiva, Countess
Godric*	Lincoln, bishop of
Gytha	York, archbishop of
Haldane*	Lincoln, bishop of
Harding	Aubrey, Earl
Harold, Earl	Hugh, Earl
Leofnoth	Lincoln, bishop of
Leofric	Henry de Ferrers
Leofric	Guy de Reinbudcurt
Leofric	Meulan, count of
Leofric son of Leofwin*	Geoffrey de la Guerche
Leofwin	Meulan, count of
Leofwin	King
Morcar	Robert de Bully
Morcar, Earl	King
Ralph	Lincoln, bishop of
Osgot	King
Ralph, Earl	Peterborough, abbot of
Ralph, Earl	Hugh de Grandmesnil
Ralph, Earl	Robert de Bucy
Ralph, Earl	Mainou the Breton
Rolf, Edwin	Durand Malet
Saxi	Meulan, count of
Thorkell*	Judith, Countess
Three thegns	Robert de Bucy
Toki*	Geoffrey Alselin
Two brothers	Hugh de Grandmesnil
Ulf*	Hugh de Grandmesnil
Ulf*	Drogo de Beuvrière
Waltheof	Hugh de Grandmesnil
Waltheof, Earl	Henry de Ferrers
Waltheof, Earl	Judith, Countess
Wulfgeat*	Lincoln, bishop of

Note: Where two or more names are given in an entry, it is likely that only one, possibly the first, was the king's thegn. The others probably held loanland (OE *laenland*) from them. An asterisk indicates sake and soke explicitly noticed in the text.

eighteen different tenants-in-chief by various routes.[117] But, with the exception of illegal seizures, it is generally only in the transfer of royal and comital
estates that individual interests were divided. Tosti/Morcar's estates in
Lincolnshire, for example, were retained by the king, but those in the vicinity of Nottingham were granted to William Peverel.[118] In the East Midlands
the division of comital estates may reflect pre-Conquest patterns of tenure,
for the region was subject to the claims of rival earldoms in the reign of Edward
the Confessor.[119] But there can be no doubt that the redistribution of bookland estates, both by division and amalgamation, was immediately related
to post-Conquest political and strategic concerns. However, the degree of
discontinuity should not be overstressed. It was probably no different in kind
or extent from tenurial upheavals of the first half of the eleventh century and
was almost certainly underpinned by the survival of existing tenurial nexus
and relationships.

As has been seen, king's thegns had full rights over the estates of lesser thegns
before the Conquest. In Yorkshire many of these subordinate holdings were
apparently ministerial. The lands of the so-called *taini regis*, for example, are
explicitly assigned to the royal demesne in the Yorkshire Summary, and a
parallel entry suggests that a further 332 manors postscriptally appended to
the king's breve were thegnages. Indeed, in the north the lesser thegns paid
the same relief as the drengs of the land between the Ribble and Mersey and
their status may have been very similar.[120] The incidence of forinsec services
south of the Humber does not preclude similar tenures elsewhere; drengs are
found in Kent and radknights in the West Midlands, while the common record
of renders from manorial commodities like the mill indicates the reservation
of dues to the overlord throughout the country. But something akin to laenage
was probably more common in the south since rights to *terra* in the form of
sokeland were attached to the thegn's hall.[121]

In both types of tenure the nature of renders and services owed to the
booklord are rarely explicit, but the main outlines are clear. All tenants were
in the soke of their lord to whom their forfeitures, whether in a private or
communal courts, belonged. Some TRE drengages, like Wharram Percy in
Yorkshire, were later held by sergeancy in the feudal army and may therefore have owed military obligations, and escort duties and the like are found

---

[117] Williams, 'A West Country Magnate of the Eleventh Century', 41–68, esp. at 63–5.

[118] GDB 337c, 338a, 338c, 280a, 287c: *DB Lincs.*, 1,1;4–6;26,65; *DB Notts.*, B2.10,18. For the history of Tosti's Nottingham fee, see Roffe, 'Anglo-Saxon Town and the Norman Conquest', 35–7.

[119] Roffe, 'Nottinghamshire', 256–60.

[120] GDB 269d, 298d: *DB Cheshire*, R1,40g; *DB Yorks.*, C40. Although called king's thegns, these individuals did not have their 'soc' and must therefore be distinguished from the holders of bookland.
They were in fact the king's median thegns and are hereafter referred to as *taini regis* to distinguish
them from the more privileged *ministri*.

[121] Stenton, *First Century of English Feudalism*, 145–7; Roffe, 'Domesday Book and Northern Society',
328–33.

TABLE 2.3. *Values in LDB, Bury C, and the Kalendar of Abbot Samson*

	LDB		Bury C	Kalendar
	TRE	TRW		
Timworth	30s	20s 0d	26s 0½d	30s 1½d
Tostock	10s	10s 8d	3s 9½d	12s 10½d
Hessett		40s 0d	48s 1d	51s 0d
Woolpit		10s 8d	10s 11d	12s 4d
Rushbrooke	16s	21s 11d	19s 2d	25s 2d

elsewhere.[122] Domesday Book, however, suggests that all, if only notionally, rendered dues to their overlord in recognition of his right. Throughout the country *valuit* figures, the value of estates in 1066, are generally expressed in round sums and are clearly conventional. Occasionally, they are explicitly called renders,[123] and in some East Anglian estates they can be shown to be soke dues. In the Suffolk folios of LDB the lands of free men of Bury St Edmund's are occasionally separately valued, and in most cases the same tenements can be identified in Bury C, a schedule very close in date to the Domesday inquest (Table 2.3). In this document each free man is named and the amount of land that he held is recorded along with a sum of money. Totals are given for these sums and, although neither they nor the aggregates of the individual figures equate exactly with the LDB values, they are all of the same magnitude and some are very close. They can be further traced in the Kalendar of Abbot Samson, a late-twelfth-century inventory of the dues of Bury St Edmund's in the hundreds of its Suffolk liberty,[124] and there they are identified. The renders were additional to a series of light labour services and a food rent called foddercorn and were known as hidage, sheriff's aid, carriage, and wardpenny. LDB makes it clear that the abbey has the soke of these men and it seems clear that Bury C and the Kalendar preserve a record of the sorts of due that made up their Domesday value. Sheriff's aid, carriage, and wardpenny can be characterized as public duties which were incumbent on all land; in financial terms they were of minor value and were probably not included in the Domesday valets. Hidage, by contrast, was a more substantial source of income which was confined to sokeland. Here it was a hundredal due, having its origins in the renders that free men and sokemen made to the king,

---

[122] Roffe, 'Wharram Percy'.

[123] Commonly in the *terra regis*. LDB and GDB at times, however, hint at a significant usage for the terms since both figures are occasionally given, the render usually being more than the 'value' (Lennard, *Rural England*, 113–23).

[124] *Kalendar of Abbot Samson*.

but it seems to represent the soke dues that were conferred by the right of sake and soke. Some sokemen may have paid in addition a manorial rent, but by and large hidage seems to have represented their full value.[125]

Bury's free men held directly from the abbey and were valued separately from the manor to which they belonged. The renders of Burton Abbey's men c.1125 appear to be directly comparable and there they represent the full value of the GDB manor.[126] This was probably the norm. The render of £150 that the queen's soke of Rutland made to the crown seems to have been the sum total of the value of the manors in the liberty, not all of which were held by Queen Edith,[127] and elsewhere the value of an estate is on occasion explicitly identified as a payment that was rendered. In Osmaston by Derby, for example, the value of the estate was divided in the ratio of two to one between the king and Henry de Ferrers in 1086.[128] Henry was apparently heir to the earl's share, and the render was therefore almost certainly of pre-Conquest origin, for the earldom was in the king's hands for much of William's reign. Within this context, the occasional attachment of the value of one manor to another becomes immediately comprehensible: the 'valuation' of a manor was a sum that went out of the estate to an overlord in recognition of a soke relationship.

The terms of tenancy after the Conquest were generally not markedly different. By the second half of the twelfth century most tenanted manors were held in hereditary fee by knight service. However, although each tenant-in-chief was probably responsible for a *servitium debitum* in 1086, it is doubtful that such a radical change in the nature of tenure was far advanced at the time of the Domesday inquest. First of all, it is clear that many pre-Conquest families continued to hold their estates. In almost every county a number of tenements in the hands of *taini regis* were held by the same individuals in both 1066 and 1086, and many others passed to sons and heirs. However, these were only the ones who held of the king, and many more can be identified. In some breves there are one or two lesser thegns who survived the Conquest to hold their manors of a tenant-in-chief. But Domesday Book probably hides many others, for tenants are only erratically recorded in the text. Colle, for example, held Youlgreave in Derbyshire in 1066, and no tenant is recorded at the time of the survey, but in the twelfth century the manor was held by Colle's grandson.[129] Likewise, the Cromwell family was enfeoffed in Nuthall and Toton in Nottinghamshire which had been held by their *antecessor* Aldene

---

[125] Ibid., pp. xxxii–xlvii.   [126] 'Burton Surveys'.

[127] The total TRW value of the constituent estates less those held with sake and soke (including Peterborough Abbey's sokelands of Oundle) is £152 8s. Cain ('Introduction to the Rutland Domesday', 27) equates the farm with the TRE value of the Martinsley and Witchley estates alone of £156 12s.

[128] GDB 275d: *DB Derby.*, 6,88.

[129] GDB 275c: *DB Derby.*, 6,76; *Monasticon Anglicanum*, vi. 468.

before the Conquest.[130] Many other tenants may have been sons of TRE holders, for a large proportion of tenants in 1086 had English or Anglo-Scandinavian names. In Nottinghamshire, for example, some 40 per cent were apparently of native stock.[131]

All of these continued to hold their lands under much the same conditions as before the Conquest. References are occasionally found to tenure in thegn-age and in the Nottinghamshire folios many are specifically distinguished from the foreign tenants, for they are said to 'have their land under', or 'hold from', as opposed to being 'men of' the tenant-in-chief.[132] Further, a high proportion of the estates emerged in the thirteenth century as socages or sergeancies. In Yorkshire, for example, whole groups of manors were held by various personal services and several characteristics of tenure suggest that many more estates were of this kind.[133] Thus, large numbers of military fees were primarily assessed in carucates, and feudal dues were calculated by set formulas: in Holderness, fourteen or sixteen carucates to the knight fee was the norm, while ten, twelve, and twenty-four are found elsewhere.[134] Feudalism was just a thin veneer: ministerial tenure was apparently the essence of these manors, and it is likely that they had their ultimate origin in pre-Conquest thegnages and drengages.[135]

By far the majority of tenants, however, were newcomers. Nevertheless, it must be doubted that many held under radically different terms. The evidence is most unequivocal in ecclesiastical estates. In the lands of the bishop of Worcester, for example, Normans seem to have held laenages in exactly the same terms as their English predecessors; Westminster and Hereford charters indicate that grants of land were non-hereditary; and again at Ely there was no enfeoffment since the *servitium debitum* was discharged by household knights.[136] But there are indications that this was also the norm in lay estates. As late as 1166 not all barons had enfeoffed enough knights to cover their *servitium debitum*, but, nevertheless, it is clear that many of their estates were still tenanted. Brailsford in Derbyshire, for example, was in the tenure of Elfin in 1086, but it was not until c.1140 that it was granted in hereditary fee;[137] the land was presumably only held for a life or term of lives before this date, although the family may have had a presumptive right to the estate.

[130] GDB 287c, 287d: *DB Notts.*, 10,25;40; *Documents Relating to Newark*, p. xxx.
[131] Roffe, 'Nottinghamshire', 95.
[132] Stenton, 'Introduction to the Nottinghamshire Domesday', 230; Roffe, 'Nottinghamshire', 95.
[133] Campbell, 'Some Agents and Agencies of the Late Anglo-Saxon State', 210–13.
[134] Roffe, 'Wharram Percy'; Hollister, *Military Organization of Norman England*, 48; *Early Yorkshire Charters*, i. 172; North Yorkshire Record Office, Outfac 125; *Charters of the Honour of Mowbray*, p. xxxviii, nos. 366–7, 374.
[135] Roffe, 'Wharram Percy'; *Charters of the Honour of Mowbray*, pp. xxxix, xl.
[136] GDB 172c: *DB Worcs.*, 2,1; *Westminster Charters*, 108–9; Galbraith, 'Episcopal Land-Grant of 1085', 353–72; Miller, *Abbey and Bishopric of Ely*, 67–8.
[137] Statham, 'The Brailsfords', 67–8; *Red Book of the Exchequer*, 338. For Yorkshire examples, see Michelmore, Faull, and Moorhouse, *West Yorkshire*, 243.

Precarious tenure of this kind is in fact implicit in post-Conquest legal treatises. In the Leis Willelme (1090–1135) the vavassour is contrasted with the *baro* and appears to represent the lesser thegn, while in the Leges Edwardi Confessoris (1115–50) the knight was apparently in the frankpledge of his lord who had sake and soke, and right was done in his court instead of that of hundred or wapentake.[138] Military service was still essentially personal and was performed by the household knight or by tenants under the terms which they could best negotiate.[139]

The greatest indication of continuity, however, lay in renders due from the estate itself. Every manor had a value in 1086, and this was still a sum which went out of the estate. Thus, the value of Onibury in Shropshire in 1086 was the annual value that Roger de Lacy agreed to pay the bishop of Hereford for the estate in the previous year, and the 10 shillings at which Ticknall and Stanton by Newball in Derbyshire were each valued was the rent that two tenants paid to Burton Abbey in the early twelfth century.[140] Indeed, the sums are again sometimes called renders. In Worcestershire, for example, it is explicitly stated that the sheriff rendered sums from each of the king's manors, and the income that the king derived from estates in the county (which is noted in the account of the City of Worcester) is within a few shillings of the sum total of the renders and values (the *reddit* and *valet* figures) recorded in his breve.[141] It is clear that, although the sums owed often changed dramatically, the tenant-in-chief levied the same types of due from the manors of his honour, both demesne and tenanted, which had been collected by his predecessor in 1066.

This continuity is reflected in post-Conquest legal treatises and law codes. In the late twelfth and thirteenth centuries tenure *per baroniam* was distinguished by four characteristics. First, although it could be held in parage, the barony had an identity as a group of fees regardless of the descent of the lordship. As a consequence, it rendered services and dues to the king as a unit and, unlike the tenement held by knight service, was legally indivisible. Secondly, its lord paid a relief at the will of the king, subsequently fixed at a hundred pounds, as opposed to a relief of five pounds for an ordinary estate. Thirdly, a single manor was designated as a *caput* and could not be divided between collateral heirs. Finally, the baron was exempt from juries and was only amerced

---

[138] *Die Gesetze*, i. 507, 647; Stenton, *First Century of English Feudalism*, 141. For a discussion of the emergence of hereditary fees, see Thorne, 'English Feudalism and Estates in Land', 193–209; Hudson, 'Life Grants of Land and the Development of Inheritance', 67–80.

[139] Chibnall, *Anglo-Norman England*, 28–34; King, 'Peterborough "Descriptio Militum" (Henry I)', 94–5.

[140] Galbraith, 'Episcopal Land Grant', 357; 'Burton Surveys', 240; GDB 273b, 274b: *DB Derby.*, 3,7.6,21.

[141] GDB 172a, 172b–c: *DB Worcs.*, C2.1,1–4. The sheriff of Worcester is said to have rendered £123 4s from the king's estates, while the total of the *reddit* and *valet* figures in the king's *breve* is £124 6s. Kinver (Staffs.) appears to have rendered in Worcestershire, but Tardebrigge and Clent (Worcs.) in Staffordshire.

before the king's council.[142] By this time the rationale of the form had been forgotten, and its imposition was merely a matter of record, but it is significant that the tenure shared these characteristics with tenure by book. Above all, barony was likewise grounded in the tenure of sake and soke. The *Leges Henrici* broaches the subject in two passages. In c. 9.11 it asserts: 'As to the soke of pleas, there is that which belongs properly and exclusively to the king's fisc; there is that which it shares with others; there is that which belongs to the sheriffs and royal bailiffs as comprised in their farms; there is that which belongs to the barons who have their sake and soke.'[143] Again in c. 20.2:

archbishops, bishops, earls, and other persons of high rank have sake and soke, toll and team, and infangthef in the lands of their own bailiwicks, but in others acquired by purchase or exchange or in some other way, they have sake and soke in common causes and such as belong to hallmoots, over their own men and in their own [bailiwick], and sometimes over men of another, especially if they have been taken in the act or accused without delay, and thence they shall have the proper fine.[144]

As Reid has shown, in origin the essential feature of barony was sake and soke, and it was the close relationship between crown and tenant-in-chief that this entailed that characterized the tenure.[145]

It is evident, then, that baronies represent pre-Conquest estates in both form and composition. Some embraced two or three pre-Conquest bookland estates, and, with but few exceptions, they were subject to new lords. But in its essential the honour was a pre-Conquest institution. In 1086 title was generally founded in English law and drew upon a recognized succession to bookland estates. As a series of jurors and witnesses in Hampshire asserted, 'they refused to accept any law but King Edward's until it is defined by the king'.[146] By and large title was already established. Restructuring of honours was still possible. William de Warenne gave up land to make way for William de Braose in Sussex; Roger the Poitevin seems to have surrendered land in the region known as Between Ribble and Mersey, in Amounderness, Derbyshire, and Norfolk.[147] In both cases, however, there seems to have been a recognition of right, for William de Warenne was compensated with the grant of estates in Norfolk and Roger the Poitevin subsequently received the lands in the northwest that became the honour of Lancaster. Some tenants-in-chief had held

---

[142] *Glanvill*, 108; *Bracton*, i. 8; ii. 39.

[143] *Leges Henrici Primi*, c. 9.11. Translation after Reid, 'Barony and Thanage', 173.

[144] *Leges Henrici Primi*, c. 20.2. Translation after Reid, 'Barony and Thanage', 174.

[145] Reid, 'Barony and Thanage', 170–3. Reid's analysis has been criticized on the ground that the tenure of sake and soke was never a test of barony in the thirteenth century (Sanders, *Feudal Military Service in England*, 66–8). However, it was the 'nighness' to the king which conferred the special status of barony. From the late eleventh century franchises were being created within honours, but the tenure of jurisdiction within that context did not forge a direct relationship with the crown.

[146] GDB 44d: *DB Hants.*, 23,3.

[147] Holt, '1086', 59; Mason, *William the First and the Sussex Rapes*, 15–16; Lewis, 'Introduction to the Lancashire Domesday', 36–8.

their lands for almost twenty years, most could look back on fifteen years of tenure. During that time they had defended their title to individual estates year after year by rendering the geld and services assessed upon them, and they no doubt felt that their right was as secure as that of their predecessors. Few could demonstrate hereditary right in the narrowest sense. Roger de Lacy had succeeded to the lands of his father, Walter, probably in 1084,[148] but most tenants-in-chief were first-generation grantees. Nevertheless, sake and soke offered them the presumption of the *ius perpetuum* that their predecessors had enjoyed. By and large title was established by 1086.

Domesday Book and Right to Land

The small number of claims in the Domesday corpus is witness enough that title was not an issue in the Domesday inquest. But, if doubt persists, it is dispelled by the treatment of problems of right in the Domesday sources, notably in Domesday Book itself. A lack of interest in title, not to say a cavalier attitude, is most apparent in the widespread incidence of duplicate and parallel entries. The same parcel of land is commonly attributed to two or more tenants-in-chief throughout GDB and LDB.[149] Sometimes the phenomenon is simply a function of unexplained tenurial relationships: it is usual to find land entered in two places when the soke is held by one tenant-in-chief and the land itself by another. In other instances a change in tenure in the course of the inquest is responsible. In the Lincolnshire folios thirteen carucates and six bovates of land in Holbeach and Whaplode are entered in the king's chapter with the note that part had been held by Count Alan. The same land is described in Count Alan's chapter where he is said to hold five carucates. A postscriptal addition to the entry, however, indicates that the land was deraigned to the king's use, but a further entry in the *clamores* provides the information that the king had granted the land to Count Alan for one manor.[150] It would therefore seem that the land had been taken away from Count Alan, probably at the start of the inquest, and subsequently returned to him. But time and again the distinction between what was held and what was claimed as of right is not made explicit. The church was generally assiduous in asserting its rights. Accounts of much of the land taken away from Ely Abbey in Cambridgeshire, for example, find themselves in the abbot's breve.[151] But laymen were equally keen to make good their tenure, usually without any indication of disputed tenure.

In many of these cases there is often no record of a communal presentment on the matter. It might, then, be argued that the compiler of Domesday

[148] Wightman, *The Lacy Family*, 168.
[149] Williams, 'Apparent Repetitions in Domesday Book', 90–2.
[150] GDB 338b, 348c, 377d: *DB Lincs.*, 1,32–3.12,84.CK71.
[151] GDB 190c–192b: *DB Cambs.*, 5.

Book was unaware of the inconsistencies to which the aspirations of tenants-in-chief gave rise. It must be suspected, however, that ignorance was usually not the issue, for he was at no greater pains to establish right where the verdicts of juries were recorded in his sources and were dutifully copied by himself. Of the 339 cases of suits between subjects analysed by Patrick Wormald, sixty-six are too obscure to allow further comment; the remaining 273 cases break down into sixty (apparently) successful defences and 213 wins by plaintiffs.[152] As might be expected, the lands in dispute in the former are duly found in the chapters of the defendants in Domesday Book. But no less than 156 of the latter are still entered in the fee of the defendant and aggressor. In the Hampshire folios, for example, it is recorded in the account of six hides in Bramshott held by Edward of Salisbury that: 'William Maudit claims one hide of this land which lay in Hartley Mauditt. The hundred and the shire testify to this.'[153] Despite the fact that both the hundred and shire bore witness in William's favour, the land is nevertheless entered in Edward's chapter as one of his estates. It must be doubted that all of Wormald's cases involved recognitions, but at least some of the presentments in the *clamores* of the northern folios were intended to be resolutions of the matters in hand.[154] The outcome of disputes was clearly not of primary interest to the compilers of GDB and LDB. Nor, moreover, was action consistently taken to make good the plaintiffs' rights after the survey. Pleas did proceed on Domesday evidence in the reign of William Rufus, but title was not always corroborated. Neither William Maudit nor his successors gained seisin of the hide in Bramshott and their experience was not exceptional. In Huntingdonshire and Cambridgeshire Eustace the sheriff retained almost all his estates despite the apparently successful pleas of those whose lands he had appropriated;[155] Ely was never able to regain many of the estates seemingly adjudged to it in Domesday Book;[156] and in Lincolnshire the land of as many as 95 per cent of apparently successful plaintiffs failed to pass into their fees.[157]

It is thus evident that the Domesday inquest had not resolved conflicts of right and that the compiler of Domesday did not strenuously strive to record rightful title. Here and there, it is true, the text is annotated to indicate claims; in the northern county folios some entries are marked with a K for *kalumpnia*, 'claim', but the device is not systematically used. Domesday Book can hardly have been intended as a register of title for the new regime where claims were treated in quite such a casual fashion. From the outset it would seem that the

---

[152] Wormald, 'Domesday Lawsuits', 78–94.   [153] GDB 46c: *DB Hants.*, 27,1.
[154] In the South Riding of Lincoln the verdicts are specifically said to be *concordia* (GDB, 376b: *DB Lincs.*, CW). See below, pp. 50–1, 83–4.
[155] GDB 208a–b: *DB Hunts.*, D1;2;12;19–21;25.   [156] Miller, *Abbey and Bishopric of Ely*, 66–7.
[157] The analysis has been confined to land since forinsec soke, the subject of the majority of pleas, is rarely noticed in later sources.

inquest had merely recorded tenure, and this remained the principal concern of the compiler of Domesday Book.

Domesday, then, fails the test as an executive process in the central matter of title. Right was not an issue in the majority of cases, and in those in which it was, Domesday only concerns itself with tenure. An executive procedure is defined by what it achieves, and within the terms of the debate hitherto it would seem to have achieved nothing. The solution to the conundrum is plain: the inquest was of its nature no executive instrument.

3

The Inquest and Government

DOMESDAY BOOK, WITH near-contemporary sources, described itself as a *descriptio*, that is, a writing down. The nearest English term is perhaps 'survey', and indeed the word is widely used of the process that was set in train in 1085.[1] Historians further characterize that survey as an inquisition or inquest. The term *inquisitio* does not appear in English sources until the twelfth century, but it is used with some reason in this context.[2] It signifies a questioning and in its essentials it consisted of a panel of jurors drawn from the local community who were sworn to answer truthfully to the questions put to them by the king or his agent.[3] It was a device that was widely used in England throughout the medieval period. The verdict became the touchstone of a host of legal and administrative activities that impinged on almost every aspect of public life. As an instrument of government it was particularly effective, for it harnessed the local community to the crown. Much of the Angevin revolution in government was founded on the device, and in consequence it has often been seen as both the cause and effect of the formation of a powerful monarchy in England. Superseding the more primitive procedures of Old English law, the inquest brought the king into the business of the shire and shone a light of reason into the mire of tribal custom.

This is, of course, a parody of the facts, but it is a parody that embodies a perception of the inquest which has influenced in one way or another almost all examinations of the Domesday process. It cannot be doubted that the sworn jury was an important source of information in the inquest of 1086. In folio after folio the declarations of the community are a commonplace. Juries of shire, riding, lathe, and hundred are ubiquitous; less common, but equally important are Englishmen, Frenchmen, and thegns. The procedure was of a kind that would not be out of place in the reign of Edward I at the height of the Plantagenet experiment in interventionist royal government. The use of the jury is manifest. Its role is to all appearances equally transparent. It is implied in most discussions of the origins of the inquest in England that the

---

[1] See LDB 450a: *DB Suffolk*, 77,4. For references to Domesday Book as a *descriptio* in other documents, see Galbraith, *Making of Domesday Book*, 183–4. The term probably also implies the idea of assessment ultimately derived from the Vulgate rendering of Luke 2: 1 'there went out a decree from Caesar Augustus that all the world should be taxed' as *ut describeretur universus orbis* (Davis, 'Domesday Book: Continental Parallels', 15).

[2] Latham, *Revised Medieval Latin Word List*, 252.

[3] Pollock and Maitland, *History of English Law*, i. 140–5.

device was the antithesis of compurgation. In Old English law truth was determined in folk courts by the weight of support as measured by oath helpers and their status. After the Conquest this procedure was superseded by judgement within royal courts by the king or his agents and the decision was based upon the verdict of a competent jury. For an older generation of scholars, the implications of this assumption for an understanding of the Domesday inquest were plain. The procedure was a Norman importation and in essence an executive instrument. More recently, evidence has been adduced to show that the jury was known in pre-Conquest England, but the idea of the inquest as an executive process has persisted. It is still widely asumed that the jurors of the Domesday texts produced verdicts which were of legal force to determine truth, and it thus follows that the survey was intended to settle the matters in hand; title was to be established and liberties confirmed. The case is eloquently put in a recent examination of Domesday Book and the Norman settlement.

Oral testimony was central to the purpose of the inquest, and it provided the means through which neighbours of all social classes and peoples witnessed and recognised the permanence of the Norman settlement: and the inquest rather than the book became the means though which the whole of the tenurial revolution (much of which had been accomplished without written order or public sanction) came clearly and finally into every man's view, and it was the way in which the Conquest was at last fit snugly and publicly within the law.[4]

As a replacement of compurgation, the outcome of an inquest was, by its nature, a recognition with equivalent force.

It is here argued that this antithesis of inquest and compurgation is misconceived. The inquest was no super-court of law that determined right; its function was more modestly to inform. Where the community's evidence was uncontested, its verdict had the force of a judgement, but otherwise it did not supersede routine legal process. It was normally the beginning of action rather than a determination. This at once removes the necessity to see the inquest as antithetical to compurgation, and, equally important, to place the origins of the inquest within royal courts. Evidence is presented to demonstrate that communal verdicts were employed in the context of both royal and folk law in the pre-Conquest period and were as preliminary to judgement by compurgation before the Conquest as they might be to recognition after.

Recognition and Presentment

The verdict was an integral part of both civil and criminal common law proceedings. Its most conspicuous use was in the determination of contentious matters. In Domesday Book itself there survives a record of disputes in the South Riding of Lindsey, 'and their resolution through the men who swear

---

[4] Fleming, 'Oral Testimony', 120.

[*clamores que sunt in Sudtreding Lincolie et concordia eorum per homines qui iuraverunt*]'.[5] Thereafter, verdicts of this kind informed the resolution of land disputes in royal courts with increasing frequency until they became the norm in the late twelfth century. A similar development saw the verdict supplement and then replace the cumbersome processes of appeal, ordeal, and the like in criminal cases from much the same time.[6] In both areas of law the jury's recognition informed the justice's judgement and effectively terminated the matter in hand. The device was effective precisely because it provided a relatively swift resolution of disputes within a communal context. Nevertheless, it was far from a summary process. The recognition came as the climax to complex procedures. In the grand assize, for example, it followed extensive investigations of a jury of knights of the shire, and it decided title once and for all.[7] Again, in the king's pleas of the eyre it was subsequent to pleadings and informed the judgement of the court.[8]

Here the verdict was based upon the evidence collected and, where appropriate, the subsequent pleadings. As the Latin *veredictum*, 'true saying', indicates, truth was expected. But recognition of this kind was not of the essence of the verdict. Jurors were always sworn to tell the truth but the context was as likely to be the beginning of administrative and judicial processes as the end; they might present a fact or demonstrate a prima facie case against someone, but their word did not end the matter. The jury of presentment in the sheriff's tourn named those it suspected of wrongdoing, and sureties were taken to ensure the appearance of the accused in court. But they then suffered the due process of law before the justices; the jury had to repeat its presentment and might subsequently make a recognition, with all manner of processes intervening.[9]

The *veredictum* in this context was evidentiary rather than recognitory in the narrow sense. As a declaration of truth, it might in some circumstances assume a finality that belied the context in which it was delivered. The assize of novel disseisin had been designed as a means to restore seisin where a lord had attempted to intimidate through forcible entry by establishing prior seisin while not precluding further action to determine right.[10] But the procedure became vested with such authority that the verdict pursuant to the writ constituted unequivocal evidence of tenure if not title.[11] In the course of time all uncontested verdicts took on the mantle of incontrovertible fact. However, except in recognitory contexts, they were initially all open to challenge in due process.

---

[5] GDB 376b–c: *DB Lincs.*, CW.　　[6] Pollock and Maitland, *History of English Law*, i. 151–3.

[7] *Glanville*, II.6, pp. 26–8; Pollock and Maitland, *History of English Law*, i. 147.

[8] Bolland, *The General Eyre*, 48–54.　　[9] Ibid.

[10] A view of the land was permitted if more than one parcel was held in the same vill (Stenton, *Lincolnshire Assize Roll*, p. lxvii).

[11] Warren, *Governance of Norman and Angevin England*, 119.

The force of a verdict, then, depended on the context in which it was delivered. It was what will be called here the presentment (as opposed to the recognition)[12] that lay at the heart of the inquest in the twelfth and thirteenth centuries. It informed an investigatory process that was initiated to determine fact in the absence of information or reliable documentation.[13] The procedure of the inquest in the twelfth century is largely invisible. No original verdicts survive for the Leicestershire, Lindsey, and Northamptonshire Surveys of the early years of the century,[14] and the extant verdicts of the Inquest of Sheriffs of 1170 are uninformative.[15] Roger of Hoveden, however, provides a vivid account of the inquest which was preliminary to the assessment of the carucage in 1198.

Richard, king of England, levied from each carucate or hide of land throughout all England five shillings as an aid; for the purpose of collecting which, the said king sent through each county of England one clerk and one knight who, with the sheriff of the county to which they were sent, and lawful knights elected for the purpose, making oath that they would faithfully perform the king's business, caused to appear before them the seneschals of the barons of each county, and the lord or bailiff of every vill, and the reeve, together with the four lawful men of the vill, whether free men or villeins, as also two lawful knights of the hundred, who made oath that they would faithfully and without fraud declare how many plough teams [carucarum wainagia] there were in each village, namely how many in demesne and how many in villeinage, and how many in alms bestowed upon religious houses which the givers thereof were bound to warrant or acquit, or the religious houses were to do service for. . . . All this was put down in writing and the clerk had one roll, the knight another, the sheriff a third, and the seneschal a fourth as to the land of their lord.[16]

Villeins who concealed the truth were to forfeit their best ox to their lord and pay to the king the amount that he would thereby have lost, while free men were to be in mercy.

From thirteenth-century inquest records it becomes clear how the procedure worked in practice. In the 1212 scutage survey it would appear that *milites inquisitores* compiled presentments from various sources. The Lancashire roll,

---

[12] The usage here is taken from the procedure of the eyre (Bolland, *The General Eyre*, 48–54).

[13] Holt, 'The Pre-history of Parliament', 3–5.

[14] The Lindsey Survey, BL Cotton, Claudius C.5, survives in a contemporary MS but would appear to be a fair copy. It is written throughout by one early-twelfth-century hand with the minimum of corrections and only a small number of annotations, seemingly details that were accidentally omitted in the copying process. Some entries were subsequently annotated in a late-twelfth-century hand and further additions of the thirteenth and fifteenth century are found outlining the descent of some fees. There was, however, no attempt at any point systematically to update the material. See *Lincolnshire Survey*.

[15] *Red Book of the Exchequer*, vol. ii, pp. cclxvii–cclxxxi; Tait, 'A New Fragment of the Inquest of Sheriffs', 80–3; Suggett, 'An Anglo-Norman Return of the Inquest of Sheriffs', 179; *EHD* ii. 441–8 for references.

[16] *Chronica Rogeri de Houedene*, iv. 46–7. For an account of the procedure of the inquest, see Round, 'The Great Carucage of 1198', 501–10.

for example, was sealed by seventeen knights of the shire but they derived their account from the presentments of juries of borough and hundred.[17] Thereafter, the procedure changed little. For the scutage survey of 1242–3, the inquiry into sergeancies of 1250, the survey of the royal fisc in 1255, the inquest of officials of 1258 pursuant to the Provisions of Oxford, the Ragman inquest of 1274–5, and the Hundred Roll inquest of 1279–80, it can be summarized as follows. After the sheriff received the writ to organize the inquisition, he informed the hundreds of the forthcoming inquest and caused twelve or twenty-four knights of the shire to be elected (if not nominated by the crown) to supervise the collection of data. The initial forum was probably the shire court and the knights may have been required to make presentment there. Groups of knights then went out to hundred courts to hear the verdicts of the hundred juries in response to the articles, the presentments of the representatives of the vill, and the plaints of individuals. After due weighing of evidence a verdict was drawn up and it was this which was presented to the commissioners for perusal and comment. After appropriate revision, the roll was sealed by the hundred and was then returned to central government.

In none of the inquests was the verdict the resolution of the matter in hand. In some cases the inquest was the first element in a dialectic of investigation, legislation, and enforcement. The Inquest of Sheriffs in 1170 was initiated to review the workings of local government and justice after the king's absence abroad, and resulted in the dismissal of twenty sheriffs as a result of the findings. The assessment of the carucage of 1198 has the appearance of a more bureaucratic process. An attempt to standardize the ploughland at 100 acres, however, was either abandoned or subsequent negotiation saw the imposition of the tax on the working plough.[18] The survey of sergeancies of 1250 identified lands that had been illegally alienated, and led to actions in further legal proceedings in eyre after eyre where agreement could not be reached.[19] Finally, the 1274 inquest, commissioned to determine the extent of seigneurial encroachment on royal prerogatives and regalia and to uncover the excesses of seigneurial officials, was quickly followed by the Statute of Westminster I and the Statute of the Exchequer to remedy the worse excesses revealed.[20] The new regulations were put into effect in general eyres commencing in 1278, and offenders were brought to account in the same sessions.[21] The remaining inquests were audits of royal dues of one kind or another and were the preliminaries to the collection of revenue. The early-twelfth-century surveys anticipated the

---

[17] *Book of Fees*, i. 206, 221.

[18] Harvey, 'Taxation and the Ploughland in Domesday Book', 103. Roger of Hoveden records that sergeancies were exempt, but they were to be recorded and the sergeants were summoned to London 'audituri et facturi preceptum domini regis'. For the extant reports, see *Book of Fees*.

[19] *Book of Fees*, 1163–6. The matter was regularly incorporated into the articles of the eyre from 1244 (Cam, *Studies in the Hundred Rolls*, 92–3).

[20] *Statutes of the Realm*, i. 26–39, 197–8.

[21] Maddicott, 'Edward I and the Lessons of Baronial Reform', 10–11.

collection of geld, and the 1212 and 1242–3 surveys scutage.[22] That of 1255 saw a more general review of the royal fisc that resulted in a sale of resources of the Royal Forests and probably an increase in the increments charged on the farms of the shires.[23] In short, the inquest provided information but did not resolve contested matters; it was a source of authoritative evidence for subsequent action.[24]

The inquest was typically employed in extraordinary circumstances where the usual machinery of local government could not provide the information required or its officers could not be trusted. By the late thirteenth century it had begun to be used for bureaucratic ends. The Hundred Rolls inquest of 1279 was apparently designed to produce a land register for the use of Edward I's ministers.[25] But it was probably on that account that it failed to make progress and the whole enterprise was abandoned in the following year. Generally, however, the inquest was a point of dialogue between the crown and the local community. Thus it was that the collection of evidence was only tangentially related to the purpose to which it was to be put. Indeed, initial findings sometimes clarified the problem to such a degree that a redefinition of the terms of reference was thought advisable. In 1255, for example, King Henry III was short of revenue after repeated refusal by the Council to grant him an aid. His first resort was to the resources of the forest, but sale of timber led to a fall in prices and the inquest that he had ordered was suspended, only to be resumed some months later as part of a more general audit of his regalia.[26] Edward I ordered an inquiry in similar terms in January 1274, but disorder within the realm was such that on his return to England in July he was forced to abort the initial commissions and reissue them in terms that addressed popular demands for action against royal and seigneurial bailiffs.[27] The inquest provided the facts, but the action that was taken was to a greater or lesser degree a matter of negotiation. It was this characteristic that lay at the heart of the inquest as an instrument of government. It is manifest from its first recorded use in England in the pre-Conquest period.

The Origins of the Inquest in England

Following the German historian Brunner, Maitland considered that the inquest was a Norman importation into England and that it was ultimately derived from tenth-century Frankish practice.[28] In France and Germany the

---

[22] Round, *Feudal England*, 181–224; *Book of Fees*, 52–65, 637–53.
[23] Roffe, 'Hundred Rolls of 1255', 201–10.
[24] Roffe, 'Hundred Rolls and their Antecedents', 179–87.
[25] Raban, 'The 1279–80 Hundred Rolls', 130–1.   [26] Roffe, 'Hundred Rolls of 1255', 205–6.
[27] Cam, *Hundred and the Hundred Rolls*, 37; Maddicott, 'Edward I and the Lessons of the Baronial Reform', 9–11.
[28] Pollock and Maitland, *History of English Law*, i. 139–44.

crown had long assumed the prerogative to inquire into the extent and management of its regalian rights; it had further used it to investigate breaches of the king's peace and could even by royal grace grant it to individuals to resolve disputes between its subjects. Parallels for the Domesday inquest itself have been sought in the polyptych surveys of the Carolingian period. Like GDB, they were characterized as *descriptiones* and were similar in form; they usually furnish a detailed account of the demesne in terms of livestock, resources, and workforce, but accord a more summary treatment to freely held land and *beneficia*, the estates farmed to clients and protectors.[29] None of these surveys, however, is as comprehensive as Domesday. Charlemagne may have formulated plans to 'write down' the whole empire, but it is doubtful whether this was anything more than pious aspiration. The extant surveys are confined to the lands of individual religious houses, and appear to be purely ad hoc. None provides a precedent for the survey of a realm. Moreover, it is unlikely that ducal government availed itself of the inquest in Normandy before the Conquest.[30] The origins of the Domesday inquest are to be found in Old English society.

The inquest is little evidenced in Old English law codes; the declaration of dooms and compurgation are the normal processes of law. It is, however, not unknown. Maitland himself acknowledged that something like the inquest was found in the Danelaw. In a law code probably promulgated at Wantage *c*.997, III Æthelred, 3.1, it is declared that 'a meeting is to be held in each wapentake, and the twelve leading thegns, and with them the reeve, are to come forward and swear on the relics which are put into their hands that they will accuse no innocent man nor conceal any guilty one'.[31] Penalties for breach of the peace were calculated on a sliding scale depending in what assembly it had been given.

1.1 The peace which the ealdorman and the king's reeve give in the meeting of the Five Boroughs, that is to be atoned for with twelve hundred.
1.2 And the peace which is given in the meeting of one borough is to be atoned for with six hundreds; and that which is given in an alehouse, is to be atoned for, if a man is killed, with six half marks, and if no one is killed, with twelve *oras*.[32]

The hundred in question was a long hundred (120) of sixteen-pence Danish *oras*, that is £8 in all, and it was the sum that gave its name to a peculiar

---

[29] Percival, 'Precursors of Domesday: Roman and Carolingian Land Registers', 5–27; Davis, 'Domesday Book: Continental Parallels', 15–39. Davis provides a preliminary list (30–9).

[30] Stenton, *English Justice between the Norman Conquest and the Great Charter, 1066–1215*, 15; Bates, *Normandy Before 1066*, 162–72. The inquest is first attested in Normandy in 1070 × 1079 (*Regesta Regum: Acta*, no. 149). The procedure employed was very close to that of the Domesday inquest suggesting that Norman tenants-in-chief were not completely unfamiliar with the device in 1086. The fact may have facilitated their manifest co-operation with the king (Bates, 'The Conqueror's Charters', 15).

[31] Robertson, III Æthelred, 3.1; *EHD* i. 403.

[32] Robertson, III Æthelred 1.1, 1.2; *EHD* i. 403.

institution of the Northern Danelaw, the twelve-carucate hundred.[33] This was a unit of administration below the wapentake which had many of the characteristics of the vill. It is clear from Domesday Book that it was responsible for the payment of the fine for breach of the peace, and although there is no explicit evidence that it did so, it seems likely that it acted as a tithing, that is, it was responsible for presenting crimes within its confines, in the pre-Conquest period.[34]

Comparable evidence for other regions is absent, but provisions of a similar kind seem to have been applied. In Æthelred's Woodstock Code, the English counterpart of Wantage, sureties were apparently as much responsible for the presentments of wrongdoers as guaranteeing law-worthiness. It provided that: 'Each free man shall have trustworthy surety, that the surety hold him to all justice, if he be accused; if he be suspect, let him go to the threefold ordeal.'[35] By the reign of Cnut something very like a frankpledge system was in place in which the functions of surety and presentment were attached to tithings and hundreds:

20. And it is our will that every free man who wishes to have right of exculpation and to a wergeld if anyone slays him, be brought, if he is over twelve years old, into a hundred or tithing; otherwise he is not to be entitled to any rights of free men.
20a. Whether he has a home of his own, or is in the following of another, each is to be brought within a hundred and under surety, and the surety is to hold him and bring him to every legal duty.[36]

What were known as *ville integre*, 'whole vills', in the later Middle Ages had many affinities with the twelve-carucate hundred of the north and may have been remnants of the system.[37]

The emergence of the jury of presentment in criminal cases is a significant straw in the wind. Historians, it is true, have tended to view it as a special case divorced from the use of the inquest in so-called civil and fiscal contexts. Maitland thought it inconceivable in this type of process that the juries could have evolved out of doomsmen, but this is precisely what happened in manorial courts. The function of the suitors of such courts seems to have been not only to declare the truth in criminal and civil cases, as in the courts of the later common law, but also to state the custom of the manor. Originally, the lord's steward merely sat as president, but in the course of time he assumed

---

[33] Stenton, 'Introduction', *VCH Derbyshire*, i. 320; Roffe, 'Hundreds and Wapentakes', 33.

[34] Roffe, 'Lincolnshire Hundred', 27–36; Roffe, 'Origins of Derbyshire', 110. What explicit evidence there is for the hundred as tithing is late. In 1371, for example, the hundred of Sleaford in Lincolnshire made its own presentment to the justices (*Sessions of to the Peace*, 181–2).

[35] Robertson, I Æthelred 1.1.   [36] Robertson, II Cnut, 20, 20a; *EHD* ii. 421.

[37] Lees, 'The Statute of Winchester and the *Villa Integra*', 98–103. Recent arguments in favour of the pre-Conquest origin of the *murdrum* fine, a penalty imposed on the hundred for the death of an unidentified individual, further imply the ubiquity of a frankpledge system (O'Brien, 'From *Morðor* to *Murdrum*: the Pre-Conquest Origin and Norman Revival of the Murder Fine', 321–57).

the role of judge.[38] That development may well have been influenced by the processes of the common law, but manorialization, the extension of the rights of the lord over the land of his tenants, must have been equally important. With the increasingly common practice of the territorialization of rights from the late tenth century onwards, lords cannot have been content passively to accept the dooms of their tenants and must have frequently intervened in their affairs.

The context, however, is presentment rather than recognition, and in reality it is anachronistic to separate criminal from civil and fiscal matters. They were but aspects of a developing relationship between the Old English crown and local communities. Up to the late ninth century royal government was largely confined to the receipt of tribute. *Ville regales*, administered by a royal reeve, received food rents from the *regiones* in which they were situated. There may have been courts in these centres, but the main right that the king had over the *regiones* was the three common burdens, that is, army service, defence of boroughs, and bridge building. It was these dues that were transformed under the impact of Viking attacks in the ninth century. King Alfred built a network of boroughs in Wessex to counter marauding bands of Danes and instituted a formal garrison system and militia by exploiting the rights. Many of his foundations were short lived, but the principle informed local defence into the next century. With the reconquest of Mercia and the Danelaw the system was remodelled and extended to the whole of England south of the Humber, and elements were introduced into Northumbria after its fall to West Saxon rule in 954.[39]

Concern for the defence of the realm, if not from the start then soon, translated itself into a more general concern to keep the peace, and instruments were devised to oversee the king's interests: shire reeves or sheriffs were appointed to act as the king's representative in county courts and writs were used to communicate the king's wishes through him to the community of the shire. By 1066 England had the most highly developed system of local government in northern Europe. The whole of England south of the Tees was governed through a network of shires. Not all were constituted in the same way, for their antecedents were various, but they shared common characteristics as instruments of royal power in the localities.[40] They were generally in the charge of an earl, who commanded the county's levies on the king's behalf, while the sheriff, as the king's representative, collected taxation and supervised the maintenance of the king's peace. Between them they administered an integrated system of local government. The main forum was the shire court, to which the greatest landowners of the shire paid suit of court. Held in the county town, it was there that the king's pleas were heard, felonies were tried, and

---

[38] Vinogradoff, *Villeinage in England*, 370–1.
[39] Loyn, *Governance of Anglo-Saxon England*, 131–69.   [40] Ibid. 131–47.

weighty matters that affected the interests of the king were determined. More mundane business, both judicial and administrative, was delegated to local courts. In hidated England and carucated East Anglia they were known as hundreds; the wapentake was the equivalent in the Northern Danelaw. Hundred and wapentake were both competent to determine minor trespasses and pleas of customary land, and their officers supervised the policing of the area and the muster of their levies.

All duties and obligations within this system were based upon assessment to the geld. From at least the seventh century kingdoms had been assessed in hides, each being notionally the land of a single family. The quotas assigned to each kingdom, as set out in the late-seventh-century document known as the Tribal Hidage, are all conventional sums, being multiples of standard units of 300 or 7,000 hides, and they probably represent the tribute which was owed to their overlord.[41] How these assessments were distributed between individual holdings, if indeed they ever were, is unknown. The size of estates is often expressed in terms of hides in early charters, and there is some evidence from the North Midlands to suggest that each, if represented by the term *mansio*, was represented by a vill in the eleventh century.[42] But by and large there is not enough evidence to reconstruct the hidation of any of the known kingdoms.

Elements of this ancient cadastration survived in some areas of southern England where estates, mostly held by privileged religious foundations, had a continuous history into the eleventh century. Fladbury in Worcester-shire, for example, was assessed at forty-four hides in the late seventh century and still gelded for forty in 1086.[43] However, this was probably the exception. Early assessments were more generally superseded by a hidation, and in the Danelaw a carucation, related to the new circumstances of the burghal system in the course of the tenth century. Although modified by reassess-ment, it is this hidation that is recorded in Domesday Book.

It was a sophisticated assessment. Each tenurial unit was rated, generally according to the vills in which it was situated, in hides and virgates or caru-cates and bovates or sulungs. The term *geldum*, geld, has a root meaning of 'payment'. In modern historiography it is usually taken to refer to the land tax known as Danegeld.[44] Indeed, in the twelfth century the word may have been largely confined to that impost. In the later Middle Ages, however, its derivative *geldabilis* and its variants referred to land that owed suit of court and rendered various communal taxes such as cartage and sheriff's aid.[45] In 1086 *geldum* also bore these wider connotations. The Burghal Hidage, a

[41] Ibid. 34–8.   [42] Roffe, 'Place-Naming in Domesday Book', 52–3.
[43] S76; GDB 172d–173a: *DB Worcs.*, 2,15.
[44] For honourable exceptions, see Abels, *Military Obligation*, 113–4, and, more recently, Faith, *English Peasantry and the Growth of Lordship*, 89–125.
[45] English, 'Government of Thirteenth-Century Yorkshire', 95–9.

ninth- or tenth-century document which lists the number of hides attached to various Wessex boroughs, hints at a close relationship between military service and the hide in the provision that one man is provided by each hide.[46] Domesday confirms the principle, if not the exact equation. The borough of Stamford is said to have gelded for twelve and a half hundreds, that is 150 carucates, 'for army service and boat service and Danegeld [*in exercitu et navigio et in danegeld*]'.[47] In Berkshire a similar relationship seems to have obtained: 'If the king sent an army anywhere, one soldier only went from five hides, and for his supply or pay 4 shillings were given to him for two months from each hide; they did not send this money to the king, but gave it to the soldiers.'[48] Again, in Chester it is stated that: 'For the repair of the city wall and the bridge, the reeve used to call out one man to come from each hide in the county. The lord of any man who did not come paid a fine of 40s to the king and the earl. The forfeiture was outside of the farm.'[49] Assessment to the geld may also have determined whatever responsibilities the local community had for policing. The fine of eight pounds that the twelve-carucate hundred paid for breach of the peace in the Northern Danelaw can only have been distributed pro rata in proportion to the number of carucates and bovates held. Likewise, royal farm was also calculated on the basis of assessment to the geld. Tenements that owed farm to Curry Rivel in Somerset paid at the rate of one sheep and one lamb per hide;[50] Ewell in Surrey was assessed at fifteen and three-quarter hides TRE and thirteen and a half hides TRW (*Tempore Regis Willelmi*, in the time of King William, that is, between 1066 and 1068) for the king's farm; Reigate answered for thirty-seven and a half hides TRE and thirty-four hides TRW 'for the king's work [*ad opus regis*]'.[51] *Geldum*, in short, was used as a generic term to express all the obligations of an estate or tenement to the hundred, shire, and crown.

There is no contemporary evidence to illustrate how hidation was determined. Computer analysis of the Domesday data using sophisticated statistical techniques has shown a correlation between assessment to the geld and various other items of Domesday data with a high degree of statistical confidence throughout the country.[52] It is clear that the value and resources of an estate are consistently matched by proportionate assessment to the geld. It is concluded that hidation reflects the economic potential of each estate and was, by implication, determined by national survey. According to the Historia Croylandensis, a fourteenth- or fifteenth-century work fostered on Ingulf, a late-eleventh-century abbot of Crowland, such a survey was commissioned by King

---

[46] Rumble, 'Edition and Translation of the Burghal Hidage', 30.

[47] GDB 336d: *DB Lincs.*, S1.   [48] GDB 56c: *DB Berks.*, B10.

[49] GDB 262d: *DB Cheshire*, C21.   [50] GDB 92a–b: *DB Somerset*, 19,17;23,25;27.

[51] GDB 30b, 30c: *DB Surrey*, 1,7;9. Demarest ('The *Firma Unius Noctis*', 82) assumed that the assessment to the Danegeld followed the farm.

[52] MacDonald and Snooks, *Domesday Economy*, 45–124, esp. at 72–4.

Alfred.[53] The extract quoted from it, however, is clearly derived from the Domesday inquest, and there is no evidence for a pre-Conquest Domesday Book.[54]

Nevertheless, there seems little doubt that Anglo-Saxon lords were capable of executing elaborate surveys. There survives a pre-Conquest terrier of Tidenham in Gloucestershire of uncertain date. It lists the extent of demesne and tenanted land in terms of hides, records the number and location of fisheries that belong to it, and provides an elaborate customal of the manor in which is set out in minute detail the services due from the tenantry.[55] The early eleventh-century Rectitudines Singularum Personarum is a more generalized statement of the dues and services of various ranks of society, but it was probably drawn up for the purposes of estate management and would therefore suggest a high degree of competence in survey.[56] Neither document indicates a measured survey that any matching of geld assessment to economic resources would imply; the sort of survey undertaken by eighteenth-century improvers was clearly meaningless in the context of a primarily tributary society. Both, however, demonstrate an awareness of potential within the confines of the given estate structure. LDB and the Leicestershire folios of GDB record pre-Conquest ploughs (however conventional the figures might be), and it is not impossible that more-or-less accurate 'ploughland' figures were generally available to inform the distribution of geld. The units of assessment certainly imply such an under-standing. The hide was notionally the total landed resources of a family, but with the great reassessment of the ninth and tenth centuries it probably became more closely identified with the yardland, a unit of ploughing.[57] The carucate, the latinized form of Anglo-Scandinavian *plogsland*, and sulung, from Old English *sulh* (plough), are more explicitly related to the plough.[58]

In these terms survey was local and confined to the counting or estima-tion of a key commodity. However, it did not constitute the assessment itself; rather, it was the basis for assessment. There is abundant evidence to indic-ate that the rate of hidation was determined from above. According to the Burghal Hidage the assessment of a borough's territory was determined by the size of the defences: each pole (16½ feet) of wall was manned by four men with each hide providing one.[59] No doubt this was a notional arrange-ment; claims have been made for an exact correlation,[60] but the assessments of the Burghal Hidage are almost all round sums, and it is hardly credible that defences were determined by fiscal rather than military considerations. The assessments of the County Hidage, a list of the hidage of a number of Midland counties dating from some time before the Conquest, are likewise

[53] *Rerum Anglicarum Scriptores Veteres*, 80.   [54] Roffe, 'Historia Croylandensis', 93–108.
[55] *EHD* ii. 817; *Anglo-Saxon Charters*, 205, 451.
[56] *Die Gesetze*, i. 444–53; *EHD* ii. 813–16; Harvey, 'Rectitudines Singularum Personarum', 1–22.
[57] See below, p. 159.   [58] Stenton, 'Introduction', p. x; Stenton, *Anglo-Saxon England*, 281–2.
[59] Rumble, 'Edition and Translation of the Burghal Hidage', 30.
[60] Hill, 'The Nature of the Figures', 80–7.

TABLE 3.1. *Five-hide units in Normancross Hundred, Huntingdonshire*

Number of holdings in each vill	Assessment in hides	Number of holdings in each vill	Assessment in hides
Yaxley (1)	15	Haddon (1)	5
Stanground (1)	8	Morborne (1)	5
St Mary's, Huntingdon (1)	2	Folksworth (1)	5
Old Fletton (1)	5	Stilton (3)	5
Woodston (1)	5	Caldecote (1)	5
Botuluesbrige (1)	5	Denton (1)	5
Orton (6)	30	Washingley (2)	5
Alwalton (1)	5	Lutton (1)	2½
Chesterton (2)	9	Sawtry (4)	22
Water Newton (1)	5	Glatton (1)	8
Sibson (2)	5	Conington (1)	9
Stibbington (2)	2½	Woodwalton (1)	5
Elton (1)	10		

all in round sums.[61] They are often duodecimal and can sometimes be directly related to the Domesday assessment. The 1,200 hides of Worcester, for example, are matched by twelve hundreds and a Domesday assessment of 1,189 hides, and Northampton's 3,200 hides correspond to the twenty-two hundreds, two double hundreds, and four hundreds and a half, that is thirty-two hundreds (22 + 4 + 6).

By the time of the Domesday inquest some counties had experienced a reduction in assessment. Northamptonshire, for example, seems to have had its overall burden of taxation lowered by almost two-thirds, although this was by no means pro rata.[62] Other counties, by contrast, retained the same assessment. The Domesday hidation of Bedfordshire, Huntingdonshire, Gloucestershire, Worcestershire, Warwickshire, Oxfordshire, and Staffordshire all more or less equate with the County Hidage figures, and it is therefore possible to discern patterns of geld distribution. What is immediately apparent is the high incidence of a five-hide unit of assessment. In the Huntingdonshire hundred of Normancross, for example, nineteen out of twenty-five vills are assessed at five hides, a fraction, or multiple thereof, and a further two at a combined figure of five hides (Table 3.1); almost half of the vills in the county exhibit a similar pattern of assessment.[63] It is a pattern that is widespread. In a sample of a further eight counties the proportion varies between 40 per cent and 62 per cent.[64]

[61] Maitland, *Domesday Book and Beyond*, 524–9. [62] Hart, *Hidation of Northamptonshire*, 39–43.

[63] Roffe, 'Introduction to the Huntingdonshire Domesday', 11. For suggested combinations of vills, see Hart, 'Hidation of Huntingdonshire', 55–66.

[64] Leaver, 'Five Hides in Ten Counties: A Contribution to the Domesday Regression Debate', 533.

The carucated Danelaw exhibits similar characteristics, although there a duodecimal cadastre is apparent. The land which was attached to York in 1086, for example, was assessed at seven groups of twelve carucates.[65] For large areas of Lincolnshire the whole pattern of carucation can be reconstructed in this way.[66] Many of the basic units of assessment encompassed more than one holding; in some areas as many as eight tenements with seemingly precise assessments combine to make up a twelve-carucate hundred. Despite much interest in patterns of hidation and carucation, much still remains to be discovered about such patterns. Nevertheless, it is already clear that basic units of assessment were not even locally always of uniform size. As difficult as it is to determine, the burden of taxation seems to have varied from area to area. Derbyshire and Nottinghamshire, for example, were each assessed at 504 carucates, while Lincolnshire was rated at a significantly higher rate of 3,900.[67] Even there, though, there were wide variations. The three ridings of Lindsey were rated low at 600 carucates each compared with Kesteven at 1,800 and Holland at 300; using population in 1086 as an index, there were 0.15 carucates per person in Lindsey, 0.27 in Kesteven, and 0.31 in Holland, while the range within the wapentakes of Kesteven varies between 0.19 and 0.44.[68] The imbalance was recognized in 1194 when the principle was re-established that Kesteven should only pay at the same rate as Lindsey.[69]

It is clear that quotas of hides or carucates were assigned to each unit of administration and the burden of taxation was distributed pro rata. The high correlations that the computer analyses have demonstrated are, then, indicative less of a tuning of assessment to economic potential than of an equitable local distribution of a quota. While the burden of taxation was independently determined, it was fairly shared out, probably through local survey, amongst the community of the shire or its subdivisions. The hidation and carucation of England cannot have been executed by detailed national survey.

This is not surprising. Neither uniformity nor fairness is a medieval idea. Ability to pay dues and taxes was, of course, a consideration; no kingdom could be said to be well ruled if subjects refused to pay. But the primary concern of kings was to maximize the receipt of dues, and this was usually effected through negotiation on the basis of customary renders. Assessment to the geld was one such custom, and it survived with some degree of its original integrity for so long because it was flexible. The adjustment of the carucation of Lincolnshire in 1194 was not an isolated instance of beneficial

---

[65] GDB 298b: *DB Yorks.*, C22.

[66] Thomas Longley's reconstruction, intended as the second volume of the Lincoln Record Society edition of the Lincolnshire Domesday (Stenton, 'Introduction', p. xlv), survives in MS (Lincoln Archives Office, Longley 7). But for caveats, see Roffe, 'Hundreds and Wapentakes', 33–9. Longley was unaware of the fact that royal demesne estates existed outside the cadastre.

[67] Roffe, 'Origins of Derbyshire', 106, 109–10. The figures exclude royal demesne which was extra-hundredal (Roffe, 'Hundreds and Wapentakes', 32–42).

[68] Roffe, 'Lincolnshire Hundred', 34–5.   [69] *Pipe Roll 1194*, 118.

hidation. It has been suggested that the reduction in the burden of geld in Northamptonshire was related to political forces within the community of the shire; it favoured the northern hundreds, which are perceived as the areas of greater Danish settlement.[70] It must be doubted that the county was quite so ethnically stratified, and perhaps other explanations for the pattern should be explored. There can be no doubt, however, that the support of lords could be sought by selective exemption. In 1086 much of the manorial demesne, that is, the land farmed directly by the lord of the manor, was exempt from the geld. Sometimes it was land that had never been hidated; there are numerous examples of *carucatae numquam geldantes* in Exon and elsewhere, and it would seem that certain types of demesne, probably that of bookland, had always escaped assessment.[71] In many areas the hidation of tenanted inland, for which the lord usually paid geld, had been further reduced.[72]

The geld, then, was not a bureaucratic imposition which operated by executive fiat. To a greater or lesser degree it functioned by negotiation, and it could do so precisely because it embodied common interests on both sides. Through it regalian dues were articulated. But it also articulated rights and interests of those who gelded. First and foremost it was the touchstone of freedom and therefore the qualification for participation in the free society of the shire. Failure to render geld in all its forms was tantamount to condemnation to servile status. Beneficial hidation transferred geld from king to lord and may thus have been a potential danger to the villein's freedom.[73] By extension, the render of geld had implications for title to land. II Cnut 79 indicates that the performance of military service constituted a presumptive right to land: 'He who with the cognizance of the shire has performed the service demanded from a landowner on expeditions either by sea or by land shall hold [his land] unmolested by litigation during his life.'[74] Hemming, the compiler of the earliest survivng Worcester cartulary, recorded that laymen often appropriated land before the Conquest by paying the geld due on it.[75] Here and there in Domesday Book reference is indeed made to land lost in this way.[76]

In its essentials geld mediated relationships between the crown and the various communities over which it exercised sovereignty. How it worked in practice is unrecorded, but its very nature suggests that it had always been

---

[70] Hart, *Hidation of Northamptonshire*, 43–5. Hart suggests that inundation in the 1060s was the reason for geld reduction in six of Cambridgeshire's sixteen hundreds (Hart, *Hidation of Cambridgeshire*, 29–30).

[71] Faith, *English Peasantry and the Growth of Lordship*, 15–55.

[72] Welldon Finn, *Liber Exoniensis*, 105–7; Welldon Finn, 'Inquisitio Eliensis', 391. See below, pp. 149–65 for a fuller discussion.

[73] See below, p. 162.   [74] Robertson, II Cnut 79.   [75] *Hemingi Chartularium*, i. 278.

[76] GDB 141a, 216c: *DB Herts.*, 36,9; *DB Beds.*, 46,1. It has been doubted that there was any continuity between the reign of Cnut and the Domesday inquest in this area, on the ground that there was a discontinuity in the collection of geld between 1051 and 1066 (Hyams, ' "No Register of Title": The Domesday Inquest and Land Adjudication', 128). However, while the collection of *Danegeld* may have been suspended in the reign of Edward the Confessor, other dues were, of course, still levied.

an active process. The assessment or reassessment of geld must have been founded in some mutuality of interest such as opposition to a common enemy. Equally, the process must have been the occasion for conflict. Most obviously, a local community might object to the extent of the demands made upon it; in the Conqueror's reign the burden of taxation was widely resented.[77] But it must also have brought the freeholders of the shire into conflict with each other; where payment of geld conferred title to land, no geld inquest can have been free of pleas.

Although there survive no records of the use of the inquest in the assessment and collection of the geld, there is one pre-Conquest text that appears to be the record of a fiscal inquest. What has become known as Æthelred's fourth law code is a composite document that is broadly concerned with London matters.[78] Of its four sections, the first is a series of first-person statements in the past tense of the tolls payable in the city that has every appearance of being replies to a series of questions by citizens. In the second and third it is still the citizens who are speaking, and they agree to follow certain procedures when crimes are committed. The last is a more formal declaration of the law as regards minting issued by the king and the council. As it stands the document cannot have been produced by either the king or council alone, and the best interpretation seems to be that it was produced by an intermediary between them, that is, the king's reeve or the bishop of London.[79] Here are apparently the presentments of an inquest and something of the decisions that were based upon them.

There are also references to presentments in relation to title before the Conquest. In 1052–3 the rights of the abbots of Ramsey and Thorney in the Huntingdonshire fen were resolved by an examination of the boundary between their two holdings along Kingsdelf. Each party was represented by monks and men, but special weight was attached to the testimony of 'old men' who are identified as Thurulf the fisherman of Farcet, Lefstan Herlepic of Whittlesey, Lefsi Crevleta, Ailmer Hogg of *Wellen*, and Wulfgeat the fisherman of Hepmangrove. They had apparently been selected as acceptable to both sides on the grounds of their local knowledge, and agreement was reached on the basis of their evidence.[80]

None of these cases directly involved the king. The context in which the presentments were sought is therefore unclear, but Ramsey felt it prudent to obtain a writ from Edward the Confessor to confirm the agreement,[81] and it would seem likely that the hundred court was the forum. Nothing in the procedure appears particularly extraordinary, and there seems no reason to

[77] *ASC* 164–5.   [78] Robertson, IV Æthelred.
[79] Wormald, 'Ethelred the Lawmaker', 62.
[80] *Cartularium Monasterii de Rameseia*, i. 188; iii. 38; Cambridge, University Library, MS 3021, the Red Book of Thorney, f. 372.
[81] *Anglo-Saxon Writs*, no. 62.

doubt that the soliciting of evidence in this way was common where the need demanded. The complex interrelationship between the crown and the local communities as articulated through the geld in all of its multifaceted aspects suggests that the presentment within the inquest was the main organ of communication in all matters that touched on that relationship.

In this context it is likely that much of the data relating to the reign of King Edward the Confessor in Domesday Book ultimately emanated from pre-Conquest inquests.[82] Dr Sally Harvey has forcefully argued that what are essentially copies of the inquests themselves have survived in documents from Abingdon Abbey and Bath Abbey.[83] Doubt must be expressed about the identity of these sources,[84] but nevertheless it is clear that the Domesday commissioners had access to geld records. The use of one such is noticed in the GDB account of Huntingdonshire: 'In Hurstingstone Hundred the demesne ploughs are exempt from the king's geld. The villagers and sokemen geld according to the hides written in the record, except in Broughton where the abbot [of Ramsey] gelds with the others for 1 hide.'[85] It is impossible to be certain whether this particular geld list pre-dated the Conquest. However, in many counties, Huntingdonshire included, geld figures are explicitly TRE assessments, and it is therefore likely that their ultimate source was pre-Conquest documents.

The record of TRE holders of land must have come from similar sources. With some notable exceptions, the account of every manor in Domesday Book notes the lord of the land in 1066; the information is also given for some subordinate tenements where title was disputed or dues were shared between a number of lords. The name forms are frequently eccentric, sometimes betraying French phonology, and it is thus conceivable that many of the names were provided by tenants-in-chief and hundred juries in the course of the inquiry.[86] Norman lords often derived their title from a king's thegn whose lands had been granted *en masse* by William the Conqueror, and it was therefore natural that they should know and name this their *antecessor* when they made claim to their lands. Likewise, local juries brought their collective memory to bear on matters where such claims to land conflicted. The *clamores* in the Kesteven division of Lincolnshire provide one of many examples of the presentment of names in this context: 'Alfred of Lincoln claims one carucate of land in Quadring against Count Alan. The men of Holland agree with the same Alfred, both because it was his predecessor's and also he himself was seized thereof in the time of Earl Ralph.'[87] Nevertheless, naming of pre-Conquest holders of land in this way was probably exceptional, their eccentric

[82] Galbraith, *Domesday Book*, 28–9.
[83] Harvey, 'Domesday Book and its Predecessors', 755–63.
[84] For a critique, see below, pp. 109–10.   [85] GDB 203b: *DB Hunts.*, B21.
[86] Sawyer, 'Place-Names of the Domesday Manuscripts', 483–506.
[87] GDB 377d: *DB Lincs.*, CK68.

orthography being a function of either transcription by francophone scribes from dictation or of the latinizing programme of the Domesday scribes.[88] TRE tenants are rarely noted in documents that emanate from the earliest stages of the inquiry. Furthermore, they are often linked with assessment to the geld. In the Cornwall folios, for example, they are explicitly said to have gelded for so much: 'Thurstan holds Gurlyn from the count [of Mortain]; Doda held it before 1066 and gelded for one virgate of land.'[89] Similar formulas are found in a dozen or so counties.[90] As the Huntingdonshire reference to 'the hides written in the record' implies, geld lists also contained the names of those who were liable to pay the tax and renders due.

If such data were by necessity the subject of inquest before the Conquest, there is little to suggest that jurors could also make recognitions. In all the cases cited there was a more-or-less amicable resolution of the matters in hand, and there was therefore no call for a formal resolution.[91] Compurgation, by contrast, terminated one of the earliest disputes in which a communal presentment was made. It is found in the Liber Eliensis.[92] In the late tenth century unnamed sons of a certain Boga of Hemingford laid claim to Ely Abbey's estate of Bluntisham in Huntingdonshire. They claimed it by right of their maternal uncle Tope who, they asserted, ought to have had it by inheritance from his grandmother. However, it had been unjustly forfeited to the king, even though before her marriage the grandmother had made the requisite submission to Edward the Elder at Cambridge. This plea was contradicted by 'the wise old men of the shire [*sapientes illius provincie et senes*]'. They declared that Edward the Elder had acquired Huntingdon before Cambridge and therefore any submission made at the latter could not have indemnified the grandmother in her tenure of lands in Huntingdonshire. The jurors found in favour of Wulfnoth, who had granted Bluntisham to Ely. A shire court was then convened and the plea was again aired. Wulfnoth gathered in his support all the best men of six hundreds and over a thousand men undertook to swear on his behalf. The sons of Boga were then unwilling to proceed, and all declared their support for Wulfnoth's title and right to grant the land.

Although this account was written in the twelfth century, there seems no reason to doubt its essential authenticity: Tope is apparently an historical figure,

[88] Clark, 'Domesday Book—A Great Red-herring', 317–31.

[89] GDB 123a: *DB Cornwall*, 5,4,18.

[90] See below, pp. 196–7. The usage is clearest in the account of the northern shires where it is stated that the TRE holder had so many carucates. In the south-west the formula '*B tenet x, a tenuit et geldebat pro y hidis*' is often translated as '*B holds x, a held and it gelded for y hides*'. But 'he gelded' is equally possible in many instances.

[91] It has been implied that the verdict of the old men in the dispute between Ramsey and Thorney was a recognition (Chibnall, *Anglo-Norman England*, 109). But it seems to have been the agreement that followed that terminated the matter.

[92] *Liber Eliensis*, 98–9.

and the salient details of Edward the Elder's East Midland campaign are confirmed by the Anglo-Saxon Chronicle.[93] The context in which the initial presentment was made is not clear, but here is compelling evidence for what was effectively an inquest which informed the due course of law. The men of the countryside delivered a verdict and pleas could then ensue, but it was compurgation rather than recognition that completed the process and confirmed title. Clearly, the inquest was not incompatible with procedure by compurgation.

The Domesday Inquest

The sophistication of English royal government before the Conquest was of an order that was largely unparalleled elsewhere in Europe at the time; only in Sicily were contacts between king and local communities unmediated by territorialized lordships to such an extent.[94] Much of the attraction of England to successive invaders from the late tenth century onwards was a system of local government and administration which could readily harness the wealth of the country. The vestiges of geld records that the Domesday corpus preserves illustrate the interlocking interests of king and subjects that made that system so effective. It is a sophistication of which it is difficult to conceive without the inquest. The crown could not have extended its competence had it depended on the unsupported word of local communities. Equally, the free man of the shire must have used the extension of the king's peace to protect his own tenure against local lords and kins.

The Domesday inquest lies squarely in this English tradition of 'kingship in the community'. Some of the verdicts recorded in GDB were clearly intended to be recognitory. But they serve to show that most were merely presentments. Thus, for example, in the Lincolnshire folios the wapentake [of Skirbeck] declared that a tenement in Drayton which had belonged to the abbot of Ramsey had been held by Bishop Wulfwige of Dorchester on Thames, but they did not know through whom he held it. Neither Remigius, Wulfwige's successor, nor Ramsey had tenure, however, and their right was only recognized in a subsequent session recorded in the *clamores*.[95] The repeated and signal failure of the Domesday scribes to take cognizance of apparent declarations of right is consistent with the workings of the inquest. Its business was to collect evidence for further action, whether it be fiscal, administrative, or judicial.

Within this context it is clear that the use of the term 'return' to describe the records of the inquest is misleading. In the Domesday canon the words used of documents produced by the inquest are *breves regis*, *rotulum*, *liber*, or

---

[93] Whitelock, 'Foreword', *Liber Eliensis*, p. xi.

[94] Clementi, 'Notes on Norman Sicilian Surveys', 55–8.

[95] GDB 348b, 377d: *DB Lincs.*, 12,59.CK65.

descriptio, while the Anglo-Saxon Chronicler refers to *gewrita*, and these terms continued to be used in the following century until the vernacular Domesday took their place. Thereafter, inquests of one kind or another attracted popular epithets generally in proportion to their fame or infamy. However, the generic term used of the inquest in the later Middle Ages was *veredictum* or simply *inquisitio*. The word *returnum* is first found in the reign of Henry II, and then it is not used to connote records of an inquest or indeed to indicate any document. Rather, in the form *retornum brevis* or *retornum brevium*, it refers to an administrative process whereby a writ was endorsed by the official to whom it had been addressed and subject to the scrutiny of the king or justices to ensure that it had been properly executed.[96] Until the late twelfth century royal government and administration was largely delegated. Instruments like the writ had been developed to make known the king's will to his ministers and subjects, but it was up to the interested party and local officials to make good its stipulations. The king's representatives in the shire were, of course, accountable to the crown for the efficient execution of their office, but this was conceived in fiscal terms, the collection of revenues due. There were no formal mechanisms to ensure that they had performed their duties, and there was little that a plaintiff could do to enforce his right if local officials were unwilling. The return was an innovation that made the equally novel devices of the emerging common law a potent reality in the resolution of disputes within an ever more complex feudal society.

Although anachronistic, the application of the term to the Domesday process has seemed signally appropriate. The Anglo-Saxon Chronicle records that 'the records were brought to [King William] afterwards',[97] and, with the perception of the inquest as a recognitory instrument, this could only mean that the king was reviewing the workings of local government. 'Return' was thus an accurate description of the process. The term has carried with it a considerable amount of baggage. Much of the interpretation of the Domesday process has hinged on its common law connotations, for, as the documentation of executive acts, the records of the inquest must embody the very purpose of the inquest; a geographical form betrays a primary concern with dues articulated through local government, while a seigneurial arrangement indicates a feodary. With the unpicking of the presentment from the recognition this tyranny of the texts can be disposed of. As simple presentments, Domesday verdicts embody the business of the inquest but do not necessarily express any purpose in themselves.

In the absence of explicit record that purpose is ultimately a matter of speculation. But the circumstances that provoked an investigation in 1085 are

---

[96] Stenton, *English Justice Between the Norman Conquest and the Great Charter, 1066–1215*, 32–2; Hudson, *Common Law*, 143–4; Warren, *Governance of Norman and Angevin England*, 115–16.

[97] *ASC* 161–2.

plain enough. Medieval monarchs are not noted for their curiosity, and so when an English king's thoughts turned to tenure, taxation was not far from his mind. It was indeed precisely in the context of taxation that Bishop Robert of Hereford placed the Domesday inquest, and it is not difficult to appreciate why William needed to raise income in 1085. His kingdom faced the most serious threat from invasion of his reign. According to the E version of the Anglo-Saxon Chronicle:

In this year people said and declared for a fact, that Cnut, king of Denmark, son of King Swein, was setting out in this direction and meant to conquer this country with the help of Robert, count of Flanders, because Cnut was married to Robert's daughter. When William, king of England, who was then in Normandy—for he was in possession of both England and Normandy—found out about this, he went to England with a larger force of mounted men and infantry from France and Brittany than had ever come to this country, so that people wondered how this country could maintain all that army. And the king had all the army dispersed all over the country among his vassals, and they provisioned the army each in proportion to his land. And people had much oppression that year, and the king had the land near the sea laid waste, so that if his enemies landed, they should have nothing to seize on so quickly. But when the king found out for a fact that his enemies had been hindered and could not carry out their expedition—then he let some of the army go to their own country, and some he kept in this country over winter.[98]

There was good reason why William took this threat so seriously. Large fleets had invaded England in 1069, 1070, and 1075, and all three invasions had been accompanied by serious revolts of the English and, latterly, disaffected Norman lords. Cnut's claim to the throne by inheritance from King Cnut was as good as William's from King Edward, and an alliance with Count Robert of Flanders enabled him to marshal his forces and recruit reinforcements in Flemish ports before the short crossing to England.[99] William, already assailed on all sides by enemies, was forced to leave Normandy to defend the wealthier half of his dominion.

In the event the threat did not materialize in 1085. William was not to know that the death of Cnut in the following year would lift it altogether; he was compelled to keep his forces in readiness and, although the numbers were reduced, his mercenaries could not therefore be stood down through the winter. In was in this context that the Domesday inquest was planned on Christmas Day at Gloucester. The crisis had clearly produced an urgent and continuing need for money. How many mercenaries were brought to England cannot be determined but, if the chronicler can be believed, the number must have been large enough to stretch the royal purse. That the events of the following year produced a survey of royal lands and an *inquisitio geldi* cannot be coincidental.

[98] *ASC* 161.   [99] Higham, 'The Domesday Survey: Context and Purpose', 11–16.

The most direct link between the crisis of 1085 and the Domesday inquest, however, was the method of billeting. If each vassal was apportioned mercenaries 'in proportion to his land', the assessment must have been made on the basis of existing records. Such may have included geld lists. The Northamptonshire example dating from c.1070 lists hundred by hundred the amount of land held in demesne, and, although the holders are rarely named, it is evident that local government had access to information on the resources of tenants-in-chief.[100] Further, it is possible (if difficult to demonstrate) that there were county totals for each. But they cannot have outlined resources other than demesne; income from tenanted lands of all kinds were unrepresented for, by and large, the holders of such lands discharged the geld due themselves. Of greater use must have been records, probably of central as well as local government provenance, of services due directly to the king, whether knight service or otherwise. Again, however, such services can have only approximated to resources; as essentially personal, their extent must have been contingent on relationship and any number of local circumstances. What is striking about the Domesday inquest is that it is precisely a record of all the resources of tenants-in-chief of which the billeting of 1085 could have availed itself.

In these terms it is difficult to escape the conclusion that there was a link between the crisis of mid-1085 and the initiation of the Domesday inquest at Christmas of the same year. It is a link that has not gone unrecognized. Those who have espoused a neo-fiscal view of the inquest have assumed that, as the aim of the inquest, Domesday Book embodies the assessments that were made.[101] But this can now be seen as a mechanistic and overly teleological analysis. In the following chapters the texts and processes of the Domesday inquest are re-examined as the products of an investigatory procedure that informed rather than dictated the future course of action.

---

[100] *Anglo-Saxon Charters*, 231–7, 481–4.

[101] Harvey, 'Taxation and the Ploughland in Domesday Book', 86–103; Harvey, 'Taxation and the Economy', 249–64; Higham, 'The Domesday Survey: Context and Purpose', 7–21.

4
The Domesday Texts

To ALL APPEARANCES the Domesday process is remarkably well documented. There is a handful of more or less independent accounts of the purpose of the inquiry and the methods that it employed, and, in addition to the two volumes of Domesday Book, a mass of documentation that was collected in the course of the inquest itself. The historian may wish for more, but in fact the volume of evidence is remarkable for the period. Comparison with the Hundred Roll inquiry of 1279 underlines the point. This was commissioned at the height of Edward I's experiment in interventionist government and, if it was ever finished, amounted to the most comprehensive survey of land tenure, Domesday Book notwithstanding, that was undertaken anywhere in medieval Europe.[1] And yet there is not a single reference to this momentous event in contemporary chronicles and only fragmentary verdicts survive from a dozen or so counties.[2] Even the immensely popular inquest of 1274/5, that promised the restitution of lands and rights after the civil war of 1264–5, only merited a single reference and this only to note that 'nothing came of it.'[3] The Domesday inquest was different. It attained talismanic status at an early date, and in consequence the inquest was noticed and its records preserved.

Celebrity creates its own momentum. Any analysis of the procedure and progress of the inquest has to come to terms with the fact that of the three primary accounts of the Domesday inquest, only the relatively uninformative letter of Lanfranc to the commissioner 'S' can make any claim to be contemporary with the process. The account of Robert of Hereford and the 1086 annal of the Anglo-Saxon Chronicle were seemingly written after the event, the one perhaps in late 1086 and the other ostensibly in 1087.[4] The lapse of time was small and the event in recent memory, but nevertheless they both represent perceptions of the inquest in the full knowledge of what came out of it. Neither, then, is necessarily an unimpeachable guide to the processes of the inquest and the circumstances that gave rise to it.

By necessity, the procedure of the survey has to be adduced from the extant documentation that it produced. English government in the medieval period

---

[1] Greenway, 'A Newly Discovered Fragment of the Hundred Rolls of 1279–80', 73–7; Raban, 'The 1279–80 Hundred Rolls', 131.

[2] London, PRO, SC5; *Rotuli Hundredorum*, ii.

[3] Maddicott, 'Edward I and the Lessons of Baronial Reform', 1–30; *Annales Monastici*, iii. 263.

[4] Stevenson, 'A Contemporary Description of the Domesday Survey', 75; Clark, *Peterborough Chronicle*, p. xxi.

was prolific in its output of national surveys and inquests. Working documents and presentments, however, are relatively rare, most surviving, if at all, as later copies. GDB, LDB, and Exon, then, are the more valuable as documents of the process itself. The physical organization of the manuscripts, the hands, scribal methods of composition, editing, and correcting, and evidence of subsequent annotation and use are invaluable clues to the purpose of a source and the procedure that produced it. For GDB the examination of such evidence is facilitated by two facsimiles, the one produced in the 1860s by the Ordnance Survey using a process known as photozincography, and the other by Alecto Editions, by invitation of the Public Record Office, with a continuous tone technique. Both have an importance beyond that of convenience. Many variations in the hand are not all readily visible in the MS, but are apparent in the facsimiles presumably because of differentials in light absorption in the production process.[5] The Alecto edition is undoubtedly the more revealing in this respect since it captures the density of the ink. However, the silhouette of the Ordnance Survey edition of the 1860s sometimes shows up differences, such as the addition of *et lx acre prati* added to the end of the account of Ainsty Wapentake in the Yorkshire Summary,[6] that are not otherwise apparent. Conversely, there are characteristics of the MS that are not apparent in either of the two facsimiles. For LDB there is only the Ordnance Survey facsimile,[7] and for Exon there is no facsimile at all.

The remaining Domesday documents all survive in later copies, and the character of the originals from which they were derived is largely invisible. For extensive sources such as ICC, what survives would appear to be a full copy of the exemplars, while others like IE and Bath A are probably comprehensive extracts of their sources. The more summary documents are more difficult to evaluate; it is not always possible to determine whether they are copies, extracts, or abstracts of their exemplars, or compilations from a number of sources, not the least of those sources being local knowledge at the time of copying. It is possible, however, to characterize *types* of document that were available and were produced in the course of the Domesday process.

Great Domesday Book

GDB is made up of some forty-seven quires or gatherings, each of a varying number of folios, which singly or in multiples are, with some important exceptions, devoted to the account of estates arranged by counties or major subdivisions thereof.[8] The order in which they are bound reflects a logical geographical sequence of four 'bands' of counties radiating out from the

---

[5] It is unfortunate that UV and infra-red photographs were not taken at the time the MS was disbound for its rebinding in 1984–5.

[6] GDB 379d: *DB Yorks.*, SW, An18.

[7] Editions Alecto is currently preparing a new facsimile as a companion to its edition of GDB.

[8] PRO, *Domesday Book Rebound*, appendix I.

south-east to the north.[9] A series of ten quires signatures of the late eleventh century running back from the end of the volume suggests that the arrangement reflects the order when first bound. There are indications, however, that the quires were extensively used as pamphlets before binding, for their outer surfaces are heavily rubbed.[10] The binding sequence, then, clearly does not represent the order of writing.

There are 383 folios in all, as a rule with two columns per side. The number of horizontal rulings varies from between forty-four to fifty-nine, although in some counties there are none at all and in many others the scribe simply ignored them.[11] With the exception of the early twelfth-century addition of the lands of Robert de Brus at the end of the Yorkshire folios,[12] it is almost entirely the work of one scribe, known as 'the main scribe'. He was responsible for the bulk of the text and probably for the subsequent rubrication of headings, place-names, and the like. The contribution of a second, the correcting scribe who may have supervised the enterprise, is modest, being confined to the addition of the odd entry and gloss with but relatively few corrections.[13] The hand of this latter scribe is late-eleventh-century Norman in character.[14] That of the main scribe, by contrast, has insular characteristics and has often been described as 'curial'.[15] In reality, however, it is a book hand that has nothing in common with the output of the Anglo-Norman Chancery.[16] It occurs in only one other document in the Domesday canon, on two folios in Exon.[17] But it has been identified in three further manuscripts, Oxford, Trinity College, MS 8, fos. 89v–91r,[18] London, British Library, Harley MS 12, fos. 141r–143v, and Hereford Cathedral Library, MS P.1. 10, f.0v. All three have connections with Durham,[19] and hands from nine other late-eleventh-century manuscripts from Durham share stylistic characteristics with the main scribe of GDB. He would appear to have come from the north. He was, moreover, a northerner who was fully conversant with English. His spelling of place-names and personal names was subject to the misreadings, mishearings, and confusions to which all scribes were prone, but he sometimes reveals a knowledge of etymology absent in his sources that suggests, if not native descent, then bilingualism.[20]

[9] Galbraith, *Making of Domesday Book*, 55.
[10] Rumble, 'Palaeography of the Domesday Manuscripts', 29.
[11] PRO, *Domesday Book Rebound*, appendix II.   [12] GDB 332c–d: *DB Yorks.*, 31.
[13] Gullick, 'Manuscripts', 98–104. For a list of the larger contributions of the correcting scribe, see ibid. 103.
[14] Ibid. 103.
[15] Ibid. 98; Galbraith, *Domesday Book*, 47; Welldon Finn, *Domesday Inquest*, 179–87.
[16] Rumble, 'Palaeography of the Domesday Manuscripts', 45; Gullick, 'Manuscripts', 99.
[17] Exon, 153v, 436v; Welldon Finn, 'Successive Version of Domesday Book', 561–4. All three entries are additions which exhibit the forms of GDB.
[18] Gullick and Thorn, 'Scribes of GDB', 78–80.
[19] Chaplais, 'William of Saint-Calais and the Domesday Survey', 73–4.
[20] Dodgson, 'Domesday Book: Place-names and Person Names', 121–38; Sawyer, 'Place-Names of the Domesday Manuscripts', 483–506. Many of the apparent shortcomings are a function of a programme of Latinization of names (Clark, 'Domesday Book—A Great Red-herring', 317–31).

By and large, the main scribe produced a neat and carefully drafted text, but he was no mere copyist. He constantly reviewed the material before him and checked and rechecked his account, making corrections and additions and adding glosses as he saw the need. To date there has been no systematic examination of all such editorial changes throughout the volume.[21] Corrections are relatively easy to identify. Occasionally a knife was used physically to remove the surface of the parchment where an error was located, and the corrected material was then overwritten; sometimes the previous entry can still be read,[22] but usually not. More commonly, the erroneous material was cancelled by ruling through in black ink and entering the corrected version in the margin or between the lines where space permitted. Likewise, glosses present few problems of identification. There interlineation was the preferred method and it is extensively used to clarify material. In the Northern Danelaw counties *comes*, *stalre*, and the like are regularly interlined to distinguish TRE holders of land of high status from others of the same name, or possibly to clarify the status of a holding. A similar device is common in Kent, while in Oxfordshire the surnames of ecclesiastical tenants who were tenants-in-chief are interlined clearly to identify them.

The addition of material presents more formidable problems. The initial and most important is identification. Following detailed codicological analysis subsequent to the disbinding of the manuscript in the early 1950s, additions entered on a separate sheet and tipped into a quire can now be readily identified.[23] In Surrey, for example, lands of St Peter of Chertsey in Wallington and Brixton Hundreds were omitted and subsequently entered in this way.[24] This expedient, however, was the last resort; where space permitted addenda were inserted into, or appended to, the existing text. Additions to margins and interlineations are self evident, but less obvious are those that are entered in a space in the text, appended to the foot of a column or at the end of a chapter, or inserted in an empty column. Sometimes when it was appropriate the scribe used a sign to indicate the context of an accidentally omitted entry or series of entries. In the Lincolnshire folios where the need to ascribe every parcel of land to a manor was acutely felt, crosses, stars, and numerous other devices are used to point the reader to the right place.[25] More usually, no such indication is given, and it is only variations in the hand and layout that betray an addition; a change of pen, compression, a difference in alignment, variation in pressure, the absence of rubrication, a change in format are all the clues that the text affords.

---

[21] A detailed study by Caroline Thorn is under way.

[22] See e.g. GDB 302a where an erasure appears to be the end of the Aldborough entry, a continuation of an account begun on 299d, and the whole of that of Knaresborough. It would seem that after the insertion of the two sheets 300–1 the entries were entered anew on 300a and the originals were then redundant (*DB Yorks.*, 1Y18–19; Palliser, 'Introduction to the Yorkshire Domesday', 11).

[23] PRO, *Domesday Book Rebound*, appendix 1.   [24] GDB 33, *DB Surrey*, 8,23–6.

[25] The device was also used where in writing a current component of the text the scribe realized it should have been entered with a parent manor that he had already entered. For annotations of this kind, see C. Thorn, 'Marginal Notes and Signs', 113–35.

Many additions merely remedy an accidental omission. Where entries have been appended to a fully drafted text, it seems most reasonable to conclude that they came to light through a process of checking against an exemplar. In other contexts, however, different explanations are appropriate. Occasionally, it might be suspected that the scribe has consulted a separate source; the postscriptal addition of jury verdicts or other indications of a claim are most obviously of this kind. Sometimes a change of plan might be suspected. In the Yorkshire folios the account of 332 manors is appended to the king's breve, but their form and corresponding entries in the Yorkshire Summary suggest that they were originally earmarked for the section entitled *taini regis*. Subsequently, though, as untenanted thegn lands it was thought more apposite to enter them with the king's estates.[26] The reasons for other additions are simply irrecoverable. Hundredal rubrics, for example, occur only sporadically, and can often be shown to be half-hearted additions to an already compiled text. Thus, in Lincolnshire they are found in four chapters and there they are only entered systematically from the point at which lands in Kesteven are described. In chapter 12, the land of Count Alan of Brittany, it can be seen that they have been carefully added to the text where space permitted: blank lines were preferred, but they might otherwise be appended to a half-line, interlined, or entered in the left margin.[27] Why especial interest should have been taken in these lands alone is unclear.[28]

By and large, additions of this kind can be characterized as ad hoc. Many, by contrast, were foreseen. The most obviously examples are the county boroughs. In many shires the lands of the king and tenants-in-chief were entered first, but a space was left for the subsequent addition of the account of the county town. Often that account proved to be longer than expected and the scribe had to compress his work. In Lincolnshire, for example, the entries for Lincoln, Stamford, and Torksey were written on fifty-two lines as against the standard forty-two of the rest of the text.[29] Famously, space was left for the accounts of London and Winchester but the information was never entered; it was either not collected, arrived too late for inclusion, or proved too difficult to abbreviate in the span allotted.[30] An account of Hastings seems to have been lost to similar considerations.[31] Foreseen additions are also found throughout the text, but they are most common in the *terra regis*. In Lincolnshire the manor of Grantham was squeezed into a space at the appropriate place in the text,[32]

---

[26] GDB 300a–301d: *DB Yorks.*, 1N1–1W73; Roffe, 'Domesday Book and Northern Society', 324.

[27] GDB 347a–348d: *DB Lincs.*, 12; Roffe, 'Hundreds and Wapentakes', 34.

[28] The fact that hundreds are not indicated at all in the south-western counties of Cornwall, Devon, Dorset, Somerset, and Wiltshire has been interpreted as a significant difference in the procedure of the inquiry in that area (Galbraith, *Making of Domesday Book*, 24, 72). However, it is as likely to be a function of editorial processes in the production of GDB.

[29] GDB 336a–337a: *DB Lincs.*, C, S, T.

[30] GDB 37, 37ᵛ, 126, 126ᵛ. For London, see Martin, 'Domesday London', 22; Winchester, *DB Hants.*, notes.

[31] Martin, 'Domesday Book and the Boroughs', 157.   [32] GDB 337d: *DB Lincs.*, 1,9.

while in Yorkshire many of the sokelands of the king's demesne manors appear
to be postscriptally entered on lines left for the purpose after almost every
entry.[33] Occasional gaps in the text show that the scribe sometimes forgot to
add the material he had intended to insert or could not find what he was
looking for.

It is sometimes assumed that such material was only added later because
the scribe had to await the return of the information. This is, of course,
formally possible, but in many cases it seems more likely that the scribe
had to consult another source, not necessarily at hand, to find the data.[34] In
Northamptonshire a space was left for an account of a parcel of land called
Portland which pertained to the borough of Stamford in Lincolnshire. It gelded
with the Northamptonshire hundred of Witchley but was in fact the west field
of Stamford, and its account was most probably provided by the burgesses.[35]
In the account of York a complex stratigraphy of discrete sections, as indicated by variations in the hand, can best be explained as compilation by the
main scribe from disparate sources (Table 4.1).[36]

The use of diverse schedules and documents may be suspected in other
contexts. Many current breaks in the drafting of the text are apparent from
variations in the hand of much the same kind that point to postscriptal
additions. Some, probably the majority, of these must be a function of the
scribe's pattern of work, whether they indicate a mead-break or the end of the
working day. Some, however, correspond with a different type of information.
The account of Count Alan of Brittany's fee in the Yorkshire Summary is a
case in point.[37] Most of the document consists of a list of fees and their assessments wapentake by wapentake and vill by vill, with the name of each lord
interlined. It is largely a fair copy with but few additions and there is nothing
to suggest that the Count Alan section is necessarily postscriptal. Nevertheless, the hand is lighter and somewhat more tentative than the text both above
and below it, and it is in a different form; the assessment of each parcel of
tenanted land is interlined. The most probable explanation for these peculiarities is that the fee was constituted as a liberty, as it was in the early twelfth
century, and therefore made a separate presentment which the scribe consulted.[38]

Nevertheless, although additions are common throughout the text and in
some counties, such as Yorkshire, hint at a less than perfect mastery of sources,
the text is generally a neat and carefully drafted fair copy uniform in its

---

[33] GDB 299a–d: *DB Yorks.*, 1Y; Palliser, 'Introduction to the Yorkshire Domesday', 11.

[34] Harvey, 'Domesday Book and its Predecessors', 770.

[35] GDB 219c: *DB Northants.*, 1,5. The land was carucated, whereas elsewhere in Northamptonshire
the hide was the unit of assessment. It would seem that the land had been surveyed with Stamford.
For the complex redefinition of administrative boundaries that lies behind the entry, see Roffe and
Mahany, 'Stamford and the Norman Conquest', 5–9.

[36] Roffe, 'Domesday Book and Northern Society', 314. The variations in the hand, differences in
pressure, alignment, and the like, are easier to perceive than describe.

[37] GDB 381b: *DB Yorks.*, SN,CtA.   [38] Roffe, 'Yorkshire Summary', 255–6.

TABLE 4.1. *The opening folios of the Yorkshire Domesday*

Entry number	Subject-matter	Variation in hand
C1–2	Customary land, the city proper	A
C3–19	Non-customary land, city fees	A
C20	Value of the city	A
C22	Assessment of land associated with the city; account of 6 carucates of C2	A
C23–35	The 84 carucates of the city	A?
C36	Holders of sake and soke, toll and team	B
C37	Customs in demesne manors; roads	C
C38–40	The king's peace; reliefs	B
L	List of tenants-in-chief	B

Note: Each line represents a one-line space in the text.

content and span. The basic unit of organization is the county. Thirty in all are described, covering the whole of England south of the Tees except the three East Anglian shires of Norfolk, Suffolk, and Essex. Extra-shrieval regions, liberties, and other anomalous areas are also described and are appended to the account of the county with which they were most closely associated. Parts of Wales and the land between the Ribble and Mersey are described in the Cheshire folios and further Welsh lands in those of Herefordshire and Gloucestershire;[39] Craven and Amounderness and Lancashire appear in the Yorkshire folios;[40] *Roteland* is appended to the Nottinghamshire folios, as are the New Forest and the Isle of Wight to those of Hampshire.[41]

[39] GDB 268d–270b, 179b, 180d–181a, 162a–b: *DB Cheshire*, FD, FT, G, R; *DB Hereford.*, A1–10; 1,48–60; *DB Gloucs.*, S, W1–19.
[40] GDB 301d–302a, 332a–b: *DB Yorks.*, 1L; 30.
[41] GDB 293c–d, 38d–39b, 40a, 50d–54a: *DB Rutland*, R; *DB Hants.*, 1,26–38; 1W; NF; IoW.

Each shire north of the Thames begins with an account of the county borough or boroughs; in the south and west the practice varies, with some boroughs appearing at the head of the county folios and others in the body of the text, or a mixture of both.[42] Sundry customs of a regional nature are often recorded in this section. In Kent, Nottinghamshire, Derbyshire, Lincolnshire, and Yorkshire lists of TRE and TRW holders of sake and soke are given,[43] in the Cheshire folios the customs of the county are set out in great detail, whilst in Berkshire and Worcestershire regulations relating to the performance of military service are recorded.[44] All these matters directly relate in one way or another to the dues of the crown in the shire. Thereafter, however, rights in land become the main focus of the text. A list of landholders in the county acts by way of an index, not always entirely accurate,[45] to a series of chapters relating to the land of each. The *terra regis* is invariably the first to be entered. It is followed by the fees of the tenants-in-chief in a strict order of precedence. The lands of clerics, the archbishops and bishops, take priority before the greater abbeys and churches. Lay lands follow. The order of entry is largely determined by local importance. The great earls and barons, like the count of Mortain, the king's brother, and Count Alan of Brittany, are rarely relegated to a low position, but regional lords with a large amount of land in the area join their company where, on a national level, their status would not merit it. With the lesser nobility the order of entry is pragmatic, with lords of the same forename being grouped together. Women, regardless of their wealth or status, are invariably found towards the end of the county folios. The final chapter is usually devoted to the lands of *taini regis*, the large class of minor thegns who held their estates from the king in return for various services, and almsmen if not entered with the ecclesiastics.

Within the account of the king's lands demesne is usually described first and is then followed by that of tenanted estates and sundry fees held as forfeitures or in custody by the king. The same form is also occasionally found in the chapters of tenants-in-chief. Peterborough Abbey's chapters, for example, are so divided in Lincolnshire, Northamptonshire, Leicestershire, and Huntingdonshire.[46] On the whole, however, no systematic interest is manifest in honourial tenants. They are rarely given distinguishing surnames or cognomens, and then only postscriptally, and subtenants are conspicuous by their absence outside of the great castleries.[47] Each chapter is emphatically

---

[42] Martin, 'Domesday Book and the Boroughs', 156–61.

[43] GDB 1c, 337a, 280c, 298c: *DB Kent*, D25; *DB Lincs.*, T5; *DB Notts.*, S5; *DB Yorks.*, C36.

[44] GDB 262c–d, 56c, 172a: *DB Cheshire*, C3–21; *DB Berks.*, B10; *DB Worcs.*, C5.

[45] The lists were probably drawn up at an early stage in the compilation of the text and therefore do not always take account of fees that came to light in the process (Galbraith, *Making of Domesday Book*, 190–8).

[46] GDB 345c–346b, 221b–222a, 231b, 205b: *DB Lincs.*, 8; *DB Northants.*, 6; *DB Leics.*, 5; *DB Hunts.*, 8.

[47] Lewis, 'Domesday Jurors', 32–4.

TABLE 4.2. *The order of entries in the Cambridgeshire breves*

Chapter	Hundredal sequence
1. King	1,2,3,10,11,14,7,2,1,5,6,8,9,12
3. Lincoln, bishop of	7,13,14
5. Ely, abbot of	4,1,3,5,6,8,9,10,11,12,13,14,15,16
6. Bury St Edmund's	15,16
7. Ramsey, abbot of	11,12,13,15,16
9. Crowland, abbot of	13,14,15
11. Chatteris Church	8,1,10,12
12. Mortain, count of	7,10,13,14
13. Roger, Earl	9,10,11
14. Alan, Count	5,6,7,8,9,10,11,12,13,14,2,3,1,4
15. Eustace, Count	7,8,10
17. Giffard, Walter	3,10
18. Warenne, William	4,6,8,1,16
19. Richard son of Count Gilbert	12,6,9
21. Robert Gernon	6,7,8,10,12
22. Geoffrey de Mandeville	5,7,8,1,9,10
25. Eudo son of Hubert	6,7,9,10,11
26. Hardwin of Scales	3,1,4,6,7,8,9,10,11,12,14,4,3,5,8
29. Aubrey de Vere	2,3,6
31. Guy de Reinbudcurt	9,10,11
32. Picot of Cambridge	3,6,7,8,9,10,11,12,13,14
38. Robert Fafiton	6,8,10,11,14
39. David de Argenton	11,14
41. Judith, Countess	2,4,6,7,8,9,11,12,13,12,14
44. Erchenger	10,11

Note: Fees with land in only one hundred are omitted.

concerned with the lands and interests of the tenant-in-chief. Demesne and tenanted lands are usually admixed.

They were generally entered in a geographical sequence that was common to each and every chapter. In the Cambridgeshire folios, for example, it can be reconstructed as: 1. Staploe; 2. Cheveley; 3. Staine; 4. Radfield; 5. Flendish; 6. Chilford; 7. Whittlesford; 8. Thriplow; 9. Armingford; 10. Wetherley; 11. Longstow; 12. Papworth; 13. Northstow; 14. Chesterton; 15. Ely I; 16. Ely II. Variations appear in many chapters (Table 4.2).[48] It would seem that Staploe's position was changed early in the course of compilation. In Count Alan's chapter the sequence is broken, and in the king's and Hardwin of Scales's it is repeated. In other counties inversion is also found, but common to all is

[48] Hart, *Hidation of Cambridgeshire*, 15–16.

TABLE 4.3. *The order of vills in Longstow Hundred, Cambridgeshire*

Vill	Breve number						
	5	7	14	25	26	32	39
Eversden			46		37		
Kingston			47	8	38–9	21	
Toft, Hardwick	36–7		48			22	
Gransden	38			9			
Bourn		1	49			23	
Caldecote			50		40		1
Longstowe		2	51		41		
Caxton					42		
Croxton					43		2
Eltisley							
Gamlingay				9			
Hatley St George			52	10		24–5	

Note: The numbers refer to entries in *DB Cambs*. Eltisley was held by the canons of Bayeux who held no other estates in the county.

an underlying geographical structure. Within hundreds a further sequence of vills can often be detected. Land was generally entered in a geographical sequence that was common to each and every chapter regardless of tenurial status. Thus, in the Cambridgeshire hundred of Longstow, where most vills were divided between a number of lords, a consistent order is observed in the chapter of every lord who held land in the hundred (Table 4.3).[49]

The basic unit of textual organization within the chapter is not uniform throughout the work. In the folios relating to the northern counties the organizing principle is what is termed the *manerium*, the manor.[50] In Derbyshire, Huntingdonshire, Lincolnshire, and Nottinghamshire, the estate centre, identified by a marginal Lombardic M, in which the lord's hall was situated is described first. There then follows an account of often widely dispersed manorial appurtenances in separate entries, first the berewicks and then the land in soke, identified by a marginal B or S (and where combined, B and S). William Peverel's manor of Wollaton in Nottinghamshire, for example, is enrolled in four consecutive paragraphs.[51] The first is concerned with the lord's home farm in Wollaton itself and is followed by a berewick in Cossall and two parcels of sokeland in Bramcote and Sutton Passeys. Diplomatic forms and calligraphic conventions emphasize differences in status. 'Manorial' entries are of the form

[49] Ibid. 17–19.
[50] For the following, see Roffe, 'Domesday Book and Northern Society', 313–21.
[51] GDB 287d: *DB Notts.*, 10,35–8.

'In x [the place] A [the TRE tenant] had y carucates to the geld.' The initial 'I' of 'In' is usually square in form, while the place-name is written in large rustic letters and through-lined in red. By way of contrast, subordinate entries are of the form 'In x y carucates of land', the initial 'I' is rustic in form, and the place-name is written in minuscule and is in no way distinguished from the rest of the text. The value of the estate is recorded in the first entry, since the lord's hall was the tributary nexus of the manor.

The structure of manors is intermittently explicit throughout the text. Usually, however, despite evidence of fully articulated estates in many areas in the eleventh century, tenurial relationships are neither explicit nor implied in the format of the account. It is diplomatic that is the main indicator of status. Exact formulas differ from shire to shire and region to region, but two basic forms predominate.

1. A [the tenant-in-chief] holds x; y hides to the geld.
2. In x y hides.

In both, place-names tend to be in large rustic letters, and calligraphic devices are not consistently used to distinguish one from the other. Form 1 and its variations is by far the most common and is found throughout GDB. It is used of the tenant-in-chief's demesne estates as well as those held by his tenants (a holds x from A). In many counties it is associated closely with the formula *pro manerio*, 'for a manor', and it would therefore seem that it signals the *caput* of an estate with some degree of autonomous identity. Form 2 is less common. In Cornwall, Devon, Dorset, Hampshire, Kent, and Surrey it is largely absent, in Oxfordshire and Warwickshire it is rare, while elsewhere it is sporadic. Its significance varies. In Cambridgeshire, Hertfordshire, Bedfordshire, and Buckinghamshire it is merely a variation on form 1 occasioned by the sources employed.[52] But in other counties it often signals a dependent holding. Its use in the Upton and Kenilworth entries in Warwickshire apparently signals the subordination of the lands to the king's manor of Stoneleigh,[53] in the Cold Ashby, Kilsby, and West Haddon entries in Northamptonshire to the church of Coventry's manor of Winwick,[54] in the Highway entry in Wiltshire to the church of Malmesbury,[55] and in eight consecutive entries in the Worcestershire folios to the abbot of Westminster's manor of Pershore.[56]

Both forms of entry contain much the same types of information in a more or less standardized format. An assessment to the geld is universal, and a record of ploughlands, 'land for so many ploughs', is usual except in Gloucestershire, Herefordshire, Worcestershire, Amounderness, and Craven in Yorkshire, and in individual chapters in Kent, Shropshire, and Leicestershire where the information is absent. There is then a statement of the demesne plough teams,

---

[52] See below for a discussion of ICC, pp. 98–9.   [53] GDB 238b: *DB Warks.*, 1,8–9.
[54] GDB 222c: *DB Northants.*, 12,1–4.   [55] GDB 72b: *DB Wilts.*, 41,4.
[56] GDB 174c–d: *DB Worcs.*, 8,1–9.

where appropriate (there was often no demesne on tributary lands), and an enumeration of the villagers, bordars, cottars, and the like and their teams, and of sundry sokemen, riding men, and similar free men, the assessment of their land, and their teams. Manorial appurtenances follow, usually ranked by value. Churches and mills, the latter often with a record of value, are noticed first as the most valuable of the lord's commodities; meadow, pasture, wood-land, marsh, and waste follow in descending order of importance and value. Other commodities are fitted in according to their perceived worth. Communal assets are less closely described, if recorded at all. All manorial entries, and many subsidiary ones, then record the value of the land, usually in 1066, always for 1086, and often for an intermediate period 'when the land was received'. The pre-Conquest holder is usually named in main entries and frequently in subsidiary entries, in some areas with an elaborate account of his interest in the land and his status. There is, however, no standard position for the information.

Despite appearances to the contrary, entries do not necessarily have cor-relates in estate structure, that is, relate to hamlets or villages with their own economic resources or to well-defined divisions of the manor.[57] An identify-ing name is sometimes that of an estate. Contemporary charters and leases indicate that large demesne holdings, like the church of Worcester's manors of Fladbury and Bibury, consisted of numerous townships and vills, but either the estate name alone is used in GDB or the various elements are noticed only incidentally in the same entry.[58] Smaller fees, by contrast, such as the Worcester monks' demesne and enfeoffed land which encompassed whole vills or part thereof are identified by vill names or probably, in some cases where they were different, by township names. Where the structure of local govern-ment can be reconstructed, it is often clear that entry formation is a direct function of it. In the Lincolnshire wapentake of Elloe, for example, inland and sokeland entries are invariably in a different twelve-carucate hundred from the manorial caput unless a parcel of land had a discrete identity within the manor.[59] There is thus only one entry per vill, and land is described within it regardless of status. It was proximity rather than status that informed entry formation; the free men and sokemen who are described in manorial entries are not necessarily different in kind from those who appear in subsidiary entries, and are not more or less integrated into the manorial economy than their counterparts.

The standard format of GDB, clearly designed to facilitate its use as a work of reference, did not leave much room for information beyond its chosen scope. Anomalous material, nevertheless, does appear. In a significant number of

---

[57] Roffe, 'Place-Naming in Domesday Book', 47–60.
[58] Hamshere, 'The Structure and Exploitation of the Demesne Estates of the Church of Worcester', 44–5.
[59] Roffe, 'Lincolnshire Hundred', 30, 32.

entries, some thousand or so, the evidence of shire, hundred, and vill juries is given. Four general concerns are addressed: 1. the assessment of the tenement in question to the geld;[60] 2. its value and that of its appurtenances; 3. its holder before the Conquest; and 4. its holder at the time of the survey. In the majority of cases, the verdict attests a dispute (less than a dozen are concerned with economic statistics).[61] A small number, however, are explanatory. Title to land in Oakley in Buckinghamshire, for example, was derived from a grant of Godric the sheriff to a girl called Ælfgeth who was to teach his daughter gold embroidery in return.[62] Yet others are seemingly acknowledgement of liberties or privileges such as exemption from the geld.

For the counties of Huntingdonshire, Lincolnshire, and Yorkshire there exist additionally three series of what are twice called *clamores*, 'disputes'.[63] In the first they are appended to the end of the county Domesday in the body of the text without explanatory rubric, but the second and third are entered together in a separate quire at the end of the volume after the Lincolnshire folios. In all three instances they record the verdicts of shire and hundred (Huntingdonshire) or wapentake (Lincolnshire and Yorkshire) on matters of disputed title within a sequence of hundreds or wapentakes which is largely identical with that of the *breves*. The Yorkshire series is a compilation from various sources and is demonstrably incomplete; those of Huntingdonshire and Lincolnshire are fair copies (Table 4.4).[64] The cases themselves overlap with presentments preserved in the body of the text, but there is no exact correlation; disputes are found in the one that are not noticed in the other and vice versa. While there is no doubt that these *clamores* belong firmly within the Domesday process, in the Lincolnshire instances at least, they were heard independently of the presentments in the text and probably on a later occasion, for the twelve-carucate hundred, ubiquitous in the text, is absent. They are, furthermore, ostensibly settlements.[65] The Lincolnshire section opens with the cases in the South Riding and it is entitled 'Disputes which there are in the South Riding of Lincoln, and their settlement by the men who swear [*Clamores que sunt in Sudtreding Lincolie et concordia eorum per homines qui iuraverunt*]'.[66] Verdicts were clearly intended to have effect. Thus, it is recorded in the Count Alan's *breve* in the body of the text that the wapentake [of Skirbeck] had declared that a tenement in Drayton which had belonged to the abbot of Ramsey had been held by Bishop Wulfwige of Dorchester on Thames, but they did not know through whom he had held it. Neither Remigius, Wulfwige's successor,

[60] See e.g. GDB 38a–39b, 100b–c, 75b, 64d: *DB Hants.*, 1,2;17;21;27;41;43–4; *DB Devon*, 1,7;11; *DB Dorset*, 1,2–6; *DB Wilts.*, 1,1, where the hidage was not known or no account of it was rendered.

[61] Fleming, *Domesday Book and the Law*, 3.   [62] GDB 149b: *DB Bucks.*, 19,3.

[63] GDB 208a–c, 373a–377d: *DB Hunts.*, D; *DB Lincs.*, CS, CN, CW, CK; *DB Yorks.*, CE, CN, CW.

[64] Roffe, 'Domesday Book and Northern Society', 325–6.

[65] Some, probably many, cases, however, were deferred for later judgement. See GDB 377c–d: *DB Lincs.*, CK50;66;69.

[66] GDB 375a: *DB Lincs.*, CS1.

TABLE 4.4. *The composition of the Huntingdonshire, Yorkshire, and Lincolnshire clamores*

Reference	Location	Lines	Pen
Hunts.		44	A
Y CN1–CW4	YNR, YER YWR	52	B
Y CW5–20	YWR	52	C
Y CW21–36	YWR	52	?
Y CW37–9	YWR	52	?
————————————(Incomplete column)————————————			
Y CE34–52	H	52	D
Y CW40–2	YWR	52	E
L CS1–4	LSR	52	F
L CS5–20	LSR	52	F
L CS21–38	LSR	52	F
L CS39–40	LSR	52	F
L CN1–30	LNR	52	F
L CW1–20	LWR	52	F
L K1–71	K, Ho	52	F

Notes: K = Kesteven, H = Holderness, Ho = Holland, LNR = Lindsey North Riding, LSR = Lindsey South Riding, LWR = Lindsey West Riding, YER = Yorks East Riding, YNR = Yorks North Riding, YER = Yorks West Riding. Each line represents a one-line space in the text.

nor Ramsey had tenure, and it is only in the *clamores* entry relating to the case that their right was recognized.[67]

After the Lincolnshire *clamores*, there is enrolled an even more anomalous source which is usually known as the Yorkshire Summary.[68] A geographically arranged skeleton list of landholdings and their lords, it is written in its entirety by the main scribe, but variations in the hand define three separate sections which, lacking substantial postscriptal material, appear to be fair copies of

[67] GDB 348b, 377d: *DB Lincs.*, 12,59.CK65.   [68] GDB 379a–382b: *DB Yorks.*, SW, SN, SE.

previously drafted documents.[69] The first section covers most of the county of York: the eighty-four carucates that belonged to York itself; the West Riding, with the exception of most of Craven which, with Amounderness and related lands to the west of the Pennines, does not appear in the text; the North Riding, less the land of Count Alan of Brittany in Richmondshire; and the East Riding, except for the land of Drogo de Beuvrière in Holderness.[70] Only the lands of Hugh son of Baldric and Count Robert of Mortain are occasionally, and Roger the Poitevin's estates consistently, omitted. It is arranged by wapentakes in the West and North Ridings (which are not explicitly recognized), and each subsection is indicated by blank lines in the text and an identifying rubric. Further groups of vills within wapentakes are signalled by enlarged square I's which usually follow half-lines or a space in the text: Agbrigg, Strafforth, and Burghshire in the West Riding are each divided in two in this way, and in like wise three groups are defined in Langbargh, and two each in *Dic*, *Maneshou*, and *Bolesforde* in the North Riding. Almost all of the areas so delineated are territorially discrete and appear to indicate subdivisions of each wapentake.[71] The East Riding is divided into hundreds, again signalled by rubrics. The wapentakes of the twelfth century were probably already in existence, and these hundreds may correspond to the vestigial subdivisions of the other two ridings, thus pointing to a change in textual organization adopted by the scribe in the course of his work.[72]

Throughout the whole section identical diplomatic forms are employed. Smaller capital I's superficially appear to indicate entries, but these are of little significance, for they only mark the beginning of each line, and generally individual items seem to be of equal status. Written in black ink in Carolingian minuscules, holdings are identified by reference to the vill in which they were situated and their assessment is noted, whilst the lord in 1086 is indicated by an interlineation in red in the same hand. All the land in the same vill is normally entered consecutively regardless of fee. Non-royal large sokes, however, are commonly enrolled as estates, that is, berewicks and sokelands are entered with the parent manors. The group is signalled by an enlarged initial rustic I, and very occasionally a rubricated upper-case place-name, and there are significant variations in form; the assessment of the *caput* is an integral element of the text, but those of the appurtenances are either totalled or interlined above the relevant place-name in black ink. The section, then, is neither completely tenurially nor geographically arranged.

The second and third sections are confined to the land of Count Alan in Richmondshire and Drogo de Beuvrière's fee in Holderness.[73] The former

[69] For what follows, see Roffe, 'Yorkshire Summary', 242–60.

[70] GDB 381b, 382b: *DB Yorks.*, SN,CtA.SE,Hol.

[71] *Gereburg* 'Wapentake', if not an alternative name for Skyrack or Burghshire, may be the name of one such subdivision (GDB 379a: *DB Yorks.*, SW,Sk2).

[72] Roffe, 'Yorkshire Summary', 246.   [73] GDB 381b, 382b: *DB Yorks.*, SN,Ct.SE,Hol.

was entered in a column at the end of the account of the North Riding which was presumably left for the purpose, and is divided into two by a blank line in which the rubric [*Terra*] *Eiusdem Comitis* was subsequently added. The areas defined are identical with the thirteenth-century boundaries of the wapentakes of Gilling and Hang and would therefore seem to indicate a geographical element within the account. The Holderness section is appended to the end of the document with no indication of lordship, and, by contrast, exhibits no subdivisions or obvious underlying geographical structures. Both are tenurially arranged, Richmondshire within its two divisions, and share the same form as the grouped entries in section one: the assessment of the *caput* of each fee, usually marked by a rustic I outlined in red and a rubricated place-name, is a current component of the text, but those of berewicks and sokeland are interlined in black ink. Nevertheless, they probably have a different origin, although not necessarily a different function, from section one. Indeed, two vills in Hallikeld Wapentake in the body of the document are duplicated in the account of Count Alan's land, and an abstract is given, albeit postscriptally, of the salient statistics of the estates within and without the castlery of Richmond.[74]

With the exception of the lands of the king's thegns which are indifferently ascribed to the king himself, most of the information that is given is consistent with the details of the relevant GDB passages. The few discrepancies, however, indicate that section one is anterior to GDB. Tanshelf, for example, is ascribed to the king in the Summary, but was held by Ilbert de Lacy in the text in succession to the king.[75] Further, there is evidence that it was used in the compilation of the Yorkshire folios. Regardless of the tenurial status of the land, the order of entries in most chapters is identical to that of the Summary, but irregularities indicate that the former drew directly upon the latter or its exemplar. The account of the count of Mortain's estates in the North Riding, for example, is divided into eight sections by spaces in the text. When entries are numbered according to their appearance in the Summary, the same order is found in each of the individual sections. However, overall the various sections overlap (Table 4.5). Such repetition clearly indicates that a Summary-like document was a basic source of the Yorkshire folios in GDB which was read a number of times with a different purpose in mind, and the process presumably accounts for the frequent omission of material in GDB that is enrolled in the Summary.

The account of Amounderness and estates to the west of the Pennines may substantially represent a fourth section, or a similar document, which was incorporated into the text itself.[76] A later addition at the end of the king's Yorkshire chapter, it exhibits some of the forms of the compiled GDB text,

---

[74] GDB 380b, 381b: *DB Yorks.*, SW,H4.SN,CtA39;45.
[75] GDB 316c, 379c: *DB Yorks.*, 9W64.SW,O15.   [76] GDB 301d–302a: *DB Yorks.*, 1L.

TABLE 4.5. *Groups of manors in the count of Mortain's Yorkshire breve*

Breve no. 5	Summary	Vill no.
N1	Langbargh	15
N2–28	Langbargh	17–108
N29–32	Langbargh	105–62
	Dic	8–9
N33–44	Dic	55–6
	Manshowe	4–53
	Bolesforde	4
N45–54	Manshowe	31–57
	Bolesforde	5–10
N55–7	Bolesforde	10–18
N58–68	Bolesforde	14–38
N69–76	Bolesforde	66
	Gerlestre	17–22
	Allerton	63?
	Bolesforde	67
	Gerlestre	23–5

such as the use of a marginal M to indicate manors. The account itself, however, is as terse as the Summary and is in the same form as its sections two and three with the addition of TRE holders. There is a brief account of the resources of Preston, but only to note that it was largely waste; significantly, no ploughlands are given.[77] It is likely that the missing Craven section is also to be found in the text. The GDB entries in the chapters of the king and Roger the Poitevin's are identical in form with the Amounderness account and equally postscriptal.[78]

GDB was apparently compiled as a register, for its forms and conventions are all designed to facilitate efficient reference. County by county, it provides a list of the lands of the king and each tenant-in-chief in a form that enables the reader easily to access its data: information is standardized and layout, notably the capitalization and rubrication of place-names, draws the eye to pertinent detail.[79] Its sources are ostensibly the findings of the Domesday inquest. But it is a considered work and, as one that was executed largely by a single scribe, it clearly post-dates that process. The volume is probably first noticed

---

[77] GDB 301d: *DB Yorks.*, 1L1. Three churches are also noted. Churches on the *terra regis* are often accounted as separate items within a hundredal structure. In Norfolk and Suffolk, for example, they appear at the end of the hundredal sections of the king's chapter (LDB 116a, 283a: *DB Norfolk*, 1,60; *DB Suffolk*, 1,20–2). They were probably farmed independently of the manors.
[78] GDB 332a–b: *DB Yorks.*, 30.   [79] Holt, '1086', 50–4.

in an authentic writ, dating from 1099–1100, which refers to Hayling Island which Queen Emma gave to the cathedral priory of Winchester 'as the king's book testifies [*sicut liber regius testatur*]'.[80] When it was commenced is unknown. It has been estimated that an experienced hand might be able to write six columns in an eight-hour day, and such a work-rate would suggest that GDB could not have been written in less than 240 days.[81] It seems hardly credible, then, that 'the writings' that were brought to William before he left for Normandy in August 1086 were the present volume when the collection of data was only begun in early 1086. It has often been asserted, therefore, that work continued after the king's departure, and was terminated incomplete on his death in September 1087.[82] In reality, however, there is no firm evidence that the work was even started by then. Claims have been made that the Surrey section must already have been written when William issued a writ, *post descriptionem tocius Anglie*, which set the assessment of Westminster Abbey's manor of Pyrford in Surrey at eight hides, for in GDB the scribe originally recorded its liability as sixteen hides, only subsequently to add postscriptally that 'it now gelds for 8 hides'.[83] The assumption, however, is unwarranted. The writ clearly sets a *terminus post quem* for the addition, but can hardly provide a *terminus ante quem* for the text itself. At most it can be said that the information was not in the scribe's original source. That source noted that the men of the hundred had not seen or heard a writ which sanctioned a previous reduction in assessment from twenty-seven to sixteen hides, and the comment could have prompted the scribe to look for one at any time.[84] Such tangible indications as there are point to a later date for the composition of GDB. Two postscriptal entries in the Staffordshire folios were seemingly written after the forfeiture of Thorkill of Arden in 1088,[85] and two current references to William de Warenne as earl of Surrey indicate that the Sussex and Huntingdonshire folios cannot have been completed before his preferment to the earldom by William Rufus between late 1087 and mid-1088.[86] It is becoming increasingly clear that the scribe was still engaged on the task in the reign of William Rufus.

---

[80] Galbraith, 'Royal Charters to Winchester', 389.   [81] Gullick, 'Manuscripts', 105.

[82] e.g. Galbraith, *Making of Domesday Book*, 205.

[83] *Facsimiles of English Royal Writs*, no. 24; Galbraith, *Making of Domesday Book*, 206; Holt, '1086', 52 n.

[84] Mention of the Pyrford charter clearly indicates that this note was written after late 1086, but it would be absurd to claim that it indicates that the chapter to which it is appended was therefore written in early 1086 or before.

[85] GDB 250b: *DB Staffs.*, 12,31; Gullick, 'Manuscripts', 106. Drayton is said to be held of William son of Ansculf by a certain Thurstan, where in the Oxfordshire folios a current entry ascribes it to Thurkill (GDB 160c: *DB Oxon.*, 57,1). Gullick also suggests that a postscriptal Hampshire entry (GDB 39c: *DB Hants.*, 1,46) which assigns land to Roger the Poitevin may have been written after Roger's return to England in early 1088. For the restructuring of Roger's honour, see Lewis, 'Introduction to the Lancashire Domesday', 36–8.

[86] Lewis, 'The Earldom of Surrey and the Date of Domesday Book', 327–36.

Little Domesday Book

The 450 folios of LDB contain the accounts of Essex, Norfolk, and Suffolk. It is a fair copy, with few additions and emendations, and was executed by seven scribes, six of whom apparently worked together; the seventh was responsible for the running heads and the colophon at the end of the Suffolk folios (Table 4.6).[87] Their orthography reveals that they wrote in a different tradition from that of the GDB scribe. Quirks like the use of *Ph* for initial *F* are unparalleled, but the unvoicing of final *d* to *t* hints at a continental influence. Generally, nevertheless, LDB exhibits both personal and place-name forms that are often closer to OE usage than equivalents in GDB. The scribes were clearly not ignorant of the English language.[88] There has been no detailed study of the work of each, but it is likely that two had supervisory roles in the production of the text.[89] Scribe 1, who wrote almost all of the Essex folios, corrected the work of the other scribes in those of Norfolk and Suffolk. It was probably scribe 2, however, who was in overall charge. The diplomatic of the sections that he wrote departs from that of the others (he omits the otherwise general statement that land was held 'for a manor [*pro manerio*]' and 'for so many carucates [*pro* x *carucatis*]'), suggesting perhaps a greater degree of independence. More significantly, he wrote indices to the contents of individual quires, and drafted the lists of tenants-in-chief at the head of the accounts of Norfolk and Suffolk. Like GDB, it would seem that LDB was not originally bound, and he provided an ad hoc guide to the contents of some of the gatherings in the process of ordering them.

In overall form the text is similar to GDB. Each county section is divided into chapters which, with the exception of an account of *invasiones*, 'invasions', at the end, are each devoted to the lands and incomes of a single individual, or, in the case of ministerial and lesser tenants, a class of individuals such as the *vavassores* or the free men. As is proper and usual, the lands of the king are described first, but it is only in Essex that the remaining chapters conform to the strict order of precedence that is evidenced in GDB. In Norfolk and Suffolk the greatest lay holders—the bishop of Bayeux (a cleric by rank but holding a lay fief), the count of Mortain, Count Alan, Count Eustace, Earl Hugh, Robert Malet, William de Warenne, Roger the Poitevin, William of Ecouis, and Roger Bigod—follow the king, displacing the clerics to a lower position. Bishops, abbots, and other clerics are succeeded by the lesser tenants-in-chief. These are not grouped by Christian-name as in GDB, but are enrolled in a seemingly haphazard way, apart from the lumping together of sergeants such as the crossbowmen.

[87] Rumble, 'Domesday Manuscripts', 98–9; LDB 450a: *DB Suffolk*, 77,4.

[88] Sawyer, 'Place-Names of the Domesday Manuscripts', 497; Feiltzen, *Pre-Conquest Personal Names of Domesday Book*, 6.

[89] Rumble, 'Domesday Manuscripts', 92.

TABLE 4.6. *The scribes of LDB*

Section		Scribe	Text	
DB Essex	L–2,9	1	Essex	list of tenants, caps. 1–2
		2		partial list of tenants
	3,1–8,11	1		breve nos. 3–8
		2		partial list of tenants
	9,1–90,1	1		breve nos. 9–90 (part)
	90,2–3	3		breve no. 90 (part)
	90,5–87	1		breve no. 90 (part)
	B	3		Colchester
DB Norfolk	L–1,7	2	Norfolk	list of tenants, cap. 1 (part)
	1,8–9	4		breve no. 1 (part)
	1,9–7,21	2		breve nos. 1 (part) –7
	8,1–14	3		breve no. 8 (part)
	8,15–138	5		breve no. 8 (part)
	9,1–5	1		breve no. 9 (part)
	9,6–37	2		breve no. 9 (part)
	9,38–45	5		breve no. 9 (part)
	9,46–78	2		breve no. 9 (part)
	9,78–87	5		breve no. 9 (part)
	9,88–104	2		breve no. 9 (part)
	9,104–115	1		breve no. 9 (part)
	9,115–234	6		breve no. 9 (part)
	10,1–16	1		breve no. 10 (part)
	10,16–13,24	5		breve nos. 10 (part)–13
	14,1–19,8	1		breve nos. 14–19 (part)
	19,9–65,17	6		breve nos. 19 (part)–65
	66,1–91	1		breve no. 66 (part)
	66,91–99	2		breve no. 66 (part)
	66,99–108	1		breve no. 66 (part)
DB Suffolk	L	2, 1	Suffolk	list of tenants
	1,1–115	2		breve no. 1 (part)
	1,115–121	1		breve no. 1 (part)
	1,122a–g	5		breve no. 1 (part)
	2,1–20	2		breve no. 2
		1		partial list of tenants
	3,1–56	2		breve no. 3 (part)
	3,56–9	1		breve no. 3 (part)
	3,59–95	2		breve no. 3 (part)
	3,95	1		breve no. 3 (part)
	3,96–4,1	2		breve no. 3 (part)–4 (part)
	4,1–3	1		breve no. 4 (part)
	4,3–9,3	2		breve nos. 4 (part)–9 (part)
	9,4	1		breve no. 9 (part)

TABLE 4.6. (cont'd)

Section	Scribe	Text
10,1–13,7	2	breve nos. 10–13
14,1–167	5	breve no. 14
	2	partial list of tenants
15,1–16,48	5	breve nos. 15–16
17,1	1	breve no. 17
18,1–21,105	5	breve nos. 18–21
22,1–3	1	breve no. 22
23,1–76,23	5	breve nos. 23–76
77,1–4	2	Malet/Bayeux dispute
	7	Colophon

Source: After A. R. Rumble, 'The Domesday Manuscripts: Scribes and Scriptoria', in J. Holt (ed.), *Domesday Studies* (Woodbridge, 1987), 98–9.

Within each chapter the structure of the text is almost entirely hundredal. With few exceptions, no attempt was made to group manorial appurtenances in berewicks and the like with the manorial *caput*. Except in the account of the lands of the king and some of the greater landholders, such as the bishop of Thetford in Norfolk, in which various sections are found,[90] lands in each hundred are generally described together in separate paragraphs regardless of estate structure, and in each of the three counties there is a common sequence of hundreds. The name of each hundred, with but a handful of exceptions, was carefully and consistently recorded by successive scribes in the course of their work (few of the hundred rubrics are obviously postscriptal as they are in many folios of GDB), and calligraphically they are the only part of the text which is emphasized, each being written in capital letters and rubricated in red ink.

Overall, the visual impression is of a geographically arranged source. However, within each hundred there are more complex organizing principles. Generally, the estates held by the tenant-in-chief, whether they be demesnes or tributary holdings, are described first. They are followed by the manors on which tenants had been enfeoffed or otherwise settled, and finally land which was the subject of disputed tenure, or was in some other way anomalous, was enrolled. William de Warenne's lands of the Lewes exchange, for example, are distinguished by position in the text in this way.[91] It is not unusual, then, to find that tenements in the same vill are not always described together. Nevertheless, at root a common sequence of vills can be detected. Within the

[90] LDB 191a–193a: *DB Norfolk*, 10,1–19 is entitled 'Land of the bishop of Thetford belonging to the bishopric before 1066', while 20–93 is entitled 'Land of the fee of the same'.

[91] LDB 157a–172b: *DB Norfolk*, 8,2–4;10;13;18–19;26;32;40;45–6;48;50–1;53;58;60–1;68–70;80;84; 88;90;112. Exceptions probably attest unremarked tenurial relationships.

TABLE 4.7. *Entry forms in LDB*

VIIA	*X* [the place] held *Y* [TRE holder] for *z* carucates . . .
VIIB	*X* held *A* [TRW tenant] which *Y* held for *z* carucates . . .
VIIC	A berewick *X* of *z* carucates . . .
VIID	In *X* holds *A* *z* carucates which held *Y* a free man TRE . . .
VIIE	In *X* a free man *z* acres TRE. . . .

divisions of demesne, tenanted, and disputed fees individual places are noticed in much the same order from one chapter to the next. In Clackclose Hundred in Norfolk, for example, Marham, Fincham, and Barton Bendish appear first, if a lord held land in those vills, and Upwell and Outwell last.[92]

    The basic unit of textual organization is what can be here only loosely termed 'the entry'. Although the account of each hundred is written as a paragraph, a *paragraphos*, that is, a gallows sign, is often employed to signal the start of the account of discrete parcels of land. This, however, is by no means universal, and in the absence of the distinctive treatment of place-names as in Great Domesday, it is only diplomatic forms and content which punctuate the account. Although exact wording varies, individual entries tend to be of five types. They are most immediately characterized by the opening statement (Table 4.7). Only form VIIC invariably points to the status of the land described; it exclusively refers to berewicks, that is, land held and directly exploited by the lord which is in one way or another divorced from the estate centre. It is, however, not the only form associated with such land, only being employed in the account of the larger estate centres. Form VIIA, relating to land personally held by the tenant-in-chief, and form VIIB, the tenanted counterpart, usually refer to manorial centres, that is, the lord's hall and home farm and the infrastructure associated with them. Indeed, the *pro manerio* formula often makes the fact explicit. But it may occasionally refer to dependent holdings. The account of an estate in Hunworth could be taken for a manor, but it was valued with Count Alan's manor of Saxthorpe and was presumably a berewick.[93] Likewise, Wramplingham, which was held by one of Gyrth's sokemen, was probably sokeland despite its form.[94] Forms VIID and VIIE are more usually found in such entries and their subordinate status is regularly indicated by an explicit notice of the manorial centre. The forms are also used of land held by free men TRE and at the time of the survey. But again, that usage is not universal. The description of Fakenham, a royal manor of the first rank, is couched in the same words as dependent holdings, as is Mellis in Suffolk which is explicitly called a manor.[95] In Norfolk and Suffolk both manorial and dependent forms

[92] Dodwell, 'The Making of the Domesday Survey in Norfolk: The Hundred and a Half of Clacklose', 79–84.

[93] LDB 146a: *DB Norfolk*, 4,21.   [94] LDB 145a: *DB Norfolk*, 4,10.

[95] LDB 323b: *DB Suffolk*, 6,227.

may be primarily related to the form of the sources of LDB.[96] In Essex forms VIIA and VIIB are by far the most common types of entry and they may therefore have no significance at all.[97]

It is only in the information recorded that the status of any particular parcel of land becomes clear. Demesne land, whether an estate centre, inland, or newly tenanted free men's land, is recorded in much greater detail than the lands of most sokemen and of free men. All entries tend to list population, ploughs, commodities, and details of infrastructure in mills, churches, and the like. But demesne entries record all this information, where known, for 1066, an intermediate period, usually when the estate was acquired by the tenant-in-chief, and 'now', that is, for 1086. Furthermore, elaborate details are given of the livestock kept on the lord's home farm; heads of cattle, pigs, sheep, horses, and goats all regularly make their appearance. Such information is sometimes given for sokeland, and less often for land of free men, where it had been granted to a tenant or supported a demesne, but altogether less interest was taken in such land. In the majority of such entries it is difficult to determine whether the information given refers to 1066, 1086, some intermediate date, or all three. Ploughlands are not explicitly recorded at all.

It is again tempting to see entries so defined as discrete units in settlement or estate structures. In neither Norfolk nor Suffolk can the subdivisions of the hundred, the leets, and the vills of which they were composed be reconstructed with any degree of confidence,[98] and it is therefore impossible to determine precisely what effect they had on the structure of the text. Nevertheless, it may be suspected that those units of local government had a similar role. Thus, although as a rule sokemen and free men are enrolled in separate entries, they are not infrequently described within the entry relating to the lord's demesne, and settlements that were joined together to form a vill are usually found in tandem wherever they appear.

The *invasiones* sections at the end of the account of each county list lands and dues appropriated by tenants-in-chief, and are arranged by fee (if not always competently) but in a different order from that of the text. However, within each fee there is a hundred order which is largely identical with that of the bulk of the text. Details of land are given in much the same terms as the rest of the text; the resources of the manor are recorded along with its value, and there is often an outline of the nature of title given. Similar material is found in the *breves*, but there is little duplication. In the Essex and Suffolk sections the invasions are said to be *super regem*, and it is clear that some of the lands in question were in the hands of the king or had been granted to

---

[96] See below, pp. 177–9.

[97] The Essex folios are peculiar in other aspects of their diplomatic, notably in the use of *tenuit* in the context of TRE holders of land. This form normally indicates a king's thegn, but it is so common in Essex that it may be of little significance. Alternatively, there may have been a high proportion of such lords in the county. If so, the predominance of the 'manorial' entry formula might reflect an extraordinary degree of high status.

[98] *Kalendar of Abbot Samson*, pp. xv–xxx.

a third party at previous hearings.[99] Often, however, there were still matters outstanding. Berengar, for example, was in the king's mercy for the annexation of land and men in Uggeshall, but was ill and could not attend the plea (*placitum*).[100] Other lands were still held by the aggressors, and pledges were accordingly given.[101] Unlike in the *clamores* of GDB, here there is little indication of pleadings in any of the three sections and recognitions by local juries are largely absent. Thus, Roger of Auberville annexed a free man in Finborough who was taken into the king's hand until the matter could be adjudged.[102] The *invasiones* sections should perhaps best be characterized as business in progress.

The production of the LDB text is seemingly dated by the colophon at the end of the volume:

This survey [*Ista descriptio*] was made in the year 1086 from the Incarnation of the Lord and the twentieth of the reign of William, not only through these three counties but also through the others.[103]

It should be noted, however, that it is far from clear that the words *ista descriptio* refer to the volume itself. The demonstrative *ista*, 'that' (as opposed to *haec*, 'this'), if applied according to classical usage, would suggest something other. The passage is, moreover, postscriptal, and scribe number seven who wrote it only otherwise rubricated LDB. The colophon is a *post hoc* comment by one who had no hand in the production of the text. A later date for the volume is not precluded.

The Liber Exoniensis

Exon is preserved as MS 3500 in Exeter Cathedral Library, where it has probably been kept since the eleventh century.[104] The MS consists of 552 folios written on both sides in a single column arranged in a number of irregular quires. There are no signatures to indicate the original order of binding, and the present arrangement probably dates from 1816 when it was last rebound. Textual links indicate that a small number of quires were associated with others, but generally the content of each gathering is discrete and it would appear

---

[99] LDB 14b, 99a–b, 100b, 276b, 278b, 279b, 448b–449a: *DB Essex*, 6,8.90,2;7;8;9;28; *DB Norfolk*, 66,64;86;99; *DB Suffolk*, 76,13–16;19.

[100] LDB 449a: *DB Suffolk*, 76,19.

[101] LDB 99a, 100b, 101a, 103a, 274a, 278a, 280a, 448b–449a: *DB Essex*, 90,1;2;29;41;42;74;78; *DB Norfolk*, 66,5;84;86;106; *DB Suffolk*, 76,14;15;17;19.

[102] LDB 448b–449a: *DB Suffolk*, 76,16.   [103] LDB 450a.

[104] Welldon Finn, *Liber Exoniensis*, 1. The hand of the scribe who worked on the Wiltshire Geld Accounts B and C, however, is represented at Salisbury (Ker, 'The Beginnings of Salisbury Cathedral Library', 34–8), and there might also be links with Bath Abbey, for one of the hands of the two major scribes is similar to the hand of Bath A (Welldon Finn, 'The Exeter Domesday', 368). See also Rumble, 'Palaeography of the Domesday Manuscripts', 43.

TABLE 4.8. *The contents of Exon*

Folios	Content
1–3^v	Wiltshire Geld Summary A
7–9^v	Wiltshire Geld Summary B
11–12^v	Dorset boroughs
13–16^v	Wiltshire Geld Summary C
17–24	Dorset Geld Summary
25–62^v	Twelve Dorset fees and one Wiltshire
63–4^v	Lists of hundreds in Devon, Cornwall, and Somerset
65–71	Devon Geld Summary
72–3	Cornwall Geld Summary
75–82^v	Somerset Geld Summary (part)
83–494^v	Fees in Devon, Cornwall, and Somerset
495–506^v	*Terre Occupate* in Devon
507–8^v	*Terre Occupate* in Cornwall
508^v–25	*Terre Occupate* in Somerset
526–7^v	Somerset Geld Summary (part)
527^v–31	Summaries of fiefs
532–532^v	Index lists of 26 fees and headings

Note: Folios not described are blank.

that they were originally used as separate pamphlets.[105] The text is written by two main scribes and a dozen or so minor ones (one being the main scribe of GDB) in late-eleventh-century Carolingian minuscules.[106] Their orthography exhibits a marked continental influence, notably in the unvoicing of final *d* to *t* and the use of a prosthetic *e* before initial *s* when followed by another consonant, and it would therefore seem that they came from an Anglo-Norman rather than an English background.[107] The scribes do not seem to have worked to any discernible pattern, one taking over from another between entries and even within entries, as the need demanded. The text, however, was corrected as the material was entered and subsequently, and there is a mass of emendations, glosses, and additions where space permitted. Exon is clearly not a copy of a fully drafted exemplar and would therefore seem to be a series of working documents compiled from a variety of sources.

Its content is diverse. The volume relates to the shires of Cornwall, Devon, Dorset, Somerset, and Wiltshire, but there are distinct types of material deriving from different documents and activities (Table 4.8). The series of summary geld accounts emanated from what in one place is termed an *inquisitio*

[105] Rumble, 'Palaeography of the Domesday Manuscripts', 31–2.
[106] There is only one detailed analysis of the hand to date (Welldon Finn, 'The Exeter Domesday and its Construction', 360–87).
[107] Sawyer, 'Place-Names of the Domesday Manuscripts', 484–95.

geldi. Three, A, B, and C, survive for Wiltshire, and one each for the counties of Cornwall, Devon, Dorset, and Somerset. They are arranged by hundred, but vary in formula, form, and the detail of content. Nevertheless, each generally notes the total number of hides in every hundred, those held in demesne by the king and his barons which were apparently exempt, the amounts for which geld was owing or had not been paid at the time of the inquest, and the sum received and for how many hides.[108] Eyton, who first studied the geld accounts in detail, believed that they referred to the geld of 6s per hide which was levied in 1084,[109] This remains possible (although an unrecorded geld in 1085 is equally likely),[110] but the records themselves relate to an audit of 1086. The entry for Cullifordtree Hundred in the Dorset account notices one hide 'which Bishop Peter [of Chester] held',[111] and he appears to have died in 1085, while Manasses the cook, who seems to have died in the course of the Domesday inquest, is recorded as a tenant in the Dorset section, but a former tenant in the Somerset.[112] Similar entries occur for Serlo de Bucy, who likewise died sometime in 1086, and possibly for Odin the chamberlain.[113] Furthermore, much of the language of the accounts echoes that of the corresponding GDB entries. In the Warminster section, for example, the geld account records 'et hic est inventa i hida que non reddidit geldum postquam Willelmus rex habuit regnum. Eam tenent Anfridus et Rainboldus', where GDB has 'Rainboldus tenet de Ernulfo Opetune. . . . In hac terra est dimidia hida comprehensa quae geldabat TRE. Sed postquam rex W. in Angliam venit geldum non reddidit.'[114] The geld accounts and GDB, or more precisely the sources from which it was compiled, are evidently closely related.[115]

The bulk of the text is devoted to accounts of the lands of the king and tenants-in-chief in Dorset, Devon, Cornwall, and Somerset, with a single Wiltshire entry. The holders of land are those who appear in GDB and much of the substance of the description of their estates is identical with the passages therein. The form, however, is different. The overriding principle of organization was the fee, that is, the account proceeds landholder by landholder for the whole region rather than county by county. Tenements in the same hundred tend to be entered together, although there are no hundredal rubrics, and there are indications of a common hundredal sequence, especially within the Devon sections.[116] In general, entries are more expansive than their GDB

[108] Welldon Finn, *Liber Exoniensis*, 98.
[109] Eyton, *Domesday Studies: Somerset*, 87–93; id., *A Key to Domesday*, 4–5, 109.
[110] For which, see Galbraith, *Making of Domesday Book*, 87–101.
[111] Exon, 24.   [112] Exon, 22ᵛ, 78.
[113] Mason, 'The Date of the Geld Rolls', 283–9.   [114] Exon, 1ᵛ; GDB 70b: *DB Wilts.*, 25,23.
[115] Bates ('The Conqueror's Charters', 4) suggests that an unpublished charter granting Piddle Hinton in Dorset to Notre-Dame of Mortain, which he re-dates to the reign of William II, provides further corroboration. It states that there were 6 hides in demesne which is nearer to the 5 hides and 3 virgates of the *inquisitio geldi* than the 5 hides of GDB (Exon, 19; GDB 79b: *DB Dorset*, 26,20).
[116] Welldon Finn, *Liber Exoniensis*, 36–44.

counterparts. Phraseology is looser; there is *reddidit geldum* for *geldabat, possunt ararare* x *caruce* for *terra est* x *carucis, ea die qua rex Edwardus fuit vivus et mortuus* for *TRE*. Vocabulary is distinctive; *mansio* is used for *manerium, pascua* for *pastura, nemus* for *silva, nemusculus* for *silva minuta*. Content is more comprehensive; extensive details of villagers' land is given, livestock is enumerated, more precise dating of the values of manors is afforded, and details of how they were held.

GDB has information that is not found in Exon and frequently it exhibits a different organization. Nevertheless, there is compelling evidence that the main scribe had the manuscript before him when he composed the West Country folios of GDB, and that he used it as his principal (if not only) source. Both Welldon Finn and Galbraith believed that there must have been an intermediate recension to account for the additional information.[117] But Caroline and Frank Thorn, following in the footsteps of Baring, have demonstrated the direct dependence of certain passages in GDB on the Exon manuscript.[118] Thus, numerous items of information that are misplaced in Exon are similarly so in GDB; slaves, for example are grouped with the pigmen in the accounts of Nympton and Merton in Devon rather than with the demesne or villagers in both MSS.[119] Marginal entries which were current corrections of the text, that is, written with the same pen by the same scribe as the surrounding text, are occasionally similarly postscriptal in GDB; in the case of Barlington, for example, the main scribe of GDB seems to have missed the addition at first and subsequently had to add it.[120] Errors in personal names, place-names, figures, bad grammar, and confused constructions in Exon are often copied in GDB. Peculiarities of formula, such as the five virgates instead of one hide and one virgate of East Down, in Exon find themselves in GDB.[121] Finally, the GDB scribe occasionally uses a standard construction but erroneously includes an Exon reading; *ferrarios*, 'the smiths', in the North Molton entry, for example, is entered in the accusative case as (correctly) in Exon, where the GDB formula demands the nominative *ferrarii*.[122]

Related to the account of fees are two further sections. The *terre occupate* consist of lists of lands which had been added or taken away from a manor or honour or which had withheld farm. They survive for the three counties of Devon, Cornwall, and Somerset, and most of the information is also found in the account of the fees. The material, however, is generally organized by hundred in a sequence that approximates to that which underlies the rest of the text. The inclusion of information that is not found there, such as 'a virgate of land called *Ledforda*' which had been added to the royal manor of

[117] Ibid. 28, 52–54; Galbraith, *Making of Domesday Book*, 31–2.
[118] *DB Devon*, Exon Introduction; Baring, 'Exeter Domesday', 309–18. See also Sawyer, 'Place-Names of the Domesday Manuscripts', 484–8.
[119] GDB 102a–b: *DB Devon*, 2,21.3,5. [120] Exon, 124ᵛ; GDB 102b: *DB Devon*, 3,19.
[121] GDB 113c: *DB Devon*, 31,1. [122] Exon, 94ᵛ; GDB, 100d: *DB Devon*, 1,27.

Williton,[123] indicates that the source of the material was closely related to, but other than, Exon itself.[124] Although the *terre occupate* have usually been equated with the *clamores* of GDB, they are closer in form to the *invasiones* of LDB. The description of each estate is confined to the details of tenure and value (only in the *terra regis* is stock noticed), but, as there, there is no indication of pleadings, and recognitions by local juries are absent. They represent a collection of evidence for later resolution.

Finally, there is a series of what are termed 'summaries' for a handful of fiefs. Each totals the resources of the demesne, tenanted, and customary estates in each county, listing within the three categories the total number of manors, usually equating with the number of TRE holders of land in the body of the text, their hidage, the number of teams in demesne, men's teams, the number of villagers, bordars, and slaves, the total value, and the number of ploughlands therein for the whole fee. Similar summaries are found in IE, in the account of the area between Ribble and Mersey, and vestigially (no population statistics are given) in section two of the Yorkshire Summary.[125] It is impossible anywhere to harmonize the information they give with any surviving text, but they are often sufficiently close to indicate that they were derived from sources contemporary with the Domesday process.[126]

The Inquisitio Comitatus Cantabrigiensis

ICC survives in one late-twelfth-century manuscript from Ely and consists of a Domesday-like description of estates in Cambridgeshire. Unlike the GDB account of that county, however, it is arranged by hundred and vill. Twelve hundreds are described in full, the account ending midway through Northstowe, the thirteenth (the last leaves of the manuscript are missing), and the order in which they occur is substantially identical with the underlying hundredal sequence of the GDB text.[127] The account of each hundred commences with a list of the jurors who swore in the hundred, and then proceeds vill by vill; again the order is all but identical with the villar sequence of GDB.[128] Where there were several lords, the account of each vill is prefaced by a statement of its assessment to the geld TRE and any reduction that it had enjoyed since. Otherwise, the lord of the vill is named and the assessment of his estate is recorded in like wise. Fees are described in much the same terms as in the parallel entries in GDB but, like LDB and Exon, there is additional detail, notably a record of demesne livestock and the names of sokemen. In the thirteen hundreds that it encompasses all fees are described except the demesne estates of the king.

---

[123] Exon, 509ᵛ.   [124] Welldon Finn, *Liber Exoniensis*, 56–60.
[125] *ICC* 121–4; GDB 270b, 381b: *DB Cheshire*, R7; *DB Yorks.*, SN,CtA45.
[126] Welldon Finn, *Liber Exoniensis*, 124–9.   [127] Hart, *Hidation of Cambridgeshire*, 15–16.
[128] Ibid. 17–19.

Although ICC is a carefully drafted and rubricated text, there are numerous errors that suggest that the copyist had difficulties interpreting his exemplar.[129] Nevertheless, it seems clear that it is a comprehensive copy thereof. The royal demesne manors were certainly absent from the source. In the account of Soham in the hundred of Staploe it is said that the vill was assessed at 11½ hides of which 'the king has 9½ in his record [*in breve suo*]'; the estate is duly entered in GDB as one of the king's demesne manors.[130] Likewise, the reader is referred to the king's record for an account of the manor of Kingston.[131] Furthermore, there is a drastic economy of expression and uncertainty of diplomatic in the account of the first hundred that suggests a scribe formulating and writing a text in haste. Similar characteristics are found in IE which, in its Cambridgeshire section, appears to be an independent copy of the same exemplar in so far as it relates to Ely lands. ICC is evidently as close to its source as its copyist was capable of making it.

The exemplar of ICC, or a document very like it, clearly precedes the GDB account of Cambridgeshire. By analogy with Exon, the record of livestock which is absent from GDB would suggest an earlier origin. But more conclusive is the form of the text. The identity of the sequence of hundreds and vills with the underlying structure of GDB must indicate that, at the very least, the two documents share a common source. Common diplomatic, however, indicates that the ICC exemplar is in fact the immediate source of the GDB text.[132] The formula 'X [the place] defends itself for y^1 hides' of a tenement in a vill held by a single lord in GDB is clearly taken from the formula 'X defends itself for y^t' of the undivided vill in ICC. Thus, in Staploe Hundred the account of Badlingham opens: 'In this hundred Ordmer from Count Alan [holds] Badlingham. It defended itself for 3½ hides TRE and now for 2½ hides . . .', while the parallel GDB entry is 'Badlingham Ordmer holds from the Count. It defends itself for 3½ hides TRE, now 2½ hides . . .'[133] It can indeed be seen that the main scribe was at times confused by his source. He duly entered an account of the king's manor of Soham from the *breve regis* at the beginning of the king's chapter, but when he started to use the ICC exemplar for the tenanted royal manors he entered the ICC note that Soham could be found in the king's record, misreading the assessment in the process: 'In Soham King William has 6 hides and 40 acres in his record [*in breve suo*].'[134] In the absence of the manuscript, it is not possible to prove beyond doubt that the ICC exemplar was the document from which the main scribe abbreviated his text, but there is no compelling reason to believe that it was not.[135]

---

[129] Round, *Feudal England*, 6–27.   [130] *ICC* 6; GDB, 189b–d: *DB Cambs.*, 1,1;13.

[131] *ICC* 85.   [132] Palmer, 'Domesday Manor', 143–4.

[133] *ICC* 2; GDB 195c: *DB Cambs.*, 14,67. The formula is sometimes used of the major holding in a divided vill, presumably echoing the opening formula of such entries (Palmer, 'Domesday Manor', 144).

[134] GDB 189b–d: *DB Cambs.*, 1,1–13; Galbraith, *Making of Domesday Book*, 131.

[135] Galbraith (*Making of Domesday Book*, 131) insists that a seigneurial return was the immediate source of the GDB text, but he provides no evidence beyond the imperative of his schema.

The Inquisitio Eliensis and Bath A

The Inquisition Eliensis survives in three late-twelfth-century Ely manuscripts, A, B, and C, of which B is the most accurate.[136] Despite the name by which it is known, IE is a compilation of various sources. It opens with a prologue which claims to set down the questions asked in the Domesday inquest, the so-called articles of inquiry, and a list of the hundred jurors in fifteen Cambridgeshire hundreds and four in Hertfordshire.[137] There then follows an account of Ely's lands and those that it claimed in Cambridgeshire;[138] summaries of assessment, ploughs, value, and the like shire by shire for the estates it held in six counties, with the addition of some summaries for other Cambridgeshire and Hertfordshire fees;[139] its lands and claims in Essex, Norfolk, and Suffolk, again with summaries; and an account of lands in Huntingdonshire.[140] The document closes with a series of five schedules of lands and assessments and an account of the Ely pleas of the 1070s.[141]

Apart from the pleas, and possibly the list of fisheries that precedes it, all of the sections appear to be related in one way or another to the Domesday inquest. The prologue, jury lists, summaries, and schedules are discussed elsewhere.[142] The remaining sections, the accounts of Ely's lands and its claims, constitute the bulk of the document. Manor by manor in the Cambridgeshire, Essex, Norfolk, and Suffolk sections, they are similar, although not identical, in content to the parallel entries in ICC and LDB; they are full descriptions of all the estates that the abbey held, including extensive details of the livestock on the manorial demesnes. The Hertfordshire and Huntingdonshire sections are likewise full accounts with considerably more information than the parallel GDB entries. There can be no doubt that the work was substantially extracted from Domesday sources. But it is not impossible that material was interpolated at the time of compilation, and it is therefore difficult to describe an exact relationship between its parts and other Domesday sources.

The Huntingdonshire and Hertfordshire sections are similar in form to the known precursors of GDB and are therefore clearly earlier than their counterparts therein. Neither in themselves provides any further clues as to their origins in the Domesday process. Detailed comparison of the Cambridgeshire entries with ICC suggests that the former were not derived from the latter. Some references to sokemen may have been supplied by local knowledge, but more generally the two texts seem to Box and Cox in the provision of additional information and glosses. The implication seems to be that they were independently copied from a fuller common source.[143] Such a relationship between the East Anglian sections and LDB has also been urged, but the demonstration that the one contains information that the other does not hardly proves

---

[136] Welldon Finn, 'Inquisitio Eliensis', 385–88.   [137] ICC 97–101.
[138] ICC 101–21.   [139] ICC 121–4.   [140] ICC 125–73.   [141] ICC 174–95.
[142] See below, pp. 114–16, 121–2, 180–3, 106–12.   [143] Round, *Feudal England*, 12

the point.[144] The fact that Bergh Apton appears in IE but not LDB may be indicative of an earlier source, but it is just as conceivable that local knowledge was responsible.[145] Disjunctions in the sequence of entries probably afford a better indication of origin. For the Cambridgeshire, Essex, and Norfolk lands IE substantially retains the villar and hundredal sequences of GDB and LDB, but in Suffolk the former is largely maintained within a muddled hundredal sequence.[146] Clearly, the IE order cannot have been derived from LDB itself through any straightforward process of extraction. Rather, the form suggests that both were derived from loose sheets on which the estates of each hundred were entered.

Bath A is entered in the first cartulary of St Peter of Bath in an early twelfth-century hand which Welldon Finn believed had affinities with one of the hands (principal scribe A) of Exon,[147] and is an account of seven demesne manors held by the house. In form and content it is close to the Exon account of the same manors, but neither is a simple copy of the other.[148] The manors are entered by hundred, in an order diverging from that of Exon, but within hundreds the places are entered in the same order, merely omitting the tenanted estates. Its language is distinctive. Bath A has *se defendebat pro . . .* for *reddebat gildum pro . . .* , *Tempore Regis Edwardi*, for *die qua rex Edwardus fuit vivus et mortuus*, *coceti* for *bordarii*, *homines* for *villani*. Moreover, within entries the material is differently organized. Where Bath A lists demesne and villagers' hides followed by demesne and villagers' ploughs, Exon regroups the information so that the demesne assessment and ploughs come first. Each contains details that are not found in the other; no values are given for the last three entries of Bath A where Exon supplies them, while other values are different. Some deviations in Exon are clearly scribal errors but others suggest a revaluation; the substitution of *x libras* for *viii libras* in the account of Weston, for example, is difficult to explain in terms of a misreading.[149] On balance, it seems likely that Bath A is slightly earlier than the more tightly formulated Exon.

The Crowland Domesday

The Crowland Domesday is incorporated in a late-fourteenth or early-fifteenth-century Historia Croylandensis which purports to have been written by the late-eleventh-century abbot Ingulf of Crowland. Transcripts of three manuscripts survive (A, B, and C) with variant readings from a fourth (A¹), of which A, the Fulman text, is the oldest.[150] It is an account of the Domesday lands

[144] Galbraith, *Making of Domesday Book*, 140; Welldon Finn, *Eastern Counties*, 82.
[145] *ICC* 136.   [146] Sawyer, 'Original Returns', 189   [147] Welldon Finn, *Liber Exoniensis*, 27.
[148] For a full description, see Lennard, 'A Neglected DB Satellite', 32–41; *DB Somerset*, 381–87.
[149] Exon, 185ᵛ.
[150] *Rerum Anglicarum Scriptores Veteres*, i; London, British Library, Arundel 178; *Rerum Anglicarum Scriptores Post Bedam*.

of the abbey of Crowland in Lincolnshire, Northamptonshire, Huntingdonshire, Hertfordshire, and Leicestershire, which is closely related to the corresponding entries of GDB.[151] In the course of copying various misreadings have crept in, and at some point an attempt was made to standardize the language. There are, moreover, differences in detail and, in the Lincolnshire and Leicestershire sections, order. But by and large the form of entries, their expression, and detail closely follow those of Domesday Book. GDB is clearly the principal source of the account.

It is, however, not the only source.[152] All the extant texts contain a body of additional material of substance. First, details have been added to GDB entries. A record of the seat of the abbey and its liberties precedes the account; parish churches are recorded where they are absent in GDB; and a note is appended to the description of Algarkirk to the effect that the land was waste on account of inundation from the sea. Secondly, wapentake and hundred names are consistently recorded. The forms given are frequently different from those of GDB (where the hundreds are named elsewhere in the text), and on one occasion a more precise name is given: in Northamptonshire South Navisland identifies the southern portion of the undifferentiated double hundred of Navisland. Thirdly, and more substantially, additional entries are found. Details are recorded of marshes and woodland in Uptongreen Hundred in Northamptonshire, and estates in Pinchbeck, Rippingale, Laythorpe, and Kirkby La Thorpe in Lincolnshire, and Peakirk, Addington, and Glapthorn in Northamptonshire. Echoed in the account of Odger the Breton's *breve*, only the Rippingale entry finds a parallel of sorts in Domesday Book,[153] and it alone of the additional entries records the manorial stock of the estate.

At the outset, it would appear that the author drew upon an account of the abbey's lands in which the additional material was already fully integrated. Throughout the GDB folios of the five counties in which Crowland held land the text is tightly structured: each estate or part of an estate is accorded a separate entry and distinctive phrases and letter forms are used to signal the status and integrity of each.[154] Although some elements survive,[155] this form has been woefully misunderstood in the Pseudo-Ingulf text. The last two words of entries in which it is stated that the value in 1086 was the same as in 1066 (*similiter modo*) have been transposed to the following entries to read 'Likewise now in . . .' The misreading is unlikely to relate to the transmission of the Historia, for it is found in all manuscripts, and, since Pinchbeck, an additional

---

[151] GDB 346d, 222c, 204a, 231b: *DB Lincs.*, 11; *DB Northants.*, 11; *DB Hunts.*, 5; *DB Leics.*, 7.

[152] For the following, see Roffe, 'Historia Croylandensis', 93–108.

[153] GDB, 364c, 377b–c: *DB Lincs.*, 42,13.CK48.

[154] Roffe, 'Domesday Book and Northern Society: A Reassessment', 310–36.

[155] In the Fulman and Savile editions hundred names, place-names, berewick, inland, and geld are printed in black-letter capitals, presumably reflecting the forms of the manuscripts employed. There is no perfect correspondence with the use of rustic capitals in the Domesday text, although enough to suggest that the one is derived from the other.

entry, is treated in the same way, it would therefore seem that the source was a continuously written account. Editorial additions and glosses there certainly were at some point in the process of compilation or copying. The record of Crowland's liberties are not found in GDB and, while generically not unparalleled in GDB,[156] it looks like a post-eleventh-century addition. In particular, the termination *-que* is used for *et* ('and'), a usage which is not found in Domesday Book, and the partial repetition of the entry in the Northamptonshire section smacks of overkill.[157] The consistent record of churches may likewise reflect concerns at the time of writing. However, none of the foundations noticed was the subject of a famous dispute and some were probably already integral parts of fees in 1086. Sutterton, for example, first noticed in 1150, was probably the church of the Dowdyke estate in the eleventh century.[158] In substance the Pseudo-Ingulf text is probably a straight copy of its exemplar.

That exemplar is clearly derived from a late-eleventh-century source. Although most of the place-names have later medieval forms, some exhibit authentic early forms. *Aswardetierne* is an exclusively eleventh-century spelling of Aswardhurn; *Anford*, a variant reading in A[1] for Hamfordshoe, is only otherwise found in the Northamptonshire Geld Roll of *c*.1070; *Pegekirk*, for Peakirk, had given way to *Peiekirk* and similar spellings by the early twelfth century; and *Achumesbiry*, for Alconbury was superseded by Al- spellings from the same period.[159] Much of the additional material must also be of an early date. Of the entries which are not paralleled in Domesday Book, only that relating to Peakirk has an early name form. However, although no firm dates can be assigned to the grant of the estates concerned, all were probably in the possession of the abbey at around the time of the Domesday inquest.

---

[156] See e.g. the account of the Church of Worcester's liberties in Oswaldslow Hundred in Worcestershire (GDB 172c: *DB Worcs.*, 2,1).

[157] The marshes that are noticed in the two entries were the subject of famous court cases in the late twelfth and early thirteenth centuries. Crowland Abbey claimed the island of Crowland and the two western fens of Goggisland, to the north of the Welland in Lincolnshire, and Alderland, to the south and in Northamptonshire, as demesne and had a charter to the effect from Henry II. However, Spalding Priory and the men of Holland claimed the eastern part of the island (probably the present Great Postland Fen east of St James Drain), and litigation ensued from 1189 to 1204 without conclusive outcome (*Rerum Anglicarum Scriptores Veteres*, 454–71; Stenton, *English Justice Between the Norman Conquest and the Great Charter, 1066–1215*, 148–211). Alderland was claimed by Peterborough Abbey, which gained seisin in 1206 (*Rerum Anglicarum Scriptores Veteres*, 471–2; *Rotuli Hundredorum*, i. 270). The lord of Deeping seems to have made similar, and equally successful claims to Goggisland (*Rerum Anglicarum Scriptores Veteres*, 475–6; *Rotuli Hundredorum*, i. 270). Crowland tradition portrays the actions as naked aggression, but it seems likely that intercommoning practices lay at the root of the problems. Although there is probably some truth in the claim that the island and the marsh were the pre-Conquest sanctuary of the monastery, attempts to assume demesne rights may have been prompted only by the division of the fen in the eleventh and twelfth centuries (Roffe, 'On Middan Gyrwan Fenne: Intercommoning around the Island of Crowland', 80–6).

[158] *Papsurkunden in England*, iii. 207. However, it had been claimed by the subdeacon Haldane in the mid-twelfth century (ibid., iii. 223, 265).

[159] GDB 337d: *DB Lincs.*, 1,15; Anderson, *English Hundred Names*, 122; Gover, *The Place-Names of Northamptonshire*, 241; Mawer and Stenton, *The Place-Names of Bedfordshire and Huntingdonshire*, 230.

According to the late-twelfth-century Guthlac Roll,[160] Hallington was given by a certain Geolfus. This name, which appears to be the rare Anglo-Scandinavian name Jaulfr, is an unlikely fabrication, and the grantor was probably the individual of the same name who held land TRE in the immediate vicinity of Hallington and was the predecessor of Rainer de Brimou.[161] Rippingale had been a Crowland holding in 1066 by witness of GDB.[162] Peakirk, although absent from the Northamptonshire Survey, was already a Crowland demesne in 1116,[163] as was the additional land in Addington at about the same date,[164] whilst Glapthorn was probably a member of Elmington from which it was administered throughout the later Middle Ages, and it may have thus escaped early notice.[165] No records survive for the other grants, but the lands appear in the first papal confirmation of Crowland's estates in 1147, suggesting an early date.[166]

Other details can be more closely dated. Hallington is said to lie in the soke of Tathwell which was held by the earl of Chester in 1086; forinsec soke of this kind had largely become redundant by the early twelfth century and is never explicit after the Lindsey Survey.[167] Likewise, soke of Belchford in Bucknall is noticed, which is not recorded in Domesday Book. The account of Odger the Breton's tenure of Rippingale adds authentic detail of a different type. He is said to hold at farm, a transaction that a religious foundation might be reluctant to admit after the early twelfth century.[168] The most revealing entry, however, is that relating to Badby. The manor is said to lie in Alwardesley Hundred Gravesend. As it stands this is nonsense. But a comparison of the GDB text with the Northamptonshire Survey shows that the manor was moved from Gravesend Hundred to Alwardesley between 1086 and sometime in the reign of Henry I. Clearly, the source had been corrected by a gloss, subsequently misconstrued and incorporated into the text and copied in full by the compiler of Ingulf, sometime before Alwardesley itself was transferred to Fawsley in the reign of Henry II at the time when the Northamptonshire Survey

---

[160] London, BL Harleian MS Y 6; *Memorials of St Guthlac of Crowland*, plates.

[161] GDB 364a–b: *DB Lincs.*, 40. In the thirteenth century the land was held by Crowland from the earl of Chester (*Book of Fees*, 174). It is likely, then, that Jaulfr's grant was not absolute, that is, rights were retained over land as well as soke, and that the land appears in Earl Hugh of Chester's breve in GDB (GDB 349a–d: *DB Lincs.*, 13).

[162] GDB 364c, 377c: *DB Lincs.*, 42,13.CK48. According to the *clamores*, the manor had been held on an annual lease from the abbey by Hereward (the Wake), but the abbot had retaken possession before Hereward fled the country.

[163] Peterborough, Dean and Chapter MS 1, The Book of Robert of Swaffham, f. 118; *VCH Northants.*, ii. 520.

[164] *VCH Northants.*, i. 388.   [165] Ibid., ii. 578.   [166] *Papsurkunden in England*, iii. 196–7.

[167] Roffe, 'From Thegnage to Barony', 157–76.

[168] The abbey would seem to be claiming that Odger the Breton was inheriting the rights and obligations of his predecessor Hereward. The tenant-in-chief, however, did not acknowledge his limited right (GDB 377c: *DB Lincs.*, CK48). Crowland was not the only interest to suffer from the acquisitiveness of this lord (GDB 377b: *DB Lincs.*, CK43).

was annotated.[169] An early-twelfth-century revision of the Ingulf source may well indicate a late-eleventh-century original.

That that original was intimately associated with the Domesday process is indicated by an apparent mistake. The estate in Bucknall is said to lie in the South Riding (of Lindsey) in the Wapentake of Haverstoe. This is at variance with the available evidence. In 1212 the settlement was situated in the wapentake of Gartree, while its neighbouring vills were assigned to the same in the Lindsey Survey of 1115 in which Gartree is said to be situated in the North Riding.[170] Its context in 1086 is not explicit in the Domesday text, but the order of entries and the numerous references to the verdicts of wapentake juries indicate that there had been no change in the structure of local government between 1086 and 1115.[171] In common with Ingulf, however, GDB also assigns a Gartree estate to the remote Haverstoe; a postscriptal rubric identifies this as the wapentake in which the *caput* of Ivo Taillebois's manor of Belchford was situated.[172] Given the apparent independence of the Ingulf account of wapentakes and hundreds from Domesday, the coincidence suggests that both mistakes stem from a common source. It can be hazarded that a geographically arranged account of Gartree estates which was used by the Domesday scribe in the compilation of GDB and subsequently by the Ingulf scribe had been loosely associated with Haverstoe because, although locally in the South Riding, it gelded with the North, and the wrong wapentake name was assigned to it in error.

It is clear, then, that the Historia's account of Crowland's Domesday estates incorporates material drawn from a geographically arranged Domesday source, recording hundred and estate names, assessments, and, given the occasional difference in figures and the curious use of *valebat*, possibly values. The record of inundation at Algarkirk may indicate that communal and/or seigneurial presentments were also included, but the absence of further information in the additional entries suggests that nothing else was recorded. The Pseudo-Ingulf identifies the source as 'the Rolls of Winchester [*rotuli Wintonienses*]', which he describes as a Domesday-like survey arranged by counties, hundreds, and tithings which was commissioned by King Alfred the Great (871–99). The attribution is clearly mistaken, but his claim to have excerpted the Crowland Domesday from GDB and the 'hundred rolls' suggest that the two sources were kept together in the Exchequer.

---

[169] GDB 222c: *DB Northants.*, 11,6; *VCH Northants.*, i. 370–1; Anderson, *English Hundred Names*, 128. The reference to Fawsley in the Northamptonshire Survey rubric is probably an emendation of the reign of Henry II which was copied into the extant MS as an integral part of the text. For other examples, see *VCH Northants.*, i. 357–64.

[170] *Book of Fees*, 169; *Lincolnshire Domesday and the Lindsey Survey*, 252–3.

[171] Roffe, 'Hundreds and Wapentakes', 33–9.

[172] GDB 350d: *DB Lincs.*, 14,46. Wapentake rubrics are postscriptal additions to the Lincolnshire folios which were not always entered in the right place (Roffe, 'Hundreds and Wapentakes', 34).

Schedules and Other Domesday Texts

The remaining Domesday texts are diverse in their form and content, but all in one way or another are more circumscribed in the information that they contain than the sources so far considered. Each presents formidable problems of analysis and interpretation in its own right, and most, both individually and collectively, have been the subject of several lengthy discussions.[173] All have been examined as ancillary documents subordinate to the making of GDB or LDB. They are here, by contrast, described as schedules without any prejudice as to their nature or origin and are examined as types. Their forms and content are tabulated in Table 4.9. Only one has a distinct identity that marks it out from the rest. Ely D is one of the schedules attached to MS C of IE and is a list of lands of the abbey of Ely that had been taken away by various tenants-in-chief. It has been asserted that it is a continuation of Ely C,[174] but that document seems to be a schedule of lands leased to tenants-in-chief or sokelands over which the abbey only had soke. There the lands themselves were in the one instance entered in the abbey's *breves* or in the other in those of the named tenants-in-chief. Ely does not seem to have made any claim to these latter as forinsec sokelands in 1086, and since most of the estates appear in the memorandum of the Ely sessions of 1071–3 (Ely E), they would seem to be those which rendered services 'after the land was sworn' in recognition of Ely's rights.[175] Ely D, by contrast, relates to claims that had yet to be settled. It exhibits much the same form as the *invasiones* sections of LDB, with the invasions of each lord listed together. The resources of each parcel of land are cursorily drawn, with population, assessment, and occasionally churches, mill, meadow, and the like noted. The order of entries, however, deviates from that of the corresponding entries in GDB and LDB and all other Ely sources. A reference to what is probably something like Ely D, or its source, is found in IE. There the Essex claims section is prefaced by the comment 'the abbot of Ely claims these lands according to the records of the king [*secundum breves regis*]'.[176]

The remaining twenty-five documents do not readily divide themselves into well-defined types. Most exhibit a concern with the dichotomy of demesne and tenanted lands, and all but one display a distinctively English orthography that perhaps suggests a greater awareness of locality. Otherwise, no groups emerge. Some schedules preserve the Domesday order of entries, while others do not, but neither form correlates with other distinguishing characteristics such as organization by fee or hundred. Content is equally diverse. Ploughlands are rare, but otherwise the standard items of information—assessment to the

---

[173] For the most recent general discussions, see Harvey, 'Domesday Book and its Predecessors', 753–73; Clarke, 'Domesday Satellites', 50–70; Roffe, 'Making of Domesday Book Reconsidered', 153–66. For the studies of individual documents, see below.

[174] Welldon Finn, *Eastern Counties*, 81, 87.

[175] *ICC* 184; Roffe, 'Historia Croylandensis', 101 n.   [176] *ICC* 127.

TABLE 4.9. *Domesday schedules*

	Content								Forms						
	Assessment to the geld	Demesne/tenanted	Ploughlands	Ploughs	Population	Value	Presentments	Claims	Order as GDB/LDB	Order not as GDB/LDB	English orthography	Arrangement by fee	Arrangement by 100	Extract/schedule of fee	Extract from 100 roll
Abingdon A	✓	✓							✓		✓				✓
Bath B	✓	✓							✓		✓				
Braybrooke	✓	✓	✓		✓				✓		✓				✓
Burton B	✓	✓	✓		✓				✓		✓			✓	
Bury A	✓	✓		✓		✓			✓		✓				
Bury B	✓	✓		✓		✓			✓		✓				
Bury C	✓	✓		✓											
Des. Ter.	✓	✓								✓	✓			?	
DM A	✓									✓	✓			?	
DM B	✓	✓			✓					✓	✓				✓
DM D					✓					✓	✓			✓	
DM E	✓	✓			✓				✓		✓				
Ely A		✓		✓	✓				✓		✓				
Ely B		✓		✓	✓					✓	✓				
Ely C	✓	✓		✓	✓				✓		✓				
Ely D	✓	✓	✓	✓	✓			✓	✓		✓				
Evesham A	✓	✓		✓		✓	✓		✓		✓		✓		
Evesham F	✓	✓								✓	✓			✓	
Evesham K	✓						?		✓		✓	✓			
Evesham M	✓	✓				✓			✓		✓	✓			
Evesham P	✓	✓					?		✓		✓	✓			
Evesham Q	✓						?		✓		✓	✓			
Excerpta	✓	✓					✓	✓	✓		✓				
Kentish Ass. List	✓								✓		✓	✓			
Worcester A	✓	✓								✓	✓				
Worcester B	✓	✓							✓		✓				

geld, ploughs, population, and value—are all represented along with the occasional presentment of juries. Only the minutiae of manorial stocking and infrastructure in mills and the like are not regularly found.

Overall, the only characteristic that these schedules have in common is that they are in some way connected with the Domesday process or are more or less contemporary with it. Formally, there are five possible relationships: 1. the schedules may pre-date the Domesday inquiry; 2. they may be contemporary but independent of it; 3. they may relate to early stages in the inquest process as copies, extracts, or abstracts of Domesday-like texts; 4. they may copies, extracts, or abstracts of Domesday Book; and 5. they may be later and independent of it. However, these categories are not mutually exclusive. All the documents are twelfth-century or later copies, and some are demonstrably derived from a number of sources. Evesham K, for example, is probably earlier than the Domesday text, but it contains surveys of Gloucester and Winchcombe which have been partially updated to c.1100,[177] while the Kentish Assessment List would now appear to be a composite source.[178] Compilation from a variety of sources in this way may account for many variations in the information recorded. The fact that the place-name forms of one document more closely approximate to English orthography than the equivalent Domesday forms or the inclusion of detail that is not found in the GDB text does not automatically imply that the source is essentially independent or earlier. The local knowledge and archival resources of a copying scribe may have often prompted revision of a straightforward Domesday extract. On these grounds it might be suspected that Worcester B and possibly Evesham M are essentially later copies.[179]

More difficult to identify are the revisions of abstracts or extracts derived from earlier documentation. The Braybrooke Cartulary schedule raises problems of this nature. In its present form it is a compilation which probably dates from the mid-thirteenth-century when the Braybrooke Cartulary was first written. It is concerned with the eleventh-century antecedents of the estates of Henry de Braybrooke and consists of summary accounts of lands held by Guy de Reinbudcurt and his tenants, and tenants of Picot the sheriff and Eudo the steward around the time of the Domesday inquest. It is an abstract,[180] but clearly not from Domesday Book itself for, incorporating two fees that were held from other tenants-in-chief, its order is evidently derived from a geographically arranged source. Much of the detailed information which it does not share with Domesday is to be found in ICC, but not all.[181] In such cases it is often argued that neither can be derived from the other and they must therefore draw on a common source.[182] It is thus that stages of the Domesday inquiry multiply like rabbits. The inference, however, is but one possibility. It is just as likely that one document draws on the other, but selectively and as

---

[177] *DB Gloucs.*, appendix EvK notes.   [178] Eales, 'Introduction to the Kent Domesday', 5–6.

[179] *DB Worcs.*, appendix 5, Worcs. B; *DB Gloucs.*, appendix.

[180] The editor has cast the account into the past tense with *tenuit* for what must originally have been *tenet*.

[181] The mill at Meldreth, for example, does not appear in ICC.

[182] Clarke considers that the schedule is independent of the Domesday inquest ('Domesday Satellites', 60).

only one of its sources. In the case of the Braybrooke Cartulary schedule, it would appear that, exhibiting much of its phraseology, it is essentially a copy of ICC's exemplar, with personal knowledge providing details which are not found elsewhere. It is conceivable, although rarely proved, that many of the lists have similar origins.

Diversities in datable information can provide a surer ground for identifying and ordering the schedules, but they still pose difficult problems of interpretation. The ascription of estates to tenants in Bath B and the Kentish Assessment List where Domesday credits them to an heir, or states that they were previously held by the tenant, almost certainly indicates that the two documents pre-date the compilation of GDB.[183] On similar grounds it is possible that Bury A, along with the closely related Bury B, also emanates from an early stage in the inquiry. The scribe who transcribed it apparently saw it as a product of the Domesday inquest, for he wrote in explanation of the document: 'Here are the manors which St Edmund's had in their demesne. And here are the lands of their men which they held at the time when, by order of King William, a description of the whole of England was made according to the oaths that nearly all the inhabitants swore, each, when questioned declaring the truth of the land they held and its stock and [of the lands] of others in the neighbourhood.' However, some manors in Bury A are demesne where they are enfeoffed in LDB,[184] and the fact may imply that the document was actually copied from an earlier, possibly seigneurially arranged source which maintained the distinction between demesne and tenanted land.[185]

However, 'dead reckoning', the bread and butter of the charter historian, is not always valid in the analysis of such documentation. GDB and LDB themselves are often anachronistic in their record of tenure: Queen Matilda, for example, appears in Buckinghamshire as a tenant-in-chief in 1086 although by then she had been dead for three years,[186] while Bishop Odo of Bayeux appears throughout the text as a major landholder even though he had been in exile since 1082.[187] It cannot be expected that the schedules are any more consistent. Other disparities in data can be equally illusive. Again, the TRE assessments of Bath B (here in the present tense) and of parts of the Kentish Assessment List, along with those of Abingdon A, where Domesday Book has those of 1066 in the past tense or simply those of 1086, have been used to identify them as pre-Domesday assessment lists of local government provenance which informed the early stages of the Domesday inquest and effectively formulated its records by dictating the order of entries.[188] This, however, is

---

[183] For a contrary view of Bath B, see *DB Somerset*, appendix 11, Bath B, 1 n.
[184] e.g. Dickleburgh (*Feudal Documents*, 14; LDB 211a–b: *DB Norfolk*, 14,29).
[185] As suggested by Harvey, 'Domesday Book and its Predecessors', 767.
[186] GDB 152c–d: *DB Bucks.*, 52.   [187] Stenton, *Anglo-Saxon England*, 616.
[188] Harvey, 'Domesday Book and its Predecessors', 755–61.

an unwarranted conclusion. Although a reduction in hidation for defence against the geld was effected in some counties and hundreds between 1066 and 1086, the old assessments were kept for civil purposes other than the Danegeld. Thus, it is clear from ICC that some estates in Cambridgeshire enjoyed a reduction from five to four hides between 1066 and 1086 but still functioned as five-hide vills in the administration of local government, and fees in divided vills were entered under their old assessments in GDB without any indication of reduction. Steeple Morden in Armingford Hundred, for example, gelded for ten hides TRE and eight TRW according to ICC, but the fees of the bishop of Winchester, Earl Roger, and Hardwin of Scales are assessed at a total of ten hides in GDB (8 hides + 1 hide ¼ virgate + 3¾ virgate).[189] The same pattern can be discerned throughout the hundred and beyond.[190] An Edwardian assessment, then, does not necessarily imply a pre-Domesday date and may merely indicate that the purpose of the document was not primarily the collection of Danegeld at the new rate.

There is no compelling evidence to suggest that Abingdon A, Bath B, or the Kentish Assessment List pre-date the Domesday process. In all three texts the coincidences of forms and content with the corresponding passages in GDB are greater by far than the differences. and indicate no significant time-lapse between them. Divergent forms, by contrast, promise a greater potential to order texts. The seigneurially arranged Descriptio Terrarum of Peterborough Abbey, Domesday Monachorum A, Evesham F, and Worcester A all exhibit a different sequence of hundreds from that which is found in GDB, and it might be hazarded that they were in some way independent of the Domesday process. Even here, however, the obvious conclusion may be too facile. Domesday Monachorum A has little in common with GDB. Nevertheless, it informed the order of entries in Domesday Monachorum B which, whatever its identity, is clearly a product of the Domesday inquest. It is impossible to determine whether A was drawn up with the inquest in mind or was only subsequently pressed into service as a source.

These are uncertainties that apply to a greater or lesser extent to all the schedules. None of the documents provides intrinsic evidence of a relationship to the main texts of the Domesday corpus. However, four can be shown to be probably earlier than Domesday Book and similar in form to documents that are known to have been kept with it. A number of near-contemporary references allude to documentation of this type in the king's treasury. The Northamptonshire Survey of the early twelfth century cites 'the rolls of Winchester [rotul[i] Wyncestrie]' as the authority for two geld assessments,[191] and a probably twelfth-century list of Worcester demesne estates refers to hides

---

[189] ICC 51; GDB 190a, 193b, 198b: DB Cambs., 2,1.13,1.26,19.

[190] Hart, Hidation of Cambridgeshire, 56–8.

[191] Round, Feudal England, 215. As Round pointed out, this cannot be a reference to GDB since the entry for Pytchley gives an assessment of 6 hides and 3 small virgates where GDB has 5 hides and 1 virgate of land (GDB 222a: DB Northants., 6a,25).

'of the ancient hidage which is in the Winchester Roll [*de hidagio antiquo quod est in rotulo Wyncestrie*]'.[192] Material in the Crowland Domesday has already been identified as an extract from 'hundred rolls' of this type. Abingdon A is most clearly another instance. In the manuscript it is preceded by a rubric which declares that it concerns 'the hundreds and hides of the church of Abingdon in Berkshire laid out by individual hundreds as the writing of the king's treasury contains [*de hundredis et hidis ecclesie Abbendonensis in Berchescire sicut in scriptura thesauri regis continet per hundreta singula depositis*]'. The document from which it was compiled evidently cannot be the seigneurially arranged GDB, and indeed the Domesday extract that follows in the MS is specifically said to have been taken 'from the other book of the king's treasury [*in alio libro thesauri regis*]', which must, presumably, be Domesday Book itself.

Abingdon A appears to be an extract of its source. Evesham P, by contrast, is probably a copy. It is entitled: 'The number of free hides, the number that geld and are assessed for forinsec service, in Fishborough Hundred according to the Roll of Winchester [*rotulum de Winton'*]', and lists the lands of the church of Evesham in its hundred of Fishborough and those of Bishop Odo of Bayeux throughout Worcestershire. The document has been dismissed as a copy of Domesday,[193] but the reference to 'a roll' suggests that the source cannot be 'the book' of Winchester. Rather, it would appear to have been copied from a seigneurially arranged document which specifically recorded geldable and non-geldable hides.

Ely C is probably an abstract of a similar source. Listing Ely lands held by other tenants-in-chief, it records the assessment of the tenements that they held and the number of men thereon, and provides a total for each tenant along with the value of the whole holding and an analysis of the amount of thegnland and sokeland of which it was comprised. The list has more or less the same order of vills as GDB and LDB, but the tenants-in-chief occur in a different sequence.[194] Information is given that is not found in GDB and LDB, and a reference to sokemen held by Roger Bigod in Blo Norton in Norfolk, where Domesday records that they were formerly Roger's, indicates that Ely C relates to an earlier stage in the inquiry. It would also appear to antedate IE which concurs with LDB on the tenure of Norton, and it can therefore almost certainly be identified with a source to which IE refers. It notes that the Ely thegnlands and sokelands which Hardwin, Picot, and Guy de Reinbudcurt held in Cambridgeshire were 'written and valued in the abbot of Ely's breve [*scripta et appreciata in breve abbatis de Ely*]'.[195] Ely C was probably abstracted from this seigneurially arranged source.

[192] *Red Book of Worcester*, 442–3. For the date of this document, see *Cartulary of Worcester Cathedral Priory*, pp. xlvi–xlvii, and *DB Gloucs.*, Worcs. E, note.

[193] *DB Worcs.*, appendix IV, Ev P.

[194] Cambridgeshire: 32, 31, 26, 44, 41, 30, 5, 40; Norfolk: 9, 15, 15, 12, 51; Suffolk: 7, 6, 67, 21, 63, 14, 16.

[195] *ICC* 123–4.

Ely A provides the fourth link with an official document preceding Domesday Book. The title reads: 'Here is enrolled how many ploughs St Etheldreda has and how many their men have whom they now have according to the records of the king [*breves regis*] which were made in the counties in which her lands lie, and how many villagers, bordars, and slaves. And these things are distinguished just as the reeves of each hold their bailiwicks.' There are elements in the document that are probably later than 1086; the bailiwicks may have been supplied at the time of copying, and the note that a hide at Teversham was held by John for the service of two knights seems to record a settlement of a dispute that is prefigured in GDB.[196] In substance, however, the schedule is clearly independent of and earlier in the inquest process than Domesday, for the grouping of demesne and peasants ploughs is closer to the usage of LDB and IE, and the order of entries, within bailiwicks, in the Cambridgeshire section conforms to the hundredal sequence of ICC rather than that of the GDB text.[197] However, the *breves regis* are unlikely to be either of these sources. Ely A contains much material that is not found in ICC and LDB, and the term *breves regis*, usually applied to the lands of individual tenants-in-chief, would suggest that its origins lay in seigneurially arranged documents.

---

[196] *ICC* 168; GDB 191a, 201d: *DB Cambs.*, 5,13.35,2. The abbot of Ely's insistence that 'this land always lay in the church' in his own breve hints at the reality of an invasion by John son of Waleran in whose breve the land is duplicated.

[197] If the sequence of hundreds in the Ely breve is numbered according to the appearance of the hundreds in ICC (with the addition of the two Ely hundreds at the end), it exhibits the order 4, 1, 3, 5, 6, 8, 9, 10, 11, 12, 13, 14. The order within the first five bailiwicks in Cambridgeshire and a sixth in Cambridgeshire and Huntingdonshire in Ely A is A: 1, 3, 4, 5, 8, B: 4, 5, 5, C: 6, 6, D: 4, 4, E: 8, 8, 8, F: 9, 9. The remaining seven with one minor exception, are all regular.

5
The Collection of Data

DESPITE THEIR INCONSISTENCIES, both GDB and LDB are marvels of
administrative planning. Within the span of 850 folios economy of expression
is linked to a systematic format that facilitates easy use to create a formidable
work of reference. It is a work of genius and, not unnaturally, historians have
sought the mind that masterminded the enterprise. Galbraith identified 'the man
behind the survey' as Samson the chaplain, a Frenchman, probably from Bayeux,
who subsequently became bishop of Worcester. His argument is a circumstantial
one, being based on the observation that a manor held by Samson of the
bishop of Bayeux at Templecombe in Somerset was entered in an abbreviated form in Exon in the same hand as that of the greater part of GDB.[1]
Curiously, the scribe incorrectly valued part of the estate,[2] and this is perhaps
surprising had he been entering his own land. Rannulf Flambard has also
been canvassed as a candidate. He is associated with the Domesday inquest
by Orderic Vitalis, and Harvey has suggested that, as master of St Martin's,
Dover, he was responsible for an initial survey of that church's lands in 1085,
anomalously enrolled after the account of Dover at the beginning of the Kent
folios, which was to inspire the general survey in the following year.[3] Here the
evidence is selective and circumstantial—Orderic writes of a revision of the
survey of all England and dates it to 1089, whilst the peculiarities of the account
of St Martin's estates are best explained as a function of scribal confusion[4]—
and the suggestion has not gained general acceptance.[5] More recently Chaplais
has made a case for a northern cleric.[6] Identifying the affinities of the main
GDB hand with those of the late-eleventh-century Durham scriptorium, he
suggested that William de St Calais was the probable author of GDB. The
possibility that work was still in progress on GDB after William's exile in 1088

---

[1] Exon, 153ʳ; GDB, 87d: *DB Somerset*, 4,1; Galbraith, 'Notes on the Career of Samson, Bishop of
Worcester (1096–1112)', 86–101.

[2] He gave the value of Thorent as 13s where his figure of 14s in Exon is confirmed by a fuller
account of the land given by another scribe writing earlier in the Domesday process (Exon, 153ᵛ, 467).

[3] Harvey, 'Domesday Book and Anglo-Norman Governance', 191–3.

[4] *Orderic Vitalis*, iv. 172; Eales, 'An Introduction to the Kent Domesday', 4 and note. The diplomatic of the section is closely paralleled by that of the first 8 breves of the text, perhaps indicating
a not radically different origin for the text. See below, pp. 206–7. Prestwich ('The Career of Ranulf
Flambard', 309) has argued that Rannulf's involvement with Domesday Book was confined to using
it to collect geld.

[5] Prestwich, 'The Career of Ranulf Flambard', 309.

[6] Chaplais, 'William of Saint-Calais and the Domesday Survey', 65–77.

has in turn cast doubt on this analysis;[7] none of the cases is entirely satis-factory. Nevertheless, Galbraith, Chaplais, and Harvey are clearly right to hypothesize a single author. The occurrence of the hand of the main GDB scribe in Exon is a fair indication that the production of that text was co-ordinated, at some stage,[8] with the further aim of producing the abbreviated fair copy that is GDB. Further assumptions, however, are unwarranted. For both Galbraith and Chaplais (and less emphatically for Harvey) there could be no doubt that the author of GDB masterminded the whole Domesday pro-cess: each implies that their own candidate planned the inquest from its inception at Gloucester in 1085. In reality, there is no unequivocal evidence of a grand plan uniting inquest and abbreviation.

Hitherto the case has been based on what has been perceived as an unimpeachable witness to the earliest stages of the Domesday process. IE opens with what has every appearance of being the articles of inquiry:

Here follows the inquest of lands, as the king's barons made it, to wit: by the oath of the sheriff of the shire and of all the barons and their Frenchmen and of the whole hundred, of the priest, the reeve, six villagers of each village. In order, what is the manor called? Who held it in the time of King Edward? Who now holds it? How many hides? How many ploughs on the demesne? How many of the men? How many villagers? How many cottars? How many slaves? How many free men? How many sokemen? How much wood? How much meadow? How much pasture? How many mills? How many fish ponds? How much has been added or taken away? How much, taken together, it was worth and how much now? How much each free man or sokeman had or has. All this at three dates, to wit in the time of King Edward and when King William gave it and as it is now. And if it is possible for more to be had than is had.[9]

For Round, it was self-evident that here was the blueprint of the survey and Domesday Book. He believed that most of the Domesday data were presented by hundred jurors, and therefore it followed that the list must have informed the proceedings,[10] and indeed since there is no reference to the honour, the list of questions could as easily have informed the account of each fee within the vills of ICC as a GDB-like source. Galbraith, followed by Chaplais as by most historians,[11] saw it otherwise. He recognized that the recorded present-ments of jurors were confined to assessments and tenure, and argued that the bulk of the material was provided by tenants-in-chief in 'backroom sessions'. He nevertheless saw the articles as the 'terms of reference' that informed the

---

[7] Lewis, 'The Earldom of Surrey and the Date of Domesday Book', 327–36.

[8] The three entries in Exon (135ᵛ, 436ᵛ) are all additions that exhibit the forms of GDB (Welldon Finn, 'The Evolution of Successive Versions of Domesday Book', 561–4; Rumble, 'Palaeography of the Domesday Manuscripts', 47–8). There is no indication that the main scribe was involved in the inquest, although it must be suspected that his talents had not been wasted.

[9] ICC 97.   [10] Round, Feudal England, 134.

[11] For the sole sceptical view, see Welldon Finn, Domesday Inquest, 33–4.

inquiry from its inception, providing compelling evidence for the resolve and sense of purpose of William the Conqueror to produce Domesday Book.[12]

The document, however, will not support these interpretations. The so-called articles are entered by way of a prologue to the IE. Their authenticity as an early witness to the Domesday process is seemingly supported by the proximity of the section to the jury lists which, there is no reason to doubt, emanate from some stage in the inquiry. However, since IE is demonstrably a composite document, extracting and possibly even abstracting its material from a number of sources, the prologue is no more likely to be related to the lists than to any of the other sources on which IE drew. Its language is seemingly of a piece with documents which were produced at an early stage in the inquiry; like Exon it uses the term *mansio* instead of *manerium* for 'manor'. But this was not the usage of the texts that it introduces and, more significantly, it describes neither their content nor form. In IE the livestock of all the demesne estates are noted, the plough teams of the peasantry enumerated, elaborate analyses are given of the status of free men and sokemen and the renders that they gave, and ploughland figures are given for the Cambridgeshire and Hertfordshire lands, where none of these items is explicitly noticed in the prologue. Furthermore, the order of the *capitula* is nowhere reproduced. In the Cambridgeshire entries, for example, TRE holders are recorded at the end, and the manorial appurtenances in mills, meadow, woodland, pasture, and fisheries are ranked by value.

Similar discrepancies are also found in the corresponding passages in Domesday Book, and more are found elsewhere. There is no explicit reference to the lands of the king, which were apparently a primary concern of the inquest. Likewise, no special attention is paid to royal dues or the geld. Throughout GDB there are numerous references to the king's farms, renders, customs, and the like which are not comprehended by any question in the prologues. Nor are other communal assessments, like the dimension of vills in Norfolk, Suffolk, and Yorkshire which seem to be related in one way or another to the maintenance of the peace and other public duties. Any notice of boroughs is also signally absent. There is no section of Domesday Book or related documents that consistently conforms to the Ely text. The prologue cannot represent articles in its present form.

That the text was corrupted when it was copied seems unlikely; it does not give the impression of being woefully misunderstood or drastically edited. On the contrary it could easily be a literary conceit concocted to act as an introduction to an obviously authoritative text dating from the time when IE was first compiled from its disparate sources.[13] But on balance this seems unlikely. The Ely monk who wrote the manuscript in the twelfth century could not have derived it from the documents that he copied, and the distinctive

---

[12] Galbraith, *Making of Domesday Book*, 59–66.   [13] Welldon Finn, *Domesday Inquest*, 33–4.

language suggests a Domesday context. If so, it was clearly late in the proceedings. In form the prologue has affinities with the 'main' entry type (forms
VIIA and VIIB) of LDB. This commences with the name of the manor, its
TRE holder, and assessment to the geld, and then continues in approximately
the same order as outlined in IE. Above all, sokemen are (otherwise uniquely)
contrasted with free men[14] and statistics are given for the three periods specified.
However, the inclusion of demesne livestock in LDB suggests that the prologue
must be later. Indeed, its closest parallel is to be found in the standard GDB
entry of the northern counties. There, like in the prologue where the free
men are implicitly part of the *mansio*, the manor is the organizing principle of
the text; appurtenant inland and sokeland follow the account of the *caput* and
is explicitly associated with the manorial centre to which it rendered its dues.
The structure of entries mirrors that of the prologue; the name of the manor
is given first, along with the TRE holder and assessment to the geld, and
is followed by the name of any tenant, ploughs in demesne, the number of
villagers, sokemen and bordars, manorial appurtenance, and finally, value. The
information is not given for the three periods specified in the prologue except
in the occasional record of value, although there are indications here and
there that the information was originally collected.[15] The prologue is clearly
closer to GDB than the unabbreviated sources from which it was derived,
and it is perhaps best interpreted as a template for the abbreviation of the
Northern folios.

It therefore provides no compelling evidence for the early stages of the inquest. It can scarcely be doubted that there was some plan, but IE clearly
does not afford a record of it. This conclusion has far-reaching implications
for the analysis of the Domesday inquiry and its relationship with Domesday
Book. Hitherto confidence in the IE prologue as an accurate record of the
terms of the inquiry has fostered the notion that all Domesday texts other
than Domesday Book itself are 'satellites', that is, they were means to the end
of producing GDB. For some, even LDB must, by definition, be categorized so
since it was never abbreviated into the standard form. The notion has not
only directed research but has also prejudiced its conclusions. The key to an
understanding of the purpose and processes of the Domesday inquest has been
sought in a taxonomy of the Domesday texts which assumes that, like chronicles, all the sources have a single typological stemma. It is a logic that demands
that if two documents share material but each contains data that are not found
in the other, then they must be independently derived from a third source.
So the Braybrooke Cartulary schedule has given birth to a proto-ICC and

---

[14] In GDB the distribution of the two classes is mutually exclusive, suggesting some high degree
of equivalence.

[15] See e.g. GDB 337d, 355b: *DB Lincs.*, 1,9; 24,46. Certain items of manorial stock are said to have
been 'found' by a lord, the implication being that they were what was there when they received the
land concerned.

Exon to an intermediary before GDB. The effect has been to create hypothetical documents, which in their turn attest more complex stages in the Domesday process. The picture that has emerged has largely depended on the choice of a starting-point. IE, Exon, Evesham A, and assorted schedules have come and gone as the key to Domesday.

With the rejection of the IE prologue as the articles of the inquiry, the taxonomic approach to Domesday loses its rationale. It must be abandoned. A chronology of composition can be established for the more important texts and it can be shown that some drew on others. It is clearly significant, however, that both geographically and seigneurially arranged schedules of demesne and tenanted estates on the one hand, and similarly arranged lists of the more important manorial appurtenances on the other were produced which are different in form from GDB and LDB and were perceived at the time of copying as distinct therefrom. There is no intrinsic evidence of an integrated process and in the following analysis no grand hierarchy is assumed. Rather, an attempt is made to identify activities within the corpus to which individual documents can then be tentatively assigned.

Forums and Organization

Throughout the Middle Ages the inquest was an administrative nightmare which, at the local level, devolved on the sheriff and his staff. By its nature the process required a careful marshalling of information for the smooth working of the inquiry and its speedy execution: as a response to crisis, it was of little use as an instrument of government if it took more than a few months to complete. Unlike the cumbersome processes of justice, essoins (excuses for absence) could not be allowed to hold up the proceedings and complex arrangements were necessary to ensure that juries and other interested parties were present, suitably prepared, to deliver the evidence required. As has been seen,[16] within a hundred years of the Domesday inquest knights of the shire were enlisted to help the sheriff in his onerous duties. It was these *milites inquisitores* who were responsible for the collection of much of the data.

Although there are references to the activities of the sheriff and occasionally to his men here and there in Domesday Book,[17] the complexities of local organization in 1086 are largely invisible. Nevertheless, the Domesday process can have differed very little from the late-twelfth- and thirteenth-century pattern. The sheriff would certainly have been expected to make ready the routine records of the shire, and its suitors, the free men of the shire, must have been associated with preparation. Indeed, in Wiltshire verdicts

---

[16] See above, pp. 52–3.

[17] See e.g. GDB 193c: *DB Cambs.*, 13,8; LDB 118a, 208a, 393a: *DB Norfolk*, 1,66.13,21; *DB Suffolk*, 25,53; GDB 172c: *DB Worcs.*, 1,3b. It is often impossible to determine to what date a particular act of a sheriff is to be assigned. Likewise, references to *ministri* may disguise their activities.

are recorded which are said to have been given by 'thegns of the shire', 'thegns', and 'Englishmen',[18] while 'Frenchmen' are found elsewhere.[19] It is probable that the local worthies and power-brokers who constituted the backbone of the community of the shire were further charged with the initial collection of data under the supervision of the sheriff. Bishop Robert's assertion that others were sent to unfamiliar counties to check the results of the survey clearly implies that the first stage of the inquest fell to the shrieval administration.[20]

Hundred courts have often been cited as the principal forum, and continue to be so.[21] The regular sequence of vills and hundreds of the text often has the appearance of something more than a procedural artefact. In Norfolk, for example, it describes eight geographically discrete groups of hundreds which proceed from the north to the south of the county in a seemingly logical fashion.[22] In Yorkshire the succession of wapentake, hundreds, and vills is so regularly geographical that common place-names like the ubiquitous northern *Torp*s, the bane of the local historian and onomastician, can readily be identified from their position in the text.[23] It has been argued from these and similar patterns that commissioners perambulated through the shires. But such an arthritic procedure is not consonant with the presumed speed with which the survey was executed. Further, Domesday Book not infrequently reports the verdicts of a number of juries which seemingly gave evidence at the same time. In Kent, for example, the hundred, the burgesses of Dover, the men of the abbot of St Augustine's, and the Eastrey Lathe all seem to have been present to adjudge the assessment of a tenement in Atterton in Newchurch Hundred.[24] No reports of court scenes have survived, but the jostle and bustle of hundreds of assembled people occasionally emerges from the text. A claim in Hampshire seems to have led to a lively and acrimonious debate among the various witnesses: William de Chenet claimed a tenement as parcel of the manor of Charford and adduced as evidence the testimony from 'the better and old men of the whole county and hundred'; Picot, by contrast appealed to the witness of 'the villagers, the common folk, and the reeves'.[25] Whether it was the greybeards or hoi polloi who prevailed is not recorded, but the debate seems to have been real enough. It was evidently jurors who repaired to a central court rather than inquisitors to the hundred, and the regular

---

[18] GDB 66d, 69a, 69c, 70c, 71b, 74d: *DB Wilts*, 7,15.23,7.24,19.26,19.28,10.68,23.
[19] See e.g. GDB 114a: *DB Devon*, 34,5; Exon, 117. In ICC and IE four of the eight jurors for each hundred were Frenchmen (Lewis, 'Domesday Jurors', 19).
[20] Welldon Finn conceived of this possibility (Domesday Inquest, 96–7).
[21] Round, *Feudal England*, 120. For the most recent expression of the idea, see Welldon Finn, *Domesday Inquest*, 49.
[22] Roffe, 'Introduction to the Norfolk Domesday'.
[23] Darby and Maxwell, *The Domesday Geography of Northern England*, 473–94.
[24] GDB 13a: *DB Kent*, 9,9. For others, see Wormald, 'Domesday Lawsuits.'
[25] GDB 44d: *DB Hants.*, 23,3.

sequence in which they appear was probably a function of the use of a geld list to call them.[26]

The shire court was almost certainly the principal forum, and much of the business of the early stages of the inquiry was probably conducted there. There seem, however, to have been circumstances in which separate sessions were held. In Yorkshire there may have been a special procedure for some lordships in the shire.[27] Richmondshire, held by Count Alan of Brittany in 1086, was a castlery of some importance in the north, and, although there is no evidence for its liberties in the eleventh century, the separate administration that it enjoyed from the twelfth may well have dated from its creation in the early 1080s.[28] Likewise, Holderness, held by Drogo de Beuvrière in 1086 and designated a county (*comitatus*) by Orderic Vitalis, probably enjoyed similar privileges from an early period.[29] The Domesday accounts of both are incorporated into the Yorkshire folios of GDB, at times somewhat clumsily, but references to them in the Summary and *clamores* are postscriptal and anomalous in form; in the one both sections are seigneurially arranged and assessment, as opposed to the lord, is interlined above each entry, while in the other disputed lands appear as a schedule.[30] The scribe clearly drew the information for the two fees from distinct sources, and it is likely that the areas were the subject of separate inquiries, either in the shire court or, more likely, within the liberties themselves.[31]

Similar procedures are probably indicated by anomalous sections elsewhere in GDB. Amounderness and northern Lancashire stood outside the shrieval system. The region was not divided up into hundreds or wapentakes and, again according to Orderic Vitalis, it was organized as an earldom.[32] An account of the area was appended to the king's Yorkshire breve after the bulk of the Yorkshire text was written, but its anomalous forms and terse content indicate that it came from a source other than that of the body of the text.[33] Distinct subsections of county Domesdays are more easily appreciated as a function of discrete sources. The accounts of the Welsh land annexed in the Conqueror's reign are appended to, but not integrated into, the Marcher county folios: Flintshire and part of Gwynned appear in Cheshire, Archenfield in Herefordshire, and much of what later became Monmouthshire in Gloucestershire.[34] The areas remained largely extracomital and unhidated in 1086,

---

[26] The Yorkshire Summary, the formal prototype of the Yorkshire folios, was ultimately derived from a geld list (Roffe, 'Yorkshire Summary', 251–5).

[27] Roffe, 'Yorkshire Summary', 255–7.   [28] Kapelle, *Norman Conquest of the North*, 144.

[29] *Orderic Vitalis*, ii. 264; English, *Lords of Holderness*, 57–97, 111.

[30] GDB 309a–313b, 323c–325a, 38ab, 382b, 374b: *DB Yorks.*, chaps. 6, 14; SN,Ct; SE,Hol; CE34–52.

[31] Roffe, 'Yorkshire Summary', 256.   [32] Ibid. 257; *Orderic Vitalis*, vi. 30.

[33] Roffe, 'Domesday Book and Northern Society', 315–18.

[34] GDB 268d–269b, 179b, 180d–181a, 162a–b: *DB Cheshire*, FD, FT, G; *DB Hereford.*, A1–10.1,48–60; *DB Gloucs.*, S, W1–19; Lewis, 'Introduction to the Herefordshire Domesday', 8–9.

and on that account presumably were enrolled in separate documents.[35] The account of the land Between Ribble and Mersey, like the Welsh lands, was tacked onto the end of the Cheshire folios, but it was held in its entirety by the king and, with its own semi-shrieval administration, was therefore quite distinct from Earl Hugh's county of Chester.[36] *Roteland*, the northern part of the later county of Rutland, was appended to the Nottinghamshire folios. It was administered by the sheriff of Nottingham, but it was an ancient royal estate, dower land of the queens of England, and retained a separate administrative identity.[37] The accounts of both Ribble and Mersey and *Roteland* are anomalously geographical in form, and are clearly derived from sources other than those of county folios to which they are attached. Finally, in the south the New Forest, entered in a separate section of the Hampshire folios, was the hunting preserve of the king and was subject to its own administration.[38] An attempt to integrate the material into the seigneurial breves in the normal way was apparently abandoned after the compilation of the king's breve.[39] A similar attempt was made with the Isle of Wight. The west of the island is entered in the king's breve and the east in a discrete chapter at the end of the Hampshire folios.[40] In both cases, the integration of separate documents into the text proved too difficult.

Evidence was invited from all levels of society: barons and Frenchmen, free men, sheriffs, bailiffs, reeves, thegns, hundredmen, and villagers.[41] Presentments of individuals are relatively poorly represented in GDB and LDB. Much of their evidence was probably accepted at face value. The surviving verdicts largely relate to disputed fact and are therefore those of local juries, for it was to the witness of the shire, hundred, and vill that appeal was made where there was a conflict of evidence. As in the later Middle Ages, data were collected from all and sundry but its veracity was vouched for by the community of the shire.[42] Neither GDB nor LDB outlines the social status or composition of such juries. Of the shire juries, only the Wiltshire references

---

[35] Lewis, 'Introduction to the Herefordshire Domesday', 5.

[36] Lewis, 'Introduction to the Lancashire Domesday', 9–12. Lewis suggests that Cheshire and Between Ribble and Mersey shared a sheriff like Nottinghamshire and Derbyshire, but were otherwise administratively separate.

[37] GDB 293c–d: *DB Rutland*, R1–21; Phythian-Adams, 'Emergence of Rutland', 5–12; Cain, 'Introduction to the Rutland Domesday' , 27–30.

[38] GDB 38d–39b: *DB Hants.*, 1,26–38; NF.

[39] *VCH Hants.*, i. 446; *DB Hants.*, Appendix. Round argued that the section was postscriptal, but, as Mumby has pointed out, it is as likely to be a planned addition to the text given the initial attempt at integration. The last five forest entries on f 50d are postscriptal and may have misled Round. There is nothing to suggest that the main section was not written continuously after the completion of the lands of the king's thegns of Hampshire.

[40] GDB 39c–40a, 52b–54a: *DB Hants.*, 1W; IoW.

[41] At least in this respect the IE prologue seems to represent reality; the witness of all these parties is scattered throughout the text.

[42] Roffe, 'The Hundred Rolls and their Antecedents', 179–87.

to 'thegns' give any hint of the types of person empanelled.[43] The implications of the term, however, are unclear. In a pre-Conquest context, 'thegns of the shire' might imply king's thegns of both local and regional standing. The term *tainus* is used in post-Conquest law codes as a synomyn for *baro* and such a usage would point at the swearing of tenants-in-chief or honourial barons, that is, the sort of knight who became 'knights of the shire' in the latter Middle Ages.[44] In a Domesday context, however, 'thegns of the shire' could as easily point to those *taini regis*, the minor royal tenants, both English and French,[45] who, performing sundry personal services for the king, are entered at the end of each county Domesday.[46]

The juries of riding and division of Yorkshire and Lincolnshire remain mysterious, as they are throughout much the Middle Ages.[47] Nor is Domesday Book more forthcoming on the composition of borough juries. A document entitled 'the rights and laws of the church of York', dating from about the same time as the Domesday inquiry and possibly associated with it, was witnessed by twelve named Englishmen and six Frenchmen.[48] None has been identified, but some twenty years later a similar presentment was made by twelve lawmen of York.[49] Lawmen are noticed in the GDB accounts of Lincoln, Stamford, and Cambridge, and 'judges' in the account of Chester.[50] These individuals are best explained, in origin or practice, as the doomsmen noticed in the Wantage Code of *c*.997.[51] In 1086 they enjoyed sake and soke, toll and team, and held extensive urban properties. Some were even in possession of small rural manors. Agmundr son of Valhrafn, lawman of Lincoln, for example, was Gocelin son of Lambert's predecessor in a dozen or so estates in Lincolnshire.[52] These are the types of person who are most likely to have represented urban communities in 1086. In 1275 two of the descendants of the lawmen of Stamford were empanelled to give their verdicts in the Ragman inquest.[53]

More is known of hundred jurors. Those of Cambridgeshire and Hertfordshire are noted in IE,[54] and, since the Cambridgeshire group are largely identical with the individuals named at the head of the account of each hundred in ICC, there is little reason to doubt their authenticity.[55] Each hundred was represented by eight jurors (sixteen in double hundreds), and half were French

[43] GDB 66d, 69a, 69c, 70c, 71b, 74d: *DB Wilts.*, 7,15.23,7.24,19.26,19.28,10.68,23.
[44] *Leges Henrici*, 35.1a, 41.1b, 80.9b, 87.5; Roffe, 'Thegnage to Barony', 158–9.
[45] For French thegns, see Exon, 462ʳ.   [46] Roffe, 'Wharram Percy'.
[47] Roffe, 'Hundreds and Wapentakes', 32–3.
[48] York, Minster Library, MS. L2(1), part 1, f. 61; Liebermann and Peacock, 'An English Document of About 1080', 412–6; Palliser, *Domesday Yorks.*, 6–8,25.
[49] Southwell, Minster Library, MS 1, pp. 18–20; Leach, *Vistations of Southwell Minster*, 190–6.
[50] GDB 336a, 336d, 189a, 262a: *DB Lincs.*, C2–3.S5; *DB Cambs.*, B13–14; *DB Cheshire*, C20.
[51] Tait, *English Medieval Borough*, 43–4; Roffe, *Stamford in the Thirteenth Century*, B3.
[52] GDB 336a, 359a–c, 362a, 376b: *DB Lincs.*, C2.28.33,1.CW3.
[53] Roffe, *Stamford in the Thirteenth Century*, 20–1, 23, 25.   [54] *ICC* 97–101.
[55] *ICC* 1–95 *passim*.

and half English. Naming patterns distinguish both from the highest ranks of society as from the lowest; the majority were local freeholders whose tenements were not explicitly noticed in Domesday (forty-three out of seventy-eight Frenchmen and sixty-nine out of eighty Englishmen).[56] Where their lands can be identified, they held a modest amount of land, averaging a few virgates with a range of between three hides and half a virgate. Typically, it would seem, they were tenants of undertenants. By far the majority of recorded verdicts are those of the hundred, and it must be supposed that they were the principal source of information.

According to the IE prologue, the reeve, the priest, and six *villani* were sworn from each village. This is consonant with the few references to the witness of the vill in GDB and LDB and later practice.[57] In an eleventh-century context *villani* is best translated as 'villagers' rather than 'villeins'. They were probably all personally free, for they demonstrably rendered geld. In some parts of Huntingdonshire, for example, as elsewhere, each *villanus* is represented by one fiscal virgate in GDB.[58] None, however, is likely to have been any more highly privileged than the ordinary sokeman. Although the verdict of the vill is occasionally joined with that of higher courts, as in the thirteenth century, its presentments were only ever evidential. William de Chenet's witnesses from 'the better and old men of the county and hundred' were unwilling to accept the judgement of 'the villagers, common folk, and reeves' in respect of Hugh de Port's claim to land in Fordingbridge Hundred, Hampshire, saying that they refused to countenance any other law than King Edward's unless the king deemed otherwise. In this case the outcome is not explicit (although, of course, William's successors seem to have held the land).[59] The evidence in Lincolnshire, however, is clearer. In the text there are numerous records of the presentment of the twelve-carucate hundred, the local equivalent of the vill, but in the *clamores*, the subsequent sessions to determine disputed title, the hundred is not represented.[60]

The number of people involved in the Domesday inquiry was huge. It has been calculated that there were probably some 3,000 individuals named in the text as holding land in 1086, either in chief or as tenants.[61] Most must have attended sessions and many may have brought their own bailiffs and even their whole households: the monks of Chertsey, Abingdon, and St Augustine's, Canterbury, attended *en masse* in Surrey, Berkshire, and Kent, while monks of Old Minster, Winchester, were present at the Hampshire sessions.[62]

[56] Lewis, 'Domesday Jurors', 17–24.
[57] GDB 44d: *DB Hants.*, 23,3; LDB 392b–393a: *DB Suffolk*, 25,52.
[58] See below, pp. 156–7.   [59] GDB 44d: *DB Hants.*, 23,3.
[60] Roffe, 'Introduction to the Lincolnshire Domesday', 8.
[61] Keats-Rohan, *Domesday People*, 23. Those of continental origin account for 2,468. There are 992 names of people of native descent. The number of individuals, while clearly smaller than this total, has not been determined.
[62] GDB 34a, 59b, 47a: *DB Surrey*, 8,30; *DB Berks.*, 7,38; *DB Kent*, 5,149; *DB Hants.*, 29,9.

Of the representatives of the community of the shire, there were probably at least twelve jurors from each of thirty-four shires, an equal number from the twenty-six riding, rape, lathe, and other area assemblies, eight from each of 767 hundreds, and twelve or eighteen from about sixty-five cities and boroughs, making a total of, at a minimum, 7,600. The number of vills in 1086 is impossible to calculate with any degree of precision. It is not until 1316 that there survives a comprehensive list, the Nomina Villarum,[63] hundred by hundred and shire by shire, and by then the structure of local government at the lowest level had changed out of all recognition. In large part due to the impact of manorialization of the eleventh and twelfth centuries, the large tithing groups of the eleventh century had become fragmented to approximate more closely to settlement structure.[64] Hidation totals may, however, give some idea. If the conservative estimate of ten hides or twelve carucates to the vill is made, then there were some 4,561 vills in hidated England and 1,927 in the carucated area (Kent is excluded).[65] With 6,488 notional vills, there must have been almost 52,000 villagers who gave evidence. In all, over 60,000 witnesses were probably heard in the course of the Domesday inquiry.[66] The writer of the preface to Bury A was clearly exaggerating when he claimed that 'almost all the inhabitants of the land' swore.[67] Nevertheless, the inquiry must have touched in one way or another every law-worthy person in the realm.

At some point in the proceedings, as the Anglo-Saxon Chronicler and Robert of Hereford attest, commissioners were dispatched to oversee the process. Here and there throughout Domesday there are references to *barones* and *legati*, and both terms are usually translated as 'commissioners'. Neither term, however, is likely to have a precise referent or legal usage. In some cases the reference is to justices dispatched before the Domesday inquest; in others it may mean nothing more than the king's local representatives, the sheriff and his men.[68] But significantly in one passage events are related to the time 'when *barones* came into the county',[69] and clearly many similar notices must be to commissioners. None is named in GDB or LDB, but some are known from other sources. Bishop Remigius of Lincoln (accompanied by a clerk and two

---

[63] *Feudal Aids, passim.*   [64] Roffe, 'Hundreds and Wapentakes', 42.

[65] The geld totals are derived from Maitland, *Domesday Book and Beyond*, 464.

[66] Fleming suggests 7,000 or 8,000 ('Oral Testimony', 105), but does not seem to have considered the villagers.

[67] Douglas, *Feudal Documents from Bury St Edmund's*, 3.

[68] See e.g. LDB 7a: *DB Essex*, 1,28. The hundred of Uttlesford in Essex witnessed that Robert Gernon held two free men with 2½ hides of land, but 'it does not know how he should have them because neither a writ nor a *legatus* came on the king's behalf to the hundred to declare that the king had given him the land [*hundredum nescit quo modo eos habuerit quia neque breve neque legatus venit ex parte regis in hundredro quod rex sibi dedisset illam terram*]'. The *legatus* here is clearly not a Domesday commissioner and was probably a royal reeve or the sheriff. The same is probably true of the *legatus* of GDB 262c: *DB Cheshire*, C3.

[69] LDB 377a: *DB Suffolk*, 16,34. A further reference is somewhat ambiguous (LDB 97b: *DB Essex*, 77,1). For a discussion, see Welldon Finn, *Domesday Inquest*, 97.

TABLE 5.1. *Domesday circuits*

I	South-east	Kent, Sussex, Surrey, Hants., Berks.
II	South-west	Wilts., Somerset, Dorset, Devon, Cornwall
III	East Midlands	Cambs., Herts., Beds., Bucks., Middlesex
IV	Midlands	Leics., Northants., Warks., Oxon., Staffs.
V	West	Gloucs., Worcs., Hereford, Salop., Cheshire
VI	North	Yorks., Lincs., Notts., Derby., Hunts.
VII	East Anglia	Norfolk, Suffolk, Essex

monks), Earl Walter Giffard, Henry de Ferrers, and Adam, the brother of Eudo the king's steward, officiated in Worcestershire, and 'S', possibly Samson, in East Anglia, while William de St Calais, the bishop of Durham, was probably active in the south-west and Bishop Osmund of Salisbury in the East Midlands. No others have come to light.[70]

It would seem that a number of shires was assigned to each group of commissioners, for Archbishop Lanfranc refers to 'the counties' which were entrusted to 'S'.[71] Characteristics of the Domesday corpus suggest that there were seven groups in all (Table 5.1). Exon, the main source for the south-west in GDB, interweaves the accounts of Wiltshire, Dorset, Somerset, Devon, and Cornwall, and it thereby suggests that those five counties constituted one such. Much of the form of the corresponding GDB folios is derived from its author's well-realized concept of structure and expression, but peculiarities crept in from his sources. In the Wiltshire and Dorset folios, for example, the assessment of the demesne is consistently recorded, a rarity elsewhere in GDB, ICC, and IE, but the norm in Exon. Quirks of form and content of this kind indicate five further groups of counties. The distinctive opening formula *In X habuit Y . . .* of groups VI is found in the Huntingdonshire section of IE but not consistently elsewhere, while the forms of III are directly related to ICC, a source of the Cambridgeshire folios, and common to all five counties is the otherwise unique admeasurement of meadow in ploughlands. Group I is characterized by the record of the TRE tenant at the beginning of the entry, as in the Domesday Monachorum B, a possible precursor of the Kent text, and the likewise unique admeasurement of woodland in swine renders. Groups IV and V are more difficult to distinguish the one from the other, but are ultimately defined by the placing of the record of TRE tenure at the end or the beginning of entries. Finally, the seventh group is defined by the many peculiarities of LDB which are only otherwise found in the parallel passages of its precursor, IE.

[70] *Hemingi Chartulorum*, 287–8; Barlow, 'Domesday Book: A Letter of Lanfranc', 284–9; Welldon Finn, *Liber Exoniensis*, 101; GDB 87c: *DB Somerset*, 2,9; *Regesta Regum: Acta*, no. 189. For a speculative assignation of William's bishops to circuits, see Loyn, 'William's Bishops', 229.

[71] *Letters of Lanfranc*, no. 56; Barlow, 'Domesday Book: A Letter of Lanfranc', 284–9.

'Cross-enrolments' confirm the integrity of the groups and further define them. In a significant number of instances estates in one shire are described in the folios of another (Table 5.2). Anomalies of this kind may sometimes be illusory, for eleventh-century county boundaries were often different from those of the later Middle Ages; settlements were frequently moved from one county to another in the twelfth century and later to bring divided settlements or tenurial units into a single jurisdiction.[72] But the enrolment of estates in deepest Dorset in the Wiltshire and Somerset folios clearly arose because the scribe misread his source; Exon is arranged by fee, and it was easy to miss the marginal rubrics that indicated the transition from one county to another. Cross-enrolments of this kind suggest similar types of source elsewhere or similar processes, and their incidence and distribution therefore indicate something of their scope. On these grounds Staffordshire, which is usually associated with group V,[73] can be firmly placed in group IV. Descriptions of Warwickshire and Oxfordshire estates are found in its folios, while some of its own estates appear in those of Warwickshire and Northamptonshire, sometimes with the appropriate Staffordshire hundred name.

The seven groups of counties have been seen by some historians as a function of compilation as opposed to data collection.[74] There are no explicit references to supracomital activities, and much of the Domesday information is of a local character. It has been pointed out that the units of woodland admeasurement in Cheshire, for example, are different from those of Shropshire, Herefordshire, Worcestershire, and Gloucestershire. The conclusion is drawn that the commissioners collected data shire by shire, and the identity of group V was merely a chance association of the five counties derived from the subsequent report that the commissioners made to central government.[75] In reality, however, the similarities are as striking as the differences. Thus, the record of the minutiae of manorial stock may differ in group V, but common to all of its counties is a unique record of parks, heys, and hawks' nests, among other distinctive characteristics. Here surely is an echo of a regional policy of data collection.

The groups of counties have every appearance of circuits, and indeed there is implicit evidence of common sessions within them as a second forum of the survey. It has already been noted that the account of *Roteland* is geographical in form and appended to the Nottinghamshire folios. Its anomalous forms point to a discrete and probably local court hearing. Much of the material, however, some eight entries, is duplicated in similar but not identical terms

---

[72] Many other such anomalies survived into the nineteenth century. See e.g. the Huntingdonshire/Northamptonshire boundary (Roffe, 'Introduction to the Huntingdonshire Domesday', 1–2).

[73] Stephenson, 'Notes on the Composition and Interpretation of Domesday', 6–7. Eyton's earlier intuition was clearly correct (Eyton, *Domesday Studies: Staffordshire*, 1–2). He was followed by Ballard (*Domesday Inquest*, 12–3).

[74] Welldon Finn, *Domesday Inquest*, 35–41.

[75] Thacker and Sawyer, 'Domesday Survey', 293–7.

TABLE 5.2. *Cross-enrolment within circuits*

Circuit	County	Cross-enrolment
I	Berkshire	Wiltshire: Shalbourne+
	Sussex	Hampshire: Warblington
	Surrey	Sussex: Worth
II	Devon	Cornwall: Landinner, Trebeigh
	Somerset	Dorset: Over or Nether Compton
		Wiltshire: ?Yarnfield
	Wiltshire	Dorset: Gussage, Gillingham
		Berkshire: ?Coleshill+
		Hampshire: Tytherley+
III	Hertfordshire	Buckinghamshire: ?Shenley
		Cambridgeshire: ?Stetchworth
	Buckinghamshire	Oxfordshire: Caversfield+
IV	Northamptonshire	Oxfordshire: Charlton on Otmoor, Cottisford, Finmere, Glympton, Hethe, Heyford, Mollington, Shelswell, Shipton, Sibford, Wootton, Worton Staffordshire: West Bromwich, Lapley*, Marston* Warwickshire: Berkswell~, Over, Sawbridge, Whichford, Whitacre
	Oxfordshire	Buckinghamshire: Ibstone+, ?Boycott, ?Lillingstone
	Staffordshire	Oxfordshire: Drayton, Sibford Warwickshire: ?Harborne, Perry Barr, Handsworth
	Warwickshire	Staffordshire: Quatt, Romsley, Rudge, Shipley, Chillington*, Essington*
V	Gloucestershire	Herefordshire: Kingstone
	Herefordshire	Gloucestershire: Forthampton Worcestershire: Bushley*, Eldersfield*, Feckenham*, Hollow Court*, Martley*, Pull Court*, Queenhill*, Suckley*
	Shropshire	Herefordshire: Farlow
	Worcestershire	Herefordshire: Suckley
VI	Lincolnshire	*Roteland*: Ashwell~, Burley~, Exton~, Market Overton~, Stretton~, Thistleton~, Whissendine~, Whitwell~
	Nottinghamshire	Derbyshire: Derby
VII	Essex	Suffolk: Sudbury
	Suffolk	Norfolk: Gorleston, Gillingham

Notes: * = hundred rubric indicated; + = located on the county boundary and either divided between two counties or eleventh-century context unknown; ~ = parallel entries found in the appropriate county.

in the Lincolnshire folios.[76] This account is completely integrated into the Lincolnshire text—it has its own place in the common sequence of wapentakes—and it must be supposed that presentments were made at the same time as those of Lincolnshire. Since *Roteland* belonged to the bailiwick of the sheriff of Nottingham, Nottinghamshire was presumably present at the same time. Here is evidently the record of a second session, and it was clearly a joint one. Elsewhere there is no such unequivocal evidence, but the best explanations for the Domesday groups is that they are a function of similar circuits proceedings.

Counties were frequently joined together for judicial and administrative purposes in the eleventh century. It is recorded in GDB itself that Bishop Wulfstan had proved his claim to Alveston in Warwickshire 'before Queen Matilda, in the presence of four sheriffdoms'.[77] The shires involved are not named, but can be identified as Warwickshire, Oxfordshire, Gloucestershire, and Worcestershire and the meeting-place as Four Shires Stone in *Gildberg*, where the boundaries of the four shires met until 1931.[78] The probably ancient association of the four counties does not seem to have influenced the procedure of the inquiry in 1086, for two of the counties were in Circuit IV and two in Circuit V. None of the Domesday groups is known to have had a political or administrative reality in 1086, but there are indications that their composition may in part have been influenced by existing or earlier institutions. Cambridgeshire, Bedfordshire, and Hertfordshire in Circuit III may have long been associated in 1086, for their meeting-place at Guilden Morden where their boundaries march has every appearance of antiquity.[79] The association of hidated Huntingdonshire with the carucated shires of York, Lincoln, Nottingham, and Derby in Circuit VI was probably of more recent origin; all five counties had been held by the earl of Northumbria up to 1075. It is unlikely that any supracomital organization survived the fall of Earl Waltheof in that year,[80] and it is therefore probable that, if the Domesday group of shires was any more than coincidental, its composition was determined by existing records. Similar processes may have influenced the composition of Circuits II and VII which had also been constituted as earldoms. No rationale has been detected in the remainder, and they were probably a product of the inquiry.

This should occasion no surprise. In the tenth and eleventh centuries expediency was as common a factor as tradition in the meeting of joint courts.

---

[76] GDB 349d, 355d, 358c, 366b, 366d–367a: *DB Lincs.*, 13,38.24,78.27,47.51,10.56,11–13;17–18. For the differences, see *DB Rutland*, appendix. Part of Thistleton is not paralleled in the Nottinghamshire section (GDB 358c, 367a: *DB Lincs.*, 27,49.56,21). Called 'the other Thistleton' in GDB, the land was subsequently in Lincolnshire and known as South Witham (Roffe, 'Introduction to the Lincolnshire Domesday', 34 n).

[77] GDB 238c: *DB Warks.*, 3,4.   [78] Ibid. 3,4 n.   [79] Ibid.

[80] Nottingham and Derby regularly met in joint sessions, but there is no evidence that other shires were associated with them in anything more than an ad hoc way.

Shires and hundreds were called together as the need required.[81] Five counties were evidently considered to be the suitable size of the circuit in 1086 (with the three left over in the seventh circuit), and customary associations could not therefore always be observed.

The Royal Fisc and the Inquisitio Geldi

Data were collected in both local and regional forums. The business of the first is exemplified by the Nottinghamshire account of *Roteland*. In content this exhibits the standard litany of names, assessments, manorial appurtenances, and value. It is in its geographical arrangement that a distinct focus is discerned. The account commences with a statement of the geld assessment of the whole area.

In Alstoe Wapentake there are two hundreds, in each of which are twelve carucates to the geld and twenty-four carucates can be. Half of this wapentake is in Thurgarton Wapentake and half in Broxtow Wapentake.

In Martinsley Wapentake is one hundred in which there are twelve carucates to the geld and forty-eight ploughs can be apart from the king's three demesne manors in which fourteen ploughs can plough.

These two wapentakes are attached to the sheriffdom of Nottingham for the king's geld. *Roteland* renders to the king £150 blanched.[82]

The entries that follow are ordered by twelve-carucate hundred (Table 5.3). The assessment of successive estates in Alstoe, held by the king and six tenants-in-chief, divide themselves into two groups of twelve carucates, the two hundreds of the prologue. Martinsley, held in its entirety by the king, is apparently assessed at thirteen carucates, but one carucate held by Leofnoth in Oakham is a duplication of one of the four carucates of the king's demesne manor in the same place.[83]

This anomalous form appears to be directly related to rights of the crown. Although much of the land was held by tenants-in-chief, *Roteland* was a royal soke. From at least the late tenth century the district had constituted one of the dower estates of the queens of England; it was held by Queen Edith until her death in 1075 and had only come to the king on the death of Queen Matilda in 1083.[84] The £150 blanch rendered in 1086 seems to be represented by the value of the individual estates in Alstoe and Martinsley along with those of Witchley Hundred in Northamptonshire which was anciently part of the soke.[85] For reasons that are now unknown, a division of the soke had been effected before the Conquest, and only the Nottinghamshire section was enrolled as

[81] Fleming, 'Oral Testimony', 103–6.   [82] GDB 293c: *DB Rutland*, R1–4.

[83] Roffe, 'Nottinghamshire and the North', 64; Roffe, 'Introduction to the Nottinghamshire Domesday', 7.

[84] Phythian-Adams, 'Emergence of Rutland', 5–12.

[85] Cain, 'Introduction to the Rutland Domesday', 27.

TABLE 5.3. *The* Roteland *Domesday*

Hundred	Manor	Lord in 1086	Assessment		
			Carucates	Bovates	
Alstoe I	Greetham	King	3	0	
	Cottesmore	King	3	0	
	Mk Overton				
	Stretton	Countess Judith	3	4	
	Thistleton	Countess Judith	0	4	
	Ibidem	Alfred of Lincoln	0	4	
	Same hundred (Teigh)	Robert Malet	1	4	12 car.
Alstoe II	Whissendine	Countess Judith	4	0	
	Exton	Countess Judith	2	0	
	Whitwell	Countess Judith	1	0	
	Awsthorp	Oger son of Ungomar	1	0	
	Burley	Gilbert de Gant	2	0	
	Ashwell	Earl Hugh	2	0	12 car.
Martinsley	Oakham (5 berewicks)	King	4	0	
	Ibidem	Fulchere Malsor	1	0	
	Hambleton (7 berewicks)	King	4	0	
	Ridlington (7 berewicks)	King	4	0	13 car.

Note: Words in brackets are interlineations.

a separate entity in GDB. Unlike the parallel entries in the Lincolnshire folios, the focus of the document or, more precisely, its formal exemplar, is these the king's dues. The interests of the tenants-in-chief are secondary. Their lands are indicated by the marginal and postscriptal addition of the roman numbers I, II, III, and IIII, probably to match the list entered at the beginning of the Nottinghamshire folios, but the attempt to indicate lordship is half-hearted and muddled and it would seem that originally there were no such distinctions. The primary concern of the account was the dues of the king in tribute and geld.

The *Roteland* Domesday is not entirely unique. In the vicinity of York there were twelve vills which were assessed at eighty-four carucates. Individual tenements were held by the king and five tenants-in-chief, and eight out of fifteen of the latter are enrolled in the appropriate breve.[86] An account of the whole area, however, is appended to the description of York, commencing with the assessment to the geld: 'In the geld of the City [of York] there are eighty-four carucates of land, and each one used to render as much as one house in the city. They were [liable] for the king's three works with the citizens'[87] Like *Roteland*, the following account is similar to the usual GDB entry in terms of content,

[86] GDB 313a, 301b, 328b, 313a–b, 301b: *DB Yorks.*, 6W4.1W1.23N36.6W5–6.1W2.1W8.6W2.
[87] GDB 298b: *DB Yorks.*, C22.

but its form deviates from the Domesday norm. The area is described vill by vill, each commencing with a statement of total assessment before proceeding to an account of the land held by the tenants-in-chief within it, and distinctive language is employed.[88] As an integral element of the City of York, it would seem that the land was also in the soke of the king.[89]

Why the two royal sokes were entered into GDB in this form is unexplained.[90] It is clear, however, that the accounts were not the function of an entirely extraordinary procedure. In Exon the account of the *terra regis* is explicitly confined to royal demesne (witness the headings *Dominicatus Regis ad Regnum Pertinens in Devonescira, Dominicatus Regis in Devenesira, Terra Regis Dominiciae in Cornugallia*).[91] Nevertheless, some tenancies are noted. Lands that 'could not be separated' TRE are entered as integral parts of the king's estates. Tenements held by the bishop of Coutances and Ælfric in succession to Wulfward and Wulfmer in the manor of Keynsham in Somerset were of this order.[92] Freely held land, by contrast, is summarily noticed but, as in Rutland and York, is more fully described in the appropriate seigneurial context. In the account of the king's manor of Axminster in Devon, for example, dues from Charlton, Honiton, Smallridge, Membury, and Rawridge are noticed, but the lands themselves are more fully described in the breves of the bishop of Coutances, the count of Mortain, Ralph of Pomeroy, William Cheever, and the church of St Mary of Rouen.[93] A similar pattern is found in the account of lands tributary to the royal manor of Winnianton in Cornwall. Some twenty parcels of land were held by the count of Mortain and they are each more fully described in his own chapter.[94] Here, however, the GDB scribe suppressed the duplication, only noticing the lands in the king's breve.[95]

A detailed analysis of the hands of the *terra regis* sections of the Exon will go a long way towards identifying the precise relationship between the two versions.[96] Nevertheless, in outline it seems clear that the anomalies of both Exon and the northern folios of GDB point to a more general survey

[88] Notably the use of *halla* instead of *aula* for hall (Roffe, 'Domesday Book and Northern Society', 314).

[89] For sokes of this kind attached to boroughs, see Roffe, 'Introduction to the Derbyshire Domesday', 19–24; id., 'Introduction to the Huntingdonshire Domesday', 19–22.

[90] The most likely explanation is that there was no other account of the king's lands—in neither case are they duplicated—and the scribe merely copied the whole document as it was presented to him. For the uncertainties in the Yorkshire folios, see Roffe, 'Domesday Book and Northern Society', 323–8.

[91] Exon, 83, 88[v], 93, 99.   [92] Exon, 113[v], 114; GDB, 87a–b: *DB Somerset*, 1,28.

[93] Exon, 84[v], 135, 216[v], 343, 111, 195.

[94] Exon, 99–100, 224–7. For a comparison of the accounts, *DB Cornwall*, 1,1 n.

[95] GDB 120a: *DB Cornwall*, 1,1.

[96] Welldon Finn believed that scribes G and A were responsible for much of the writing, but he is less than clear as to what other sections were written by them. He does aver, however, that the Winnianton section in the king's breve was the work of G, while A and C were responsible for the corresponding entries in the count of Mortain's chapter ('The Exeter Domesday', 368, 385). Further comment must await an entry-by-entry analysis.

of regalia.[97] Reference to such a survey is found in ICC. One of the defining features of this document is its limited account of the king's lands. Those tenements which were held in custody by the sheriff or were let at farm to sergeants are all described, but the demesne estates, with the possible exception of Exning,[98] are conspicuous by their absence. The text provides the explanation: an account of the missing estates is to be found in the *breve regis*.[99]

There are only two other unambiguous references to the king's breves: it is noted in the Worcestershire folios that Martley and Suckley rendered their farm in Herefordshire 'and are described in the king's breve', and IE alludes to claims in the same.[100] Nevertheless, others can be detected in the various accounts of *terra regis*. The dichotomy of demesne and tenanted land is sometimes reflected in the form of the text, with each in separate sequences: in Yorkshire the account of 332 thegnages is a postscriptal addition.[101] More significantly, there are variations in expression. In the Cambridgeshire folios of GDB the entries taken from the king's breve are quite distinctive in form.[102] The manors are enrolled hundred by hundred in the same order as that of ICC. The diplomatic, however, departs from both ICC's and that of the rest of GDB. Normally there is a simple statement of geld assessment, land is said to be worth (*valet*, *valuit*) so many pounds, and the pre-Conquest lord or tenant is said to 'have held [*tenuit*]' the land. In the description of the demesne estates, by contrast, entries commence with the statement '*X* is a royal demesne vill', elaborate details of food farms are given, value is expressed in terms of an annual render in the form 'its renders [*reddit*] *a* pounds', and the pre-Conquest lord is said to 'have had [*habuit*] the manor'. In almost every shire the account of royal demesne exhibits similar variations in expression. In Gloucestershire, for example, formulas almost identical with those of Cambridgeshire were employed, whereas most of the text conforms to the Circuit V norms. Separate reports were clearly made throughout the country.[103]

The scope of the survey that produced them was wide. Although possibly supplemented by additional material, the account of the six hundreds between Ribble and Mersey in the Cheshire folios probably represents the substance of the sessions in South Lancashire.[104] Accounts were drawn up of the more important tenants and the services they rendered; in West Derby all the thegns

[97] Welldon Finn, 'The Exeter Domesday', 386.

[98] The manor is held by King William in 1086, but it had belonged to Edeva the Fair (GDB 189d *DB Cambs.*, 1,12).

[99] *ICC* 6, 83; GDB 189d: *DB Cambs.*, 1,13.

[100] GDB 178a: *DB Worcs.*, X3; *ICC*, 127. In the Somerset folios 'the witness of the *brevis regis*' is cited (GDB 87b: *DB Somerset*, 1,35). The context, however, suggests that the reference is probably to a writ.

[101] GDB 300a–301d: *DB Yorks.*, 1N1–1W73.   [102] GDB 189b–d: *DB Cambs.*, 1,1–13.

[103] GDB 162b: *DB Gloucs.*, 1,1. The common usage is probably coincidental; there seem to be no forms that constitute a consistent diplomatic peculiar to the king's lands.

[104] GDB 269c–270b: *DB Cheshire*, R1–7. The summary at the end of the account is postscriptal and probably draws on additional material (Lewis, 'Introduction to the Lancashire Domesday', 12).

paid two *oras* of pence for each carucate, and were obliged to repair the king's hall, fisheries, woodland enclosures, and stag beats, and cut the king's corn in August. The customs and sokes from which the king derived an income were recorded; failure to acquit services incurred a fine of 4s, absence from the hundred one of 5s, and rape, bloodshed, or absence from the shire moot 10s. Finally, an account was made of the value of individual holdings and the renders that the king received from each hundred.

Much the same sorts of information were collected throughout the country. Renders in kind are frequently noticed, and details of their management are recorded in the accounts of the farms of one night (the food rents owed to the king) in the western and south-western shires.[105] Hundredal jurisdiction is also regularly noticed. In Oxfordshire, for example, the number of hundreds attached to Benson, Headington, Kirtlington, Wootton, Shipton-under-Wychwood, Bampton, Bloxham, and Adderbury are recorded.[106] In Worcestershire the shire presented that seven of the twelve hundreds were exempt, and the sheriff complained that he thereby lost much in farm.[107] In Norfolk the farms and soke of each hundred are noted at the end of each hundredal section.[108] In Gloucestershire a careful account is given of all land that had been taken out of the king's farm and brought into it since 1066, along with the circumstances of each change.[109]

Boroughs were also surveyed. Like the *terra regis*, they are often omitted from the Domesday documentation and their descriptions are anomalous in form. They are usually enrolled before the breves, often postscriptally in a space that was left for them, and are entirely different in their diplomatic. Thus, for example, Gloucester and Winchcombe, like the royal demesne, are said to have rendered and render (*reddit, reddidit*) so much to the crown where the rest of the text expresses value in terms of worth (*valuit, valet*).[110] As with the borough proper, customary land, that is, the tenements which rendered dues and services to the king,[111] are entered first, and in some cases, as in Derby,[112] the farm of the borough and the other renders that it made are immediately recorded. The surveys may originally have been very detailed: numerous burgesses are named in the accounts of Norwich, Thetford, Ipswich, and Colchester in LDB, along with a record of the amount of land that each held.[113] In GDB numbers only are usually given. There then follows an account of non-customary land which rendered its dues to tenants-in-chief. In some cases the information is postscriptal, and it must often be suspected that it was drawn from other sources. Alfred of Lincoln's fee in Stamford is more or less duplicated in his breve, while the order of fees in Buckingham is almost exactly

[105] Demarest, '*Firma Unius Noctis*', 78–89.   [106] GDB 154c–d: *DB Oxon.*, 1,1–7a.
[107] GDB 172a: *DB Worcs.*, C3.   [108] LDB 109b–141b: *DB Norfolk*, 1.
[109] GDB 162d–164b: *DB Gloucs.*, 1.   [110] GDB 162a, 162c: *DB Gloucs.*, G, B.
[111] Mahany and Roffe, 'Stamford' , 200–1.   [112] GDB 280b: *DB Derby.*, B2.
[113] LDB 104a–107b, 116a–118a, 289a, 290a: *DB Essex*, B; *DB Norfolk*, 1,61–6; *DB Suffolk*, 1,116;122.

the same as the breves themselves, and in some counties the land is actually found in the relevant chapters.[114] Finally, the farm of the borough is recorded if not entered before.

The survey, however, was not confined to the specific issues of royal manors and boroughs. More general fiscal matters were probably also reviewed. In most counties very little of the material was entered into Domesday Book, but in some various notes outlining the services the king could expect and the dues that they brought with them were added to the account of boroughs where space permitted, or, as in the Oxfordshire folios, appended to the king's breve.[115] In Worcestershire and Berkshire there are detailed accounts of the military obligations of the various classes of society and the fines and penalties they paid if negligent in their duty.[116] In Kent, Lincolnshire, Nottinghamshire, Derbyshire, and Yorkshire the holders of sake and soke, toll and team are listed.[117] The purpose was not merely to record liberties; the franchise conferred forfeitures and the like on the holder, but more importantly he himself made his forfeitures to the crown, and the list therefore records the dues that the king might expect.[118] Similarly, in Lincolnshire various legal customs are also noted along with the customs, that is, the profits of justice, of the ridings and divisions of Lincolnshire.[119]

These regalities must have been of considerable value, but they were not the most substantial source of income. This was the geld, and there seems no doubt that the *inquisitio geldi* noted in Exon constituted the most important element in this stage of the Domesday process. Hitherto this conclusion has been resisted. The record of exemption from the geld is a commonplace, occurring in almost every county surveyed, sometimes in considerable numbers. Galbraith was in no doubt that these data were derived from the geld inquest but, anxious to prove that Domesday Book was no geld book, was of the opinion that that information was a late addition to the text; he assumed that the geld accounts postdated the Domesday inquiry, seemingly on the grounds that the former contained less information than the latter.[120] Dr Harvey has concurred. For her the progress of the geld inquest can be traced in GDB by the incidence of reassessment as indicated by TRW geld figures. The pattern of distribution is patchy. In Circuit II, for example, reassessments are only found in the folios relating to Cornwall, which was probably the last county in that circuit to be surveyed. Harvey concludes that the *inquisitio* was still in progress in the course of the Domesday inquiry, that the commissioners

[114] GDB, 336d, 358b, 143a: *DB Lincs.*, S11.27,35; *DB Bucks.*, B1–13; Martin, 'Domesday Book and the Boroughs', 143–63.

[115] GDB 154d: *DB Oxon.*, 1,12;13. Whether the section is postscriptal is unclear; 13 was probably written before 12, but the exact stratigraphy of the text at this point is uncertain.

[116] GDB 56c, 172a: *DB Berks.*, B10; *DB Worcs.*, C5.

[117] GDB 1c, 337a, 280c, 298c: *DB Kent*, D25; *DB Lincs.*, T5; *DB Notts*, S5; *DB Yorks.*, C36.

[118] See above, pp. 32–5.   [119] GDB 336c: *DB Lincs.*, C28–33.

[120] Galbraith, *Making of Domesday Book*, 87–101, esp. at 92.

made use of its findings where available, but that the whole enterprise was a separate initiative.[121]

Neither argument is forceful. It is a categorical error to assume that because one of two related texts is less informative then it must be derived from the other. GDB was a compiled text and its sources were manifold. A stemma clearly cannot be defined by content alone. Assessments are an even less certain basis. The record of a TRE figure does not preclude a reassessment, as the Cambridgeshire folios amply demonstrate.[122] Even more to the point is the fact of reassessment. It is far from clear that the geld of Cornwall had been recently reviewed. The normal entry in the county is of the form 'Richard holds Cartuther from the count [of Mortain]. Cola held it TRE and gelded for ½ hide. There is there, however, 1½ hides.'[123] In the king's breve the formula is a significant variation: 'The king holds Pendrim. There is one hide there, but it gelded for ½ hide.[124] The implication is that TRE the land had compounded for the geld at a lower rate than its actual assessment. Such an arrangement is explicit in the account of Judael of Totnes's manor of Froxton,[125] where it is simply stated that there are three ferlings of land but it gelds for only one, and it seems likely that this was the reality throughout most of the county.[126] Beyond Cornwall there is no more convincing evidence of a reassessment. Throughout Circuit VI TRE geld figures are given and they were used for various fiscal purposes without change throughout the Middle Ages and, in some cases, into the eighteenth century. Above all, the geld accounts of the south-west clearly relate to the payment and collection of the geld. Thus, the thegns of Walter de Douai gave evidence that a holding belonged to the hundred of Bempstone; Lambert of Wheathill was adjudged to be quit for a hide by the testimony of the collectors; lands of the count of Mortain in Cornwall had always been exempt from the geld according to the testimony of the hundredmen.[127] There are numerous other references of a similar kind, but little to suggest a reassessment.

It remains true that the geld accounts may be contemporary with the production of the circuit reports ('the returns') from which GDB was compiled.[128] But the process that produced them was ongoing. Of the three accounts of Wiltshire, C appears to be earlier than A and B, for it records sums which were outstanding that had been discharged in the other two.[129] All, however, drew on earlier sources from which they were abstracted. Thus, much of the detail given is perceptibly earlier than the GDB state of affairs. In the three Wiltshire geld accounts the king is credited with four hides in Highworth Hundred, but the king does not seem to hold it in GDB; in Swanborough Hundred the king is accorded fifty-five hides, but the sole royal manor of Rushall

---

[121] Harvey, 'Domesday Book and its Predecessors' , 768–9.
[122] See above, p. 110.　　[123] GDB 122c: *DB Cornwall*, 5,3,5.
[124] GDB 120b: *DB Cornwall*, 1,7.　　[125] GDB 125b: *DB Cornwall*, 6,1.
[126] Welldon Finn, *Liber Exoniensis*, 113.　　[127] Exon, 77ᵛ, 81ᵛ, 72, 72ᵛ, 68ᵛ.
[128] Welldon Finn, *Liber Exoniensis*, 100.　　[129] Darlington, 'Wiltshire Geld Rolls', 171–2.

is assessed at thirty-seven hides; the assessment of Robert of Mortain's manor of Thornfalcon in Somerset is given as seven hides, but GDB makes it six only, with the missing hide correctly restored to the royal manor of North Curry.[130] Galbraith made much of the chronological signficance of a passage in Wiltshire Geld Roll A. In the account of Chedglow Hundred it is stated that the four collectors of geld retained 15s 6d and A adds: 'and from those who collected the geld Walter and his colleagues recovered 5s 3d besides 8s 9d which the bishop [William de St Calais] and his colleagues found.'[131] Walter is identified with Robert of Hereford's second wave of inquisitors and, Galbraith concluded, he represents a special Treasury panel to collect the arrears of the geld.[132] The geld inquest was an ongoing process. However, in reality it is far from clear that Walter succeeded Bishop William, but, more to the point, both seem to have been on the ground after much of the business of the inquest, as represented by Roll C, was complete.

There seems, then, no grounds for necessarily assuming that the references to geld exemption are late and ad hoc additions to the Domesday process. The Anglo-Saxon Chronicler is explicit in his linkage of a survey of royal lands and farms with 'how many hundred hides there are in the county',[133] and indeed traces of the process can be found throughout the Domesday texts. The geographically arranged account of *Roteland* and York both hint at a concern with taxation, preserving as they do a record of geld quotas and what is presumably the structure of geld accounts. The intimate connection between the geld audit and the survey of royal estates is explicit in the account of the City of Lincoln. In the midst of the description of urban fees, a geld account is given:

Those written below have not paid the king's geld as they ought:

The land of St Mary on which Teodbert dwells in the high street has not paid geld; nor has the bishop's land situated at St Laurence's paid geld in respect of 1 house.

The abbot of Peterborough has not paid geld in respect of 1 house and 3 tofts.

Earl Hugh has not paid geld in respect of all his land; nor Thoraldr of Greetwell, nor Losoard, nor Ketilbjorn.

Hugh son of Baldric has not paid geld in respect of 2 tofts; nor Geoffrey Alselin likewise in respect of 2 tofts.

Nor has Gilbert paid geld in respect of 3 houses. Nor has Peter de Valognes in respect of his house. Nor has the Countess Judith in respect of her house. Nor has Ralph Pagenel in respect of 1 house. Nor has Ralph de Bapaume in respect of his house. Nor has Ertald in respect of his house.

The house in respect of which the abbot of Peterborough has not, as they say, paid geld, Norman Crassus claims as of the king's fee, for Guthrothr his predecessor had it in pledge for 3½ marks of silver.[134]

[130] Welldon Finn, *Domesday Inquest*, 150.   [131] Exon, 2; Darlington, 'Wiltshire Geld Rolls', 196.
[132] Galbraith, *Making of Domesday Book*, 94–5.   [133] *ASC* 161–2.
[134] GDB 336b–c: *DB Lincs.*, C20–1. Although this entry is slightly misaligned with the column above, it does not seem to be postscriptal.

Within its urban context this is a direct parallel of the geld accounts of Exon.

References to non-payment of geld elsewhere in GDB and LDB are rare. A half-virgate of land was added to the manor of Eastleigh in Devon, but 'it has been concealed with the result that the king had no geld from it';[135] in Essex Ralph held a manor of 1 hide from Robert Gernon which 'has never rendered geld and did not render the last one';[136] in Gloucestershire geld was withheld from three hides in *Duntisbourne*.[137] Geld collection does not figure widely in GDB and LDB. But the incorporation of exemption data suggests that many, if not most, of the geld assessments of Domesday Book were taken from the geld inquest. In this context, it therefore seems likely that the Yorkshire Summary represents something of the substance of the inquest in Yorkshire. Demonstrably earlier than the Yorkshire folios of GDB, it reproduces the geographical form of the eighty-four carucates attached to York at the very beginning, and in the same section notes TRE tenants like the comparable summary lists of lands in Amounderness and Craven. Thereafter it is more limited in scope. Nevertheless, it seems likely that it was the source of the assessments of the Yorkshire text. Thus, for example, the order of entries in the GDB account of the inland of Northallerton is derived from an inter-lineation (probably carried over from its exemplar) in the Yorkshire Summary.[138] As the formal archetype of the GDB text, the Summary may have been abstracted from its exemplar to guide the compiler in the composition of the Yorkshire folios. But in its essentials it probably represents the business of the geld inquest in Yorkshire.

As such, its forms hint at the sources on which the geld inquests drew. The most important were clearly geld lists. Each hundred or wapentake tends to begin with the vill in which the court met, and the accounts proceed in an ordered geographical circuit; even where estates are entered as a whole and settlements appear twice in the Summary, a common villar sequence in the compound estate entries reveals underlying geographically arranged taxation lists (Table 5.4). The type is alluded to in the Huntingdonshire folios,[139] but it was not the only source. The enrolment of complete estates in the Yorkshire Summary, like Howden and Beverley which stand outside of the neat villar structure, suggests that some sort of presentment was also made by tenants-in-chief.[140] Domesday Monachorum A, the Descriptio Terrarum of Peterborough, Evesham F, and Worcester A may be examples. Domesday Monachorum A can be most closely tied into the Domesday process. A

---

[135] GDB 110b: *DB Devon*, 19,6. For the reading of *habuit* for *habet*, see 19,6 n.

[136] LDB 66b: *DB Essex*, 32,29.　　[137] GDB 166d: *DB Gloucs.*, 31,7.

[138] GDB 299a, 381a: *DB Yorks.*, 1Y2;SN,A1.　　[139] GDB 203b: *DB Hunts.*, B21.

[140] GDB 381c, 382b: *DB Yorks.*, SE,How1–11; SE,Th10–14; SE,No; SE,Mid; SE, So. At least one reference in LDB suggests that tenants-in-chief had to make claims to their lands: free men in Bircham in Norfolk were in the hands of the king 'because there was no one to claim them' (LDB 222b: *DB Norfolk*, 19,9).

TABLE 5.4. *Order of vills in the Yorkshire Summary account of the hundred of Howden*

Manor of Howden	Other manors	Lord
1. Howden		
2. Hive		
3. Owsthorpe		
4. Portington		
5. Burland		
6. Cavil		
7. Eastrington		
8. Kilpin		
9. Yokefleet		
10. Cotness		
11. Saltmarshe		
12. Laxton		
13. Skelton		
14. Barnhill		
15. Belby House	26. Belby House	King
16. Thorpe		
17. Knedlington		
18. Asselby	27. Asselby	Mortain
19. Barmby		
20. Babthorpe		
21. Brackenholme	28. Brackenholme	Tison
	34. Brackenholme	Earnwine
22. Hagthorpe	30. Hagthorpe	Tison
23. Bowthorpe		
24. Barlby	37. Barlby	King
25. Riccall	38. Riccall	Archbishop of York

Note: The place-names have been numbered consecutively as they appear in *DB Yorks.*, SE, How.

schedule of the estates of the archbishop of Canterbury, the bishop of Rochester, and the monks of Christchurch in Kent, and their assessments, it appears to have dictated the order of the entries in Domesday Monachorum B which, as a fuller Domesday-type source, was a precursor of the GDB text.[141] Domesday Monachorum A, however, has a completely different order of entries from the remaining Canterbury Domesday texts and GDB itself, and it therefore seems likely that it precedes the hundredal inquest.

In like wise, the order of entries in the other two texts deviates from that of the corresponding Domesday entries, and they may also have similar origins. The Descriptio Terrarum of Peterborough is a list of the abbey's lands

[141] Harvey, 'Domesday Book and its Predecessors', 757–8.

in Lincolnshire, which is arranged by settlements as opposed to the manors and twelve-carucate hundreds of the Lincolnshire folios. It cannot be dated precisely; a *terminus ante quem* is provided by the notice of Earl Hugh of Chester who died in 1101, and a reference to a queen could just refer to the wife of Henry I. But King William Rufus never married, and it is more likely that the reference is to William the Conqueror's queen Matilda who died in 1083. An association with the geld inquest is perhaps suggested by the Descriptio's preoccupation with geld: throughout, each entry carefully distinguishes between the presumably exempt demesne and the sokeland.[142] This concern also characterizes Worcester A, a list of the holdings of the church of Worcester in Gloucestershire. The distinction between demesne and tenanted land is only explicit in the entry relating to Westbury: the bishop held thirty-five hides and his *milites* fifteen. However, the location of the men's lands are noticed, and comparison with Domesday Book reveals that the appurtenances that are recorded in the other manors also relate to land of the same type. Only Aust is not mentioned, and its subsequent enfeoffment would seem to indicate that Worcester A is earlier than GDB.[143]

If correctly identified, these sources demonstrate that the geld audit was no mere formal exercise in accounting. Tenants-in-chief had to identify their demesnes and, by implication, justify the exemption they enjoyed on them. In the Devon folios Bishop Osbern of Exeter is recorded as doing precisely that: he produced charters to show that his church held the manor of Crediton before the reign of King Edward and after.[144] The process is not surprising. Given the intimate relationship between geld liability and title to land, any review had to be cast in terms of the inquest, with the resulting claims and counter-claims made against the backdrop of communal presentments. The presentments of shire, hundred, and vill preserved in the Domesday texts are of the type that might be expected. Many, probably most, must have emanated from the geld inquest.[145]

It seems likely, then, that the *inquisitio geldi* produced what was effectively a fully annotated geld list in which explicitly fiscal data were combined with presentments on title and tenure. Several Domesday texts exhibit such characteristics and may therefore preserve something of the records of the geld inquest. Bury A and B, lists of the demesne and enfeoffed lands of the abbey of Bury St Edmund's, provide details of hundred verdicts on the tenure of land and the carucates which were quit. Exhibiting much the same order of entries

---

[142] Roffe, 'Descriptio Terrarum', 1–16.   [143] *DB Gloucs.*, Appendix, Wo and notes.

[144] GDB 101d: *DB Devon*, 2,2. He is said to have presented his evidence 'before the king's barons [*coram baronibus regis*]'. Exon, however, reads *testimonio francigenorum*, that is, 'by witness of the Frenchmen or free men' (Exon, 117). See *DB Devon*, 2,2 n. The context is clearly the first stage of the inquest.

[145] In this context it is significant that Ely claimed lands *secundum breves regis* in IE, indicating that the claims were in documents separate from the verdict from which the scribe was extracting (*ICC* 126–7).

as the corresponding entries in LDB, they appear to be derived from a seigneurially arranged source. Bury A, however, is explicitly ordered by hundred and it is therefore likely that its ultimate source was a hundredally arranged document. Both A and B record the land that was held by free men and sokemen who acquitted the geld upon their own holdings, perhaps indicating that this information might also be recorded in the *inquisitio geldi*. In Huntingdonshire the liability of villagers and sokemen was noted 'in the records'.[146] Elsewhere in Domesday Book the enumeration of the peasantry is often separately recorded; in LDB, for example, they follow the assessment to the geld. It might therefore be suspected that such details were a matter of official rather than seigneurial record.

Domesday Monachorum B and the Excerpta of St Augustine's, Canterbury, are similar in form, being derived from hundredally arranged sources, but additionally record the value of estates in 1066, when acquired, and in 1086. This information too may have been the subject of official interest as an index of royal income. Values were certainly a matter of common knowledge. There are three references to the presentment of data by the shire and hundred in Domesday Book.[147] A further eight by Englishmen, Frenchmen, or English and Frenchmen could refer to presentments by the vill, hundred or shire,[148] while one to 'the men' is presumably a reference to a seigneurial source.[149] This last is instructive. The evidence of the men is opposed to the recorded value and it would therefore suggest that there was an input from both shrieval and seigneurial sources. What evidence Domesday affords indicates that values were not entirely the privileged data of estate management. That they were in some sense public is inherently likely. Values are consistently given for 1066 and when the estate was acquired, and yet these were statistics that tenants-in-chief cannot regularly have been in a position to know. They can only have been a matter of official record or communal presentment or both. The reason is sometimes transparent. As has been seen,[150] values represent soke dues and were in origin probably shares of a royal farm. Where estates, like those in the soke of *Roteland*, were not held with sake and soke the render was made to the king. Otherwise, the lord received the king's share. But the earl, in the north at least, retained his right to the third penny, and this could confer on him a share of the farm. Thus, the earl had the third penny of the customs of the soke of Clifton in Nottinghamshire, while the value of Osmaston by Derby in Derbyshire was divided between the king and Henry de Ferrers (as the successor to the dues of the earl).[151] Whether a portion of the value of an estate was always reserved to the earl (or the king

[146] GDB 203b: *DB Hunts.*, B21.
[147] LDB 15b: *DB Essex*, 7,1; GDB 166c: *DB Gloucs.*, 28,7; LDB 343a: *DB Suffolk*, 7,121.
[148] LDB 18a, 38b: *DB Essex*, 9,7.23,2; GDB 2c, 65a–b, 70b: *DB Kent*, 1,1; *DB Wilts.*, 1,10–12.26,5.
[149] GDB 66c: *DB Wilts.*, 7,1.   [150] Above, pp. 41–2.
[151] GDB 280c, 275d: *DB Notts.*, S6; *DB Derby.*, 6,88.

where no earl was appointed after the Conquest) is unclear, but it is evident that the information was a legitimate item of interest to the crown.

Nevertheless, neither Bury A, Bury B, Domesday Monachorum B, nor the Excerpta of St Augustine's, Canterbury, can be identified with certainty as an actual product of the geld inquest. Although all claim, implicitly or explicitly, to be extracts from their sources, the possibility remains that they are in fact abstracts. Indeed, Domesday Monachorum B occasionally hints at a more expansive exemplar in its references to mills and the like.[152] However, the two texts that approximate most closely to the suggested form of the geld inquest records provide independent corroboration of the existence of the type. Abingdon A, a schedule of the lands of Abingdon Abbey in Berkshire, details manors and appurtenances, their assessments, and the names of tenants who held them. Despite its TRE assessments, it is very close in diplomatic, form, and content to the corresponding GDB entries, and is therefore unlikely to be very much earlier. Its overt concern is with the demesne and tenanted lands of Abingdon and their respective assessments. There is only one record of TRE tenants and no presentments, but it was abstracted from a hundredally arranged source which is explicitly contrasted with GDB, 'another book in the king's treasury'. The geographical element in the Crowland Domesday is again said to be derived from hundred rolls kept with Domesday Book, and it appears to have included all details of tenure, assessment, hundredal presentments, and possibly value.

The Estates of the Tenants-in-Chief

The second forum of the Domesday inquest before the commissioners in regional session is represented by the Lincolnshire section of the *Roteland* Domesday. Here there is no notice of the king's land or dues. Only the estates of the tenants-in-chief are duplicated, and the accounts are fully integrated into their respective breves. It would therefore seem that it was the economic resources of estates that was the subject. For Round, as for most of the early students of Domesday Book, it was axiomatic that the data, as with every item of information found in GDB and LDB, was presented by local juries in open court sessions.[153] During the early years of the twentieth century this view was reinforced by research into the operation of the general eyre in the thirteenth century. There the procedure was seemingly transparent. The numerous juries jostled and crowded each other outside the hall of pleas, while the representatives of the vill and individuals attempted to catch their eye in order to ensure that their complaints were duly and correctly enrolled. At

---

[152] It must be noted, however, that mills are often separately valued in GDB and LDB, and they may therefore have been considered discrete units of tenure. Mill soke is of relevance in this connection.

[153] Round, *Feudal England*, 1–27.

the appointed hour each jury was called before the justices, and the foreman, quaking with fear, gave its replies to the articles put to it. The scribe noted everything down, and when the justices were satisfied, the jurors attested the truth of their verdict by appending their seals to the roll.[154] The comparison is, however, misleading. The eyre was a largely formal process in which the presentments of the community were checked against records of the royal officials in order to levy amercements when discrepancies were detected. The inquest, by contrast, was an investigative process.[155] Galbraith was the first to grasp the significance of the distinction. He recognized that local juries were hardly qualified to pronounce on the essentially privileged details of estate structure and management. He believed that the tenants-in-chief made returns in what he termed 'backroom sessions'.[156]

The presentments recorded in the Domesday texts are consistent with this perception. Although it must be allowed that they are a selection dictated by the purpose of GDB and LDB, it is significant that no jury appears to have pronounced on the stocking of seigneurial estates.[157] A number of references confirm that the information was normally provided by the tenant-in-chief or his agents. In the Herefordshire folios it is recorded that the bishop of Hereford's men rendered no account (*rationem*) of thirty-three hides of land;[158] in Gloucestershire Earl Hugh is said to have had two manors in Longtree Hundred, but no one had made an account of them and they were valued by the Shire at £8, while in Swinehead Hundred there was no one to answer for the manor of Roger son of Ralph;[159] in Sussex there was no account of the count of Mortain's manor of Hankham;[160] in Suffolk Count Robert of Mortain's servant Nigel had died and there was therefore no one to answer for eleven acres of land in Stow Hundred.[161] All these entries exhibit the salient details of assessment to the geld and TRE holder, but otherwise have a minimal or non-existent account of the manorial appurtenances.

The process required close co-operation between tenant-in-chief and commissioner. Variations in the account of estate structure and resources from circuit to circuit in GDB and LDB are probably a function of the commissioners' understanding of what was required. Common to all, however, is some record of the ploughs on the estate, both those of the lord and of his tenants, of the villagers who worked them, and the issues of the estate (if not derived

---

[154] Bolland, *The General Eyre*, 48–54; Cam, *Studies in the Hundred Rolls*, 15, 30, 127–38; Cam, *The Hundred and the Hundred Rolls*, 39–46.

[155] Roffe, 'Hundred Rolls and their Antecedents', 179–87.

[156] Galbraith, *Making of Domesday Book*, 82.

[157] In Cambridgeshire a jury reported that Aubrey de Vere had appropriated land in Abington in the king's despite and Picot the sheriff, some three years earlier according to ICC, adjudged it against him. Of the stock which he took from it, Aubrey still kept 380 sheep and one plough at the time of the inquest (*ICC* 32; GDB 190a: *DB Cambs.*, 1,16). This, however, is a presentment of misappropriation rather than of stock *per se*.

[158] GDB 182b: *DB Hereford.*, 2,57.   [159] GDB 166c, 170b: *DB Gloucs.*, 28,7.75,2.

[160] GDB 22b: *DB Sussex*, 10,82.   [161] LDB 291b: *DB Suffolk*, 2,8.

from the geld inquest). It was these items of information which constituted the main concern of the commissioners. A day and a time was probably appointed for each tenant-in-chief to make his presentment. Thus, in the Norfolk folios Robert Malet speaks of the day on which he was enrolled (*inbreviatus*).[162] It is likely that every lord was required to make a personal appearance at some point in the proceedings. But the sheer volume of data must suggest that the detail of their estates was presented in written form. Archbishop Lanfranc communicated with 'S' about his estates in East Anglia by letter; the matters he addressed were details of tenure in the widest sense.[163] Four further texts may represent something of the presentments made to the commissioners. Bury C outlines the lands and renders of the free men of Bury St Edmund's and, although in aggregate the dues recorded may have been in the public domain, the details of the men and tenements that rendered them can only have emanated from the abbey. However, since much of it is unique, it cannot be directly related to the Domesday inquest. Ely A and B, lists of estates, tenants, and their ploughs of Ely Abbey, are of a similarly privileged character and may also have been drawn up at this point in the proceedings. But again they cannot be precisely placed; although unequivocally related to the Domesday process, they cannot be proved beyond doubt to pre-date GDB. Bath A can make the best claim to emanate from the seigneurial-report stage of the inquiry. It is a full, Domesday-like account of the abbey's estates, but is perceptibly earlier than Exon.

Throughout GDB and LDB vestiges of the presentments are probably to be found in modifications to standard forms.[164] The description of the Lincolnshire lands of the bishop of Lincoln starts with its principal demesne manor of Stow St Mary, where it should have commenced with Welton by Lincoln had it observed the wapentake sequence of the county.[165] The bishop's presentment might naturally begin with his main estates, and it may here therefore have dictated the order of the text. Likewise, the separation of the demesne from the tenanted lands of Peterborough Abbey within the common hundredal sequences of the Huntingdonshire, Leicestershire, Lincolnshire, and Northamptonshire folios is probably also a function of the information the abbot or his bailiffs gave to the commissioners.[166] Sometimes presentments may have completely superseded the norms. The GDB account

---

[162] LDB 276b: *DB Norfolk*, 66, 61.

[163] *Letters of Lanfranc*, no. 56; Barlow, 'Domesday Book: A Letter of Lanfranc', 284–9.

[164] Marginalia, such as *f, n, f.r., n.f.r, fd.* etc, have been interpreted as referring to returns or their absence (*VCH Norfolk*, ii. 2; Galbraith, *Making of Domesday Book*, 82). However, there seems to be no consistency in the use of the marks, and it is likely that there is no one meaning (Welldon Finn, *Domesday Inquest*, 86–8; Thorn, 'Marginal Notes and Signs in Domesday Book', 129–31).

[165] GDB 344a: *DB Lincs.*, 7,1;8.

[166] GDB 205b, 231b, 345c–346b, 221b–222a: *DB Hunts.*, 8; *DB Leics.*, 5; *DB Lincs.*, 8; *DB Northants.*, 6. The form is occasionally found in Circuit IV (see below, p. 210), but is not a characteristic of Circuit VI.

of Glastonbury Abbey's lands in Somerset is arranged by location, starting with Glastonbury and the estates in its vicinity, but does not observe the normal hundredal sequence of the Somerset text. Its form presumably reflects the administrative structures of the abbey and must therefore be derived from the abbot's presentment.[167] The bishop of Worcester's Worcestershire breve clearly had a similar origin.[168] Its diplomatic is entirely different from that of the rest of the county and, anomalously, it is arranged by manor. Above all, its place-name forms exhibit an orthography that suggests an intimate knowledge of English unparalleled elsewhere.[169] Although the account is entered in GDB by the main scribe, he was clearly copying from a document drafted by an official of the church.

These peculiarities, however, are by far the exception. The lands of tenants-in-chief in GDB and LDB are entered in a common hundredal sequence. The implication must be that their presentments were at some stage correlated with, and organized by, official records. Hitherto Evesham A has been cited as proof that the presentments of hundred and shire of LDB and GDB were solicited precisely for the purpose of validation.[170] The document is a late-twelfth-century abstract of a survey of Worcestershire estates. It is arranged by hundred and possibly vill, but is fragmentary being confined to the hundreds of Esch, Fishborough, Pershore, and part of Came. Entries typically record the place, assessment to the geld, and value; plough teams are recorded more spasmodically, as are the names of subtenants, while a handful of entries give extensive accounts of appurtenances that are not paralleled in GDB. The order of entries is substantially the same as that of GDB except in the hundred of Esch and in Westminster Abbey's two hundreds of Pershore. In the former the lands of each tenant-in-chief have been brought together, but their order of appearance deviates from that of GDB, while in the latter demesne estates are listed first, followed by partly enfeoffed vills, and then wholly enfeoffed vills where GDB makes no distinction. From these discrepancies the editor of the text concludes that Evesham A is earlier than GDB, and probably represents a stage in which full seigneurial returns were ordered by hundred before they were confirmed in the hundredal inquiry.[171]

That the presentments of the tenants-in-chief were tried before the communal representatives of the shire is clear. In ICC the jurors of each hundred are explicitly said to have presented the composite verdicts which follow the record of their names. Hemming, writing in the late eleventh century,

---

[167] GDB 90a–91a: *DB Somerset*, 8; Welldon Finn, *Domesday Inquest*, 82.

[168] GDB 172c–174b: *DB Worcs.*, 2.

[169] Sawyer, 'Original Returns', 183; Feilitzen, *Pre-Conquest Personal Names*, 7.

[170] Sawyer, 'Evesham A', 8–10; Clarke, 'DB Satellites', 60–1. Sawyer and Clarke both consider that Evesham A is an accurate copy of its exemplar and they thus assume that it provides an indication of the varying types of information that tenants-in-chief returned.

[171] Sawyer, 'Evesham A', 7–10.

describes the session in Worcestershire. After an account of the liberties of the church and the duties of its tenants, he goes on:

The whole shire of Worcester confirmed this evidence through a sworn oath, with the exhortation and encouragement of the most holy and wise father, lord Bishop Wulfstan, in the time of the elder King William, before the same King's leading men, that is Bishop Remigius of Lincoln, Earl Walter Giffard, Henry of Ferrers, and Adam, brother of Eudo the king's steward. They had been sent by the king himself to seek out and set down in writing the possessions and customs, both of the king and of his leading men, in this province and in several others, at the time when the said king had (details of) the whole of England set down in writing.[172]

The oath of the whole shire should perhaps be here understood as the witness of all the hundreds instead of, or in addition to, that of the shire court. In the later Middle Ages it was common for composite verdicts to be formally sealed by the hundred juries alone; it was they who were the legal voice of the community regardless of whether the information that they presented had been furnished by the knights of the shire, villagers, or individuals.[173] The procedure was largely formal, and it is perhaps unsurprising that it has left few traces in the surviving Domesday documents.

    These verdicts were the culmination of the sessions before the commissioners. There are indications that the presentments of the tenants-in-chief were already hundredally arranged in what was to become substantially the GDB order before they were witnessed by the shire. The evidence of Evesham A is scant and at best equivocal. That the exemplar of the text emanates from an early stage in the Domesday process is clear. It cannot have been abbreviated from GDB with the addition of additional material, as Round suggested, since abstraction using the Domesday rubrication would not produce the order of the text, and the additional material is similar to that found in Exon which was subsequently edited out to produce GDB. However, Evesham A is so fragmentary that it is difficult to draw firm conclusions as to its place in the Domesday process. Nevertheless, the discrepancies cited are as much indicative of the hundredal inquest as of its preliminaries. The disjunction in ordering in Esch Hundred is less real than apparent. The sequence of lords is immaterial to the analysis, for even in GDB there are discrepancies between the list of tenants-in-chief at the start of county Domesdays and the chapters which follow, and the GDB reorganization of the lands of Evesham Abbey and the bishop of Worcester (two of only three lords with more than one estate in the hundred) seems to be largely a matter of grouping appurtenance with *caput*, a process suggestive of subsequent seigneurial presentments. Likewise, the separation of demesne and enfeoffed lands in the two hundreds of Pershore

---

[172] *Hemingi Chartularium*, 287–8. Translation from *DB Worcs.*, Appendix V, Worcs. F.
[173] Roffe, 'Hundred Rolls and their Antecedents', 179–87; Roffe, *Stamford in the Thirteenth Century*, 12–19.

is redolent of the concerns of the *inquisitio geldi*, as is the naming of subtenants who paid the geld in preference to the tenants-in-chief.[174]

Evesham A affords no compelling reason for supposing that the common hundredal sequences of the Domesday texts are secondary to the seigneurial presentments. Bishop Robert of Hereford clearly conceived of the local survey as antedating the sessions of the commissioners sent in to vouchsafe their veracity, and indeed the *terra regis* surveyed at that time usually exhibits the sequences of the rest of the text.[175] The influence of the *inquisitio geldi* on the presentments of tenants-in-chief is most palpably evident in the processes of GDB entry formation.[176] Entry formation was simple in areas of the country in which manor and vill were coterminous; there was, as a rule, one entry per holding. In areas of more complex estate structures, by contrast, it was determined by the structure of local government; in the absence of distinguishing features of a parcel of land, such as enfeoffment, the number of entries was determined by the number of vills, that is, geld-paying units, into which the manor extended. In a tributary society it is sometimes difficult to determine what constituted units of estate management. It seems clear, however, that they did not always correspond with these largely artificial manors in GDB. The Lincolnshire estates of Peterborough Abbey illustrate the point. In GDB the demesne and enfeoffed estates are described separately, but each exhibits the standard wapentake sequence of the Lincolnshire text. Appurtenant inlands and sokelands are grouped with their respective manorial *capita*, and where local twelve-carucate hundreds (the vill of the Northern Danelaw) can be reconstructed, it is evident that the entries were formulated in accordance with them. The manor of *Adewelle* (later known as Careby), for example, is entered in three entries corresponding to the three hundreds of *Bredestorp*, Witham, and Little Bytham.[177] In the Descriptio Terrarum of Peterborough Abbey, however, a completely different structure is found. Identified as probably a presentment to the *inquisitio geldi*, it is clearly a Peterborough document and its preoccupations are the settlement.[178] There are no references to the manors of GDB and place-names occur that are not found therein. Peterborough Abbey saw its estates in different terms from the compiler of GDB.

This perception and representation of management units is not entirely unknown in GDB. The large sokes of Nottinghamshire and Derbyshire were anciently divided into duodecimal groups of settlements, and where this structure survived into the late eleventh century they are recorded in GDB.

---

[174] Roffe, 'Yorkshire Summary', 258 n.

[175] Sawyer ('Original Returns', 182 and note) counted eleven counties, but, with the completion of the Phillimore edition of the text, in which the hundreds of 1086 have been systematically reconstructed and omitted rubrics restored in the text, it can be seen that the coincidence of order is general and significant.

[176] Roffe, 'Place-Naming in Domesday Book', 47–60.

[177] Ibid. 51–2.   [178] Roffe, 'Descriptio Terrarum', 5.

Southwell, for example, was granted to the archbishop of York in 956 with its twelve berewicks, and its structure is represented in much the same terms in 1086.[179] But commonly the account of estates was forced into the strait-jacket of geld liability. Ploughs, population figures, and the details of man-orial resources are all given in units that must often have deviated from those used in estate management. The implication must be that tenants-in-chief generally made their presentments on the basis of schedules drawn from the *inquisitio geldi* which were supplied to them by the officers of the shire or, perhaps more likely, the Domesday commissioners.[180]

The Somerset and Worcestershire breves of the abbot of Glastonbury and the bishop of Worcester indicate that this procedure was not universal. It is significant, however, that in Bath A, the text most likely to represent evidence presented by a tenant-in-chief, the order of entries within hundreds conforms to that of Exon. The issuing of a schedule of lands requesting a full account was probably the norm. Four documents in the Domesday canon may rep-resent examples. Ely C and Evesham P have already been identified as discrete, seigneurially arranged documents from an early stage in the Domesday process. Evesham K appears to be a series of such documents relating to the seventy-eight tenants-in-chief in Gloucestershire. It lists place-name and assess-ment, and above each entry the hundred in which the estate was situated is noted. The order of entries is very close to that of GDB, although irregularit-ies indicate some revision, but the order of fiefs deviates considerably. The Kentish Assessment List is of the same form. It is a schedule of estates in Kent and their assessments, again arranged by tenant-in-chief but in an order other than that of GDB. All four documents would have produced schedules for each tenant-in-chief which would have ordered seigneurial presentments and thereby account for the hundredal sequence of the relevant sections of GDB. Evesham K and the Kentish Assessment List, however, are both com-posite documents and, including details of the king's demesne, they may have been derived most immediately from a later stage in the Domesday process.

---

[179] S659; GDB 283a: *DB Notts.*, 5,1; Roffe, 'Introduction to the Derbyshire Domesday', 8–14; Roffe, 'Place-Naming in Domesday Book', 52–3.

[180] The process probably accounts for a number of anomalies in GDB and LDB. Numerous name forms are found for almost every hundred in the country. To take but one example Clackclose Hundred in Norfolk variously appears as *Clachelosa*, *Claclelosa*, *Clacheslosa*, and *Clakeslosa*. It is unlikely that such variations in orthography would have occurred if verdicts had been checked against a single source.

6

Commissioners and the Limits of
Their Commission

As an instrument of government the inquest was an extraordinary enterprise. Although it might avail itself of the usual processes and personnel of
central and local government, it was not bound by normal procedures. The
commissioners were the king's representative, his *legati* or *barones*, and were
free within the bounds that the commission assigned them to expedite the
business in hand. Like justices in eyre, they were empowered to call all
manner of witness before them. They were no mere chairmen presiding
over the business of others. They were the occasion and the instrument of
definition and were therefore both conduit and agent. Through them the
inchoate was realized. The commissioners were a vital element in the process that was set in train in 1085. Their actions were various.

In the later Middle Ages the inquest was often preceded by a purge of local
government; in both 1258 and 1274/5 the removal of the incumbent sheriffs
was a preliminary to major inquiries into their activities. The clearing of the
ground in this way facilitated the collection of evidence. Nevertheless, commissioners probably always took further precautions to ensure that witness
was not suborned or intimidated. In 1198 villeins who concealed the truth were
to forfeit their best ox to their lord and pay to the king the amount that he
would thereby have lost should they conceal the number of plough teams in
each vill, while free men were to be in mercy.[1] Conversely, juries could expect
protection from the commissioners. In 1275 the juries of Elloe and Skirbeck
Wapentakes petitioned the king through William de St Omer and Warin de
Chaucombe to seek a remedy against the bailiffs of the wapentakes who dis-
trained them because of the verdict they gave.[2] In Yorkshire commissioners
themselves even came under threat of violence:

Gilbert de Clifton, bailiff of the wapentake of Staincliffe, used the most shameful words
against William de Chatterton, justice assigned to take these inquests, because he,
William, had told the jurors of the countryside fearlessly to tell the whole truth about
the bailiffs of the earl of Lincoln. Gilbert said that if he had been present when this
announcement was made he would have pulled the justice by his feet, and that before

---

[1] *Chronica Rogeri de Houedene*, iv. 47.   [2] *Rotuli Hundredorum*, i. 276b, 308b.

half a year was up the justice would be wishing that he had lost all his lands rather than be a commissioner.[3]

Commissioners took action to counter threats that undermined the whole business of the inquiry.

More subtle was their intervention in the process of eliciting evidence. In theory, their task was simple: they merely had to pose the questions asked in the articles and record the answers that were given. In practice, however, circumstances dictated that they interpreted the information required. The *capitula* of inquiry were generalized and they had to be fitted to the local peculiarities of time and space. It was the discretion of the commissioners that ensured that it was the spirit rather than the letter of the inquest that prevailed. Thus, in 1255 each panel of commissioners, aware of the need to determine the issues of the shire from regalia, seem to have asked the questions that seemed appropriate rather than follow any standard list beyond a core of key matters.[4] Again in 1274/5 there were regularly thirty-nine *capitula*, but in the northern circuits the commissioners took it upon themselves to introduce a further twelve relating to matters of local interest.[5] Much of the business of data collection was delegated to local officials and the community of the hundred and shire, but resulting presentments were scrutinized by the commissioners and the jurors were subject to searching cross-examination where the relevant detail was lacking or more explication was desirable. Many of the hundred rolls are annotated with the comments and information that they elicited.

Executive action did not normally extend further. Appearances, however, could be deceptive. According to Roger of Hoveden, commissioners in 1198 estimated a ploughland at 100 acres, and from this perspective the calculation of the carucage that resulted has every appearance of being the executive action of a bureaucracy with only minimal regard for the community of the shire.[6] And yet in reality they were merely engaged on the enumeration of working ploughs (*carucarum wannagia*), as the subsequent levying of the tax on the same confirms.[7] The 100-acre equation was probably no more than an estimate where more precise information was absent or unavailable. Nevertheless, the effect of the inquest was to institute a new assessment on land based upon the plough. The business of the inquest was the collection of evidence, not judgement. But at the same time the very writing down of uncontested fact accorded data an imperative that was often tantamount to executive action.

It is in this context that the role of the Domesday commissioners must be viewed. Although no commission survives for the Domesday inquest, the

---

[3] *Rotuli Hundredorum*, i. 111b.   [4] Roffe, 'The Hundred Rolls of 1255', 201–10.
[5] Cam, *The Hundred and the Hundred Rolls*, 248–57.
[6] Harvey, 'Taxation and the Ploughland in Domesday Book', 102–3.
[7] *Radulphi de Coggeshall Chronicon Anglicanum*, 101.

commissioners were clearly vested with extensive powers and responsibilities in 1086. There is no sign of a wholesale change of local government personnel. Some predatory royal officials were inevitably frog-marched into the limelight by the processes of the inquest. Eustace of Huntingdon, Picot of Cambridge, and Urse de Abitot, sheriff of Worcester, are egregious examples of ministers who had used their office to further their own interests.[8] The Domesday records lay bare the extent of their predations, but no special action seems to have been taken against them before or during the inquest. Collectors of geld, by contrast, were apparently subject to closer scrutiny. Accounts were audited and, where shortcomings were identified, appropriate action was taken.[9] In the Dorset hundreds of Uggescombe and Eggardon collectors were obliged to furnish sureties to put matters right, while the retention of monies in Kinwardstone Hundred in Wiltshire led to the culprits being put in mercy.[10]

The Domesday corpus affords few details of the discipline that the commissioners brought to the inquest. Problems there must have been aplenty. To what extent juries were nobbled is impossible to determine. As the men of powerful tenants-in-chief, many jurors must have been open to influence.[11] There is, though, no record of complaints of intimidation. By and large, all concerned seem to have co-operated with the king's officers and commissioners. It is reported from time to time that no account was made of land, but the full details of almost every tenement attest a more or less willing participation in the process.

The commissioners' active involvement in the Domesday process is more clearly seen in the collection of data. The regional differences in the information recorded reveal at once the fingerprints of individuals striving to make sense of the commission entrusted to them and the active management of the witnesses to provide the evidence that they deemed essential. In two areas their intervention has been seen to go further than the merely interpretative. It is the role of the commissioners in the assessment of ploughlands and the adjudication of disputes that is the subject of this chapter.

The Ploughland

Of all the Domesday data the ploughland is the most difficult of interpretation and the most controversial. The protagonists have divided into two broad camps. The natural interpretation of the phrase 'land for n ploughs' and its variants is that it refers to land pure and simple, and this position has been taken by what can be termed the realists. Historiographically, they can be classified as realists past, present, and future. Maitland (in part, at least) exemplifies the first, arguing from the Leicestershire folios and LDB that ploughlands

---

[8] Abels, 'Sheriffs, Lord-seeking and the Norman Settlement', 33.
[9] Welldon Finn, *Liber Exoniensis*, 100–2.   [10] Exon, 17^v, 18, 9^v, 16.
[11] Fleming, *Domesday Book and the Law*, 17–28.

relate to the number of ploughs in 1066,[12] while the last is represented by Vinogradoff who, latching on to the phrase z *caruce possunt esse*, believed that they refer to the potential for assarting.[13] Both positions are now no longer espoused. Ploughlands are expressed in the present tense, and to relate them to any other period introduces insuperable problems of interpretation. The realist position is now occupied by those who believe in the real presence. For Dr John Moore, and most recently Dr Nicholas Higham, ploughlands represent the arable that was worked in 1086.

Opposing them are the nominalists. They point to the patent artificiality of many ploughland figures and contend that they must therefore be fiscal units. The camp is again divided, here into two groups of nominalists past and nominalists present. Round was the first to assign ploughlands to the past.[14] He noticed that there was a constant ratio between hides and ploughlands throughout much of Northamptonshire, and since the latter were larger, he argued that they must be an ancient geld assessment preceding that of 1086. The idea was subsequently developed by Dr Cyril Hart, who attributed them to the distant past of the Danish settlement and English reconquest of the southern Danelaw.[15] Both views have been criticized in much the same terms as the comparable realist position, and belief in the nominal presence now leads the camp. Stenton was the first to articulate the argument,[16] but it has been most comprehensively advanced by Harvey,[17] for whom the ploughland figures represent a fiscal assessment designed to broaden the base of taxation in 1086.

The most effective criticism of the realist position has focused on the phenomenon of overstocking. Where ploughlands exceed the number of recorded ploughs of the demesne and tenanted land there are no obstacles to a realist interpretation; it would merely indicate the unsurprising fact that the available land was not fully exploited. But where recorded ploughs exceed ploughlands difficulties arise. A realist view must suppose that more ploughs were being maintained than there was land for them to plough. Given that the plough team was the most expensive item of stock, which, by its nature, had to be fed through the winter, the position seems untenable. Higham has countered that overstocking occurs precisely in those areas where dispersed settlement patterns would suggest that the exploitation of the arable was far from efficient. He concludes that the ploughland figures were designed to point

---

[12] Maitland, *Domesday Book and Beyond*, 482–513. Maitland, of course, believed that there was a great deal of estimation based upon whatever figures were available.

[13] Vinogradoff, *English Society in the Eleventh Century*, 153–74.

[14] Round, 'Hidation of Northamptonshire', 83; *VCH Northants.*, i. 266.

[15] Hart, *Hidation of Northamptonshire*, 28.

[16] Stenton, 'Domesday Survey', *VCH Notts.*, 211–13; Stenton, 'Introduction', *Lincolnshire Domesday*, pp. xv–xix.

[17] Harvey, 'Domesday Book and Anglo-Norman Governance', 186–9; Harvey, 'Taxation and the Ploughland in Domesday Book', 86–103.

to inefficiencies of this kind and prompt a more rational exploitation of the land.[18] Nevertheless, this defence, elegant as it is, is more the stuff of eighteenth-century enlightenment than medieval inquests, Farmer George rather than Farmer William. Eleventh-century government had neither the interest nor the competence to advise on agricultural practice, let alone conduct an evaluation of farming methods.

Conversely, the nominalists have been criticized in their turn. The Anglo-Saxon Chronicle and Robert of Hereford, along with numerous twelfth-century writers, have been cited in evidence of the connection of the Domesday inquest with excessive taxation, but this hardly proves that a new assessment was levied. Suspiciously, there is no unambiguous trace of the ploughland in large parts of many counties, notably Gloucestershire, Worcestershire, and Herefordshire, and it is apparently completely absent from Norfolk, Suffolk, and Essex and the north-west.[19] Furthermore, there are no vestiges of a reassessment in twelfth-century sources.[20] The Northamptonshire, Leicestershire, and Lindsey Surveys all use the Domesday geld assessments, as do the early monastic terriers. There is precious little tangible evidence of a reassessment in 1086.

Neither realist nor nominalist, then, provides a wholly convincing explanation of the ploughland. In fact, the dichotomy is probably misconceived. There seems no doubt that the datum of the ploughland was 1086, and, moreover, as far as the lands of the tenants-in-chief are concerned, late in the proceedings. Ploughlands are recorded in the *terra regis* sections of Exon and in reference to the same land in the geld accounts. However, they appear in none of the other documents that have been tentatively identified with the geld inquest and are found in only one schedule of the lands of tenants-in-chief, Burton B, which is of doubtful origin.[21] An identity as a pre-Domesday fiscal assessment is, therefore, unlikely. In Exon and ICC, by contrast, it occurs as a matter of course, but indubitably its earliest appearance in a seigneurial context in the surviving records is in Bath A. If correctly identified as a seigneurial presentment, this document provides compelling evidence that the ploughland was an item of information provided, or that could be provided, by the tenant-in-chief. GDB hints at a similar origin. In the Leicestershire folios the statement of ploughing potential is variable, but the distribution of forms is largely by breve. Thus, in nos. 4, 5, 7, 13, 21–3, 25, and 41 the usual *terra z carucis* is employed, while there is no record of ploughlands in nos. 1, 2, 8, and 43 and the number of TRE ploughs is seemingly substituted in 11, 12,

[18] Higham, 'Settlement, Land Use and Domesday Ploughlands', 33–43.

[19] Welldon Finn, *Domesday Inquest*, 127.   [20] Green, 'Last Century of Danegeld', 243–4.

[21] A pre-Domesday date has been urged by its editor, but there is little evidence to support such a contention. The document styles itself *Scriptura sicut continetur in libro regis*. Moreover, ploughlands are recorded in the form 'terra *n* carucis' which, in the north at least, was developed in the course of composition of GDB itself. Burton B would therefore seem to be an abstract from GDB; it can probably be associated with the survey of 1114 with which it is enrolled (Walmsley, 'Another Domesday Text', 115–19).

14, 29, 30–40, 42, and 44 in the form *TRE erant ibi* z *caruce* or *ibi* z *caruce fuerunt*. Many lords, it seems, had failed to provide the data. The ploughland was evidently an item of information that was primarily related to the estate and its management.

It was, moreover, an item of information that the tenant-in-chief understood as land. The practice of measuring land in terms of the ploughs that tilled it was probably a common practice. In the first Burton Abbey survey compiled in 1114 (Burton Survey B), inland is consistently measured in such terms.[22] The formula employed, with minor variations here and there, is 'there is as much inland where three ploughs can be; now there are two ploughs there [*tantum inlande ubi possunt esse aratra iii*].' Likewise, Ramsey Abbey measured its demesne in comparable terms in its early-twelfth-century terrier. At Elsworth in Cambridgeshire, for example, there were said to be 'three carucates of land in demesne [*tres carucatae terrae*]'.[23] The same formula is used of its other demesnes or the number of teams is simply stated. In both surveys the context is seemingly agricultural. In the Burton Abbey estates ploughs do not always equate with ploughlands, but the deficiency is made up by inland held by *censarii*. In Stretton, for example, there were three ploughlands and two ploughs in demesne, but a further eight bovates of inland were held by Ulnod, Edric, and Steinchete who were rent-payers.[24] Typically, the statement of ploughlands and ploughs is followed by a record of the demesne stock before the yardlands of the tenants are described. There is nothing to suggest that the ploughland of the early twelfth century was a specifically fiscal unit.

Whether the Burton formula echoes Domesday usage is impossible to determine. Ploughlands are expressed in similar terms in Exon and sporadically throughout GDB, but there are few comparable statistics in the two accounts of the lands of Burton Abbey: only in Okeover is the warland assessed in ploughlands in the Burton Survey, and there the land for two ploughs may equate with the two ploughlands of the Staffordshire Domesday.[25] However, demesne is measured in directly comparable terms in the GDB account of Hurstingstone Hundred in Huntingdonshire. The Bluntisham entry is typical: 'Manor. In Bluntisham the abbot of Ely had 6½ hides to the geld. Land for 8 ploughs, and, apart from these hides, [he had] land in demesne for 2 ploughs [*M. In Bluntesham habuit abbas de Ely vi hidas et dimidiam ad geldum. Terra viii carucis et exceptis his hidis, in dominio terram ii carucis*].'[26] Here the point of reference is 1066, but the context is the same. In Hurstingstone Hundred the demesne was quit of geld and ploughing capacity was a measure of extent.[27] In the Welsh Marches the ploughland or carucate is similarly used of land that had

[22] 'Burton Surveys', 209–47.   [23] *Cartularium Monasterii de Rameseia*, iii. 248.
[24] 'Burton Surveys', 217–8.   [25] GDB 247c: *DB Staffs.*, 4,8.
[26] GDB 204a: *DB Hunts.*, 4,2. The editor appears to have read 'land' as a nominative. There is, in fact, a suspension mark over the final 'a' both here and elsewhere in the Huntingdonshire folios where the phrase occurs. 'He had' must be understood since this is the reading in IE (*ICC* 166).
[27] GDB 203b: *DB Hunts.*, B21. IE shows that the GDB scribe substituted *terram ii carucis* for *ipse abbas habuit ii carucas exceptis predictis hidis* (*ICC* 167).

never been hidated.[28] Thus, Clifford Castle 'is in the kingdom of England and does not belong to any hundred or customary due', and in consequence its land is measured in ploughlands: there was land for three ploughs, although there was only one there.[29] In the absence of an alternative, it was used of newly acquired lands. In much of Atiscross Hundred in North Wales the plough was the only measure of land, and in entry after entry the reality of the admeasurement is emphasized by the statement that the ploughs were actually there. In Whitford and Bychton, for example, it is recorded that 'there is land for 1 plough. It is there with 2 villagers and 12 male and female slaves [*In Widford et Putecain est terra i caruca. Ibi est cum ii villanis et xii inter servos et ancillas*]'.[30] The implications are clear: as in the twelfth century, the ploughland was a non-fiscal measure of land.

The Huntingdonshire demesne formula is rare. In all but one manor[31] in Hurstingstone Hundred and in the odd entry in Toseland[32] there was land outside that assessed to the geld, but elsewhere there is notice of only a handful of parcels of demesne measured in ploughlands, in Buckinghamshire, Northamptonshire, Oxfordshire, Dorset, and possibly Rutland.[33] Land in demesne, of course, is a commonplace, occurring in just about every entry in GDB outside the northern county folios. But such was evidently geldable land. In Huntingdonshire beyond Hurstingstone Hundred the fact is frequently made explicit. In Spaldwick in Leightonstone Hundred, to take an example that follows the Bluntisham entry quoted above, it is stated that: 'In Spaldwick the abbot of Ely had 15 hides to the geld. Land for 15 ploughs. There is now in demesne 4 ploughs on 5 hides of this land [*M. In Spalduice habuit abbas de Ely xv hidas ad geldum. Terra xv carucis. Ibi nunc in dominio iiii caruce in v hidis istius terre*].'[34] Similar information is given in the Wiltshire and Dorset folios and it is found throughout Exon from which Circuit II was abbreviated, where the hides in demesne and those of the peasantry regularly add up to the total for which the estate defended itself. Elsewhere it is only sporadic. The implication is nevertheless clear. Where GDB states that a tenant-in-chief holds x and it defends itself for y hides, land for z ploughs, in demesne d ploughs, that demesne is to be understood to be part of the geldable land.[35]

---

[28] Lewis, 'Introduction to the Herefordshire Domesday', 5.

[29] GDB 183b: *DB Hereford.*, 8,1.   [30] GDB 269a–b: *DB Cheshire*, FT2, 8.

[31] GDB 203c: *DB Hunts.*, 1,1. As royal land the whole manor may have been extra-hundredal.

[32] GDB 204d: *DB Hunts.*, 6,19.

[33] GDB 151d, 219c, 155b, 75d, 77c, 293c: *DB Bucks.*, 31,1; *DB Northants.*, 1,9; *DB Oxon.*, 6,6; *DB Dorset*, 2,2.8,1; *DB Rutland*, R2. In *Roteland* reference is made to 14 ploughlands on three demesne manors, but the referent is almost certainly to the demesnes of the three manors, for a ploughland figure is also given for the whole fee.

[34] GDB 204a: *DB Hunts.*, 4,5. This seems to correct the IE reading, where the land is probably represented by thegnland outside of the geld (*ICC* 166). The assessment of the demesne in GDB as 5 hides has been taken from another source.

[35] The 1 hide of warland in demesne in Cowley (Oxon.) would seem to be the norm rather than the exception (GDB 160d: *DB Oxon.*, 58,25). Its use here is interesting in the light of a number of references to inland in the Oxfordshire folios.

It is clear from the records of the geld inquest in the south-west, nevertheless, that the demesne of GDB held by tenants-in-chief did not pay geld. In hundred after hundred the non-gelding land can be equated with the land *in dominio* in Exon and GDB.[36] That this was the norm in the reign of William the Conqueror is illustrated by the pre-Domesday Northamptonshire Geld Roll, in which substantial amounts of 'inland' which were integral elements of hundred quotas did not pay.[37] It would appear that the Domesday demesne was warland that had been exempted. The demesne ploughlands of Huntingdonshire, by contrast, had never gelded. Land of the same type is found elsewhere in GDB where, albeit occasionally hidated, it is called inland. It is most frequently recorded in Oxfordshire, where it is seemingly contrasted with the demesne. The account of Stanton Harcourt exemplifies the type. 'The same bishop [of Bayeux] holds Stanton. 26 hides there which gelded TRE. There is land for 23 ploughs. Now in demesne 1 hide and 1 virgate of this land beside the inland [*Idem episcopus tenet Stantone. Ibi xxvi hide que geldebant TRE. Terra est xxiii carucis. Nunc in dominio de hac terra i hida et una virgata preter inland*].'[38] With the possible exception of 231 acres of arable and 100 acres of meadow in Lincoln,[39] the inland of Lincolnshire and Yorkshire is synonymous with berewick and, as geldable land, is therefore not comparable.[40] But similar formulas are found in Northamptonshire and Warwickshire.[41]

The type, however, was not a local phenomenon of limited import as this handful of references might imply. The inland of the Burton Surveys measured in ploughlands was evidently of the same status.[42] In entry after entry it is contrasted with the warland of the men which, a comparison with the Staffordshire and Derbyshire folios of GDB shows, gelded for the same number of hides or carucates as are recorded in GDB. The one-and-a-half hides for which the land of the men of Wetmore defended itself, for example, is matched by a similar assessment in the Staffordshire folios.[43] In two instances it is even opposed to demesne: in Appleby there was no inland (there defined as land 'which is without the king's geld [*que est sine gildo regis*]'), but

---

[36] Darlington, 'Wiltshire Geld Rolls', 169–221. For comment, see ibid. 178.

[37] *EHD* ii. 483–6; Hoyt, *Royal Demesne*, 52–8; Round, *Feudal England*, 147–56.

[38] GDB 155d: *DB Oxon.*, 7,3. For other references, see GDB 155b, 155c, 155d, 156d, 158b, 159a: *DB Oxon.*, 6,4;6;15.7,2.9,7.28,1;5.32,1.

[39] GDB 336b: *DB Lincs.*, C12.

[40] Stenton, *Types of Manorial Structure*, 5, 10–11. More recently it has been argued that the inland of the north was comparable, but was assessed to the geld since so extensive (Faith, *English Peasantry and the Growth of Lordship*, 53). As will become clear, it is less the status of land than its assessment to the geld, a function of the rate of hidation, that is the decisive point here.

[41] GDB 219c, 242d, 243b: *DB Northants.*, 1,8–10; *DB Warks.*, 22,28.29,1. A reference to inland in Shropshire is obscure (GDB 254c: *DB Salop.*, 4,3,15). For the inland of the Northamptonshire Geld Roll, see Round, *VCH Northants.*, i. 258–60, and Hoyt, *Royal Demesne*, 36–51, esp. at 45.

[42] It has been suggested that the inland of Burton was land that had been recolonized between 1086 and 1114 (Moore, 'Population of Domesday England', 323). In reality it is no different from the inland of GDB.

[43] 'Burton Surveys', 219; GDB, 247c: *DB Staffs.*, 4, 3.

thirty-four virgates in demesne, while in Willington there was similarly no inland with seven bovates in demesne.[44] Likewise, the Ramsey demesnes are entities distinct from the geldable land. Only in Ramsey Abbey's Huntingdonshire estates is there any sign of this land in GDB. Domesday was a survey of geldable land. It was to this, the warland, that the ploughland figures relate.

The fact is, of course, implicit in every GDB entry in which ploughland figures are given. In Circuits III and sporadically in Circuit V shortfalls in the number of ploughs employed are recorded in the context in which the deficiency was perceived, either on the demesne or the land of the men. But the aggregate figure, the land for so many ploughs, is entered after the assessment to the geld. In the sources of GDB the close connection between the two items of information was probably explicit. In ICC many entries are of a form that anticipates GDB usage; others are more expansive. Thus, it is recorded that: 'In this village of Thriplow Hardwin [of Scales] holds under the king one hide of the supplies of the monks [of Ely] . . . In this hide is land for one plough [*In hac villa Trippelaue tenet Hardeuinus i hidam de victu monachorum . . . In hac hida est terra i caruce*].'[45] In Exon the linking of assessment and ploughlands is the norm. Entries are of the form: 'The Count [of Mortain] has a manor called Buckland [Brewer], which Edmer Ator held TRE and it rendered geld for three hides less half a virgate; twenty ploughs can plough these [*Comes habet i mansionem que vocatur Bochelanda quam tenuit Edmaratorus ea die qua rex Edwardus fuit vivus et mortuus et reddidit gildum pro iii hidis dimidia virga minus; has possunt arare xx carruce*].'[46] In GDB itself such formulas are occasionally found where the compiler followed these or similar sources rather than his own programme. In the early Yorkshire folios, for example, there are entries of the form: 'In Pickering there are thirty-seven carucates of land to the geld which twenty ploughs can plough [*In Picheringa sunt ad geldum xxxvii carucate terre quas possunt arare xx caruce*].'[47] The ploughland is clearly a non-fiscal measure of fiscal land.[48]

Ploughland figures, then, are a real measure of land. However, they are not a measure of the total arable, for inland was beyond the geld and therefore not usually assessed in these terms. Here immediately is suggested a solution to the problem of apparent overstocking. The working ploughs above and beyond the ploughlands were those of the inland. The structure of the Burton estates corroborates the conclusion. It is clear from the 1114 survey that holders of warland also rented inland in the early twelfth century. In Wetmore, for example, Godric brother of Godwin had two bovates of inland and two bovates of warland.[49] In large part the extra traction power seems

---

[44] 'Burton Surveys', 236, 244.   [45] *ICC* 43–4.
[46] Exon, 210ᵛ.   [47] GDB 299b: *DB Yorks.*, 1Y4.
[48] Walmsley claimed that the *censarii* of Burton Abbey, who rented inland, can be detected in the ploughland figures of the abbey's manors in GDB ('Censarii of Burton Abbey', 75–6). However, I have been unable to reproduce his figures.
[49] 'Burton Survey', 221.

TABLE 6.1. *Burton Abbey's overstocked manors and inland in 1114*

Manor	GDB			1114	
	P/l	P/d	P/v	P/i	P/v
Burton	2	2	2	2	2
Stretton	2	1	5	3	2
Bromley	1	1	1	2	1
Leigh	3	1	5		2
Winshill	3	2	1½	2	2

Notes: P/l = ploughlands; P/d = demesne ploughs; P/v = villagers' ploughs; P/i = inland ploughlands

to have accounted for the apparent surplus of ploughs in the five manors which were 'overstocked' in 1086. Thus, in Burton and Bromley the excess of ploughs over ploughland in GDB is matched by inland ploughs in 1114, while in the remaining three there is a close approximation (Table 6.1).

Thus far the realist analysis is correct. But it is only in the relationship between the ploughland and the hide that the meaning and function of the plough-land become clear. The fiscal tenement was no mere abstraction. It had its correlates in land and population, and it is this that the Domesday entry describes. Apart from the textual demesne (as opposed to inland), by and large the burden of the geld fell upon the peasants. Thus, for example, the Nuneham Courtenay entry in the Oxfordshire folios contrasts inland with the *terra villanorum*.[50] In most entries no rationale can be detected in the numbers recorded. In some, however, each fiscal virgate or bovate is matched by one villager. The equation is easiest to perceive in Huntingdonshire, where hides in demesne are regularly recorded. In Coppingford, for example, there were four hides of land of which half a hide was in demesne, and the fourteen villagers were therefore responsible for exactly one fiscal virgate each (14 virgates = 3½ hides).[51] In 40 per cent of Huntingdonshire entries in which there is sufficient information a similar equation is found.[52] In the south-west the hidage of demesne is regularly given, but a similar equation is only occasionally apparent and, it must be supposed, coincidental. Nevertheless, it seems clear that each peasant represents a tenement from which geld was due. In the Middlesex folios GDB records the assessment of the land of virtually every peasant. In Fulham, for example, there were five villagers with one hide each, thirteen with one virgate each, and thirty-four with half a virgate each, as well as sundry other tenants with smaller amounts of land.[53] There is, moreover, evidence that such fiscal tenements were also the unit of service in the

---

[50] GDB 159a: *DB Oxon.*, 32,1.   [51] GDB 205c: *DB Hunts.*, 11,2.
[52] Roffe, 'Huntingdonshire', 11.   [53] GDB 127c: *DB Middlesex*, 3,12.

twelfth century. In 1125 Fiskerton in Lincolnshire, for example, was assessed at eleven carucates and six bovates to the king's geld and the service of Peterborough Abbey.[54] In Holywell in Huntingdonshire c.1135 the twenty-six villagers of the GDB account are seemingly matched by twenty-five or twenty-six tenants of virgates,[55] and in Caldwell in Derbyshire the two carucates to the geld of GDB correspond with the sixteen virgates of warland in 1114.[56]

On the Ramsey Abbey estates the fiscal tenements survived as units of service into the thirteenth century and beyond. They were, however, subdivided for the purposes of agricultural exploitation. In Holywell many of the twenty-five or twenty-six fiscal tenements were held by a number of people. Godwin, Alan, Leofric, Leofwin le Savage, Robert, Reginald son of Orgar, Alfred the carpenter, Reinald son of Hagenilde, and Hereward all held their various tenements with coparceners, and others were large enough to suggest the existence of subtenants.[57] Elsewhere the hide was locally redefined for agricultural purposes as containing five, six, or seven virgates.[58] A similar expedient was adopted in the banlieu of Battle Abbey in Sussex where there were reckoned eight virgates to the hide.[59] It was this agricultural reality of which the Domesday ploughland was a measure. The correlation is often precise. Moore showed in 1964 that the twenty-four ploughlands of two manors in Laughton and Stockingham in Sussex correspond to the twenty-four hides and one virgate of ploughlands in the later Middle Ages.[60] There is a similar correspondence in some of Burton Abbey's estates. Willington, for example, was reckoned to have thirty-two bovates in the second survey where GDB records four ploughlands.[61] More often there is no neat fit of tenemental units and GDB ploughlands. Significantly, however, both are usually greater than the assessment to the geld.

Herein lies the clue to the function of the ploughland. As a more or less accurate record of the number of ploughs working the fiscal land, it can be perceived as a measure of the capacity of the warland to pay the geld assessed upon it. Where ploughlands equate with hides it would seem that each fiscal

[54] *Chronicon Petroburgense*, 164.

[55] GDB 204b: *DB Hunts.*, 6,6; *Cartularium Monasterii de Rameseia*, iii. 283–5. The holdings are of various sizes, but seem to represent land in villeinage.

[56] GDB. 273b: *DB Derby.*, 3,6; 'Burton Surveys', 243.

[57] *Cartularium Monasterii de Rameseia*, iii. 283–4. Robert the knight had half a hide and a further 3 virgates and a cotset, and Margaret had 2 virgates.

[58] Elton 5 virgates to the hide (*Cartularium Monasterii de Rameseia*, iii. 257), Upwood 4 (270), Wistow 4 (271), Broughton 6½ (273), Hemingford 6 (275), Graveley 6½, 7 (277), Wyton 5 (278), Houghton 7 (278), Ellington 5 (304), Brington 4 (310), Weston 4 (311), Bythorn 4 (313).

[59] *Chronicle of Battle Abbey*, 48. In the light of the evidence here presented, it seems unlikely that the phenomenon indicates a sliding scale of fiscal assessment for newly assarted land as previously suggested (Searle, 'Hides, Virgates and Tenant Settlement at Battle Abbey', 297).

[60] GDB 22b–c: *DB Sussex*, 10,93–4; Moore, 'Domesday Teamland', 129–30.

[61] GDB 266c: *DB Derby.*, 10,20; 'Burton Surveys', 236–7. For the grant of the land to Burton Abbey, see *Monasticon Anglicanum*, i. 275.

tenement was matched by its field equivalent. In the Northern Danelaw this was common, or at least was considered to reflect accurately the burden of taxation. In entry after entry in Lincolnshire, for example, an assessment to the geld in carucates and bovates corresponds to identical ploughland figures in ploughs and oxen. Assessment and reality coincided. Mismatch of ploughland and hide is more common, expressing varying capacity. A short-fall in ploughlands suggests a deficit of resources. In Yorkshire the situation was common, no doubt reflecting the economic impact of the Harrying of the North in 1069–70.[62] In the soke of Falsgrave, for example, the number of inhabitants fell from 108 to thirty-six between 1066 and 1086 and only forty-two ploughlands are recorded on the eighty-four carucates of land.[63] An excess of ploughlands, by contrast, indicates a superfluity of resources in relation to the assessment. It is clear in many such cases that the geld was discharged by only a proportion of the tenants, like the twenty-six villagers in Holywell in Huntingdonshire, as an obligation imposed on the fiscal tenements that they held. In others the burden of taxation may have been shared by all the tenants of the warland in common.

In both cases the ploughlands figures were probably derived independently of the number of working ploughs, at least as they are recorded in the text. Where geld was levied on specific tenements the number of ploughs may well have been confined to those available to the tenant, and they would therefore represent only a percentage of the ploughlands. In manors with a broader taxation base the record of ploughs was probably more comprehensive, but may well have also included those used on non-fiscal land. Even so, the collection of ploughland data did not necessarily involve any great effort of survey or assessment of resources; it merely required the tenant-in-chief to calculate the number of ploughs available on the fiscal land. Indeed, since it must be supposed that each plough in some way rendered dues to the lord, the figure may already have been a matter of estate record.

Nevertheless, it is clear that some tenants-in-chief experienced difficulties in furnishing the information. In Kent it is absent from the breve of the canons of St Martin's of Dover in its entirety.[64] Elsewhere in the county as much as 30 per cent of entries lack the data. In some the scribe clearly expected the figures to be forthcoming for in ninety entries he left a gap after *Terra . . .* for the number of ploughlands to be added. In the rest the ploughland formula is omitted altogether. In Leicestershire the information was also wanting in many entries. Sometimes the GDB scribe also left spaces for later insertion of the data. But here he was not always confident that the information would be forthcoming. The widespread substitution of TRE plough[65] for

---

[62] Palliser, 'Domesday Book and the Harrying of the North', 1–23.

[63] GDB 299b: *DB Yorks.*, 1Y3.   [64] GDB 1c–d: *DB Kent*, M.

[65] In all cases the abbreviation *car'* is used, which could be extended as *caruce* or *carucate*. The former, however, is to be preferred in that the clause is on occasion linked with the demesne or

ploughlands seems to represent an attempt to remedy the deficit by other means. Working ploughs in 1066 are clearly not directly comparable with TRW ploughlands but, it would seem, they were used as the evidence closest in kind.[66] And in reality they were not so wide of the mark. In entry after entry they are larger than the assessment to the geld, indicating an untapped pool of spare capacity.

This expedient is rarely used elsewhere in GDB; TRE ploughs may well have been widely recorded since manorial statistics were generally collected for the three points of reference of the survey, but ploughlands were calculated from conditions in 1086. The device is largely an idiosyncrasy of Leicestershire. Its wide use there, however, suggests that the initiative was official rather than individual. The commissioners, it would seem, took an active role in eliciting the information or, where this was impossible or impractical, in assessing capacity as best they could. It is probably in this context that the close correlation between ploughlands and assessment to the geld in some counties should be understood. The Northamptonshire evidence has dominated the discussion and has been central to the nominalist case. In the south-east of the county there is a consistent ratio of two hides to five ploughlands, while in the six-and-a-half hundreds around Northampton a ratio of one to two applies. Elsewhere less regular but nonetheless consistent relationships are found. With five and six ploughland units per vill ubiquitous, the whole structure looks artificial.[67] However, recent research has demonstrated a close correlation between both hide and ploughland to field tenements.[68] As in Huntingdonshire, the hide was subdivided in varying numbers of 'small virgates', ranging locally from ten to twenty-four. These small virgates in their turn are represented by yardlands that are readily traceable in later medieval and early modern documentation and on the ground. To take but one example, Great Billing was assessed at four hides in 1086 and there were eight ploughlands there with two ploughs in demesne, and these were represented in the seventeenth century by forty-eight yardlands of which twelve were in demesne.[69]

Just how typical Northamptonshire is remains unclear. The inference that the landscape of the county is entirely planned, and that at the time of hidation, is intrinsically implausible (although nonetheless possible). The

---

peasant ploughs. At GDB 231d: *DB Leics.*, 11,3 it follows the record of peasant teams (where elsewhere it follows assessment to the geld), while at GDB 236c: *DB Leics.*, 40,35, it is stated that *ibi una car' fuit, nunc in dominio una car'* and at GDB 237b: *DB Leics.*, 44,13 *Ibi fuit dimidia car' et tantum ibi est in dominio*. Carucates are usually indicated by the phrase *carucate terre.*

[66] Cf. Phythian-Adams, *Norman Conquest of Leicestershire and Rutland*, 32. For a more arcane discussion of the distribution of the forms, see Cain, 'Leicestershire', 10.

[67] Hart, *Hidation of Northamptonshire*, 24–8.

[68] Hall, 'Introduction to the Northamptonshire Domesday', 15–17.

[69] GDB 229b: *DB Northants.*, 57,1; Whalley, *The History and Antiquities of Northamptonshire*, 405.

intimate association of ploughland and field reality is nevertheless seemingly unassailable.[70] The ploughland was not an artificial unit in Northamptonshire. There remains the north. Attempts have been made to demonstrate the agricultural reality of the carucate (and, by implication, the ploughland) in Yorkshire.[71] But there has been no detailed analysis of the carucation of the shire, and elsewhere in the Northern Danelaw there seems no doubt that the carucate was an entirely fiscal unit.[72] It is here that the close relationship between the ploughland and the carucate seems to attest official estimation. Stenton long ago recognized that in Lincolnshire the ploughland figures were either the same as the assessment to the geld or precisely double.[73] In the soke of Ruskington, for example, almost every ploughland corresponds to a single carucate, while in the divided vills of Beckering, Swallow, Appleby, Risby and Sawcliffe, and Goxhill there are exactly two per carucate.[74] Many other estates exhibit what look like more realistic calculations, but there is a perceptible pattern to the distribution of the seemingly artificial ploughland figures. They are largely balanced by assessment to the geld in Kesteven and Holland where the rate of carucation was exceptionally high. The ploughlands of the more lowly rated Lindsey, by contrast, are generally twice the carucates to the geld.[75]

The ploughland figures of Lincolnshire would appear to be estimates of the geld capacity of the estate. The reason for the resort to this strategy is unclear. The loose bonds of lordship, the predominance of freedom amongst the peasantry, and the dispersion of settlement may have all played their part. Assessment certainly seems to have been on the basis of the settlement as opposed to estate: the relationship between geld and ploughland in most vills holds true entry by entry as well as in total. In Addlethorpe, for example, there were no less than ten parcels of land, ranging in assessment from four carucates and two bovates to one bovate, in nine of which the equation is exact (details are wanting in the tenth).[76] As the communal characteristics of the twelve-carucate hundred of the Northern Danelaw reveal, the community was *par excellence* the unit of geld assessment and payment in the north. In Lincolnshire it seems that it often superseded the estate in the workings of the Domesday inquest.

---

[70] Hall, 'Fieldwork and Field Books: Studies in Early Layout', 124–9; Foard, 'The Great Replanning?', 1–11.

[71] Sheppard, 'Pre-Conquest Yorkshire: Fiscal Carucates as an Index of Land Exploitation', 67–78.

[72] See above, p. 62.

[73] Stenton, 'Introduction', *Lincolnshire Domesday*, pp. xv–xix.

[74] GDB 369c-d, 339d, 352b, 353d, 359b, 361c, 339c, 342c, 347b, 352a, 357d, 346a, 352d, 354c, 344b, 357d, 360b, 363b, 371b: *DB Lincs.*, 64,1–14.2,15.16,18.22,12.28,30.32,12.2,10.4,27.12,15;17.16,2.27,6. 36,1.4,20.8,27.17,2.24,10.7,23.27,1.30,2.34,6.68,40.

[75] See above, p. 62.

[76] GDB 339d, 341b, 348c, 355b, 360a, 363c, 370d: *DB Lincs.*, 2,19.3,46.12,79–80.24,51.29,17;19; 23.38,8.68,10.

TABLE 6.2. *Twelve-carucate hundreds in Nottinghamshire*

Ref.	Vill	c	b	p	o	Ref.	Vill	c	b	p	o
10,63	Newthorpe	0	2	0	2	10,66	Bulwell	2	0	2	0
10,43	Watnall	1	0	1	0	*1,45*	*Arnold*	*3*	*0*	*3*	*0*
10,47	Kimberley	1	0	1	0	10,51	Basford	2	3	2	3
10,40	Nuthall	0	4½	0	4½	10,52	Basford	0	1		
30,32	Nuthall	0	3½	0	3½	30,34	Basford	0	4	0	4
10,36	Cossall	0	6	0	6	10,15	Radford	3	0	3	0
13,12	Cossall	0	6	0	6	*1,48*	*Lenton*	*0*	*4*		
10,27	Strelley	0	6	0	6	10,19	Lenton	2	0	2	0
10,28	Strelley	0	3			10,24	Lenton	0	4	0	4
30,31	Strelley	0	3	0	3	10,17	Morton	1	4	1	4
1,50	*Bilborough*	*0*	*1*			*B1*	*Nottingham*	*6*	*0*		
10,39	Bilborough	0	7	0	7						
1,49	*Broxtow*	*0*	*1*								
28,3	Broxtow	0	3	0	3						
29,2	Trowell	1	4	1	4						
30,30	Trowell	0	4	0	4						
30,50	Trowell	0	4	0	4						
30,51	Trowell	0	4	0	4						
1,47	*Wollaton*	*1*	*0*	*1*	*0*						
10,35	Wollaton	1	4	1	4						
TOTAL		12	0	11	5			12	0	11	7

Note: c = carucate, b = bovate, p = plough, o = oxen. The king's lands (italicized) were non-geldable.

The ploughland may have been similarly assessed in relation to the vill in Yorkshire. Composite ploughland figures are given for the eleven vills that gelded with York.[77] Elsewhere, the hundred seems to have been the unit. Nottinghamshire, like Lindsey, also enjoyed a low carucation: the whole county was assessed at no more than 504 carucates. It is significant, then, that ploughlands usually exceed the assessment to the geld, often by a factor of three or four. In such circumstances it is not surprising that there are a great number of 'overstocked' manors in the county, for much of the arable potential must have been ungelded and probably inland or allod. In two groups of vills in the vicinity of Nottingham, however, ploughlands correspond to the geld, and, when exempt royal demesne is subtracted, these two areas are found to be assessed at precisely twelve carucates (Table 6.2). Likewise, in *Roteland*,

---

[77] GDB 298b–c: *DB Yorks.*, C23–35. Where these entries are duplicated in the body of the text, the more usual estate-based ploughland figures are given. It is possible that a figure for the total plough-lands of each vill was provided throughout the county (and possibly beyond) in the geographically arranged recension of the Yorkshire Domesday from which GDB was compiled. The geld must have been a primary concern of this stage. See below, pp. 234–42.

administratively part of Nottinghamshire in 1086, ploughlands are distributed by twelve-carucate hundred. In the two hundreds of Alstoe Wapentake there were twenty-four ploughlands each and in the single hundred in Martinsley Wapentake forty-eight ploughlands.[78] Throughout large parts of Nottinghamshire the estate continued to be the datum of a calculated figure—in 17 per cent of entries, indeed, no figure could be supplied[79]—but in certain circumstances an estimate was made on a communal basis.

That such an expedient was employed from time to time does not detract from the argument here presented. The Domesday commissioners were not interested in the extent of arable *per se*, but rather for the light that it cast on the capacity of the warland to pay the geld assessed upon it. Where the preferred means proved ineffective or impossible, any alternative that elicited the same information was sufficient. The ultimate aim was, no doubt, to increase the yield of the geld. The *inquisitio geldi* had identified hides that had been hidden and individuals who had not paid. The calculation of ploughlands went further by investigating how much more the tax might yield to the king. Much of the geld collected never reached the treasury. In the early twelfth century the abbot of Burton retained the geld of his cotsets as well as that of the tenants of his inland.[80] The geld assessed upon his estates was charged upon a few tenements or distributed pro rata among a wider group of peasants and the surplus was diverted to his purse. It is conceivable that some peasants were entirely exempt from payment, but it seems likely that this practice was common throughout the country in 1086.[81] The Conqueror's reign had already seen a great reduction in taxation in many counties; in the Midlands it was locally based, while in the south-east it predominantly benefited the non-tenanted estates.[82] William now wished to have some measure of how much geld was appropriated by his tenants-in-chief.

The capacity of the tax system was a matter of pressing concern to a government intent on increasing its income. The omission of ploughlands in

---

[78] GDB 293c: *DB Rutland*, R1–2.   [79] Roffe, 'Nottinghamshire and the North', 130–5.

[80] As a matter of course the abbot took the geld levied on his inland. More significantly, however, he also had assumed the right to the geld from cottars' lands regardless of who held them ('Burton Surveys', *passim*).

[81] In cases of total exemption the lord seems to have levied the geld himself. Thus, Exon records (202) that Padstow in Cornwall never gelded 'except for the use of the church [of St Petroc]'. LDB records that the geld of Bury St Edmund's was diverted to the monks of the church and this arrangement seems to have been a function of the exemption of the vill by King Cnut in 1021 (LDB 372a: *DB Suffolk*, 14,167; S980). For a more ambiguous reference, see GDB 174a: *DB Worcs.*, 2,74. 'Underassessment' was probably no different in kind. Urban tenements that belonged to rural manors certainly paid their geld to the lord, for *geldum* was apparently one of 'the customs' that he enjoyed. In Huntingdon, for example, the abbot of Ramsey, the abbot of Ely, and Ulf Fenisc had had all customs except geld, but the bishop of Lincoln (*recte* Dorchester), Earl Siward, and Gos and Hunef had held all customs and sake and soke without reservation (GDB 203a: *DB Hunts.*, B1–5, 14). An explicit reference to payment to a lord is found in the Sussex folios; a Leofwin held ½ hide of the 59 at Washington and gave geld to his lord, but the latter 'gave nothing' (GDB 28a–b: *DB Sussex*, 13,9).

[82] Harvey, 'Taxation and the Economy', 260.

some areas is, then, surprising. The deficiency, however, may be less real than apparent. The survey of the Yorkshire satellites of Craven, Amounderness, and Lancashire apparently did not proceed beyond the initial geld survey, and ploughlands were therefore not recorded. In Circuit V, by contrast, the deficiency may have been in GDB rather than the survey. In Gloucestershire, Worcestershire, Herefordshire, and the first half of Shropshire the record of ploughlands in the normal form is absent. However, it is consistently found from entry no. 4,11,17 in Shropshire (f. 257a), and is the norm in Cheshire. A scribal idiosyncrasy seems to be at work here. There is no underlying geographical or seigneurial rationale in the change in the Shropshire folios, and it is therefore clear that ploughland figures had been available for the whole of the county but had not been entered in GDB. There are indications that such was also the case in Worcestershire and Herefordshire. A statement of ploughing potential is noted in some entries in the form *ibi possunt esse* z *caruce*, which is usually added after the peasant teams. In the church of Worcester's breve in Worcestershire it is stated at the end of the Esch Hundred manors that: 'In all these manors there cannot be more ploughs than is stated.'[83] But otherwise it would seem that the reader is to understand that the ploughlands were the same as the ploughs in use unless there is a statement to the contrary. Gloucestershire alone betrays little interest in the ploughland, with only two references to the unit.[84]

LDB presents a more difficult problem. None of the standard ploughland formulas of GDB is found in its folios, nor is there any echo of the more expansive forms of ICC, IE, and Exon.[85] The only expression of arable potential is unique to the volume and then it is only intermittent. In almost every entry there is a record of the number of ploughs TRE, when the land was acquired, and TRW. Usually no further comment is made, but in a small number of instances in which ploughs are less than at an earlier period it is stated that more ploughs 'could be restored [z *caruce possint restaurari*]'. In Panfield in Essex, for example, there were 'then 4 ploughs in demesne, later and now 2. Always 5 men's ploughs. Then and later 10 villagers, now 8; then and later 8 bordars, now 15; then and later 8 slaves, now 7; woodland 120 pigs; meadow 13 acres; 2 ploughs can be restored'.[86] Where noticed at all,[87] this has been taken as a comment on a deficit of no relevance to ploughlands.

---

[83] GDB 174a: *DB Worcs.*, 2,80. The reference may also relate to the Oswaldslow manors that precede the Esch Hundred estates.

[84] GDB 165b, 165d: *DB Gloucs.*, 6,2.11,5.

[85] There is very occasionally a note of how many demesne ploughs are possible, a form that is common in Circuit III. See e.g. *DB Norfolk*, 7,3.8,40.

[86] LDB 39a: *DB Essex*, 23,6. The information is almost always given after the record of stock and applies to both demesne and tenant ploughs. In two instances, demesne and tenanted lands are treated separately (LDB 64a, 287a: *DB Essex*, 32,7; *DB Suffolk*, 1,101).

[87] Maitland, *Domesday Book and Beyond*, 485.

Instead, two further items of information have been cited as possible substitutes. In Norfolk and Suffolk each parcel of land is measured in carucates of land (*carucate terre*), and some have seen in this a reference to the ploughland, since geld liability is otherwise expressed in terms of the number of pence paid by each vill when the hundred paid £1.[88] Maitland long ago rehearsed the objections to this reading.[89] Elsewhere in Domesday *carucate terre* are always assessments to the geld. If they are not read as such in East Anglia, it is difficult to see how the sums levied on each vill were distributed between the men who were liable to pay. Moreover, if the same argument is applied to Essex (where geld was rendered in much the same fashion as in the rest of England) and the hides are read as ploughlands, then there is no statement of assessment to the geld at all. Maitland preferred his own interpretation, that the TRE plough totals were a substitute.

A careful reading of the text, however, shows that LDB is not so devoid of interest in the ploughland as it seems. Like the account of Panfield, many of the entries in which the number of ploughs that can be restored is recorded appear to account only for a deficit. In a significant number of instances, however, the potential ploughs exceed the loss recorded. In Banham, for example, sixteen sokemen held twenty-four acres of land, and there were two ploughs in 1066 and when the land was acquired and one-and-a-half in 1086. Nevertheless, two ploughs could be restored.[90] In Little Snarehill there had always been one plough in demesne and yet half a plough could be restored.[91] In total, seventeen *restaurari* entries record potential teams that cannot be the shortfall of the present from the three datums of the survey.[92] It is clear that in these cases it is understood that the ploughs in 1086 can be added to those 'that can be restored' to provide a measure of the arable potential at the time of the survey.[93]

It is this, the idea of potential as opposed to shortfall, that probably lies at the heart of the use of the *restaurari* formula. It occurs in only eighty entries in the whole of LDB, but its distinctive usage suggests that, as in parts of Circuit V, TRW ploughs were considered an adequate measure of potential at the time of the survey. Independent evidence for this view is afforded by IE. The summaries of Ely holdings in Essex, Norfolk, and Suffolk not only record the number of manors held by the abbey itself and by its knights, along with

---

[88] Jolliffe, 'Survey of Fiscal Tenements', 136.   [89] Maitland, *Domesday Book and Beyond*, 485–6.
[90] LDB 223a: *DB Norfolk*, 19,13.   [91] LDB 178a–b: *DB Norfolk*, 9,75.
[92] LDB 61a–b, 111b–112a, 115b, 118b, 120b, 136b–137a, 178b, 191b, 192b, 222a, 245b–246a, 249b–250a, 264a, 381a, 431a: *DB Essex*, 30,34;39; *DB Norfolk*, 1,19;57;69;77;78.9,75;77.10,5; 11.19,13.29,5.31,15.47,4; *DB Suffolk*, 20,1.46,5. A further 15 entries probably fall into the same category, but the failure to record explicitly that the ploughs of the men had remained constant between 1066 and 1086 makes the fact ambiguous.
[93] In three instance the form echoes intermittent usage in GDB. In Shellow Bowells in Essex it is stated that 'a further plough is possible [*adhuc i caruca posset fieri*]', and likewise in Osmondiston and Calvely in Norfolk 'two are possible' and 'the whole is possible' (LDB 61a, 176b, 214b: *DB Essex*, 30,34; *DB Norfolk*, 9,48.15,18), a form that is found in Circuit III.

figures for their total assessment to the geld, the demesne ploughs that worked them, and the number of men and their ploughs, but also a figure for overall ploughlands.[94] In Essex there was in total land for sixty-one ploughs, and this corresponds to sixty-two ploughs in LDB.[95] The correlation is not so precise in Norfolk and Suffolk; 141 and 248 ploughlands correspond to 132[96] and 224[97] ploughs respectively when the 'restored' ploughs are added in.[98] Nevertheless, the wider implication is clear: LDB, it would seem, was as concerned with ploughlands as GDB.

The determination of ploughlands in each estate, then, appears to have been a general concern of the Domesday process. Where the information was not a matter of record, could not be easily calculated, or where there were extenuating circumstances, the commissioners took it upon themselves to make an estimation which reflected perceived reality. The intention was not to provide a simple measure of arable; inland generally went unnoticed. Nor was there a reassessment to the end of superseding the geld; there was no new carucage nor tax. The process was simply intended to determine the capacity of the existing hidation to produce more. In the words of the IE prologue, it was designed to determine 'whether more could be had'.

The Resolution of Disputes

The survey of the royal fisc and the description of seigneurial estates were clearly undertaken with little regard to the determination of title. But this is not to say that disputes were not a preoccupation in the Domesday process. Regardless of the aims of the inquest, title could not fail to be an issue where taxation and service were so intimately connected with the tenure of land. Nor could the crown omit to take an interest in the matter. If the demand for justice welled up from below, the king was also aware that illegal seizures of land were a potential source of royal income. In the words of LDB, invasions were *super regem*, and continued to be a milch-cow until they were seen through to completion. Justice was at once the duty of a king and a lucrative prerogative.

---

[94] It has been suggested that these summaries were written, in part at least, when the abbey of Ely was in the hands of the king in 1093, on the ground that the figure for the increase in value during the time of Abbot Symeon is unlikely to have been recorded in 1086 when he was still alive (Galbraith, *Making of Domesday Book*, 141–2). A similar increase in value is given for the lands of Glastonbury Abbey which was in the hands of the king in 1086 (Exon, 173, 527ᵛ–528), but the information is also found for Picot the sheriff's fee in Cambridgeshire (*ICC* 123) and (as a depreciation) in the count of Mortain's in the south-west (Exon, 531). There is no reason to doubt, then, that the Ely summaries in substance emanate from the Domesday inquest.

[95] *ICC* 122.

[96] This figure includes 5 ploughs recorded in IE but seemingly omitted from LDB.

[97] This figure includes 15 ploughs recorded in IE but likewise seemingly omitted from LDB.

[98] 4¹/₂ in Norfolk and 6 in Suffolk.

Legal processes were set in train from the beginning of the survey. Matters in which the king had an interest were often quickly expedited. Several passages indicate that he took lands into his hands. In Exon, for example, it is recorded that the predecessor of the abbot of Tavistock had held the manor of Werrington in Devon, 'and the abbot had been seized of it when King William sent his barons [barones] to inquire into the lands of England; his predecessor before him had been in possession of it. He was disseized by them because the English testified that it did not belong to the abbey on the day King Edward was alive and dead.'[99] In Herefordshire, land in Yatton was said to have been thegnland TRE but that afterwards it was turned into reeveland; 'the king's agents [legati] therefore say that the land and the rent from it are being secretly withdrawn from the king'.[100] In Essex Geoffrey de Mandeville had annexed land in Mashbury, but the king had recovered the estate and granted it to a certain Wulfric.[101] Elsewhere reference is found to estates 'deraigned to the king's use' without any indication of the agency responsible.[102] In all cases the land concerned appears in the king's breve in Domesday Book, and it is therefore clear that action had been ordered. This was not always, and probably not usually, a judicial decision. Sometimes where the facts were not in dispute the course of action was tantamount to a judgement. Otherwise, it probably attests the usual processes of law. Land was taken into the king's hand pending further investigations and pleas. Thus, land in Alresford was in the king's hands awaiting a judgement, while Tavistock pleaded for its manor, recovering it in 1096.[103]

There was no fast-track procedure for the tenants-in-chief. Some of the encroachments of tenants-in-chief on their fellows may have been conceded at an early state: Wormald's fifty-seven 'away wins', that is, cases in which a plaintiff made good his claim against a sitting tenant, probably resulted from an admission that the defendant was 'fair copped, bang to rights, guv'.[104] Again, the witness of uncontested fact was tantamount to a judgement. However, judgement was clearly not perceived as a primary duty in either the geld inquest or the commissioners' survey. There was a dispute over Ashfield in Suffolk 'when the king's barons came into the county', but they merely brokered a peace 'until there is a judgement [donec sit derationatus]'.[105] The remaining cases in which the king was not directly implicated had to wait their turn. The timetable and procedure employed are obscure. Tenants-in-chief may have drawn up schedules of claims as a counterpart to their list of lands before the inquiry. Ely D is undoubtedly a schedule of claims of some kind, but it exhibits few vestiges of the Domesday order of entries, and its manifold deviations

---

[99] Exon, 178ᵛ.   [100] GDB 181b: DB Hereford., 1,75.   [101] LDB 100a: DB Essex, 90,20.
[102] GDB 348c, 367b–c: DB Lincs., 12,84.57,14; LDB 133a: DB Norfolk, 1,195; GDB 158d: DB Oxon., 29,13.
[103] LDB 25b: DB Essex, 18,44; Regesta Regum, i. no. 378.
[104] Wormald, 'Domesday Lawsuits', 78–102.   [105] LDB 377a: DB Suffolk, 16,34.

from IE, ICC, GDB, and LDB may suggest that it was drafted at Ely for presentment in the initial courts sessions.[106] There is no unequivocal evidence to demonstrate at what point official lists were drawn up. The hundredal structure of the *terre occupate* and the *clamores* sections and the unique information that they contain indicate that they were not in their entirety compiled from Exon or GDB or its precursor, and it is likely that the *inquisitio geldi* was the main source. Thus, in IE Ely claimed land in Essex *secundum breves regis*.[107] The identification of disputed lands before the enrolment of seigneurial presentments is suggested by the form of some breves. In Hardwin of Scales's Cambridgeshire lands, for example, the invasions are entered at the end of the chapter within its own hundredal sequence.[108] But schedules of claims could have been drawn up from these sources at any stage in the Domesday process.

The *invasiones* of LDB, however, suggest that proceedings were initiated at an early stage. Each of the three sections exhibits an underlying hundredal structure and may therefore have been ultimately derived from the geld survey. But their arrangement by lord and inclusion of the details of stock indicate that as they appear in LDB they were drawn up at a relatively late stage. As schedules of business in hand, they do nevertheless indicate that extensive legal wranglings had preceded them. Lands had been seized and even re-granted by the king, and offenders were in mercy;[109] warrantors had been pledged but had not supported claims,[110] while others had yet to be produced;[111] pledges were made to prove right and sureties secured;[112] in other instances the cases had proceeded no further than the fact of the claim itself.[113] Like all pleas in the Middle Ages, the workings of the law were protracted. One reason for the inclusion of the *clamores* in GDB might be that they alone were cases that were perceived to have reached a resolution. Even there, however, not all were terminated. The claims that Drogo de Beuvrière made on the lands of Morcar in the wapentake of Aveland in Lincolnshire were remitted to the king's decision, while in Kirton Wapentake in the same county pledges were given by the opposing sides to prove by ordeal or battle rival claims made by Count Alan and Guy de Craon to lands in Drayton, Bicker, and Gosberton.[114]

---

[106] Welldon Finn, *Eastern Counties*, 87–91. Neither Domesday Monachorum A, the Descriptio Terrarum of Peterborough, nor Worcester A includes claims (Roffe, 'Descriptio Terrarum', 9).

[107] *ICC* 127. Welldon Finn claims that the reference is to Domesday Book (*Eastern Counties*, 87). The following entries, however, are drawn from material pre-dating LDB. It is conceivable that its immediate precursor is the referent; the entries are undoubtedly derived from that source. But the scribe may have had a schedule of claims like Ely D in mind.

[108] GDB 197d–199b: *DB Cambs.*, 26.

[109] LDB 99a–b, 276b, 278a, 279a–b, 448b–449a, 450a: *DB Essex*, 90,4;6;8;9; *DB Norfolk*, 66,60;84;86;98;99; *DB Suffolk*, 76,13–16;19.77,4.

[110] LDB 101b, 103a: *DB Essex*, 90,48;77;78.   [111] LDB 448b: *DB Suffolk*, 76,13–15.

[112] LDB 99a, 100b, 101a, 103a, 274a, 278b, 289a, 448a–449a: *DB Essex*, 90,1;2;29;41;74;76;78; *DB Norfolk*, 66,5;88;106; *DB Suffolk*, 76,13;15;17.

[113] LDB 101a, 102b: *DB Essex*, 90,35;64;66.   [114] GDB 377c–d: *DB Lincs.*, CK50;66;69.

Most disputes probably continued after compilation. Professor David Bates has recently shown that a Ramsey case that was resolved in 1087 had been brought to light by the Domesday inquest.[115] At the time of the survey Eustace, sheriff of Huntingdonshire, held land at Isham in Northampton-shire which he had appropriated by force from the abbey.[116] In 1087 William II issued a writ to William of Cahagnes to convene a shire court at Northampton to determine whether the land had paid a farm to Ramsey; if it had, it was to be placed in the abbey's demesne, but if, on the other hand, it had been thegnland, the tenant was to hold of the abbey.[117] Abbot Æthelsige proved his right at the county court by the oath of witnesses and a second writ of the same year ordered the sheriff to put him in possession of the estate.[118] Here can be perceived the routine workings of the shire court to resolve disputes outside of the extraordinary processes of the Domesday inquest. This was of the nature of the inquest. It was not designed to resolve problems but to inform and bring them to the attention of government. The verdicts of hundredmen were not recognitions, but simple presentments, and they were returned to government as quickly as possible to inform future policy. The hares that were started were subject to the normal processes of law, with all the paraphernalia that that entailed: witnesses had to be called, views made, pledges handed over, and sureties secured. Disputes were inevitably the subject of subsequent sessions. It might be expected that the Domesday commissioners continued to be involved in the process in their capacity as ministers of the crown; as Bates has noted, William de St Calais witnessed the second Ramsey writ.[119] But the resolution of disputes was no part of the Domesday commission. Had William wished to resolve disputes in 1085 he would have initiated assizes rather than an inquest.

[115] Bates, 'Two Ramsey Writs and the Domesday Survey', 337–9.
[116] GDB, 228a: *DB Northants.*, 55,1.   [117] *Regesta Regum*, i. no. 383.
[118] Ibid., no. 288b. Davis assigned this writ to William I, but Bates has demonstrated that it must have been issued by William II between his accession and the death of Abbot Æthelsige late in 1087.
[119] Bates, 'Two Ramsey Writs and the Domesday Survey', 338.

7

Circuit Reports

By its nature the inquest was reflexive. The king issued a commission of inquiry to inform himself of the facts in question and the commissioners were bound to furnish a reply.[1] From long scholarly usage that reply is known as a return. As has been seen, however, this term is a misnomer.[2] Inquests were the start rather than the finish of enterprises, and the idea of the return, marking as it does the end of a bureacratic legal process, is hardly appropriate to the procedure. In the following discussion the word 'return' is eschewed in favour of the more neutral 'report'. What those reports consisted of is illustrated by the extant documentation of later medieval inquests.

There survive in the Public Record Office many thousands of verdicts in response to commissions relating to particular feudal matters, especially inquisitions *post mortem* and miscellaneous civil suits and disputes of one kind or another.[3] By contrast, there are relatively few that emanated from national inquests. Up to 1250 the vast majority of surveys survive as copies or abstracts incorporated into works of reference kept in the various departments of state. The chance survival of the odd verdict, like those from the Inquest of Sheriffs in 1170,[4] indicates that they could be preserved, but it must be suspected that generally they were not after they had served their specific purpose or had been engrossed to facilitate reference.[5] The exception is the mass of documents known collectively as the Hundred Rolls.[6] Encompassing formal verdicts from four inquests spanning the period 1255–80,[7] they have probably survived because the business that set them in motion was never completed.

From these it is clear that the commissioners were expected to furnish composite verdicts, culled from the various presentments of vill, hundred, and shire that had been received in the course of the inquest and from the plaints of individuals, in response to the articles of inquisition set out in the commission. By 1274 some commissioners had formalized the process. Many of the

---

[1] Holt, 'The Prehistory of Parliament', 1–28; Hall, *Studies in English Official Historical Documents*, 281–306; Glénisson, 'Les Enquêtes administratives en Europe occidentale aux XIIIe et XIVe Siècles', 17–25.

[2] See above, pp. 67–8.

[3] See *Calendar of Inquisitions Post Mortem* and *Calendar of Inquisitions Miscellaneous*.

[4] *EHD*, ii. 441–8.   [5] For others, see *Book of Fees, passim*.

[6] London, PRO, SC5, most of which are printed in *Rotuli Hundredorum*. The unprinted rolls, and those in other deposits, are currently being edited under the auspices of the Sheffield Hundred Rolls Project, Department of History, University of Sheffield.

[7] Roffe, 'The Hundred Rolls and their Antecedents', 179–87.

Ragman rolls were drawn up as questionnaires in the form of the *capitula* on the Patent Roll, and the composite verdicts were inserted in the spaces left for the purpose.[8] This, however, was perhaps the ideal. In practice, most of the rolls deviate from a standard form in one way or another. Those of 1255 mostly comprise unsealed presentments of vill and hundred and can be characterized as essentially raw data. The 1279 series, by contrast, represents a whole spectrum of material, from initial rough notes to fair copies of final reports.[9]

Diversity was largely a function of circumstance. Divergent forms sometimes betoken lack of time to complete the inquest as prescribed. The Whittlesford Hundred roll of 1275 from Cambridgeshire is geographically arranged by vill, with only vestigial notice of the articles of inquest, and it seems that it was pressed into service as the final offering from the hundred for want of anything better.[10] In other cases anomalies are indicative of material which was given to the commissioners as of interest in its own right. Although they are no longer known, rolls in the due form from the 1274/5 inquest clearly existed for all the hundreds of Essex, for they are abstracted on Extract Rolls, but the commissioners also deposited the extant raw presentments, written in French, which embody the evidence presented to *milites inquisitores* in initial sessions.[11] Time and again there are found appended to rolls schedules of all manner of tenurial and administrative matters which were not strictly germane to the articles but were evidently considered to be of some relevance.[12] Jurors, no doubt fearful of the amercements that failure to report all relevant detail might bring down on their heads, frequently erred on the side of caution by presenting all and sundry, and commissioners in their turn often seem to have been reluctant entirely to jettison what the community deemed of importance.[13] More rarely, but nonetheless significant for that, anomalous forms point to a different procedure. In the Devon series of the 1274/5 inquest the verdicts are summary in the extreme, often recording only a single salient detail and concluding with the statement *de aliis capitulis nihil*.[14] It would seem that the hundreds of the county were so small that it was not felt necessary to roll out the whole panoply of the inquest for the handful of jurors present.[15]

---

[8] This is particularly apparent in the Cambridgeshire series (London, PRO, SC5/Cambridge/Chapter House).

[9] Greenway, 'A Newly Discovered Fragment of the Hundred Rolls of 1279–80', 73–8; Raban, 'The 1279–80 Hundred Rolls', 123–41.

[10] London, PRO, SC5/Cambs/Chapter House/4. There was clearly no other verdict since the entries relating to the hundred on the king's Extract Roll were derived from this account (*Rotuli Hundredorum*, i. 55).

[11] *Rotuli Hundredorum*, i. 136–65.   [12] See e.g. the Lincoln rolls (*Rotuli Hundredorum*, i. 309–28).

[13] Roffe, *Stamford in the Thirteenth Century*, 12–19.

[14] London, PRO, SC5/Devon/Chapter House/1–47; *Rotuli Hundredorum*, i. 63–88.

[15] Roffe, 'The Hundred Rolls and their Antecedents', 184.

The form and nature of the documentation that found its way back to central government, then, was various. Although the king might have a general idea of what he wanted to find out, commissions were not usually tightly focused, and what came back depended on the perceptions of the process of the many people involved and the time and resources available. On the whole, it must be supposed that government got what it wanted, but it was not always in a standardized form. There is no reason to believe that the Domesday inquest was any different in this respect. Although the 'terms of reference' of the IE prologue can be rejected as the articles of inquiry, it cannot be doubted that articles of some kind were drawn up at various stages to guide the jurors, ministers, and commissioners who collected the evidence. It is nevertheless clear that they were differently interpreted, for the categories of data and the terms in which they were expressed varied from circuit to circuit. Perception of what was required and circumstance must have been equally variable. It cannot be expected that the writings sent to William were necessarily any more uniform than the records of thirteenth-century inquests. The taxonomic approach to Domesday documentation has given rise to intense debate about the nature of 'the original returns'. In reality, there was no one form.

The Breves Regis *and the Geld Schedules*

If the survey of the royal fisc and the *inquisitio geldi* were carried out by the officers of the shire, as seems likely, the records that they produced would not have been unique. The sheriff was responsible for the management of the king's demesne estates, and his duties were more than nominal. Domesday Book indicates that the sheriff of Essex looked after the king's salt-houses in Thurstable Hundred, while his counterpart in Gloucestershire changed the structure of the manor of Chedworth by adding eight villagers and three bordars to the manpower.[16] Numerous references of a similar kind indicate that the sheriff was not a passive administrator of farms, but was actively involved in the day-to-day running of the royal estates. It must be supposed, then, that he kept records of the issues of each manor that he administered. Similarly, he accounted for all the issues of the crown in the shire, and thus must have had access to all manner of accounts relating to geld and the other revenues that accrued from the king's regalia.[17]

To what extent these were royal records is debatable. Central government clearly knew the farm of each shire and the amount of geld that could be raised from each; the Burghal Hidage and County Hidage are probably

---

[16] LDB 7b: *DB Essex*, 1,31; GDB 164a: *DB Gloucs.*, 1,57.

[17] The exemplar of the Northamptonshire Geld Roll preserved in the Black Book of Peterborough (London, Society of Antiquaries, MS 60) was probably an example of the type of record that was kept.

pre-Conquest examples of the documentation available.[18] Central government may also have had some idea of the value of the more extensive demesne properties. If nothing more, the matter must have come within the king's ken when he granted them out for the purposes of patronage. There is, however, no evidence that detailed accounts were routinely available within the treasury. It is clearly significant, then, that ICC calls the survey of the king's demesne manors the *breve regis*.[19] This was a record that in some way especially touched the king, and it is likely that it was independently deposited with central government. Elsewhere, the evidence is more equivocal. The *terra regis* of the south-west, although entered in separate quires, is bound in with the land of the tenants-in-chief in Exon as presently constituted.[20] It could, then, have been returned to central government as part of a larger report. There seems little doubt, however, that the *inquisitio geldi* found its way to Winchester, for both Abingdon A and the Crowland Domesday were derived from the documents which were kept in the treasury with Domesday Book.[21]

Circuit Reports

Where tenants-in-chief answered to lists of estates supplied by the commissioners, the subsequent process of enrolment, or 'inbreviation' as LDB calls it, must have been a relatively simple matter. The commissioners' schedule dictated the order of the presentment and supplied the essential details of assessment and value. Checking was probably confined to ensuring that all estates had been accounted for and that the details requested had been provided. The engrossing of the text was then confined to the imposition of a standard format.

The relationship between Exon and Bath A appears to exemplify the process. Exon is clearly a working document, its many changes of hand, revisions, emendations, and corrections and its original use as separate pamphlets suggesting a series of office files in which the materials of the survey were collected and formulated.[22] Bath A, in the seven Exon entries that it parallels, is clearly closely related to it. Its hundredal order deviates from that of Exon; the sequence Bath Hundred, Keynsham Hundred, and the Frome group of hundreds in the one is represented by Keynsham, Bath, and Frome in the other. As in many such dislocations of order, the geld survey may have been entered hundred by hundred on separate sheets which became shuffled at some point.[23] The order of entries within hundreds, by

---

[18] Rumble, 'Edition and Translation of the Burghal Hidage', 14–35; Maitland, *Domesday Book and Beyond*, 577–81.

[19] *ICC* 6, 83.   [20] Rumble, 'Palaeography of the Domesday Manuscripts', 29–32.

[21] See above, pp. 105, 111.   [22] Welldon Finn, *Domesday Inquest*, 166.

[23] Sawyer, 'Original Returns', 186.

contrast, follows that of Exon. However, Bath A is appreciably earlier, and its loose phraseology and idiosyncratic record of data are regularized in its Exon counterparts. It seems likely that it can be interpreted as the seigneurial presentment to the commissioners' schedule which was revised and regularized as it was entered in Exon.

Exon, then (insofar as it relates to the account of fees), is probably best interpreted as a product of the process of inbreviation rather than as the first attempt at compilation from seigneurial presentments and outline geld records.[24] There seems no doubt that it was the immediate source of the account of the West Country in GDB, but its constituent parts were probably conceived as the basic record of the seigneurial inquiry rather than specifically as a composite report. Exon only effectively became such when the various seigneurial files became associated with the *breves regis*, the account of the king's demesne estates which were apparently the subject of a separate survey, some time before the compilation of GDB from them.

When compared with the reports from inquest commissioners of later centuries, Exon might well be considered an ad hoc production, working documents pressed into service for want of anything better. That this was not always the case is illustrated by what appears to be a compiled report, the document known as ICC. As has been seen, this document was clearly a precursor of the GDB account of Cambridgeshire, for, regardless of whether GDB was compiled from a seigneurially arranged recension post-dating ICC, the diplomatic of the one informs that of the other. There was nothing ad hoc about ICC. Possibly like Exon, its exemplar travelled separately from the *breve regis*, but there the similarity ends. It was a fully compiled document, for, although it is feasible that each hundred was entered on a different sheet or series of sheets, each section drew upon all the various sources of which it was composed. How this was achieved cannot be determined in detail. There seems no doubt that the procedure of the inquest employed in Cambridgeshire was much the same as elsewhere in the country. The common sequence of hundreds found in both the accounts of the king's demesne and the seigneurial *breves* points to the use of a geld list, and lords presumably also provided the details of their own estates. But whether tenants-in-chief returned their lands on the basis of an official schedule, or their presentments were ordered by reference to the geld survey after they had been returned, is unclear. However, ICC must have been compiled in the form of the geld inquest itself rather than any seigneurial rearrangement of it. The whole enterprise clearly represented a perception of what the inquest required over and above the mechanism of data collection.

---

[24] See e.g. Welldon Finn, *Liber Exoniensis*, 28; Welldon Finn, *Domesday Inquest*, 166. Numerous post-scriptal entries relate to disputed lands where an attempt had been made to resolve the queries that had come to light.

Of the two surviving sources of GDB, ICC alone can be said to represent a tailor-made report. It was clearly not unique in this respect. Professor Sawyer, in his analysis of hundredal order in Domesday Book, is of the opinion that all counties were so arranged before they were cast into a seigneurial form.[25] His analysis, however, fails to appreciate the possible impact of hundredally arranged schedules of land of whatever provenance. Nevertheless, some counties other than Cambridgeshire have clearly gone through a similar recension. There is no doubt that the other counties of Circuit III (Hertfordshire, Bedfordshire, Buckinghamshire, Middlesex) were treated in the same way. All betray the same diplomatic forms derived from the *se defendit* formula that opens the account of each vill in ICC. The same formula is found in Circuit I, and it has been suggested that, again, a hundredal recension may account for the usage.[26]

Circuit VI provides more compelling evidence. The geographical arrangement of the accounts of *Roteland* and the eighty-four carucate of land attached to York has already been noticed. Since these two estates were *terra regis* of one sort or another, it might be argued that the passages are therefore exceptional. There survives, however, a third passage in the same form that relates to land held by a tenant-in-chief. The Isle of Axholme in Lincolnshire was granted in its entirety to Geoffrey de la Guerche after 1066. The account of the fee in GDB is arranged in a neat pattern of four twelve-carucate hundreds proceeding from south to north.[27] This form is clearly not derived from a seigneurial presentment for, although the relationships are explicit, no attempt was made to group inland and sokeland with manorial *caput* as is otherwise the norm in the Lincolnshire text (Table 7.1). The whole account was presumably taken from an earlier, geographically arranged source as it stood, probably because no other tenants-in-chief held in the Isle.[28]

Outside royal demesne, there were no other comparable estates in the Circuit VI shires. Vestiges of a geographical recension are nevertheless apparent in other characteristics of the GDB folios relating to the northern shires and in associated documents. The IE account of the abbot of Ely's estates in Huntingdonshire, for example, exhibits a similar diplomatic to that found in ICC. Containing details of demesne stocking which were edited out of the Domesday text, the section is somewhat earlier than the corresponding GDB entries, and deviates from it in various forms. However, significantly for the present analysis, the treatment of place-names is related to the structure

---

[25] Sawyer, 'Original Returns', 177–97, esp. at 196–7.

[26] Domesday Monachorum B and the Excerpta were both geographically arranged, but they seem to be derived from the geld survey rather than a full DB-like recension.

[27] GDB 369b–c: *DB Lincs.*, 63,5–22. A further four entries (23–5) duplicate material in entry nos. 19–21. Entry no. 14 is an addition to the text, written on line 45 at the foot of the column, and presumably duplicates land elsewhere in the hundred or beyond since it is not represented in the Lindsey Survey.

[28] There were, however, claims to land (GDB 376c: *DB Lincs.*, CW17).

TABLE 7.1. *GDB account of the Isle of Axholme, Lincolnshire*

Ref.	Vill	Assessment		Status	
		Carucate	Bovate		
63,5	Epworth	8	0	Manor	
63,6	Owston	4	0	Manor	12 car.
63,7	Haxey	3	0	Manor	
63,8	Eastlound				
	Graizelound	1	6	Two manors	
63,9	*Ibidem*	1	1	Soke of Epworth	
63,10	*Ibidem*	0	1	Berewick of Belton	
63,11	The Burnhams	6	0	Soke of Epworth	12 car.
63,12	Belton	5	0	Two manors	
63,13	Beltoft	1	0	Soke, unspecified	
63,14	Althorpe	1	0	Soke, addition	
63,15	Crowle	5	7	Manor	
		0	1	Inland of Upperthorpe	13 car.
63,16	Amcotts	2	0	Soke of Crowle	
63,17	*Ibidem*	0	3	Inland of Westwood	
63,18	*Ibidem*	0	5	Soke of Garthorpe	
63,19	Garthorpe				
	Luddington	4	4	Soke of Crowle	
63,20	*Ibidem*	1	0	Manor	
63,21	*Ibidem*	0	4	Soke of Belton	
63,22	Butterwick	3	0	Soke and inland of Owston	12 car.

of lordship. Undivided vills commence with the formula 'X [the place]. Abbot Thurstan had a manor . . .', while divided vills are of the form 'In X Thurstan has . . .'.[29] The form is at variance with the usage of GDB in its account of the Circuit VI shires, and it therefore seems likely that, like the parallel forms in Circuit III,[30] it is similarly related to a geographically arranged account.[31]

More subtle is the geographical element in the record of manorial rents and stock. Warnode is only recorded in relation to manors in Beltisloe Wapentake in Lincolnshire, although it was almost certainly a common impost throughout

[29] Colne is an apparent exception, for only Ely held within the settlement. However, it would seem that, assessed at 6 hides, it was joined with some other settlement to form a vill.

[30] Palmer, 'Domesday Manor', 143. The form is also used of the largest holding in divided vills and is probably derived from a heading indicating the start of each vill in the prototype of ICC.

[31] The dimensions of vills are also given, for which, see below, p. 223.

the area.[32] Churches are more widely noticed, but their incidence is local. In some Lincolnshire wapentakes they are conspicuous by their all-but complete absence, in others they are comprehensively recorded. In Elloe Wapentake, for example, only one church is noted, although at least five are known from others sources to have been in existence at the time,[33] while in Bolingbroke no less than fifteen out of a total of eighteen in 1256 (the first extant list of churches) are recorded.[34] Even the notice of the priests who served them was mediated by geography; in Bolingbroke only one is associated with his church,[35] while in Loveden the formula 'a priest and a church' is universal.[36] Since details of manorial rents and churches were almost certainly presented by the tenants-in-chief themselves (the information is recorded with other manorial appurtenances), the pattern in both cases points to the editing of hundredally arranged accounts of the estates.

It has been noticed that the record of churches and priests in the Cheshire folios is similarly mediated by hundredal structure.[37] In Hamestan Hundred no churches at all are noticed, but in the others a distinct pattern emerges. In Dudestan, Warmundestrou, Riseton, Wilaveston, and Tunendune a priest alone is recorded, while in Roelau, Bochelau, Atiscross, and Exestan the formula is a church or a church and priest. In like wise woodland is differently described in Shropshire from hundred to hundred. In Culvestan, Leintwardine, Merset, and Wrockwardine it is given in linear measurements, while in Alnodestou, Baschurch, Conditre, Condover, Hodnet, Overs, Patton, Reweset, and Rinlau it is given by the number of swine that it could support.[38] The GDB accounts of both counties may thus have also been derived from ICC-like precursors.

Elsewhere hundredally arranged reports are less likely. In the Circuit IV and V shires, excepting Cheshire and Shropshire, it is probable that something like the Circuit II approach was adopted. In both areas estates from one shire were frequently enrolled, apparently erroneously, in GDB in the folios of other shires. The phenomenon suggests that, as in Exon, the lands of each tenant-in-chief were inbreviated without reference to county divisions. Had a geographical recension intervened between the collection of data and the compilation of GDB such anomalies would have been identified and rectified

---

[32] GDB, 340b, 366b, 368a: *DB Lincs.*, 2,36;37;42.51,9–10.57,46. The *clamores* section indicates that the rent was also found in the wapentakes of Ness and Graffoe (GDB 376d, 377c: *DB Lincs.*, CK2,8,61). Numerous references are found to the impost in later records.

[33] GDB 377d: *DB Lincs.*, CK70.

[34] GDB 351b–d, 354d, 359d: *DB Lincs.*, 14,66;71–9;81;83;98.24,24.29,11,CK70; *Valuation of Norwich*, 228. There were ten churches in Elloe Wapentake in 1256 (*Valuation of Norwich*, 248–9).

[35] GDB 354d: *DB Lincs.*, 24,24.

[36] GDB 345a, 347d–348a, 355d, 363b, 369b–370a: *DB Lincs.*, 7,54.12,47–9.15,1.24,78.37,2.64,14–15;17.

[37] Thacker and Sawyer, 'Domesday Survey', 296–7.

[38] Lewis, 'Introduction to the Shropshire Domesday', 10. Only the demesne of Earl Roger of Montgomery breaks the rule in using linear measurements regardless of where the woodland was situated. The land was probably extra-hundredal.

(as witnessed by the absence of such cross-enrolment in Circuits I, III, and VI).[39] In all of these counties, as in the south-west, the task of reconstructing the hundreds of 1086 is far more difficult than elsewhere as a result.

Whether the relevant folios of GDB were abbreviated from working documents like Exon or more considered seigneurially arranged compilations is impossible to ascertain. With the recognition of Exon as the immediate source of the GDB account of the south-western shires, the case for such fair copies rests largely upon LDB. Its record of demesne livestock and expansive formulation immediately invites comparison with ICC and Exon, and the omission of the three East Anglian counties described in the volume from GDB might suggest that it is derived from similar locally produced reports. Opinion has differed as to whether the account defied abbreviation because of the complexity of the social structure that it documents or whether time simply ran out. Whatever the case may have been, it clearly became associated with GDB because it completed the survey, albeit in what Galbraith termed 'mongrel form'.[40] A recent palaeographical study of LDB has suggested the identity of at least one scribe who considered the problem. Rumble has shown that Scribe 7 who wrote the colophon at the end of LDB was otherwise only responsible for the rubrication and running heads. He concludes that this represents an attempt to make the best of a bad job in bringing a circuit return into conformity with the already completed, and rubricated, GDB.[41]

This reasoning has considerable force. But it does not demonstrate that the fair copy that is LDB was compiled necessarily as the report of Circuit VII. There are, indeed, a number of indications that it was not the first attempt to represent the evidence from the eastern counties. It was almost certainly preceded by a fully formulated, geographically arranged recension of the data.[42] The evidence is diverse, but together compelling. First, there is diplomatic. The usage of the Essex folios may be *sui generis*, but that of Norfolk and Suffolk Domesdays is quite distinct. It has already been noted that the overwhelming characteristic of the text of those counties is its arrangement by hundreds within each seigneurial chapter. Throughout LDB tenurial relationships of all kinds are noticed. Berewicks are explicitly linked with the demesnes to which they belonged; sokemen and free men are regularly associated with the manors to which they rendered their dues; various sokerights are made explicit.

---

[39] There are two alternating forms in Circuit IV of the same kind as those of Circuit III, but they do not seem to correlate to what can be perceived of vills, that is, the two forms are seemingly used at random. See below, p. 209.

[40] Galbraith, *Making of Domesday Book*, 205.

[41] Rumble, 'Domesday Manuscripts: Scribes and *Scriptoria*', 80–1.

[42] This conclusion is implicit in Round's analysis. Sawyer has further argued the point ('Original Returns', 188), but his argument is based on the order of the Ely claims in Norfolk which may have had entirely different origins. Dodwell, 'Domesday Survey in Norfolk', 79–84 has postulated an ICC-like recension in Norfolk, but she admits (p. 83) that her evidence does not go beyond the existence of a schedule of vills.

Nevertheless, estate structures articulated in this way have little affect on the form of the text; hundredal structure is rigidly maintained throughout. This in itself does not necessarily indicate anything more than the use of a hundredally arranged schedule. However, the layout is accompanied by diplomatic that is elsewhere associated with hundredally arranged accounts. Entry forms VIIA and VIIB of Norfolk and Suffolk (Table 4.7), 'X held Y for z carucates' and 'X holds A which Y held for z carucates', echo the 'X for z hides defends itself' formula of the GDB account of Cambridgeshire which is taken from the opening formula 'X for z hides defends itself' of the ICC account of each vill. That this usage is derived from a similar source is suggested by the distribution of these forms. Where vills are divided between a number of holdings there is a tendency for the main or principal holding alone to exhibit them. Of the five holdings in Martley in Suffolk, for example, only the account of Hervey of Bourges's manor commences with 'Martele tenuit Brihtmarus commendatus Haroldi pro manerio . . .' The remaining four holdings exhibit the formula 'In Martele . . .' of form VIID.[43]

Secondly, some Norfolk and Suffolk entries contain information that relates directly to the vill as opposed to the estate. Although each holding is given what appears to be a rating to the geld in terms of carucates or acres,[44] there is attached to some a statement of the burden of taxation in terms of the number of pence due when the hundred paid £1. The formula is linked with a statement of what is ostensibly an estimate of the dimensions. That these items of information express a villar assessment is sometimes explicit. Count Alan's holding in Foulden in Norfolk is said to be measured with the land of William de Warenne where the data are duly found, while in both Norfolk and Suffolk the formula is frequently accompanied by the statement that 'others hold here'.[45] It is also indicated by the fact that the sums add up to, in some cases, or more often approximate to, the £1 total for each hundred and fall into the 20d or 30d units owed by the leets.[46] Like entry forms VIIA and VIIB, the distribution of the information is again not haphazard. It is often associated with undivided vills and is thus appended to entries commencing with the formulas 'X held Y' and 'X holds A' of forms VIIA and VIIB. Where there was more than one holding it is almost invariably tacked on to a subsidiary entry of the form 'In X . . .' and its variants (forms VIID and VIIE).[47] The implication must be that the dimensions of the vill and its liability to the geld were at the end of a geographical account and the information was attached to the last holding in the vill when it was transferred to LDB.

[43] LDB 293b, 294a, 327b, 348a, 443b: *DB Suffolk*, 3,35;52.6,293.8,28.67,27.
[44] See above, p. 164.
[45] LDB 144b, 167a–b, 328b–329a: *DB Norfolk*, 4,3.8,90; *DB Suffolk*, 6,308.
[46] *VCH Suffolk*, i. 361; *VCH Norfolk*, ii. 6; *Kalendar of Abbot Samson*, pp. xvi–xxv.
[47] *Pace* Dodwell, 'Domesday Survey in Norfolk', 80.

Thirdly, certain expressions and items of information are mediated by hundred rather than fief.[48] Some such may have been derived from the geld survey or the schedules that were drawn up from it. In South Greenhoe Hundred in Norfolk, for example, values are given for *quando recepit* or *quando invenit*, when the land was acquired, where elsewhere the term *post* ('later') is used, while in Docking, Smethdon, and South Greenhoe carucates to the geld are frequently omitted. Others, however, must have come from a full hundredal recension. In North Greenhoe, Eynesford, Earsham, Henstead, and Loddon, in part a distinct group of hundreds within the common sequence,[49] the unusual formulation *inter omnes*, or *inter homines*, is used of the total number of teams, and in the hundreds in central Norfolk *sochemannus* is preferred to *liber homo*, where the opposite obtains in the south-east.

All of these characteristics point to the existence of a geographically arranged recension of the data from which LDB, or at least the Norfolk and Suffolk sections, was compiled. It was presumably from this source that the textually earlier East Anglian sections of the IE, ostensibly derived from a hundredally arranged source, were copied. As a compiled text itself (it was presumably drafted from a series of accounts of fees), its closest affinities must have been with ICC. Like that document, it probably omitted the *terra regis*, for in both the Norfolk and Suffolk folios of LDB the king's lands 'that belonged to the realm [*regnum*] or region [*regio*]'[50] are entered first in their own sequence of hundreds, and are followed by tenanted holdings and escheated estates held in custody in much the same way that the separately surveyed *terra regis* of Cambridgeshire was. This characteristic also provides a link with Exon, for equally there the *terra regis* was probably only contingently related to the rest of the seigneurial breves.

By the same token, LDB's affinities are decidedly with GDB. It is true that there is no way of demonstrating that the seigneurial recension was not subsequently compiled to act as the report from the commissioners in East Anglia. Equally, there is no compelling reason, beyond the demands of Galbraith's thesis, to believe that it was. In Circuit III such a recension is difficult to detect.

[48] Welldon Finn, *Eastern Counties*, 54, 59.

[49] The adjacent hundreds of Earsham, Henstead, and Loddon with Diss were nos. 21–4 in the common hundredal sequence. There is some evidence to suggest that hundreds were grouped together for some purposes. Two parts of the soke of 3 hundreds were attached to the farm of the borough of Yarmouth (LDB 118a–b: *DB Norfolk*, 1,67). This may represent a purely ad hoc arrangement, for hundreds were often joined together for especially weighty legal occasions, but it is perhaps more likely to indicate a ship soke, that is a group of 3 hundreds that provided a ship for the royal fleet. Hundredal sequences often coincide with propinquity to suggest other Norfolk groups, but no others coincide with diplomatically defined entities.

[50] LDB 119b, 144a, 281b, 289b, 408b–409a: *DB Norfolk*, 1,71.4,1; *DB Suffolk*, 1,1;120.31,44. For *regio*, see Round, *Feudal England*, 124 and *DB Suffolk*, 1,1 n, in which the term is taken as either a mistake for *regnum* or an alternative for it. The same meaning is clearly intended by the two terms, for they both refer to demesne lands administered on the king's behalf by the sheriff. *Regio*, however, probably should be translated as 'shire', the estates being those that pertain to the sheriff's bailiwick.

Indeed, the Cambridgeshire folios are so close to ICC that an intermediate stage is perhaps unlikely, and it is feasible that documents like the Yorkshire Summary and the Kentish Assessment List were used to compile GDB.[51] Be it remembered that the form of Exon was a function of data collection rather than compilation, then the inclusion of the *terra regis* and the adoption of a seigneurial form in LDB marks a signifcant change in emphasis that is most fully exemplified in GDB. There is little evidence that considered seigneur-ially arranged reports were ever envisaged by the commissioners.

The Summaries

Of the thirty-three counties surveyed in GDB and LDB, twenty seem to have gone through a geographical recension. ICC-like reports were the norm. With Exon surviving as a group of working files, it looks suspiciously as if the com-missioners in the south-west and the West Midlands failed to compile their reports in the form requested, either through lack of time or oversight. Nevertheless, it seems likely that the predominantly geographically arranged sources were usually accompanied by seigneurial summaries. Two appear in GDB itself. In the Cheshire folios there is an account of Roger the Poitevin's holdings between the Ribble and the Mersey:

In these six hundreds of West Derby, Newton, Warrington, Blackburn, Salford, and Leyland there are 188 manors in which there are 80 hides less 1 gelding. They were worth £145 2s 2d TRE and £120 when Roger the Poitevin acquired them from the king. Now the king holds and he has in demesne 12 ploughs and 9 soldiers holding a fee. Between them and their men there are 115 ploughs and 3 oxen. The demesne that Roger held is valued at £23 10s. What he gave to the soldiers is valued at £20 11s.[52]

There is little indication from which part of the survey this passage emanates.[53] The second is more informative. In the Yorkshire Summary the list of Count Alan's Richmondshire lands is followed by a resume of his interests in the rest of Yorkshire:

[51] In one instance the GDB scribe can be shown to have been responsible for the conversion of a hundredal account to a seigneurial one. Thus, the eleven berewicks of the king's manor of Northallerton in the Yorkshire folios are entered in GDB in an order which is determined by an interlineation of six holdings in the Summary which was equally written by the GDB scribe (GDB 299a, 381a: *DB Yorks.*, 1Y2.SN,A1). Vills 7 to 12—Great Smeaton, Little Smeaton, Cowton, Borrowby, Romanby, and Yafforth—were interlined above 2 to 6—Birkby, Sowerby, Kirby, Landmoth, and Thornton—and the order in the king's breve is 2, 7, 3, 8, 4, 9, 5, 10, 6, 11, 12. The entries have clearly been read in pairs from left to right rather than across in lines, and therefore the account of Northallerton must have been drawn directly from the enrolled text of the Summary.

[52] GDB 270b: *DB Cheshire*, R7. The Phillimore editor preferred 115 carucates to 115 ploughs (R7 n) on the ground that the preceding entries have *carucatae terre*. However, the latter is clearly intended unless it is hypothesized that *boves* is a mistake for *bovatas*. Nevertheless, the suspicion remains that the scribe actually meant carucates.

[53] Lewis suggests that the summary was provided by a co-ordinating authority above the hundred, by implication the sheriff or reeve, on the ground that not all the details can be derived from the information supplied by the hundreds ('Introduction to the Lancashire Domesday', 12).

Count Alan has in his castlery 200 manors less 1. Of these 108 are waste; and of these his men hold 133 manors. In total there are to the geld 1,153 carucates of land and land for 853 ploughs. Value £80. Besides the castlery he has 43 manors. Of these 4 are waste. In all there are 161 carucates and 5 bovates of land to the geld, and land for 170½ ploughs. Of these his men hold 10 manors. They are worth £110 11s 8d.[54]

The passage is postscriptal, but its survival within a geographically arranged text pre-dating the GDB account of Yorkshire suggests that it was drawn up before compilation, while its inclusion of a value and the number of tenants indicates that it post-dates the survey itself. Inbreviation is a possible context, but the hundredally arranged recension of the Yorkshire text seems more likely. The summaries in IE likewise seem to have been associated with ICC or an ICC-like recension. The Ely scribe who compiled the work copied details of fees unrelated to the abbey, and he therefore presumably found them in the geographically arranged sources from which he drew his account.[55] The Exon examples cannot be firmly associated with any of the other documents preserved in the volume, but presumably they emanated from much the same stage of the inquiry as the seigneurial breves from versions of which they must have been ultimately derived.

As a category of document the summaries are remarkably consistent in form and content. That relating to the abbot of Ely's lands in Essex is typical of those found in IE:

The same abbot has in demesne in Essex 5 manors [assessed] at 49½ hides. There are 14 ploughs in demesne, and 102 villagers, 45 bordars, 44 slaves who have 39 ploughs. The whole is worth £64 10s.

His knights have 2 manors in the same county [assessed] at 5 hides. There are 3 ploughs in demesne, and 6 villagers, 7 bordars, and 7 slaves who have 6 ploughs. It is worth £8. This land suffices for 61 ploughs [*Hec terra sufficit lxi carucis*]. It has improved in value by £9 in the hands of Abbot Symeon.[56]

It is immediately recognizable as of a similar type to that of the abbot of Glastonbury in Exon:

The abbot of Glastonbury has 20 demesne manors in Somerset of 194 hides and 3 virgates. Besides that there are there 23 hides and 40 ploughlands of non-gelding land. In these there are 75½ ploughs in demesne, and 47 villagers, 325 bordars, 108 slaves, 19 *coliberti*, and 10 fishermen having 160 ploughs. This land is valued at £288 4s.

The knights of the church have 50 manors in the same county of 160 hides less 1. In these there are 64½ ploughs in demesne, and 219 villagers, 249 bordars, 101 slave,[57] and 2 *coliberti* having 100 ploughs less ½ plough. This land is worth £146.

Of the said land thegns hold 11 manors of 31½ hides and 2 carucates of non-geldable land. In these there are 12½ ploughs in demesne, and 21 villagers, 48 bordars,

[54] GDB 381b: *DB Yorks.*, SN,CtA45.
[55] Welldon Finn, 'Inquisitio Eliensis Reconsidered', 394-7.
[56] *ICC* 122.   [57] 'c et i seruus.'

and 16 slaves having 11 ploughs. This land is worth £20 15s. This land suffices for 554½ ploughs [*Hec terra sufficit D & liiii carrucis & dimidia*]. This land has appreciated in the hands of Abbot Thurstan by £128.[58]

All the summaries, apart from that of the count of Mortain, summarize the interests of a lord in a single county.[59] Demesne is distinguished from tenanted estates, and each section begins with a statement of the number of manors held. The assessment to the geld is then recorded, the number of ploughs in demesne, the total number of each category of peasant and the number of ploughs that they held, and the value of the whole. Some indication is sometimes given of appreciation or depreciation in the time of the current tenant-in-chief. The final statistic is usually the number of ploughlands in the whole fee, that is, for both the demesne and the tenanted land.[60]

The number of manors seems to have been derived from a rule of thumb rather than any technical or textual definition. In the Cheshire folios, IE, and Exon the record of TRE tenants alone seems to have provided the statistic without any regard for the status of land.[61] The figure of 142 manors belonging to Count Alan in Yorkshire, by contrast, is probably derived from the number of settlements in which he held land, which, at 132, more closely approximates to the recorded total than the number of manors in GDB or TRE tenants named. The other statistics are simple additions. The figures are, however, usually difficult to reconcile with existing documentation, the discrepancies probably arising as much from compilation from geographically arranged sources as from the difficulties of adding roman numerals.

All these statistics were no doubt of use in one way or another to the king. But ploughlands were seemingly of some especial importance. The change of format from demesne and tenanted totals to a total for the whole fee is pointed and focuses attention on this item of information. Generally, the figures approximate to those recorded in the relevant folios of GDB except for those given for the Ely fees in Essex, Norfolk, and Suffolk which are not overtly evidenced in LDB. In GDB ploughlands are linked with assessment to the geld, but there is no indication that they were key items of data. More prominence, however, was probably given to them in the commissioners' reports. ICC, it is true, distinguishes only the assessment to the geld in its record of the liability of the whole vill at the head of each entry. Elsewhere there may also have been given the total number of ploughlands in each vill. In two of

---

[58] Exon, 528. See also f. 173 for a parallel version. It is virtually identical with the present text with the exception of the omission of the non-gelding lands in demesne.

[59] Robert son of Gerold's summary comes in three versions. One and two summarize his interests for the three counties of Wiltshire, Dorset, and Somerset separately, while the third totals the three sets of figures (Exon, 530ᵛ).

[60] On occasion it is given after the assessment to the geld in Exon.

[61] Welldon Finn, 'Inquisitio Eliensis Reconsidered', 394–7; Welldon Finn, *Liber Exoniensis*, 124; Welldon Finn, *Domesday Inquest*, 67. The 188 manors between the Ribble and Mersey are probably represented by the 182 thegns and drengs who held in 1066.

the geographically arranged sections of GDB, the account of *Roteland* and the eighty-four carucates that gelded with York, the assessment of the vill or twelve-carucate hundred is followed by the number of ploughlands in it. The summaries start with the actual assessment to the geld and the resources from which it was paid, and finish with the potential yield.

The consistency of form suggests that these summaries were not the product of administrative convenience or whim. The surviving examples emanate from no less than five of the seven circuits, and all but one (Cheshire) focus on the ploughland figures. Common language underlines the unity of concept and indicates that it was central government that dictated this bias. In Robert son of Gerold's Somerset summary ploughlands are expressed in the form y *hidas quas z caruce possunt arare* of the body of the Exon text, while in Count Alan's in Yorkshire the normal *terra z carucis* of GDB is found. But otherwise the formula *hec terra sufficit* t *carucis* is employed. This precise formulation is not otherwise found in the Domesday corpus, and it must surely point to the guiding hand of government. The summaries were one item of information that can be said to have been specifically requested from the commissioners in the language that survives.

Disputes

The record of the legal proceedings resulting from the inquiry in GDB and LDB is uneven, and it looks as if there was no systematic report of the information. Of the 339 cases examined by Wormald, no fewer than 55 per cent are found in Circuit VI and Circuit VII accounts for another 20 per cent. Circuit II comes next with 14 per cent, Circuit I with 6 per cent, Circuit V with 3 per cent, Circuit II with 2 per cent, while Circuit IV had no verdicts at all. Wormald discussed a number of possible reasons for this pattern. The preponderance of lawsuits in the eastern and northern counties could suggest that the commissioners did not have the time to resolve the problems of tenure in an area of complex estate structures, whereas elsewhere they had been able to digest the material and incorporate it into the text. This, however, he deemed unlikely. In Warwickshire there is postscriptally appended to the account of Alveston the record of a pre-Domesday plea,[62] while in Exon there are as few verdicts as there are many in LDB, which was (Wormald avers) seemingly produced at a similar stage in the Domesday inquiry. The pattern of pleas could be a function of demand, that is, their distribution echoes the incidence of misappropriation, although again he found it difficult to account for variations between areas of similar social structure like Cambridgeshire and Northamptonshire. His preferred interpretation was that the distribution merely reflects the willingness of commissioners to address the problem and

---

[62] GDB 238c: *DB Warks.*, 3,3-4.

the energy that they brought to the task. Wormald concludes that 'Disputed title in 1086 was a can of worms. What crept into the record depended on how far the lid was opened and how soon it was slammed shut again.'[63]

It is doubtful that all of Wormald's cases actually entailed recognitions; only the *clamores* are explicitly such, and even there many of those recorded had not reached a determination. Nevertheless, the distribution of cases noticed in Domesday remains decidedly eccentric. The survival of the *clamores* has clearly skewed the pattern in favour of the northern counties, but even with exclusion of these cases and the addition of others that Wormald discounted,[64] there still remains a considerable bias in favour of the northern and eastern shires. It is unlikely, however, that this distribution is a simple reflection of the level of legal activity.[65] To focus attention only on what is recorded in the body of the text is to overlook the volume of business and the interest that central government took in it.

The schedules of pleas preserved in LDB and Exon put the existence of the *clamores* and the apparent bias that they introduce into a different light. The *invasiones* do not obviously record any recognitions, but the progress of the pleas therein was as far advanced as many cases in the *clamores*. The *terra occupate* of Exon merely record the fact of what are effectively claims. The intention was, presumably, to proceed with the claims in some way, and, indeed, matters may have already been in hand, although no report was made of progress or none has survived. Alternatively, the apparent arrest of the Domesday process at the inbreviation stage may suggest that the whole proceedings were retarded in the south-west. Few of the cases in either the *invasiones* or the *terre occupate* sections are incorporated into the body of the text, and in the case of Exon they were omitted from GDB. This looks very much like an editorial decision. It seems likely, then, that the paucity of pleas elsewhere in Domesday was similarly a function of omission in the course of compilation. Schedules of disputes, along with an indication of the progress that had been made towards resolving them where applicable, were probably returned from all seven circuits. It was the compilation of GDB that introduced the bias into the evidence rather than any significant variation in the level of legal action or the reports that were made of it.

Of all the data sent back to central government, reports on the progress of pleas approximate most closely to returns. The rubric of the Lincolnshire West Riding *clamores* draws attention to the settlement of disputes, and this might suggest that the king was intent on seeing justice done. But such may not have been a primary concern. In LDB the *invasiones* are said to be *super*

---

[63] Wormald, 'Domesday Lawsuits', 69.

[64] Appendices C and D cases, 'king's pleas' and miscellaneous (Wormald, 'Domesday Lawsuits', 98–102).

[65] Total 327. I: 48 (14%); II: 17 (5%); III: 70 (21%); IV: 13 (4%); V: 20 (6%); VI: 50 (15%); VII: 119 (36%).

regem, 'on the king'. Some were certainly cases in which land or dues had been taken away from royal manors in one way or another. However, many more were clearly not matters which touched the king's title in any material sense. Time and again hundred presentments indicate that manors held by other tenants-in-chief had been despoiled by the aggressors and the invasion is occasionally said to be in the despite of a named individual. William de Partenay's *invasiones*, for example, are explicitly *super Abbatem*, 'upon the abbot [of Bury St Edmund's]'.[66] They were only invasions in the king's despite in so far as they affronted his dignity as king. It was his prerogative rights that were infringed. The invasions were, in short, a source of income. LDB attests that many of the disputed estates were already in the king's hands and aggressors had been put into the king's mercy. The continuation of the cases promised further increases in royal revenue.

The *terre occupate* section of Exon is more reticent than the *invasiones*. The aggressor is, of course, always named, and from time to time his victim is identified or implied. Roger de Courseulles and the bishop of Coutances, for example, had appropriated manors in Limington, Hutton, and Elborough 'which could not be separated from the church of Glastonbury on the day on which King Edward was alive and dead . . . They do not render any service from these manors to the abbot.'[67] As in the *invasiones*, however, a plaintiff is generally not explicit. The determination of right does not seem to have been high on the agenda and, again, the revenue accruing from the invasions was probably of primary interest. The *clamores* are more expansive in the information that they give, but they were are not inconsistent with this interpretation. Schedules of disputes, whether of those in progress or those settled, were probably perceived as a record of income from lands in custody as well as of the potential for raising more from future actions.

[66] LDB 448b: *DB Suffolk*, 76,8–12.   [67] Exon, 524.

8

The Writing of Great Domesday Book

THE MYSTIQUE THAT surrounded Domesday Book in the popular mind was in no small measure a function of the sacral connotations of the book form. Nevertheless, the extent to which such symbolism was fostered by government should not be exaggerated. In 1279 Edward I ordered his commissioners to enter the Hundred Rolls 'in books [*in libris*]'.[1] Edward was certainly aware of the power of appropriate iconography; that of his Welsh castles evoked images of a triumphant Albion.[2] But the survey of 1279 was never completed and it is therefore impossible to determine what was intended. Nevertheless, throughout the Middle Ages inquests were abbreviated and copied into books for more prosaic reasons. Almost all of the major surveys brought to light information that was of continuing interest to government, and convenient summaries were frequently made to facilitate reference. Sometimes the process was contemporary or almost contemporary. The Rotuli de Dominabus certainly date from the late twelfth century and Round believed them to be the verdicts of the inquest of 1185.[3] In reality they appear to be abbreviations (here in roll form, albeit sewn together) of the inquest, for the names of the jurors are not preserved and the rolls were apparently not sealed. More often abbreviation post-dates by many years the inquests. Thus it is that many of the twelfth- and early-thirteenth-century surveys are preserved in works of reference of the later thirteenth and fourteenth centuries.[4] The Red Book of the Exchequer, probably originally dating from the 1240s, contains the records of numerous aids and, most notably, the *carte* of 1166 (here copied from an earlier register of the reign of John). The Book of Fees of *c*.1302 abbreviates the records of carucages, scutages, and surveys of sergeancies from 1198 to 1293. Both were compiled as registers to facilitate reference to documents within the Exchequer and were designed for the management of feudal dues.

What was included and excluded in works of this type depended, of course, on what was perceived to be of more permanent interest. As in the Rotuli de Dominabus, the names of jurors are consistently omitted. In the Ragman rolls the lists are frequently annotated to indicate whether jurors were present at the subsequent eyres when the pleas which their presentments

---

[1] *Rotuli Hundredorum*, ii., frontispiece.
[2] Taylor, *Four Great Castles*.   [3] *Rotuli de Dominabus*, pp. xvii–xix.
[4] *Red Book of the Exchequer*, vol. i., pp. i–ix, xlix–liii; *Book of Fees*, pp. iii–x.

had engendered were heard.[5] None of the Extract Rolls, however, deigns to notice them.[6] Jurors were only relevant to the immediate and particular actions that inquests initiated. Otherwise, content varies. The texts of the Leicestershire, Lindsey, and Northamptonshire Surveys may well reproduce the whole substance of the verdicts that were originally given. By contrast, what appears to be an abbreviation of the 1255 verdicts in Wiltshire seems to indicate a ruthless editing of the ephemeral to retain the substance of the king's rights in the county.[7] At the same time information was often reorganized. The Lindsey Survey proceeds by wapentake, but within each the lands of the tenants-in-chief are brought together, sometimes with a statement of his total liability to the geld, representing a reordering of an original organization by vill.[8] The scutage accounts of 1242/3 were entered in the Book of Fees in both geographical and seigneurial forms.[9]

The subject of this chapter is the editorial processes that informed the production of GDB from its various sources. It is now clear that those sources were more diverse than has been hitherto allowed. The achievement of the GDB scribe lies in his consummate skill in the reorganization as well as précis of his materials. The choices that he made, and the point at which he made them, provide a necessary background to an appreciation of the relationship between GDB and the inquests on which it was based.

Format and Content

The production of GDB is now usually considered as a relatively simple process of abbreviation from more or less fully compiled drafts.[10] In reality, the scribe's sources were less homogeneous and uniform in their nature. In part at least he was almost certainly responsible for radical rearrangement of his materials, if not compilation. As such, the checking of facts and figures was probably an integral element in the process of abbreviation. Hitherto the discrepancies in information between GDB and the extant circuit reports have often been interpreted as evidence of intermediate recensions; Exon was superseded by a fair copy with additional material and ICC by a seigneurially

---

[5] See e.g. the Lincolnshire series (*Rotuli Hundredorum*, i. 241–402). The eyre did not take place until 1281, by which time many of the jurors were dead.

[6] There is a list of jurors appended to a summary roll for Kent which is preserved in the main sequence of Hundred Rolls (London, PRO, SC5/Kent/Chapter House/1 m.16). The function of this roll, however, is unclear.

[7] London, PRO, SC5/Wilts/Chapter House/1a; *Rotuli Hundredorum*, ii. 230–8. It should be noted, however, that a list of the jurors in Wiltshire is appended to this roll (*Rotuli Hundredorum*, ii. 238–41). In the absence of verdicts, it is impossible to be certain of its origin or purpose.

[8] *Lincolnshire Domesday and Lindsey Survey*, 237–60. For totals, see e.g. L5; 6/8–1; 9/1,2; 11/1; 12/1–7; 13/1–2; 14/6; 15/2. The close correlation between the total assessments of the wapentakes recorded at the head of each and the totals derived from the figures given for individual estates indicates an original survey by twelve-carucate hundred.

[9] *Book of Fees*, 654–1141.   [10] Galbraith, *Making of Domesday Book*, *passim*.

arranged version. The reasoning, however, is skewed by the assumption that the production of GDB was an integrated process from beginning to end. The fact that GDB has material that is not in ICC and Exon does not necessarily indicate a different source. The compiler clearly had access to material other than the circuit reports, notably the geld survey, and there is evidence that these were used to check the accuracy of the material that was being abbreviated. Thus, as Galbraith noted, there are instances in which ICC identifies a place differently from GDB.[11] A holding described under Foxton in the one, for example, is identified as Fowlmere in the other.[12] It is precisely such detail that the geld schedule might be expected to furnish.

Abbreviation of the circuit reports saw the realization of the GDB form for the first time. From the outset, there was a clear understanding of the format. The shire became the basic unit of organization. This caused few problems for the compiler. By and large the area of each shire was apparent from the sources at his disposal. It was only occasionally that an estate was wrongly assigned where Exon-like sources were drawn up by supracomital fee.[13] The extra-shrieval areas were merely appended to the counties with which they were most closely associated. Within the shire the geographical format gave way to a seigneurial one; the fee, with but few exceptions, became the basic unit of textual organization. Here more problems presented themselves. Some or all of the main scribe's sources probably had rudimentary lists of tenants-in-chief: Exon itself preserves one.[14] But he had his own programme which entailed the arrangement of the chapters by order of precedence,[15] and he therefore probably compiled his own lists which were appended, often postscriptally,[16] to the account of the county town to act as a finding aid for the breves that followed. Few of these lists accurately conform to the number and order of the fees. On occasion names in the one are absent in the other; the abbot of York and Rainald son of Erchenbald appear in the lists in Yorkshire and Surrey folios respectively but are only recorded as tenants in the breves, while conversely Alfred of Spain and Robert de Bucy are absent from the lists in Dorset and Leicestershire but appear in the texts. More commonly, the order of entries, especially in those of the minor fees, are different. Sometimes the variations attest checking. The status of the abbot of York as a tenant-in-chief is apparently supported by testimony of the Yorkshire Summary, but subsequent investigation seems to have shown that he held in thegnage.[17] Otherwise, it would seem that fees were sometimes accidentally

[11] Ibid. 133–4.   [12] *ICC* 45; GDB 194b: *DB Cambs.*, 14,20.

[13] Welldon Finn, *Domesday Inquest*, 168–9.   [14] Exon, 532.

[15] Exon does not exhibit the same order of fiefs as GDB, but, of course, the order is derived from its first binding rather than any contemporary order.

[16] See e.g. Dorset (GDB 75a: *DB Dorset*, L), where from no. 52 the entries are written across both columns, and Berkshire (GDB 56a: *DB Berks.*, L), where the hand is cramped.

[17] GDB 305a, 314a, 380d: *DB Yorks.*, 4N1.8N2.SN,Ma,3–14. Berengar of Tosny seems to have acquired the service.

omitted. Thus, the lands of Tavistock Abbey in Cornwall were apparently overlooked (they are entered in the inside of a quire in Exon) and were subsequently misplaced in GDB.[18] Smaller fees are commonly postscriptal additions to the texts, indicating that this was common.

Such problems were relatively simple to resolve. Other matters of format apparently threatened to undermine the scribe's taxonomy. The definition of a tenant-in-chief is seemingly transparent; he rendered services directly to the king. There were, however, others who were similarly close to the king, but were of more humble standing. Many a sokeman had no intermediate lord and there were numerous thegns and drengs of various kinds who held their lands in return for ministerial service. Ultimately, the preferred solution to this problem was to relegate tenants of this kind to a separate chapter, that of the *taini regis*. But the scribe appears to have taken a long time to arrive at it. In Yorkshire it is clear that the original intention was to enroll such lands in the king's breve, for in the Summary all of the lands are attributed to the king without qualification. Elsewhere in GDB the land of many royal tenants appears in the *terra regis*. In Yorkshire, however, it was subsequently decided to enter them in a separate chapter, noted in the prefatory list as *terra tainorum regis*. But this did not completely resolve the issue. In the course of compiling the chapter it appears to have been realized that 332 manors were not tenanted at the time of the survey, and they were thus entered on a separate sheet and sewn into the quire in which the king's lands were entered.

Vacillation to this degree was probably exceptional. But there remained nice distinctions of status to draw. In Exon various 'class' breves were created, but when the GDB came to draft his abbreviation many of the *milites, taini*, and the like were brought above the salt and, like Godbold,[19] assigned their own chapters. Elsewhere there was equivocation. In the Lincolnshire folios there was apparently no doubt that sergeants like Odo the arblaster should have their own breve, and originally so did the more important English thegns. Thus, in the Lincolnshire prefatory list Kolgrimr and Svartbrandr were entered alone, and Ketilbjorn with other thegns. In the event only the first was to retain his position in the pecking order;[20] the other two were entered together with the rest of the king's thegns.[21]

The focus of the work was to remain emphatically the lands of the tenant-in-chief. This is clearest in the treatment of tenants. Throughout GDB little attempt is generally made to distinguish one person from another. Roberts,

---

[18] Exon, 180ᵛ–181ᵛ; GDB, 120d: *DB Cornwall*, 3; Welldon Finn, *Domesday Inquest*, 169.

[19] GDB 117a–b: *DB Devon*, 47.

[20] The lands of other thegns intrude, as at GDB, 370b–c: *DB Lincs.*, 67,5;8–12;19;22;23.

[21] GDB 370d–371c: *DB Lincs.*, 68. The three divisions are, nevertheless, recognized in the breve. The chapter opens with the land of Svartbrandr arranged in the common wapentake sequence and then a blank line and an enlarged initial I signals the start of the land of Ketilbjorn. His lands are also arranged in the order of the common sequence. A second enlarged initial I at the head of column 371a marks the start of the account of the lands of the *taini regis*.

Williams, Rogers, Walters follow one after the other without any attempt to indicate separate identities.[22] This is at variance with the circuit reports. ICC and Exon more or less consistently attempt to identify individuals with a toponymic, by-name, or distinguishing epithet. Count Alan's tenants in Cambridgeshire, for example, are undifferentiated in the folios of GDB.[23] In ICC, however, almost all are positively identified the first time they appear in each hundred,[24] unless they have a very rare name, such as the Godlamb who only appears once. Exon is similarly expansive. The compiler of GDB was not particularly interested in tenancies and did not assiduously strive to record them.[25]

Content reflects the preoccupation with the lands of the tenant-in-chief. The prologue to IE, the so-called articles of inquiry, accurately conveys what was deemed indispensable; all of the items recorded relate in one way or another to the direct issues of the *mansio* or manor. Communal data found no place. In the IE account of the Huntingdonshire estates of the abbey of Ely the area of each vill is given,[26] as is the practice in LDB, but the corresponding passages in GDB do not notice the information.[27] It is generally recorded in the Yorkshire folios,[28] but elsewhere does not regularly appear.[29] More surprisingly, the details of demesne livestock were consistently omitted (the retention of the information in the occasional GDB passage is probably a function of oversight).[30] In some circuits slaves may have been similarly viewed. The class is noticeable by its absence in the Circuit VI counties of GDB. Significantly, however, slaves are recorded in the Huntingdonshire section of IE, and it is clear that they were edited out by the compiler of GDB or his sources.[31] It seems likely that they were represented elsewhere in the north but were similarly ignored.

[22] The exception is in the accounts of the great territorial lordships like Chester.

[23] GDB 193d–195d: *DB Cambs.*, 14.

[24] See e.g. Ælmar of Bourn in Longstow Hundred whose toponym is given in the entry for Bourn itself but not in those of Caldecote, Longstowe, and Hatley St George that follow (*ICC* 89).

[25] The bishop of Worcester's Worcestershire breve is an exception, but here the scribe seems to have copied what was largely a seigneurial compilation. See pp. 143, 208.

[26] *ICC* 166–7.   [27] GDB 204a: *DB Hunts.*, 4.

[28] The information is normally appended to manorial entries and immediately precedes, or more rarely succeeds, the statement of value. This is one of a number of diplomatic irregularities in the Yorks. Domesday. See below, pp. 194–5.

[29] Area is sporadically recorded in the Lincolnshire folios, once in Nottinghamshire, three times in Rutland, five times in Derbyshire, and ten times in Cheshire. Occasionally the figures are said to be of arable and pasture land (GDB, 340a–b, 345d, 346d, 355a: *DB Lincs.*, 2,33;42.8,8.11,3–4.24,36) and the referent is probably to the land of the fee (in Yorkshire the measurements are sometimes explicitly of the manor). Generally, however, where it is recorded manor and vill are coterminous, and it seems likely that the figures were accidentally copied from a hundredally arranged recension. The information is not found elsewhere. However, ICC and Exon indicate that it was either not always collected or was edited out at an earlier stage. See Darby, 'Domesday Book and the Geographer', 113–4.

[30] Welldon Finn, *Domesday Inquest*, 170. See e.g. GDB 139b: *DB Herts.*, 31,8.

[31] *ICC* 166; Pelteret, *Slavery in Early Medieval England*, 185–232.

It is tempting to see in this decided policy a firm focus on the more con-crete infrastructure of the manor. Slaves were just individuals, but villagers, sokemen, and free men represented permanent and, it must be said on their part, inalienable service.[32] Other items were included for some circuits but excluded from others. Intermediate manorial statistics, notably the value of estates 'when they were received' by the TRW holder, are common to both Exon and ICC, but only those of the latter found their way into GDB; the information is regularly found only in the GDB folios of Circuits I and III. Here there was clearly a change of mind at some point in the process of abbre-viation. Other irregularities of this kind must reflect the scope of the sources employed. Most, however, are indicative of a developing expression.

Beyond format and content, the main scribe formulated a precise diplomatic. Much was the substitution of short forms and standard phrases for commonly occurring material: *TRE*, for example, replaced *die qua Rex Eduardus vivus et mortuus fuit* throughout, and a simple statement of a place-name did service for the cumbersome *mansionem que vocatur* of Exon. The aim of such changes was simply to reduce the expansive phraseology of the circuit reports to a precise and economical form to facilitate reference. Other changes, however, hint at a more ambitious attempt to represent the reality of landed wealth of his sources. A progression in thinking can be observed as the work progressed.

Diplomatic and the Order of Writing

The present arrangement of GDB dates from the time of its first binding some time after the completion of the work. Its composition, then, does not indicate the order of writing. There are textual links between quires, but they are of limited occurrence. Normally the account of a shire was entered in its own quire or group of quires. In four places, however, a quire is shared, showing that Devon was written before Cornwall, Gloucestershire before Worcestershire, Shropshire before Cheshire, and Yorkshire before Lincolnshire. Textual links of another kind suggest that Nottinghamshire preceded Derby-shire, for Derby is described with Nottingham before the account of the cus-toms of both shires and the Nottinghamshire breves. There are no other explicit indications of a sequence of writing. Rulings, however, suggest that some quires go with others. In much of GDB the scribe carefully marked out the lines and columns of each quire, often with the aid of a template to prick the folios, before he commenced to write.[33] Four ruling patterns, as they are called, so produced have been identified by Michael Gullick.[34] Number 1 consists of

---

[32] Much has been written on the various classes of Domesday peasant and the population that they represent. There is evidence to demonstrate, however, that they often represented fiscal units. See above, pp. 156–7.

[33] Gullick and Thorn, 'Scribes of GDB', 94–6.   [34] Gullick, 'Manuscripts', 96.

eight vertical and usually forty-four horizontal lines; 1b is distinguished from 1a by the use of a template. Number 2 has seven vertical and fifty horizontal lines, number 3 six and fifty-three, and 4 has four column guides, but is otherwise unruled. The distribution of the forms is illustrated in Table 8.1.

Variations are considerable, but Galbraith postulated therefrom a progressive compression of the text with the scribe's growing awareness of the urgency of the task before him. On this basis he suggested an order of writing. Circuit III folios, with forty-four lines per column, were written first, and were followed by Circuit VI, I, and IV with fifty lines, and concluded with II and V in which the rulings were ignored altogether.[35] Unfortunately, Galbraith relied upon the figures given in *Domesday Book Rebound*,[36] and therefore failed to appreciate that the maxima and minima there given conceal significant

TABLE 8.1. *Ruling patterns in GDB*

Quire	Ruling pattern	Lines	Template
Circuit VI			
38 Yorks. 1	1b	47 or 49	
39 Yorks. 2	2	38, 40, or 43	
40 Yorks. 3	1b	44	
41 Yorks. 4	1b	44	C in parts
42 Yorks. 5			
and Lincs. 1	1b	44	
43 Lincs. 2	1b	44	
44 Lincs. 3	1b	44	
45 Lincs. 4	1b	44	
46 Lincs. 5	1b	44	
47 *Clamores*	2	52	
36 Notts. 1	1a	44	B
37 Notts. 2			
and Rutland	1a	44	B
35 Derby.	1a	44	B
26 Hunts.	1a	44	B
Circuit III			
24 Cambs. 1	1a	44	B
25 Cambs. 2	1a	44	B
17 Middlesex	1a	44	B
27 Beds.	1a	44	B
19 Bucks.	1a	44	B
18 Herts.	1b	44	

[35] Galbraith, *Making of Domesday Book*, 203–4.   [36] Appendix II, end foldout.

TABLE 8.1. (cont'd)

Quire	Ruling pattern	Lines	Template
Circuit I			
1 Kent 1	2	50	
2 Kent 2	1b	44 re-ruled with 51 or 52	
3 Sussex 1	2	50	A
4 Sussex 2	2	50	
5 Surrey	2	50	A
9 Berks.	2	50	A
6 Hants. 1	2	50	A
7 Hants. 2	2	50	A
8 Hants. 3	2	50	A
Circuit II			
10 Wilts.	3	53	
11 Dorset	3	53	
12 Som. 1	4		
13 Som. 2	4		
14 Devon 1	4		
15 Devon 2	4		
16 Devon 3 and Cornwall	4		
Circuit V			
22 Gloucs. and Worcs.	4		
23 Hereford	4		
32 Salop 1	4		
33 Salop 2 and Ches. 1	4		
34 Ches. 2 and Lancs.	4		
31 Staffs.	4		
30 Warks.	4		
20 Oxon.	4		
28 Northants.	4		
29 Leics.	2 and 3	50–4 ruled by leaf, not sheet	

Source: After M. Gullick, 'The Great and Little Domesday Manuscripts', in A. Williams and R. W. H. Erskine (eds.), *Domesday Book Studies* (London, 1987), 96.

variations, first in the rulings, and second in the actual number of lines of writing. The forty-four line format of Circuit III is in fact largely confined to rulings and it is only in a few folios that they are observed. The fewest lines are found in the Yorkshire folios, and it was in the course of their compilation that the forty-four line standard of ruling pattern 1 was established.[37] But more suspect is the assumption of haste. The suggestion that the scribe became increasingly aware of the need to compress in order to make the volume manageable is more likely.[38] Nevertheless, the evidence of rulings, and lines, can only be used effectively in conjunction with developing diplomatic.[39]

It is clear that many of the distinctive forms used in the various circuits are derived from circuit drafts. The opening formula 'In x a had y carucates to the geld' of the northern folios, for example, is not found in Exon or ICC, but is encountered in the Huntingdonshire section of IE and is therefore presumably peculiar to Circuit VI.[40] Likewise, the distinctive opening formulas of Circuits II and III are derived from the drafts from which they were compiled.[41] Other forms, by contrast, were demonstrably adopted and developed in the course of writing GDB. A number are found in the Yorkshire and Lincolnshire VI folios.

The Yorkshire Domesday opens in the normal way with an introductory section which comprises a description of the city of York and the eighty-four carucates of land that gelded with it, a note on the liberties and customs from which the king derived an income, and finally a list of the tenants-in-chief in the shire. It is written with ruling pattern 1b in two columns on forty-nine lines, and variations in the hand indicate that the scribe entered the material on at least three separate occasions (Table 4.1). Each section relates to a different type of information, and the fact may therefore indicate the use of diverse sources. Nevertheless, it is likely that all are derived in one way or another from the survey of the king's demesne and the geld inquest. The seigneurially arranged breves that follow are likewise written in two columns as is usual throughout GDB. Ruling pattern 1b is used throughout apart from quire no. 39 where pattern 2 is found. Initially the number of lines per column varies. There are forty-nine at the beginning of the king's breve, but the total falls to thirty-eight in the account of the count of Mortain's estates, to climb to forty-three in the middle of Count Alan's fee. It is only from GDB 315a, breve no. 9, that the forty-four line standard that is found throughout Circuit VI is adopted.[42] With the exception of all or parts of breves nos. 1, 2, 3, 12, 30, and 31, the account seems to have been written consecutively by

---

[37] Roffe, 'Domesday Book and Northern Society', 322. Ruling pattern 2 is used in quire no. 39.

[38] Gullick, 'Great and Little DB Scribes', 95.

[39] The following draws upon Roffe, 'Domesday Book and Northern Society', 313–23.

[40] ICC 166. The only other occurrence of the form is in the king's Gloucestershire breve, where it is highly anomalous (GDB 162d–164b: DB Gloucs., 1).

[41] See above, p. 81.   [42] PRO, Domesday Book Rebound, Appendix II.

one hand, although additions, both foreseen and unforeseen, are found throughout the text.

In the normal course of events no attempt was made to group dependent berewicks and sokelands with the manorial *caput* within each breve. Tenurial relationships were, however, expressed by an explicit notice of soke centres, and subordinate status is further indicated by distinctive forms of entry. It is usually stated that 'In x^1 there is soke of x^2; y carucates to the geld', or 'In x^1 there are y carucates of land to the geld; the soke is in x^2', and from f. 315d: 9W36 marginal lombardic B and S signal berewicks and sokelands. It is only the appurtenances of the larger sokes such as Ripon and Howden which are enrolled with the *caput*:[43] berewicks are either listed after the record of the name of the estate centre or, like tributary sokeland, are appended to the end of the entry. The normal formula is 'To this manor pertains the soke of this land . . .', a list of vills follows, with their individual assessments interlined, and the stocking of the whole soke is then outlined.

The diplomatic of manorial entries is far more variable. Twelve basic opening formulas,[44] VIA to L, have been identified which are seemingly used at random (Table 8.2). Type VIA is only found in the description of the eighty-four carucates that belonged to York. The distribution of the remaining eleven, however, reveals a remarkably consistent pattern once postscriptal entries and sections have been identified (Table 8.3). The three related forms VIB, VIC, and VIE are generally employed interchangeably up to the beginning of breve no. 5 (f. 305b). VIK appears in four places, but is found only in postscriptal sections, and VID is found in 2B (ff. 302c–303a), which again is almost certainly a later addition to the text. At f. 305d: 5N31 type VIF is introduced, and it alternates with VIC until f. 309b: 6N10 where VIG appears, which itself is succeeded in turn by VIH, VII, and VIJ. VIK again appears at f. 321a: 11W2–4 and in 12, but in both cases the entries are postscriptal. It is only from f. 325a: 14E51 that it becomes the standard formula which is used in the remainder of the Yorkshire folios, with the exception of Robert de Brus's breve which was added in the twelfth century.[45] Throughout, tenant in 1086 (if any), teams in demesne, villagers, bordars, and sokemen with their teams, manorial stock, and value are recorded in that order without significant variation.

The basic form VIK, along with ruling pattern 1b and the forty-four line column, is employed from the very start of the Lincolnshire breves, which follow on from the Yorkshire Domesday after the description of the city of Lincoln and the boroughs of Stamford and Torksey, and no further modifications were made to the standard formula. Rather, the compiler turned his attention to the problems presented by subordinate holdings. From breve

[43] GDB 303d, 304c: *DB Yorks*, 2W7.3Y4.
[44] Minor variations of word order which only appear in one entry have not been listed as separate forms.
[45] Green, 'David I and Henry I', 12.

TABLE 8.2. *GDB formulas*

Circuit VI

VIA   Survey by vills: In x there y^1 carucates which z ploughs can plough; of these a^1 had y^1 with a hall; now b^1 has them. And a^2 had y^2 . . .

VIB   In x there are y carucates to the geld which z ploughs can plough; a held it for a manor, now b and c from him.

VIC   In x are y carucates; z ploughs possible; a had a manor, now b and c from him.

VID   In x are y carucates; land for z ploughs. The manor was and is a's.

VIE   In x are y carucates; z ploughs are possible; a had and has it.

VIF   In x a had a manor of y carucates; z ploughs possible. Now c has it from b.

VIG   In x a had a manor of y carucates; [there is land for z ploughs]. Now c has it from b.

VIH   MNR In x a had y carucates, [land for z ploughs]. Now b has it.

VII   MNR In x a had y carucates, z ploughs are possible. Now b has it.

VIJ   M In x a had y carucates, z ploughs are possible. Now b has it.

VIK   M In x a had y carucates, land for z ploughs. Now b has it.

VIL   In x a^2 held y carucates from a^1, land for z ploughs.

VIM b has t^1 teams in demesne, and n^1 villagers, and n^2 bordars with t^2 teams, and n^3 sokemen with t^3 teams.

VIN b has t^1 teams in demesne, and n^1 villagers, and n^2 bordars with t^2 teams, and n^3 sokemen on y^2 carucates with t^3 teams.

VIO b has t^1 teams in demesne, and n^1 villagers, n^3 sokemen, and n^2 bordars with t^2 teams.

VIP b has t^1 teams in demesne, and n^1 villagers, n^3 sokemen, and n^2 bordars with t^2 teams . . . y^2 carucates are in soke.

VIQ b has t^1 teams in demesne and n^3 sokemen on y^2 carucates, and n^1 villagers, and n^2 bordars with t^2 teams.

VIR b has t^1 teams in demesne and n^3 sokemen, n^1 villagers, and n^2 bordars with t^2 teams.

VIS b^2 holds from b^1.

Circuit III

IIIA   M x is a demesne vill and defends itself for y hides . . . Value now, when acquired, TRE. This manor a held.

IIIB   M x b holds, y hides are there . . . Value now, when acquired, TRE. This M a held.

IIIC   M b holds x/in x, y hides are there/it defends itself for y hides . . . Value now, when acquired, TRE. This manor a held.

IIID   In x b^2 holds y hides . . . Value now, when acquired, TRE. a^2 held this land under a^1. He could sell etc.

Circuit I

IA   M b holds x/in x, y sulungs are there/it defends itself for y sulungs. . . . Value now, when acquired, TRE. This manor a held.

TABLE 8.2. (cont'd)

IB	b holds x; a held it and it defended itself for y^1 sulungs, now for y^2 . . . It used to be worth . . . when acquired . . . now.
IC	In x a held y hides and now it defends itself for/it never gelded . . . Valuit/valebat, valet.

Circuit II

IIA	B^1 holds x (and b^2 from him). A held it TRE; he/it used to geld for y^1 hides. Land for z ploughs. Of these y^2 hides in demesne . . . Valuit, modo.
IIB	B^2 holds from b^1 x. A held it TRE; he/it used to geld for y^1 hides. Land for z ploughs . . . Valuit, modo.
IIC	B^1 holds x. A held it TRE; he/it used to geld for y^1 hides. Land for z ploughs . . . Valuit, modo.
IID	B^1 holds x. A used to hold it TRE; he/it used to geld for y^1 hides. Land for z ploughs . . . Olim, modo.
IIE	B holds x. There were y^1 hides TRE. Land for y teams. In demesne y^2 hides . . . Olim, modo.
IIF	B holds x; a used to hold it TRE and he/it used to geld for y^1 hides. There are y^2 hides there, however . . . Olim, modo.

Circuit V

VA	B held x, there were y hides. In demesne . . . Valebat, modo.
VB	In x held b y hides. In demesne . . . Render.
VC	B^1 holds (and b^2 from him) x, a held and could go. There y hides gelding. In demesne . . . Valuit, modo.
VD	B holds y hides in x/b holds in x y hides, a held . . . In demesne . . . Valuit, modo.
VE	In x are y hides . . .
VF	B (b^2 from b^1) holds x. A held. There y hides gelding. Land for z ploughs . . . Valuit, modo.

Circuit IV

IVA	B (b^2 from b^1) holds x. A held. There are y hides. Land for z ploughs . . . Valebat, modo.
IVB	B (b^2 from b^1) holds x. A held. There are y hides. Land for z ploughs . . . Valuit, modo.
IVC	B^1 y hides in x/in x y hides (and b^2 from him). A held. Land for z ploughs . . . Valuit, modo.
IVD	B (b^2 from b^1) holds x. There are y hides. Land for z ploughs . . . Valuit, modo. A held . . .
IVE	B (b^2 from b^1) holds y hides in x/in x y hides. Land for z ploughs . . . Valuit, modo. A held . . .
IVF	In x are y hides/In x holds b y hides.

TABLE 8.3. *The distribution of forms in the Yorkshire Domesday*

	A	B	C	D	E	F	G	H	I	J	K	L
C23–35	+											
1Y1–1Y11		+										
1Y12–13											+	
1Y14–15		+										
1Y16–18			+									
1Y19											+	
1N–1L											+	
2A				+								
2B1					+							
2B2–7		+										
2B8			+									
2B9–18		+										
2B19–2N14			+									
2N19–25					+							
2N26–30												+
2W1					+							
2W2–6		+										
2W7			+									
2E1												
2E2		+										
2E5–7					+							
2E8			+									
2E11					+							
2E12–14		+										
2E15–17			+									
2E18–41											+	
3Y1–4		+										
3Y5			+									
3Y6–15		+										
3Y16–18											+	
4N1–3		+										
4E1–5N30			+									
5N31–44						+						
5N45–6			+									
5N47–8		+										
5N49–5E38						+						
5E39			+									
5E40–1						+						
5E42			+									
5E43						+						

TABLE 8.3. (cont'd)

	A	B	C	D	E	F	G	H	I	J	K	L
5E44			+									
5E45–64						+						
5E65–66			+									
5E67–6N9						+						
6N10–7E2			+									
8N1–5							+					
8N6–8E6								+				
9W1–5									+			
9W6–8		+										
9W9–40									+			
9W41–63										+		
9W64												
9W65–118										+		
9W119												
9W120–11W1										+		
11W2–4											+	
12											+	
13W1–14E50										+		
14E51–29W50											+	

Note: Entries in **bold** type indicate postscriptal additions to the text. Many of these entries exhibit variations in form that are not separately listed here.

no. 1 berewicks and sokeland were consistently grouped with the manorial *caput*, or signs were employed to indicate the context of a subsidiary entry where it had been accidentally misplaced.[46] Until breve no. 24 the soke centre is frequently named in each entry—the diplomatic is much the same as that used in the Yorkshire folios—but subsequently a general rubric is used of the form 'Soke of this manor' or 'Soke of *X*'. Throughout, elaborate calligraphic conventions were adopted to distinguish tributary land from demesne. Manorial entries are introduced by a square initial I, and the place-name is written in large rustic letters and rubricated. Subordinate inland and sokeland entries, by way of contrast, commence with a rustic I, and the place-name is

---

[46] A number of exceptions can be found, but, usually enrolled towards the end of breves, they are almost invariably later additions to the text which lack of space precluded from enrolment with the manorial *caput*. Forinsec soke entries, that is sokeland held by one tenant-in-chief while soke was paid to another, are entered in the breve of the tenant in Lincolnshire and are sometimes grouped with the manor from which they were exploited. More usually, however, their position in the text was determined by geography.

in no way distinguished from the rest of the text.[47] The most noticeable differences, however, are found in the treatment of 'intramanorial sokemen', that is, sokemen who are enrolled in the manorial entry, and their lands (Tables 8.2 and 8.4). Initially, the VIO form, which predominates in the

TABLE 8.4. *Distribution of sokeland forms in the Yorkshire and Lincolnshire folios*

	M	N	O	P	Q	R
Y1Y13–15			+			
2A1–2B1	+					
2W4–3Y4	+					
4E2–14E6			+			
14E15–15E4						+
16W1–20E3			+			
21E6						+
23E14–29W9			+			
L1,1–4	+					
1,5		+				
1,6	+					
1,26–4,41			+			
4,42	+					
4,43–5,3			+			
6,1					+	
7,1–35			+			
7,36	+					
7,37–8,8			+			
8,9		+				
8,15			+			
8,17	+					
8,18–12,97			+			
13,1–21				+		
13,22			+			
13,24–38				+		
13,45			+			
14,1–29				+		

[47] Roffe, 'Nottinghamshire', 37–40. Exceptions to the rule indicate otherwise unremarked relationships and subtleties of status. See e.g. GDB, 293d: *DB Rutland*, R17–18 where a rustic I indicates the subordinate status of a small manor which was appurtenant to the queen's estate of Oakham. Inland and sokeland entries with manorial forms presumably imply that the land had some special status that approximated to a manor. Square and rustic I's are seemingly used at random in the Yorkshire folios. It is possible, however, that they have the same meaning in some contexts. The dependence of Ketilbjorn's manor in Hunmanby on the major holding in the same vill, for example, which was held by Karli and belonged to Ulf Fenisc, is probably signalled by a rustic initial I (GDB 326b: *DB Yorks.*, 20E2).

TABLE 8.4. (cont'd)

	M	N	O	P	Q	R
14,30			+			
14,31–8				+		
14,39–45			+			
14,46–62				+		
14,63–5			+			
14,66–101				+		
15,1					+	
16,1–47			+			
17,2	+					
18,1–3				+		
18,4			+			
18,7				+		
18,13–23			+			
18,24				+		
18,27–22,30			+			
22,31				+		
23,1					+	
24,1–12			+			
24,13–19	+					
24,20				+		
24,24–5			+			
24,36–81					+	
24,82			+			
25,3					+	
25,5–6			+			
25,7–37,1					+	
37,2	+					
38,1–66,2					+	
67,1–12						+
67,13					+	
67,24–68,41						+
68,42					+	
68,43–8						+

Yorkshire folios, is employed.[48] From breve no. 13, VIP is the normal form until VIQ is introduced in breve no. 24. From that point VIQ and the closely related VIR are henceforward universal.

The remaining Circuit VI shires see a change from ruling pattern 1b to 1a. However, all exhibit the VIK/Q form, except in the account of a handful of

[48] GDB, 343d 351d, 354b: *DB Lincs.*, 6,1.15,1.23,1.

TABLE 8.5. *The compilation of Circuit VI*

	Folios	Quire	Forms	Textual links	
Yorks.	297–306	38	A–F	qs	K
	307–14	39	C, F, G, H, I		I
	315–22	40	J, K		H
	323–30	41	K		G
	331–5	42	K		F
Lincs.	336–40	42	K/M, N, O		F
	341–8	43	K/M, N, O		E
	349–56	44	K/N, O, P, Q		D
	357–64	45	K/Q		C
	365–72	46	K/Q		B
Notts.	280–8	36	K/Q	Derby with Nottingham	
	289–96	37	K/Q		
Derby.	272–9	35	K/Q/S		
Hunts.	203–8	26	K/Q/S		

Note: qs = quire signature.

royal manors,[49] and only one further change is found in the diplomatic. The Nottinghamshire folios are almost identical to those of Lincolnshire, although *obiter dicta* are less common and manorial entries are proportionately more numerous. There are, however, fewer sokemen and sokeland entries. The description of *Roteland*, which forms an appendix to the account of the county, is likewise regular in form apart from its geographical arrangement. Derbyshire and Huntingdonshire are again uniform with the rest of the circuit, with the single exception of the record of tenants in 1086. In both counties their names are generally appended to the end of manorial entries rather than before the enumeration of demesne teams in the form 'B^2 holds from b^1' (form VIS). In many cases, especially in Derbyshire, the information is clearly postscriptal: the record of subtenancies is noticeably patchy and is therefore frequently subject to revision and emendation.[50] In most instances, however, it is a current component of the text and seems to mark the development of a new form.

The dovetailing of evolving form and scribal revision indicates that this development of diplomatic was the work of the GDB scribe rather than the compilers of his source material. As such the pattern reveals the order in which the northern county folios were composed (Table 8.5). Yorkshire was clearly

[49] GDB 272b–c, 203c: *DB Derby.*, 1,1;13–15; *DB Hunts.*, 1,6 all approximate to the Yorkshire form VIB, although no TRE holder is noted and the developed ploughland formula is employed. The reversion to an archaic form may imply that a common diplomatic, and by implication, source, lies behind the Domesday account of the *terra regis* in the northern shires. A VIB-type form is also found at GDB 283a: *DB Notts.*, 5,1.

[50] Roffe, *Derbyshire Domesday*, 12–13, 29–30. See e.g. GDB 273b, 274a, 275d: *DB Derby.*, 2,1.6,12;95.

first, for its great variety of formulas was resolved into a form which was adopted in the remaining shires. Lincolnshire, linked to Yorkshire by a shared gathering and a series of quire signatures which run backwards from the end of the volume,[51] clearly followed, for the refinements in the formal organization of manors and the definition of the status of sokemen that were developed in its folios are otherwise universal. Nottinghamshire apparently followed, for diplomatically it is virtually indistinguishable from Lincolnshire, but is anterior to the account of Derbyshire which is interwoven with the former, but newly exhibits form VIS. Huntingdonshire would therefore appear to be the last to be compiled.

Such variations in diplomatic in a single circuit are all but unparalleled, and there are grounds to believe that the northern counties were the first to be composed in the production of GDB, for two of the conventions developed there were used elsewhere in GDB. First, marginal M (Table 8.2, forms VIJ, VIK), absent from the surviving circuit reports and only adopted in Circuit VI after much experimentation halfway through the Yorkshire folios, is thereafter employed throughout much of Circuit III. Secondly, the form 'Land for z teams' (VIK), evolved, again in the Yorkshire folios, from the more cumbersome 'z ploughs can plough there' and its variants which is the norm in Exon and has echoes in ICC and IE,[52] is all-but universal elsewhere in GDB.[53] Conversely, distinctive forms of Circuits I to V do occasionally appear in Circuit VI, but are, significantly, postscriptal in all instances. Thus, for example, at the end of the Ranskill entry in the Nottinghamshire folios appears the statement 'Godric held [it]; the archbishop [of York] holds [it] [*Godric tenuit, archepiscopus tenet*]'.[54] The entry is clearly postscriptal (it has been squeezed into a blank line between the preceding and succeeding entries and is written with another pen), and the phrase, paralleled in the Sussex folios in Circuit I,[55] was evidently written after the circuit was completed. More clear is another entry in the Nottinghamshire folios. The statement that 'Aswulf held [*Escul tenuit*]' one bovate in Basford was written by the revising scribe.[56]

It is likely that the compiler of GDB worked out the major problems of composition in the abbreviation and engrossing of the first folios that he worked on, the account of the northern counties. Thereafter, the organization of the material is generally more accomplished and there are fewer changes in

[51] They presumably relate to binding, but they may represent a perception of an appropriate order before the binding was undertaken.

[52] ICC and IE have similar formulas where actual ploughs do not match potential, but the summary statement at the beginning of fees is of the form *ibi est terra z carucis*.

[53] The form was the norm in Worcestershire and the first half of Shropshire. Other exceptions are apparently due to Homer nodding.

[54] GDB 283b: *DB Notts.*, 5,12.   [55] GDB 19a–20b: *DB Sussex*, 9,44–130.

[56] GDB 288a: *DB Notts.*, 10,52; Gullick, 'Manuscripts', 103. For other examples, see GDB 303c, 283b, 291a, 291b: *DB Yorks.*, 2N27–30; *DB Notts.*, 5,12.18,5.20,8. The form of GDB 345a: *DB Lincs.*, 7,58 is closer to Circuits I to V in its initial statement of the lord and tenant in 1086 than Circuit VI, but an exact parallel has not been observed.

diplomatic. In consequence it becomes more difficult to discern such a clear chronology of composition. There seems no doubt, however, that Circuit III was the second to be written. Like the Nottinghamshire, Derbyshire, and Huntingdonshire folios, and no other GDB quires, Middlesex, Buckingham-shire, Cambridgeshire, and Bedfordshire exhibit ruling pattern 1a and Hert-fordshire 1b. Four distinctive opening and closing clauses are found (Table 8.2, forms IIIA, IIIB, IIIC, IIID).[57] Throughout, IIIC and IIID are occasionally prefaced by an indication of the hundred in which the land was situated, 'In the hundred of *X . . .*', but it seems to mark less another form than a variation on the normal practice of identifying hundreds with a rubric.[58] In Hertfordshire marginal M occurs only intermittently.[59] As ICC shows, in substance these forms are derived from circuit drafts and they therefore exhibit no development of chronological significance for the writing of GDB. Marginal M, however, must be derived from the Circuit VI folios where the device was first adopted. It is not found elsewhere in GDB and there is nothing to suggest that it is not a current component of the text.[60]

As in the north, the manor of Circuit III sometimes had detached elements. Tenements are occasionally termed berewicks, more often they are said to 'be in' or 'lie in' a manor. Again, one piece of land might be valued in another both TRE and TRW, indicating that a tenurial nexus or soke might be reserved to a predecessor or a manorial centre. No attempt was made to group such appurtenances with manorial *caput*. Nevertheless, in Bedfordshire, Cam-bridgeshire, and Middlesex square and rustic initial I's were more or less consistently used to distinguish *manerium* from *terra*. For example, Count Alan held the manor of Abington in succession to Edeva the Fair. The entry is in form IIIB, but the initial I of the opening words *Ipse comes* is square. Four parcels of land are then described in form IIID, each beginning with a rustic I, in which the TRE tenants are said to hold under Edeva, were not free to withdraw, or owed other inalienable services to her.[61] Again, the bishop of London held the manor of Stepney in Middlesex and the initial I of the entry in which it is described is square in form. By contrast, the ten parcels of land 'in the same place' that follow (of which nine are explicitly said to have been held in demesne in 1066 or were parcel of the manor of Stepney)

---

[57] These forms are represented by T, U, V, and W in Roffe, 'Domesday Book and Northern Society', 316.

[58] There are a number of entries in Middlesex, however, and very occasionally elsewhere, in which a place-name is not noticed (GDB 127a, 127b, 128d, 129c, 130b, 130d, 197c: *DB Middlesex*, 1,2.2,3.5,2.9,2.14,2.25,2; *DB Cambs.*, 24,2). The place-name could have been accidentally omitted or a different form presented.

[59] It does not appear before GDB 137a: *DB Herts.*, 16,2 and thereafter only seven times. On at least one occasion the marginal M seems to have been used to correct the false impression given by a rustic I (GDB 142a: *DB Herts.*, 38,2).

[60] There is no difference in the hand or pen between the letters and the entries to which they refer (Thorn, 'Marginal Notes', 123–4).

[61] GDB 194a: *DB Cambs.*, 14,14–18.

TABLE 8.6. *The compilation of Circuit III*

Shire	Ruling	Lines folio by folio	Marginal M	Calligraphy
Cambridgeshire 1	1a	44, 44, 44, 44, 44, 44, 44, 44	✓	✓
Cambridgeshire 2	1a	44, 49, 48, 52, 51, 52	✓	✓
Middlesex	1a	44, 44, 48, 50, 53	✓	✓
Bedfordshire	1a	43, 52, 49, 52, 53, 54, 54, 53, 56, 61	✓	✓
Buckinghamshire	1a	na, 53, 53, 54, 54, 53, 53, 52, 50, 52, 54	✓	✓
Hertfordshire	1b	43, 44, 49, 49, 49, 58, 56, 55, 53, 51, 56		

Note: Lines have been counted for the first column in each folio except where blank or incomplete. Obvious additions to the text have been excluded as have 'overflows' at the bottom of columns. 'na' = not available.

exhibit a rustic I.[62] The calligraphic device was clearly used with purpose. Indeed, in the account of Eudo son of Hubert's manor of Gamlingay in Cambridgeshire the scribe felt it necessary to correct himself. He originally wrote a rustic I to introduce the entry, but he appears to have subsequently found that the land was a capital manor and changed the initial letter to a square I.[63] In Bedfordshire the scribe was less careful where a marginal M signalled a manor, but in the case of Stevington he similarly felt the need to amend his text.[64] It is usually impossible to reconstruct manors and their appurtenances from this type of data, but there seems to have been a clear intention to distinguish manorial from dependent land.

Square and rustic initial I's are found in the Buckinghamshire and Hertfordshire folios, but they do not always seem to be employed in any purposeful fashion.[65] If the device is a carry-over from Circuit VI, as seems likely, its absence from these two shires might suggest that they were the last of the circuit to be written. The conclusion is consonant with the limited evidence for a chronology of composition within the circuit. The occurrence of marginal M tends to indicate that Bedfordshire, Buckinghamshire, Cambridgeshire, and Middlesex precede Hertfordshire where it occurs in only three places. All four of these counties exhibit ruling pattern 1a, but the number of actual lines of writing varies (Table 8.6). Progressive compression is apparent in all as the scribe neared the end of the allotted quire. He clearly felt the need, first, to enter each county in its own booklet or booklets, and second, not to waste space.[66] The first quire of Cambridgeshire does, however, adhere to the rulings

[62] GDB 127b–c: *DB Middlesex*, 3,1–11. There is a note attached to the first dependent entry which states that 'Sired holds 2½ hides of this manor'. The reference seems to be to the *caput*; the entry is postscriptal.

[63] GDB 197d: *DB Cambs.*, 25,9.   [64] GDB 211b: *DB Beds.*, 15,2.

[65] But see a correction from square I to rustic I, or vice versa, at GDB 136d: *DB Herts.*, 15,9.

[66] In the second Cambridgeshire quire, for example, the scribe seems to have been acutely conscious of the need to save space; there are no lines between entries or indeed breves, and as his work

throughout. Might there be seen here a more relaxed scribe at the beginning of the circuit? A tentative chronology will therefore place Cambridgeshire first, followed by Middlesex or Bedfordshire, and then Buckinghamshire and Hertfordshire.

Kent and the other Circuit I counties were abbreviated next. Apart from the ploughland formula (albeit with the number of ploughlands often wanting), none of the conventions worked out in Circuit VI and adopted in III are found in the south-eastern counties. However, the scribe seems to have carried form IIIC from Circuit III into the account of the land of St Martin, Dover, and the first eight breves of the Kent Domesday as IA.[67] Here the distinctive features are a single TRW assessment to the geld and the record of the TRE holder at the end of the entry. No circuit report survives for Circuit I, but both were almost certainly at variance with the scribe's source for the Kent folios, for in Domesday Monachorum B both TRE and TRW assessments are given and the TRE tenant, where recorded, is given at the beginning of the entry in a prototype of form IB which is found from Kent breve no. 9 and subsequently in the Circuit I folios.[68] The IIIC-like form IA of Kent, then, must be derived ultimately from ICC and the similar sources of Circuit III. The scribe seems to have attempted to maintain a standardized entry by omitting TRE assessments and moving the record of the TRE tenant, but eventually gave up the struggle and surrendered to the text before him.

A further link with Circuit III is to be found in the rulings of the second Kent quire. Originally pattern 1b was used, but subsequently it was re-ruled with fifty-one or fifty-two lines which approximate to the fifty of the rest of Circuit I. It would seem that a quire was to hand which had been drawn up in the hitherto standard format, and it was modified to conform to the new pattern. Ruling pattern 2 was otherwise used throughout the circuit. Form IB is employed without chronologically significant variation.[69] The dependence of one parcel of land on another is occasionally explicit, but there is no obvious attempt to group appurtenances with manorial centre. In the count of Eu's breve in Sussex the distinctive form IC is found from ff. 19a–20c: 9,42–130, but it seems to be confined to the peculiarities of the geld-free or allodial land with which it is usually associated. Form IIID (with the value in the Circuit I order of TRE, after, and now) occurs occasionally in Surrey and

progressed he squeezed in more and more. It was only in the last column, f. 202c, that he could relax with the knowledge that he had enough space to finish his work and he celebrated by leaving a blank line before the last two breves.

[67] The valuation clause is slightly different. Kent reverses the order, starting with TRE, and substitutes *valebat* for *valuit*.

[68] *Domesday Monachorum*, 86, 88, 94: Brasted, Ulcombe, Sandlings (GDB 4b, 7a: *DB Kent*, 2,31–2.5,38). In a number of other instances the TRE tenant is given at the head of an entry but the information does not appear in GDB.

[69] In Hampshire the TRE tenant is often said to hold *in alodium*.

Sussex.[70] The initial I is rustic or square and the land is indifferently either geld-free, dependent, allodial, or a manor.[71] Significant compression is found in Berkshire, but there is little compelling evidence to frame a chronology of composition after Kent.

While shared diplomatic links the first three circuits, there is precious little for the remaining three beyond the 'land for z ploughs' formula and the commonplaces of GDB. Ruling, however, would suggest that Circuit II came next. The Wiltshire and Dorset folios exhibit ruling pattern 3, but Somerset, Devon, and Cornwall pattern 4. The change marked a significant decision to dispense with horizontal rulings which are subsequently found in GDB only in the Leicestershire folios. The writing of the Circuit II folios, then, would appear to bridge a change of policy in the layout of GDB. Diplomatic development within the circuit suggests an order of writing which reflects the break. The Wiltshire folios were clearly the first to be entered after Circuit I. With some uncertainty from ff. 65c–66a: 2,1 to 3,5[72] and anomalies in breves nos. 22, 23, and 24,[73] form IIA is generally used throughout. From breve no. 25, however, the name of the tenant in 1086 precedes that of the tenant-in-chief and the number of hides in demesne in such entries is not noticed (form IIB). This modification is carried over into the Dorset folios, but otherwise IIA is used there until breve no. 26, when IIC is introduced. IIA recurs in nos. 28, 30, and 31, giving way thereafter to IIC.[74]

This signals a change in editorial policy, for the number of hides in demesne are recorded in the parallel passages in Exon.[75] It is significant, then, that IIC (with IIB for tenanted land) is used, although not exclusively, from the beginning of the Somerset folios, indicating that it follows Dorset. In its turn it too is developed, with the *tenuit* of the TRE clause changing to *tenebat* from breve no. 25 and the substitution of *olim* for *valuit* in the valuation clause, to form IID. This is used from the beginning of the Devon folios and throughout, with the notable exception of the land that had been held by Queen Edith and those held by Drogo son of Mauger of the bishop of Coutances.[76] Cornwall was entered at the end of the second Devon quire and

---

[70] *Habet* is very occasionally substituted for *tenet*, especially in the abbot of Battle's breve no. 8, in Sussex. There is a handful of such entries in the Berkshire folios.

[71] There is a tendency for only two values, TRE (*valuit*) and now (*modo*), to be given in these entries.

[72] The TRE tenant is omitted (as it is generally where the same person held TRW as TRE). Values are given in the form *valebat* for TRE, for when acquired, and 'now'. This information was generally available but was edited out by the GDB scribe.

[73] TRE holders are recorded at the end of groups of manors in a form similar to that found in Leicestershire and Northamptonshire. In breve 23 a dependent form 'X gelded for y' hides TRE . . .' occurs. It finds parallels in Devon (GDB 100d–101c, 102b–103b: *DB Devon*, 1,25–71.3,9–85). It is perhaps significant that all three were schedules of land which were or had formerly been held as a fee. In the cases of Queen Edith *et al.* and Count Aubrey the lands were in the hands of the king.

[74] Apart from the breves of the king's thegns and servants (nos. 56 and 57) where 'B holds y hides in x' occurs.

[75] For a concordance, see *DB Dorset, passim.*

[76] GDB 100d–101c, 102b–103b: *DB Devon*, 1,25–71.3,9–85, for which see above, n. 73.

was thus the last in the circuit to be written. In the king's lands IIE, approximating to IIA, appears. In breves nos. 2 and 3 it is replaced by IIC, but from no. 5 IIF, the definitive Cornwall form, takes over. It is clearly a variant of IIA and the form therefore marks a reversion to an earlier preoccupation with the assessment of the demesne to the geld.

Little interest was taken in manorial structure throughout the circuit. The extent of large ecclesiastical manors like Taunton is implicit.[77] But there is little indication of concern with tenurial matters generally. Exon frequently records that a TRE tenant was free to go with his land and the like, but GDB normally omits the information or substitutes *pro manerio* or *libere*. Even the record of value in 1066 has been suppressed; comparison with Exon again shows that the *olim* of the text from midway through Somerset refers to the time when the tenant-in-chief acquired the land. It must be suspected that the *valuit* of the earlier folios refers to the same time.

The diplomatic of Circuits IV and V are similar, but a sequence is apparent indicating that Circuit V was written first. The sequence starts in the Gloucestershire folios with a bewildering variety of forms in the king's breve. None can be said to be a formula (most appear in only one or two entries), but all record the pre-Conquest tenant as the first or second item of information and approximate to forms VA and VB. Thereafter VA predominates until VC is introduced in breve no. 5. It is the only form until breve 32, where VD makes an appearance. Thereafter, the two forms VC and VD alternate until the end of the section. Worcestershire follows, commencing halfway through the second Gloucestershire quire. Breve no. 2, the land of the bishop of Worcester, exhibits its own diplomatic, reflecting its many other peculiarities.[78] Otherwise, apart from breve no. 8 where VE is also found, VC is used throughout with *valebat . . . et modo* in the valuation clause. As in Gloucestershire, ploughlands are not recorded,[79] but from breve no. 3 there sporadically appears, usually after the peasant ploughs, a statement of ploughing potential in the form *ibi possunt esse plus z caruce.*[80]

In the Herefordshire folios the *terra regis* goes its own way, but otherwise the Worcestershire modifications to VC are found sporadically throughout

---

[77] GDB 87c: *DB Somerset*, 2,1–9.

[78] It is arranged by manor with each introduced by the phrase *In eodem hundredo* [Oswaldslow] *tenet isdem episcopus* x . . . Subordinate entries commence with *De eodem manerio tenuit* a y *hidas ad* x, or *De eodem manerio tenet* b² y *hidas ad* x. It is also clear that in this context *Ipse* b² *tenet* y *hidas ad* x is also a dependent form. Westmancote, for example, was so held by Urso, but its dependent status is indicated by the fact that it was held by Brictwin TRE for service of the bishop. The editor of *DB Worcs.* has assumed that all these entries are manors in their own right.

[79] In the bishop of Worcester's breve it is recorded that 'In these manors there cannot be more ploughs than is stated' (GDB 174a: *DB Worcs.*, 2,80). It can perhaps be understood that the same was true elsewhere where ploughland figures are not given.

[80] Cf Circuit III. There are two entries in which *terra est z carucis* appears of which the second may be postscriptal (GDB 177a, 177b: *DB Worcs.*, 21,2.23,14).

with only the occasional intrusion of VD and VE.[81] The same is true for Shropshire until *terra est z carucis* is substituted for *ibi possunt esse plus z caruce* to form form VF. It is first found at f. 252b: 1,5 and makes a further thirty-four appearances between f. 252b and f. 257a: 1,9 and 4,11,14.[82] From f. 257a: 4,11,17 (GDB 257a), however, it becomes all but invariable.[83] There is no underlying seigneurial or geographical rationale to this change; there seems no doubt that ploughland figures were available for the whole of the county.[84] It must, therefore, be suspected that the scribe was responding differently to his source material. The *possunt esse* formula is redolent of circuit reports. Heretofore the scribe was probably following this his source closely, and here it would seem, as in ICC, the *possunt esse* formula only appeared where potential was not matched by stocking and in consequence the record of ploughlands as it became transmitted to GDB is intermittent. The reversion to the common GDB form and its universal application, then, marks the correction of an oversight and the removal of a possible ambiguity.

Cheshire was the last county in Circuit V to be written. The account begins in the second half of the second Shropshire quire and overflows into another quire to which is appended an account of lands in Wales and Between Ribble and Mersey. Form VF is used throughout the shire proper and in the account of the Deeside division of Atiscross Hundred in Flintshire. The remaining Welsh lands are anomalous in form. They were apparently not hidated and the sole measure of land is in terms of ploughing potential.[85] The usual formula is *est terra z carucis*, but there is a variety of opening clauses. Between Ribble and Mersey is also anomalous. Entries are of the form b *habuit/ tenuit/tenebat* x, or *in hundredo habuit* b, echoing the forms of the Gloucestershire *terra regis*.

The Circuit IV sequence probably starts with Staffordshire. Chapters 1 to 3 exhibit the IVA form which is identical with VF apart from the substitution of *Ibi y hidae* for *Ibi y hidae geld*. Thereafter the TRE tenant is not always recorded, but IVA, and from breve no. 9 the closely related IVB, predominate, alternating with IVC which is introduced in breve no. 11. As in Circuit V, then, the holder of land in 1066 is normally recorded at the beginning of the entry. Here and there in breves nos. 8, 10, 11, and 16 the information is recorded

---

[81] This latter is found in breve no. 2 where it is associated with a list of the land held by the canons of Hereford. The usage is similar to that of IIID, and the form is presumably derived from a schedule.

[82] Lewis, 'Introduction to the Shropshire Domesday', 17–18.

[83] *DB Salop*, 1,5 n suggests that the change cannot be due to the preferences of the GDB scribe on the ground that the two forms are not mutually exclusive. However, in Circuit III the two forms are often used together. The failure to record ploughlands after the change to the normal formula is associated with subdivisions of estates where, it might be supposed, the information is to be found in the main entry (Lewis, 'Introduction to the Shropshire Domesday', 17).

[84] Lewis, 'Introduction to the Shropshire Domesday', 19.

[85] Lewis, 'Introduction to the Cheshire Domesday', 21–3.

at the end (forms IVD, IVE), but, in at least some instances, postscriptally.[86] This characteristic is important, for it provides a link between Staffordshire and Warwickshire where forms IVB and IVC alternate in the first six breves. Thereafter, however, forms IVD and IVE take over, with the record of the TRE tenant at the end of the entry, to become the standard formulas of the rest of the circuit.[87] Warwickshire, therefore, clearly followed Staffordshire.

Oxfordshire and Northamptonshire occasionally exhibit anomalous forms in the *terra regis* and the lands of churches but are otherwise regular. From breve no. 17 in the one and throughout the other there is a tendency to record the TRE holder at the end of groups of manors and, with Warwickshire, the demesne precedes the enfeoffed lands.[88] Leicestershire shares both characteristics, but is otherwise anomalous. Form IVD and IVE are used, but ploughing potential in the form *terra z carucis* is only found in all entries in breves nos. 4, 5, 7, 13, 21–3, 25, and 41 and in most in 3, 10, and 19. Elsewhere, it is replaced by a statement of the number of TRE plough,[89] in the form *TRE erant ibi z caruce* or *ibi z caruce fuerunt*, although in a significant number of entries there is no indication of potential at all. The seigneurial distribution suggests that the scribe was following his sources, and it may be suspected that he could not always find the information he required. In Robert the bursar's breve he wrote *terra* and left a space for the number to be supplied, and in the *terra regis* he could only furnish one ploughland figure and there it is significantly postscriptal.[90] TRE ploughs were clearly not directly comparable with TRW ploughlands but, as has been seen, were probably used as the only information available.[91] The Leicestershire anomalies, then, are unlikely to represent any development in the GDB scribe's organization of his work. Only one characteristic distinguishes Leicestershire from Oxfordshire and Northamptonshire. Uniquely in Circuits IV and V its folios are ruled, and then by leaf rather than sheet, three in pattern 3 and one in pattern 2, and variously with fifty-one, fifty-two and fifty-four lines. Otherwise there is no evidence to determine the order of writing of the three shires.

---

[86] GDB 248a, 248b, 248c, 248d, 250c: *DB Staffs.*, 8,4;13;14;18–29.10,7–8.11,8.16,1. The information was probably appended to entries 10,7–8. *DB Staffs.*, 16 n asserts that all three of Nigel's lands are postscriptal. Entries 16,2–3, with the TRE holder at the beginning, certainly are. But the first entry is probably a current component of the text; the spacing is not so cramped as the entries above, but the same pen seems to have been used.

[87] IVB is only rarely found (GDB 230b, 219c, 222d, 238c: *DB Leics.*, 1,3; *DB Northants.*, 1,4.16,1. *DB Warks.*, 3,2).

[88] A blank line is often employed to distinguish the two groups and one tenant from another. See e.g. GDB, 223a–224b: *DB Northants.*, 18.

[89] In all cases the abbreviation *car'* is used which could be extended as *caruce* or *carucate*. The former, however, is to be preferred in that the clause is on occasion linked with the demesne or peasant ploughs. At GDB 231d: *DB Leics.*, 11,3 it follows the record of peasant teams (where elsewhere it follows assessment to the geld), while at GDB 236c: *DB Leics.*, 40,35 it is stated that *ibi una car', nunc in dominio una car'* and at GDB 237b: *DB Leics.*, 44,13 *Ibi fuit dimidia car' et tantum ibi est in dominio.* Carucates are usually indicated by the phrase *carucate terre*.

[90] GDB 230d, 234d: *DB Leics.*, 1,12.19,2;4–6;9;11;12.   [91] See above, pp. 158–9.

Outside the *terra regis* there are few indications of manorial structure in Circuits IV and V. Throughout, tenurial links are occasionally explicit, but it is only in Leicestershire and Northamptonshire that organizations like sokes are fully articulated. The dependent form IVF is found in this context, but otherwise it is rare and not always associated with subordinate holdings. There is some indication of the status of TRE tenants, usually the simple statement that they could go with their land, and they are occasionally said to have held for so many manors (*pro* n *maneriis*). The record of single TRE holders for a number of estates in Leicestershire and Northamptonshire, and the less common occurrence of the form in Oxfordshire and Warwickshire, suggests a shift of interest from TRE tenant *per se* to soke lord in these folios. Many of those so named are said to hold with sake and soke and can thus be directly identified as king's thegns. The tenure of most of the others is usually unqualified (*a tenuit*) and a similar status can be inferred.[92] In Leicestershire free men can often to be shown to have held in the soke of one such and they appear to have been named only because the tenure of their land was in dispute in 1086 or some other clarification was required.[93] Pre-Conquest tenure in itself is less of a feature of these folios.

The Great Domesday Book Scribe and the Manor in the North

The order of writing revealed by the MS and the development of diplomatic within it suggests an orderly progression from the north of England through the East Midlands, the south-east, south-west, and finally the west and central Midlands. The elucidation of this chronology facilitates analysis of content. The northern and eastern folios reveal details of lordship and tenure that are absent elsewhere in the country. With some justice this characteristic of GDB has been attributed in part to the idiosyncrasies of procedure from circuits to circuit. In Circuit III elaborate details of estate structure like those of the north were not collected or had been edited out by the time ICC was produced. The GDB scribe may have had access to such data, but in the event he followed his main source. In Exon even less information was given. Variation in the scope of data collection is considerable, and this has led to the belief that the form of GDB reflects the reality of the underlying societies that it represents. This conclusion is more questionable. The social and tenurial structure of Leicestershire differs little from that of south Nottinghamshire and upland Kesteven immediately to the north and east. There is little doubt that manors were as fully articulated there and that the Domesday commissioners had access to the information, for, where title was disputed, seisin turned as much on the rights of predecessor here as elsewhere.

---

[92] See above, p. 34.
[93] Roffe, 'Great Bowden and its Soke', 107–20.

And yet the GDB account of the one is as simple as the other is complex.[94] The decisive difference between Leicestershire on the one hand, and Nottinghamshire and Lincolnshire on the other, would appear to be when they were written. The former was composed at the very end of the process and the latter at the beginning.

There are, in fact, indications that the GDB scribe struggled with a central concept of Domesday Book in the composition of the first shires that he tackled. The experimentation in forms that characterizes the folios of Circuit VI is accompanied by a refinement in his understanding of the *manerium*, manor. Throughout the north the term is invariable. But its application subtly changes. In the Yorkshire folios there are proportionally more manors than are found in the Lincolnshire. That this is not merely a function of depression of status of formerly free tenants consequent on the Harrying of the North in 1069 is illustrated by the fact that all record a pre-Conquest tenant, a textual indicator of a manor in Lincolnshire and, indeed, in the whole of Circuit VI. Further, unlike in the rest of Circuit VI, there was no concerted effort to group berewicks and sokeland together with the manorial *caput* beyond the great sokes of the shire. It is unlikely that this characteristic is a function of compilation. Estate structure was probably not a matter of official record, for geld was collected on the basis of vills, and it is improbable that any panel of jurors could accurately describe the appurtenances of manors that extended into a number of vills and wapentakes.[95] Rather, the information seems to have been derived from the presentments of the tenants-in-chief, who quite naturally described their lands in terms of their management. Twenty-four out of twenty-eight of those in Yorkshire made such presentments in Lincolnshire, and it is therefore unlikely that they purposely refrained from doing so north of the Humber. It is likely, then, that the reality behind the Yorkshire manor was sometimes different from that of the East Midlands.

Throughout Circuit VI large sokes which enjoyed tribute and services from an extensive group of vills are consistently called manors. Held by the great lords of the north with sake and soke, toll and team, these were effectively bookland estates and as such appear to have presented few conceptual problems to the compiler of GDB. With extensive liberties and a discrete jurisdiction, they were readily identifiable as a type.[96] Most parcels of land which were categorized as manors, however, relate to estates that in one way or another were intermediate between such lords and the ordinary peasant. In the East Midlands the term typically denotes a nexus of tribute. The tenant held a hall at which various dependants rendered food rents, labour services, and sundry minor dues. He did not have unequivocal rights to his land, however, but held it either at farm or in return for the render of soke dues, the Domesday

[94] Ibid.   [95] Roffe, 'Nottinghamshire', 53–4.
[96] Kapelle, *Norman Conquest of the North*, 50–85; Roffe, 'Nottinghamshire', chap. 5.

valuit, from an overlord to whom the soke, *qua* jurisdiction, and *terra* were reserved.[97] The manor, then, was a point of interception of certain types of dues and tribute, and it was therefore natural to group its contributing lands with the *caput*.

It is clear that such tenures were to be found in Yorkshire. Farthegn, Alwine, and Tonni, for example, held a manor in Appleton from Wulfbert in 1066, the predecessor of Osbern de Arches, while the Count of Mortain had no right to the manor of Aldgyth because he did not hold from his *antecessor*.[98] But ministerial tenures like drengage and thegnage were probably also common. The existence of only four drengs is noticed in the Yorkshire Domesday, but drengage is referred to in other sources at Burton Agnes, Driffield, and in Howdenshire and may also be indicated by the widespread occurrence of forinsec service paid from one manor to another.[99] The tenure was almost certainly identical with thegnage, however, for the Yorkshire thegn paid the same relief as the Lancashire dreng, who was also known indifferently as a thegn, and this class was apparently extensive.[100] Thus, for example, a parallel entry suggests that the distinctive characteristic of the 332 untenanted manors which were postscriptally added to the king's breve was thegnage,[101] while the reservation to the overlord of renders from manorial commodities like the mill suggests that the relationship was common.[102] Since drengs did not intercept dues but merely administered them,[103] there was thus not always the imperative to group appurtenances with the dreng's demesne, for like the *caput* itself it was soke of the lord's estate.

Many of the manors of the Yorkshire folios, then, were probably thegnages or drengages. The numerous references in the Yorkshire folios to manors without halls becomes comprehensible in this context, although it may be suspected that the fact often worried the GDB scribe as an oxymoron.[104]

---

[97] In 1114 tenants of Burton Abbey in Ticknall and Stanton near Newhall each paid the sum of 10s for their estates, which was the value of each of the holdings in 1086 ('Burton Surveys', 240; GDB 273b, 274b: *DB Derby*, 3,7.6,21).

[98] GDB 329a, 374a, 306d, 373a: *DB Yorks.*, 25W2.CW36.5E27.CE6.

[99] Kapelle, *Norman Conquest of the North*, 69–70, 71–2.

[100] GDB 269d, 298d: *DB Cheshire*, R1,40g; *DB Yorks.*, C40.

[101] GDB 299d, 301b: *DB York.*, 1Y15.1W26. In the second version the land is said to be inland or sokeland and Stenton therefore maintained that the *taneland* of the first was a scribal error. He was inclined to the opinion that the latter tenure did not exist in the Northern Danelaw (Stenton, *Types of Manorial Structure*, 15–17). However, land in both Derbyshire and Nottinghamshire is said to be held in thegnage, and a marginal 'T' found in Huntingdonshire probably indicates the same tenure in that county. Moreover, the description of the land as 'inland' is not inconsistent with the tenure: in the account of the land Between Ribble and Mersey in the Cheshire folios thegnlands and drengages were interchangeably termed manors or inland of the king's estate (GDB 269c–270b: *DB Cheshire*, R1–7).

[102] The mill is frequently given a separate value in the account of the manor and may therefore have made a separate render to the overlord. The soke of two mills which belonged to the manor of Belton, for example, was owed to the king's manor of Grantham in Lincolnshire (GDB 370c: *DB Lincs.*, 67,15).

[103] Jolliffe, 'Northumbrian Institutions', 5, 6–8, 10–11, 14–25.

[104] GDB 305d, 306b, 307c, 308a, 309b, 312b, 312c: *DB Yorks.*, 5N35;74.5W4–5;18.6N11;125;137.

.

Incidental notices of tenants other than those of the parent manor probably indicates that there were similar intermediate tenures in the East Midlands. In Gonalston, for example, Ernuin the priest and four sokemen held five bovates of sokeland of the king's manor of Arnold in Nottinghamshire, and six soke-men in Huntingdonshire, who are identified as Alfwold and his brothers, were seized of four and a half hides of sokeland of the manor of Alconbury in Gidding.[105] Many of the sokemen who enjoyed the services of villagers and bordars at Northorpe, Brant Broughton, Barton on Humber, and Baumber in Lincolnshire, and throughout East Anglia, may have been of the same status and would probably have been assigned manors in Yorkshire.[106] Only five in East Deeping, however, are so classified,[107] and in the four instances in which an estate is specifically called thegnland, it is enrolled in a sub-ordinate entry.[108] Tenures of this kind, then, were generally unremarked in the text and the land probably appears as ordinary sokeland or, as in Somersham in Huntingdonshire,[109] was engrossed in manorial entries without comment.[110] By the time the compiler came to the Lincolnshire folios, he had apparently restricted his concept of the manor by excluding ministerial tenures and enrolling them as sokeland.

It is probably not coincidental that this refinement was accompanied by a greater concern with the status of the sokeman and his land. The process is most apparent in the diplomatic experiments in the Lincolnshire folios, but is also manifest in a more detailed record of socage tenure. In Yorkshire few sokemen are recorded. If Falsgrave, where the numbers fell from 207 to seven between 1066 and 1086, was at all typical, then many may have disappeared in the Harrying of the North and its aftermath.[111] In the rest of the circuit varying numbers are enrolled. In Lincolnshire sokemen account for almost 50 percent of the population, a proportion which is comparable to the numbers in East Anglia,[112] and significantly the form in which they are enrolled is akin to that found in the more expansive LDB. The description of the soke of Folkingham in some twenty-four entries, for example, is similar to that of Desning in Suffolk which is described in twenty-three.[113] Only the details of

---

[105] GDB 293b, 206b: *DB Notts.*, 30,49; *DB Hunts.*, 19,15. See also GDB 204b, 206c: *DB Hunts.*, 6,3.19,32.

[106] GDB 345d, 347d, 354c–d: *DB Lincs.*, 8,16.12,47.24,13;20.   [107] GDB 366b: *DB Lincs.*, 51,3.

[108] GDB 287b–c, 274d, 206a–b: *DB Notts.*, 10,15; *DB Derby.*, 6,48; *DB Hunts.*, 19,9;16.

[109] *ICC* 166; GDB 204a: *DB Hunts.*, 4,3. Demesne land is said to be held in thegnage in ICC, but the information has been suppressed in GDB.

[110] There may have been deviations from the norm. Longdendale in Derbyshire, for example, was held by a number of individuals who had twelve manors (GDB 273a: *DB Derby.*, 1,30). Only nine are named, two of whom are identified postscriptally, and tenurial and ecclesiastical structure suggests that they belonged to the manor of Bakewell or Hope. It is likely, then, that their tenure was very similar to that of the drengs in Lancashire. As such, they should probably have escaped the notice of the commissioners, but the whole area was waste, and the land was therefore described in terms of its pre-Conquest designation.

[111] GDB 299a: *DB Yorks.*, 1Y3.   [112] Stafford, *East Midlands*, 20, 158.

[113] GDB 355d–356a: *DB Lincs.*, 24,82–105; LDB 390a–392a: *DB Suffolk*, 25,3–17;35–41.

status are apparently absent. Soke, *qua* jurisdiction, however, is probably as carefully noted in Lincolnshire as in East Anglia, if only implicitly, but it was not so frequently reserved, and the record of forinsec dues is therefore less common.[114] Moreover, custom and service, that do not appear as such, are almost certainly represented by the concept of *terra*. It is only *commendatio* that does not appear in Circuit VI. In content, then, the account of Lincolnshire is probably close to the unabbreviated circuit report from which it was abbreviated.

Subsequently in Circuit VI the concept of the manor was further refined, for the commissioners' reports were apparently subject to more rigorous editing that excluded sokemen. In Nottinghamshire the class only represents some 26 per cent of the recorded population, while it falls to 5 per cent and less than 1 per cent in Derbyshire and Huntingdonshire, and the fact has been seen as symptomatic of fundamental differences in the society of the Northern Danelaw.[115] There are indications, however, that in reality their numbers were more directly comparable with those of Lincolnshire for, although no absolutely contemporary evidence survives to check the survey, early-twelfth-century estate terriers suggest that freedom was far more common than is implied in GDB. The Burton Survey of 1114 records a large group of peasants called *censarii* in Derbyshire. The services that they owed are almost identical with those of the Lincolnshire sokemen, but none is noticed in the abbot's GDB breve.[116] Likewise, there were extensive free tenements that were held by suit of court to the hundred and the shire, money rents, and boon works, services which were not dissimilar to those of sokemen, on Ramsey Abbey's Huntingdonshire estates *c.*1135 where, with one exception, only villagers and bordars are recorded in GDB; and in 1167 sokemen held land in the king's manor of Brampton, although none is noticed at an earlier period.[117] In the thirteenth century extensive free holdings are found at Bakewell in Derbyshire, and socage tenure at Godmanchester and Pilsley in Huntingdonshire, all apparently fully 'manorialized' in the eleventh century, but subsequently known as sokes of one kind or another.[118] It is unlikely that all such

[114] There were no great liberties like those of Ely and Bury St Edmund's. The franchise of sake and soke, toll and team was enjoyed by a large group of lords before the Conquest. However, some sokes reserved jurisdiction over the estates of other lords within their vicinity. Morcar's manor of Stoke Rochford, for example, was in the soke of Grantham (GDB 360c: *DB Lincs.*, 30,25). The king may have retained soke over much of the wapentakes of Bassetlaw and Oswaldbeck in Nottinghamshire (Roffe, 'Nottinghamshire', chapter 8).

[115] Stafford, *East Midlands*, 20, 158; Stenton, 'The Danes in England', 203–46; id., *Free Peasantry of the Northern Danelaw*; Kapelle, *Norman Conquest of the North*, 50–85.

[116] Walmsley, 'The "Censarii" of Burton Abbey and the Domesday Population,' 73–80; 'Burton Surveys', 229–47; Stenton, *Types of Manorial Structure*, 22–7. The services of both sokemen and *censarii* typically consist of rent, boon works, and carriage services.

[117] *Cartularium Monasterii de Rameseia*, iii. 241–314; *VCH Hunts.*, iii. 13. In the mid-thirteenth century *censarii* are found in Elton and Abbot's Ripton who may have been the descendants of such free peasants (*Cartularium Monasterii de Rameseia*, i. 267).

[118] Carrington, 'Illustrations of Ancient Place-Names in Bakewell', 30–64; *VCH Hunts.*, ii. 185, 288.

free tenures were created in the twelfth century and, indeed, the association of some of them with the custom of inheritance by Borough English strongly suggests that they were pre-Conquest in origin.[119] Only in Burton Abbey's Derbyshire estates can their presence be detected in GDB—the total number of ploughs recorded probably include those of the *censarii*[120]—but most must have been in existence in 1086. The GDB compiler, however, clearly felt that there was no need to record their presence.

The reason for this change in policy is probably not unconnected with estate structure. In 1086 Lincolnshire, like much of East Anglia, was characterized by a great complexity of interlocking interests, and to describe adequately the interests of each tenant-in-chief it was clearly necessary to note each parcel of land in order to identify the source of income. In Huntingdonshire, Derbyshire, and Nottinghamshire large dispersed sokes, mostly royal, were treated in the same way, and many sokemen are recorded. But generally estates were much less fragmented and, as in the case of the abbot of Burton's manors, it was probably felt that it was only necessary to record the population that worked the fiscal demesne since there was less chance of another tenant-in-chief claiming soke dues. It was sufficient to include the issues of sokemen in the manorial *valet*, for they were as indubitably appurtenant to the lord's demesne as the slaves who, as is clear from IE, were omitted from the abbot of Ely's manors in Huntingdonshire in the compilation of GDB. The complexities of estate structure undoubtedly played a part, but in a broader context the change in policy reflects a dawning realization on the part of the GDB scribe that the intricacies of tenure were irrelevant to his purpose.

The Great Domesday Book Scribe and the Manor in the South and West

The production of the Circuit VI folios was a *tour de force* of composition. The scribe had to think on his feet and shape his text to his growing awareness of what was apt. His achievement is nonetheless significant for that. Although he had access to a whole range of documents that had been produced in the Domesday process, his primary source was a geographical recension probably not dissimilar to ICC. In this source the soke centre to which each parcel of inland and sokeland owed its dues was probably, although not necessarily, noticed, but there was no list of such attached to each manor. Thus, in Yorkshire where the scribe did not group *caput* and appurtenances in the text, almost all inlands and sokeland record the manorial centre at which they rendered their dues, while in Lincolnshire, where by contrast manors were fully articulated, there are many stray parcels of land that are entered in accordance with geography rather than lordship. Signs were widely used in the latter and

---

[119] *VCH Hunts.*, ii. 288; Raftis, *Estates of Ramsey Abbey*, 46–8. Ultimogeniture was a basic characteristic of socage tenure (Stevenson, 'Land Tenures in Nottinghamshire', 66–71).

[120] Walmsley, 'The "Censarii" of Burton Abbey', 73–80.

thereafter to direct the reader to the appropriate context. Sometimes the task of constructing manors was almost beyond the scribe. In the abbot of Peterborough's Lincolnshire breve he was apparently unaware that sokeland belonged to the manor of Walcot near Threekingham. He then found two bovates soke of Walcot in Haythby and duly entered it after Walcot, only subsequently to find that it was in fact soke of Walcot in Alkborough, some fifty miles away. He entered the land again after that entry and marked the two entries to signal their identity.[121] This, however, was the exception. By and large, the scribe constructed his text with remarkable success, if with no little labour.

In Circuit III and thereafter he was to follow his primary sources more closely. ICC furnishes few explicit tenurial details beyond those that directly touched on the demesne: only the odd berewick is linked with its *caput*. The primary concern of the document, in so far as it records status at all, seems to have been to distinguish that demesne from freely held land. This was a preoccupation of all the sources concerned with the geld inquest and the purpose was presumably to establish whether it was the lord or tenant who paid the tax on each parcel of land.[122] It is possible that this characteristic of ICC represents the full compass of the survey in Circuit III in so far as it concerned manorial structure. However, it does seem that some details were available to the GDB scribe in one form or another. There were a few tenants who were not free to leave with their lands TRE, and the record of their commendation lord indirectly points to a manorial *caput*. More broadly, the articulation of disputes hints at an awareness of a network of personal services which must have had territorial correlates. Either the GDB scribe found it too difficult to use this information to order his text or he decided that it was not worth the effort.

Whatever the case, the manor still looms large in the folios of Circuit III, with every tenement described either as a manor or as simple land. The dichotomy has excited much comment. For Round, Tait, and Baring there was no doubt that the usage was random and that there was therefore no technical content to the distinction.[123] Dr John Palmer, however, has shown that *manerium* was used with purpose.[124] In the course of abbreviation the *terra* of ICC was reclassified as *manerium* on fourteen occasions in the Cambridgeshire folios, but only once is *manerium* emended to *terra*.[125] Palmer is clearly

---

[121] GDB 345d, 346a: *DB Lincs.*, 8,10;30. The first entry is probably not postscriptal. It records that Ivo held where the information is understood in the second, for Ivo is noted as the tenant of the main entry.

[122] Roffe, 'Descriptio Terrarum', 14.

[123] Round, 'The Domesday Manor', 294; Tait, review of *Domesday Book and Beyond*, 768–77; Baring, *Domesday Tables*, 79, 82, 94, 139–42, 177.

[124] Palmer, 'Domesday Manor', 141–2.

[125] *ICC* 15; GDB 199c: *DB Cambs.*, 29,5. Here the scribe was clearly certain of his facts, for he prefaced the entry with a marginal M. There are 15 such amendments in all relating to fees in Abington,

right to see in this pattern a coherent understanding of manorial structure that transcended ICC. But his further argument that that understanding was other than the nexus of soke of the Northern Danelaw is more suspect. The scribal emendations, he asserts, are consistent with what he terms 'four rules determining manorial status', and from these it is possible to perceive that the distribution of manors approximates to one manor, but no more than one, per vill or group of vills. No such exact correlation pertains throughout the circuit, but he concludes that the observation substantiates Maitland's view that a manor was a house at which geld was charged and that so the GDB scribe understood it.[126]

Elegant as it is, the argument adds little to the fundamental issue. Maitland built his analysis on a narrow view of soke as jurisdiction and geld as Danegeld, and no neat distribution makes up for the deficiencies. It was soke as rights over land that largely determined title in 1086, and in Cambridgeshire at least there are indications that it was articulated through the manor of the text.[127] And so, with the benefit of a chronology of composition, can the GDB scribe's understanding of the manor in Circuit III be shown to be precisely that. His diplomatic was consistent. The marginal Lombardic M and the rustic initial I to signal subordinate status were devices which the scribe had himself devised in the composition of Circuit VI to articulate the intricacies of sokeright. His continued use of them in Circuit III must indicate that he clung as much as his sources allowed him, or his inclination motivated him, to the programme that he had evolved in the abbreviation of Circuit VI. The manor as a nexus of soke was still a concept that he deemed worthy of note, and he strove to draw his readers' attention to it.

In the event the task proved to be too difficult or not worth the candle. The extent of manorial information recorded in ICC was probably typical of that collected in most of the country; Exon, at least, is similarly reticent. From the Hertfordshire folios onwards the GDB made no further attempt to highlight the manor beyond the occasional notice of its existence. Large estates, it is true, continued to be entered as such. They are particularly common in the *terra regis*. Sixteen dependencies of Leominster in Herefordshire, for example, are noted in the main entry, and there then follow twenty-seven parcels of land in a further twenty-one places that had belonged to the manor in

---

Ashley, Burrough Green, Carlton, Hildersham, Isleham, Quy, Rampton, Saxon Street, Stapleford, Stetchworth, Weston Colville, and Wilbraham. Some of these may be merely errors, but this seems unlikely. In all but one *manerium* has been substituted for *terra* (Palmer, 'Domesday Manor', 142–3).

[126] Maitland, *Domesday Book and Beyond*, 140–63.

[127] The dichotomy between manor and land is matched by a difference in the status of those who are said to have held them. 'Land' could be held by all manner of persons, from the king to the humblest peasant who was tied to the land. 'Manors', by contrast, seem to have been in the hands of king's thegns, the predecessors of the tenants-in-chief, for, with but five apparent exceptions (GDB 190c, 195a 195c, 201a–b: *DB Cambs.*, 3,6.14,53;67.32,31;33), manorial entries display the simple *tenuit* formula. The correlation is less apparent in the rest of the circuit.

1066.[128] Almost every shire can boast of comparable entries. Here, it would seem, the GDB scribe was merely following his sources by entering what had been collected in the survey of the king's demesne manors.[129] Much the same was probably true of similar entries in the breves of tenants-in-chief. The bishop of Worcester's nine manors of Kempsey, Wick Episcopi, Fladbury, Bredon, Ripple, Blockley, Tredington, Northwick, and Overbury in Oswaldslow Hundred in Worcestershire are each entered with their respective dependent lands, but the whole account seems to have been drawn, directly or indirectly, from the bishop's presentment.[130] A list of appurtenances is attached to the account of Geoffrey de la Guerche's manor of Melton Mowbray in Leicestershire. It is, however, incomplete, and the failure of the GDB scribe to group other appurtenances with the *caput* suggests that the initial list was, again, none of his doing.[131]

Diplomatic and scribal practice reflects the change. Within entries like these, and intermittently elsewhere, the scribe occasionally made use of the 'dependent' form '*In* x y *hide*'. Although the rustic initial I is normally not employed, the form indubitably signals dependence in some instances.[132] Its primary characteristic, however, is probably to mark individual items in a list. This is well illustrated by the account of the church of Hereford's breve in the Herefordshire folios.[133] It commences with the land of the bishop in a form echoing the anomalous diplomatic of the *terra regis* that precedes it: after an account of land in Hereford, manors held by Walter, bishop from 1061 to 1079, are described in the form '*X tenuit . . .*' A rubric then announces that 'these lands mentioned below belong to the canons of Hereford',[134] and the following entries are all in the form '*In* x *sunt* y *hide*'. Many of the tenements so described are explicitly manors, and it would therefore seem likely that the list is the decisive context of the distinctive form in which they are entered in GDB. It was probably ultimately derived from a schedule. By and large, however, the dependent form is not found, and in consequence it is difficult to argue that the remaining forms are necessarily indicative of manorial status.[135]

On the whole, the GDB scribe was content to follow his sources. It is true that he remained alive to the possibility of ambiguity, and sometimes amended his source accordingly. Thus, on occasion he saw fit to gloss the *pariter*, 'jointly', of Exon as '*pro* n *manerio*'. The term was not of his invention.

---

[128] GDB 180a–c: *DB Hereford*, 1,10–38. One of the parcels was in Shropshire (GDB 259d: *DB Salop*, 4,28,5).

[129] In Herefordshire the survey was particularly detailed. Royal manors like Leominster may have been units of geld management, for, in the north at least, *terra regis* did not geld with the rest of the countryside (Roffe, 'Hundreds and Wapentakes', 38; Roffe, 'Origins of Derbyshire', 106).

[130] GDB 172a–174a: *DB Worcs.*, 2, 1–80. See above, pp. 143, 208.

[131] GDB 235c–d: *DB Leics.*, 29, 3–4;18.   [132] Welldon Finn, *Domesday Inquest*, 70.

[133] GDB 181c–182d: *DB Hereford.*, 2.

[134] *Hae terrae subterscriptae pertinent ad canonicos Hereford* (GDB 181c: *DB Hereford.*, 2,4).

[135] Palmer. 'Domesday Manor', 143; Welldon Finn, *Domesday Inquest*, 70.

It is ubiquitous in LDB, occurs in ICC, and as form VIB, was common in the early folios of the Yorkshire Domesday suggesting that it was also found in the circuit report of the north. '*Pro* n *manerio*' is apparently synonymous with *libere* and being able to go with land, and the intention was, presumably, to draw attention to the fact that the tenement or tenements in question were in reality equal.[136] Such, however, was the exception. Indeed, the scribe did not always strive officiously to preserve the status and structure of estates. Exon, for example, records that Roger de Stanton held a manor of ten hides in Stanton in the king's manor of Keynsham in Somerset, but no reference is made to its manorial status in GDB.[137]

Nor, apparently, was a more expansive record of pre-Conquest tenure an alternative way of conveying the same information. The abandonment of any attempt systematically to notice manors coincides with the greater availability or use of details of the TRE status of individual holders of land. It has been suggested that the record of free tenure thereby accorded is indicative of manorial status.[138] The Circuit III folios reveal that this was far from the case; TRE free men are as often associated with 'land' as 'manors'. More to the point, however, ICC and Exon show that much of this information, like manorial structure, was a function of the evidence collected. It is possible to identify king's thegns therefrom where the unqualified *tenuit* formula is employed. But this seems not to have been a conscious purpose of the GDB scribe, for his frequent failure to transmit the details of status from Exon indicates that he took no great interest in the matter. Indeed, by the time he came to abbreviate the Northamptonshire and Leicestershire folios he often felt it unnecessary to record pre-Conquest tenure at all. After his initial engagement with the problem of the manor, the GDB scribe clearly came to feel that it was of no importance.

Great Domesday Book and Little Domesday Book

The scope of GDB is awesome; thirty counties neatly and economically described in a form that could be bound together in one volume. It is this, its very scope, however, that makes its apparent omissions the more surprising. Of England north of the Tees there is no evidence to suggest that there had ever been a survey. Cumbria was held by the king of the Scots, and, although Durham was indubitably English, it was probably simply not considered an integral part of the realm in 1086. Like the Yorkshire appendages of

---

[136] Welldon Finn, *Liber Exoniensis*, 88–93.

[137] Exon, 113ᵛ; GDB 87a–b: *DB Somerset*, 1,28. Welldon Finn (*Domesday Inquest*, 64–5) asserts that this and similar entries indicate that the GDB scribe was recognizing that Exon was inconsistent in categorizing a subordinate element as a manor. GDB, however, does not reclassify the tenements in question as *terra*. There was, of course, no inconsistency in asserting that one manor was in the soke of another.

[138] Welldon Finn, *Liber Exoniensis*, 88–91.

Amounderness and Craven, it was extracomital. But, where the king held the lands that had belonged to Roger the Poitevin in the one, he had no interests in the other. The shire was central to the Domesday inquest both in terms of procedure and purpose: either the apparatus of government to conduct a survey was absent or on that same account it was otiose.[139]

The major omission is East Anglia. Here the survey had ostensibly been conducted in the same way as elsewhere in the kingdom; LDB stands as a monument to just how successful it had been. And yet the data were never abbreviated and entered in GDB. Three related explanations have been advanced. All in one way or another impinge on the complexity of East Anglian society. First, it has been asserted that the commissioners took more time to conduct the survey and their report arrived too late for inclusion. By the time it had become available William had died and the project was discontinued incomplete. Secondly, its intricacies defied précis in any useful form; and thirdly, its size would have made the proposed volume simply unmanageable.

None of these explanations is entirely satisfactory. There is no reason to doubt that the survey, if not necessarily LDB itself, was completed in 1086 as the colophon claims. The composition of GDB itself, as is now clear, continued into the reign of William Rufus, and presumably the scribe thus had potential access to all of the data. The account of the Eastern Counties was indeed complex, but no more so than that of the northern counties which the scribe abbreviated, if not without effort then ultimately with some success. Compared with the sources which emanated from the south-western circuit, the East Anglian data were apparently well organized and orchestrated. It seems likely that a fully compiled, geographically arranged recension was available as well as LDB itself and the problems of abbreviation were probably on that account less than for some other counties. Finally, although the scribe clearly kept in mind the need for conciseness and an economical usage of space, it must be doubted that a final format for GDB was firmly fixed at the time when the work was commenced. The individual quires were evidently used as separate pamphlets, and it would seem that the problem of binding did not present itself until some time after the completion of GDB.

The GDB scribe clearly had the time and expertise to finish the job. His apparent failure to do so, then, may be due to some accident of history that is now irrecoverable. GDB is *par excellence* the work of an individual, and any personal factor may have led to its discontinuation. However, this is probably to misunderstand the context. The failure may be more in the eyes of the tidy-minded historian than of the compiler. The order of writing of GDB, from the north of England through the East Midlands, the south-east, south-west, and finally the west and central Midlands, describes a neat geographical progression. If this is not coincidental, and it shows every sign of not being

---

[139] Aird, *St Cuthbert and the Normans*, 184–5 and note.

so, the pattern is striking not least for its apparent exclusion of East Anglia. Had the scribe intended to abbreviate the account of the eastern counties it might be expected that he would have entered it either after Circuit VI or Circuit III. He did not do so, and it would therefore seem that the LDB counties never formed a part of his plan. From this it could indeed be concluded that the material was not available for abbreviation at the time at which he planned and wrote. Another explanation, however, and perhaps a more likely one, suggests itself. LDB is at once a fair copy and a complete circuit report in the form that GDB was to take. No other is known: Exon was a series of working documents and ICC was geographically arranged and, with its omission of the *terra regis*, incomplete. It is therefore probable that LDB was not abbreviated precisely because, uniquely, it was a fair copy of a seigneurial rearrangement of its ICC-like sources. As it stands it is as serviceable as GDB as a work of record, albeit lacking the finer points of rubrication. Abbreviation would have created a great deal more work, with only a minimal return that was arguably of interest only to the tidy-minded. Why it should have been produced as it was in the first place is impossible to determine, but LDB, as Round divined in 1895, is best interpreted as the prototype that was to inspire GDB.[140]

This conclusion, novel as it may seem to those, like Galbraith, who only admit of pedigree sources, begins to make some sense of that other GDB lacuna, the *clamores*. A record of disputes occurs in only three counties, and it is possible that the scribe had intended to enter similar claims in the others. On balance, however, this seems unlikely. In the Huntingdonshire folios there is no pressing reason not to believe that the *clamores* section was written after the account of the shire that it follows. The Yorkshire and Lincolnshire examples are less clearly current. They are entered on fifty-two lines in ruling pattern 2 with the Yorkshire Summary in quire no. 42, and this on its own might suggest that they were entered after the bulk of Circuit VI. However, the Summary as written was apparently used in some sections of the Yorkshire *terra regis* and an earlier enrolment must be suspected.[141] The three *clamores* sections were clearly no afterthoughts. Although the absence of similar sections for Nottinghamshire and Derbyshire has to be explained,[142] it is significant, then, that the material only occurs in the first circuit to be abbreviated, even though available elsewhere as Exon indicates. If the suggestion that LDB was the prototype of GDB is correct, the model is patent. The *invasiones* were an integral part of the East Anglian folios and therefore probably inspired the scribe to enter similar material in GDB. As with much

---

[140] *Feudal England*, 141. He presented no evidence for the assertion.

[141] Roffe, 'Yorkshire Summary', 251.

[142] The resolution of some disputes is appended to the appropriate entries and therefore a separate section may not have been felt necessary (Roffe, 'Domesday Book and Northern Society', 326). For a more sceptical, not to say perplexed, view, see Wormald, 'Domesday Lawsuits', 65–7.

else, he thought better of the decision in the course of the composition of circuit VI and subsequently omitted the material as irrelevant to his purpose. Overall, there is also evidence of a decline in interest in claims generally. In terms of numbers of those recorded in the body of the text, Circuit VI follows Circuit III, but thereafter there is a steady fall-off through Circuits I, II, and V, and by the time the scribe reached IV there are hardly any recorded at all.[143] Disputes claimed less of the scribe's time as his work progressed.

Only one further major formative influence from LDB on GDB suggests itself. The dimensions of vills are universally recorded in Norfolk and Suffolk, and so they are in the Yorkshire folios.[144] Thereafter, the information was suppressed as the scribe began to realize his purpose.[145] Nevertheless, the two volumes can be seen to form a coherent whole that embodies the developing scheme of the GDB scribe. LDB was none of his work, as far as is known, but its forms and content appear to have focused his concerns as he commenced on the writing of GDB. There his ideas became more and more refined, until at the end his account had become cut down to its bare essentials. The so-called articles of inquiry in the prologue to IE probably mark an important stage in the process. Formally close to the 'main' entries of LDB, but in content more closely approximating to the standard GDB entry of Circuit VI, they embody a distillation of the thought of the scribe at the time when he commenced on his abbreviation of the remaining circuit reports. LDB, then, probably marks one end of a development from complexity to simplicity. What is now volume II of Domesday Book should be more properly volume I.

[143] Wormald, 'Domesday Lawsuits', 65–7.

[144] Often they explicitly relate to manors, but they are clearly of a similar origin to those of East Anglia. In the account of the 84 carucates of York dimensions are those of vills. Due to the summary form of many of the Yorkshire entries, many figures are seemingly omitted and it is therefore difficult to determine their distribution. There are indications, however, that the explicitly manorial figures are often associated with the manorial entries of the Yorkshire Summary and that the remainder are associated with villar groups of estates. Further investigation is called for.

[145] It has been asserted that the areal measurements of East Anglia are related to the payment of the geld and are therefore of a different order from those of the north (Darby, 'Domesday Book and the Geographer', 113–4). However, the juxtaposition of the two items of information is probably only a function of their occurrence at the end of the account of the vill in the source of LDB. To what use the figures were put is unclear. Other LDB forms may be perpetuated in GDB. Slaves, for example, are listed in LDB with the other inhabitants of the estate and so they are in fourteen out of the sixteen places they appear in the folios of Circuit VI (GDB 272a, 275a–b, 276c, 277a, 287b, 287c, 287d, 288c, 289b, 289b, 293b: *DB Derby.*, 1,1.6,52–4;66.8,1.10,1;4; *DB Notts.*, 10,1;16;39.11,10.12,1;16;18.30,47). Thereafter they are listed as part of the manorial stock or with the demesne ploughs.

9

The Domesday Inquest and Domesday Book

THUS FAR THE analysis of the Domesday inquest has proceeded in terms of processes, namely, the collection of data, executive action, the formulation of reports, and finally, the production of Domesday Book itself. Two stages have been identified in the garnering of evidence. Initial sessions were held in local centres and were overseen by the regular personnel of local government. Their brief was limited, being confined to, in the words of the Anglo-Saxon chronicler, 'how many hundred hides there were in the shire, or what land and cattle the king himself had in the country, or what dues he ought to have in twelve months from the shire'. Thereafter, further sessions were held in regional courts before commissioners who were charged with receiving presentments from tenants-in-chief on the resources of their estates. Executive action, notably the resolution of disputes, was thereby set in train in a process which was to continue independently but in parallel with the ongoing Domesday inquest. In the meantime reports of one sort or another were drawn up and sent to a central point, and GDB was subsequently abbreviated from these materials.

All four of these processes have been recognized to a greater or lesser degree by historians as discrete activities. Nevertheless, they have been interpreted as integrated elements of a wider programme. Round is vague as to his views on the function of GDB. He was in no doubt, however, that the outcome of the survey, for him hundred rolls as exemplified by ICC, were prefigured in the deep speech at Gloucester on Christmas Day 1085. Maitland, and then more emphatically Galbraith, brought GDB into the fold and there, by and large, it has remained. Despite differences in the identification of sources and the understanding of procedure, for most historians today the aim of the Domesday inquest was the production of GDB.[1] At each stage the collection and selection of data were tailored to this, the ultimate purpose of the whole enterprise.

The rationale of the analysis is founded in the concept of the inquest as recognition. The various stages of the inquiry might produce different categories of information, but these must be subordinate to the essential matters

[1] For a dissenting voice, see Fleming, 'Oral Testimony', 120, who sees the 'real' focus of the Domesday inquest in the recognitions of the community in the forum of the local courts. Nevertheless, she still comprehends the government's aim as the production of Domesday Book (*Domesday Book and the Law*, 35).

of land tenure and title to which the inquest's respondents swore. Successive recensions saw the refinement of the central idea as expressed in the articles of inquiry. The model is essentially a bureaucratic one, something like that of an august Royal Commission set up to record once and for all the facts. That the inquest might be conceived in such terms is illustrated by Edward I's survey of land tenure in 1279/80. A number of records survive, from rough notes preliminary to court sessions, through the presentments of jurors, to fair copies of fully digested resumés. However, the more abbreviated and considered documents all seem to date from later in the process, and it would seem likely that the *libri* in which Edward had ordered the verdicts to be entered were conceived of as a fully digested register of landholding.[2] In the event this was a mistaken apprehension. Not even Edward I's bureaucracy was able to resolve all the problems of right that the inquest threw up, and the inquest was aborted in 1280. The instrument of the inquest was not designed to produce definitive record. As an investigatory procedure it was open-ended, and the records of various stages had their own peculiar validity and use. Initially, the verdicts themselves were of central importance. They afforded the information which government needed to resolve the matter which had launched the inquest in the first place. In 1275 the incoming verdicts of the Ragman inquest indicated the need for reform of procedures, and even before all the verdicts were in, a parliament passed the Statute of Westminster I and the Statute of the Exchequer to remedy the worse deficiencies.[3] The presentments also initiated more specific actions. Surviving verdicts are often annotated by justices and officials as the specific facts that they brought to light were examined and dealt with. The sole surviving roll of the 1258 inquest consequent to the Provisions of Oxford records the decisions reached in the eyre conducted in the following year by Hugh Bigod into the matters of concern brought to light.[4] The Ragman Rolls of 1274/5 were similarly annotated in the ensuing eyres, which commenced in 1279 and continued into the 1290s.[5]

The verdict was sufficient, and indeed probably always necessary, for the resolution of the immediate concerns of the inquest. The Hundred Rolls corpus again illustrates the point. The Extract Rolls were produced some twenty years after the Ragman inquest of 1274/5 and were conceived as some sort of a guide to the content of the mass of verdicts that the process had produced.[6] However, they did not supersede them, for there occurs therein the frequent exhortation to 'consult the rolls' or to make reference to 'the pleas in the rolls',

---

[2] Greenway, 'A Newly Discovered Fragment of the Hundred Rolls of 1279–80', 73–8; Raban, 'The 1279–80 Hundred Rolls', 140–1.

[3] *Statutes of the Realm*, i. 26–39, 197–8; Cam, *The Hundred and the Hundred Rolls*, 37, 225–9.

[4] Jacob, *Studies in the Period of Baronial Reform and Rebellion, 1258–1267*, 337–44. The 'Ragman Pleas' were a distinct activity in the subsequent eyres until the matters were abandoned in the 1290s.

[5] Roffe, *Stamford in the Thirteenth Century*, 10. See e.g. the Lincolnshire rolls (*Rotuli Hundredorum*, i. 241–402).

[6] English, *Yorkshire Hundred and Quo Warranto Rolls*, 2–3.

and the original verdicts continued to be the presentment on which the Ragman pleas were conducted.[7] Like cartularies, digests of surveys were of little legal force. Abbreviation was of its nature a secondary process related to the subsequently perceived usefulness of the inquest as a source of reference. It was, moreover, by necessity *post hoc*, for in an investigatory process it was not possible to perceive what is of permanent value until the verdicts were given and the results were known.

There are, then, conceptual problems in using an abbreviation to determine the purpose of an inquest. With many later instances the fact is self-evident. The Northamptonshire Survey, which is preserved in a Peterborough cartulary, was presumably drawn up for tax purposes, for it records assessment to the geld by hundred. The extant text, however, is a copy of an abbreviation (at the very least, the names of jurors have been omitted) which had subsequently been annotated for some years after initial compilation with the names of the current holders of the lands therein described. It was evidently used, if not compiled, as a feodary.[8] As evidentiary documents the verdicts themselves on which they are based are only contingently related to the aim of an inquest. It is, of course, axiomatic that the commissioners generally got the information that they asked for and that the questions that they asked were predicated on a particular problem. But the reports that the commissioners made to central government depended upon their understanding of what was relevant and appropriate. Thereafter the course of action that was taken turned on the answers that were received. An inquiry into the royal fisc could only presage a campaign to increase royal income. But the form that that might take was dictated by the deficiencies in the existing arrangements that the inquest uncovered.

In the following analysis an attempt is made to relate the four activities of the Domesday inquest to each other and to Domesday Book. In the absence of any record of statement of intent or articles of inquiry, there is no way of recovering the objectives of government in 1085 from the surviving records of the process with absolute certainty. Likewise, the understanding of those objectives by the officers of local government and the commissioners cannot be reconstructed. However, the form of documentation produced at each stage can be used to reveal something of their perception of what was required of them. Various preoccupations emerge, and these can be used in their turn to interpret the remarks of contemporary commentators. A context for the Domesday inquest can be suggested with some degree of confidence from the extant documentation. The settlement, by contrast, can only be a matter

[7] Cam, *The Hundred and the Hundred Rolls*, 225–32.

[8] Peterborough, Dean and Chapter MS 1, the book of Robert of Swaffham, f. 124; London, BL Cotton MS Vespasian E, xxii, ff. 94–9; *VCH Northants.*, i. 357–89; Round, *Feudal England*, 221. Whether it was so used by government or Peterborough Abbey is, of course, difficult to determine. The former, however, is likely since all manner of fees unrelated to the abbey are updated.

of speculation. There is no record of the negotiations at Salisbury in August 1086, and it is not inherent in the records of the inquest itself; had the terms been known at Christmas the previous year there would have been no need for the inquest in the first place. Finally, Domesday Book represents the government's perception of what it could subsequently do with the information.

The Domesday Inquest and Domesday Book

In the recensionist model it is axiomatic that the documents that were produced in the course of the inquest were 'satellites', that is, they were subordinate to the end of producing GDB. In reality it seems that they had an identity and use in their own right. The compiler of the Crowland Domesday was in no doubt that the geographically arranged document that he consulted and incorporated into his text was a discrete entity, for he attributed it, albeit erroneously, to King Alfred. The references to 'the roll of Winchester' and 'the other writing in the king's Treasury' in Evesham P and Abingdon A indicate that this was a common perception. The schedules of land were evidently preserved as documents in their own right. So, indeed, were other types of record retained by central government. The schedule of claims called the *breves regis* noticed in IE presumably informed the ongoing legal procedures of the inquest, providing, as it probably did, a record of the issues of the estates in dispute to the king during the process. Even the more extensive composite reports that the commissioners sent back to central government were manifestly the basis of executive action. In the account of the bishop of Winchester's Somerset lands in Exon it is stated that, at a meeting at Salisbury, King William ordered the bishop of Durham to write down in his records (*in brevibus*) a grant to the bishop of Winchester of additions to his manor of Taunton which he, King William, had just acknowledged.[9] The complete account is written in a hand that is not otherwise found in the manuscript, and is apparently a revised copy of the whole section occasioned by the king's intervention.[10] GDB was not finished, and may not even have been started, until the reign of King William Rufus, and the records 'brought to the king' in 1086 were therefore by necessity, *inter alia*, the circuit reports. To whatever use William the Conqueror put the Domesday inquest, executive action must have been predicated on this evidence.

The identity of each type of document is paralleled by a distinct focus. The records of the geld inquest and survey of the king's lands are broadly characterized by an interest in the issues of the royal fisc. The account of the king's demesne estates is similar to those of the tenants-in-chief recorded in GDB and LDB. To what extent this is a function of subsequent editing is unclear. Demesne lands are absent from ICC and those in LDB probably attest a later

---

[9] Exon, 175.   [10] Chaplais, 'William de Saint-Calais and the Domesday Survey', 75.

stage in the Domesday process. Only the Exon accounts survive as witness
to the form of the records of the survey of royal lands, and in substance they
are close to their GDB counterparts. In the south-west, at least, the scope of
the accounts suggests little difference. In Oxfordshire, by contrast, there are
indications that the survey was of a different order. There almost every item
of manorial stock is separately valued, suggesting something more akin to
an audit.[11] That this was of the essence of the process is illustrated by the
coupling of all of these data with the issues of boroughs and hundreds, but
is most clearly exemplified in the records of the geld inquest. The Exon geld
accounts are overtly concerned with accountancy, the principal emphasis being
on the identification of exempt demesne and the discovery of unpaid tax. The
form of the schedules may be a reflection of the same concern. The common
denominator of almost all of these documents is the dichotomy between demesne
and enfeoffed estates or sokeland. Both geld accounts and schedules are hundredally arranged (where the form is discernible), indicating that the primary
focus was the relationship of the community, as opposed to the tenant-in-chief,
with the king.

The survey of the lands of the tenants-in-chief was self-evidently a change
in subject matter. But the preoccupations of the process are remarkably close
to those of the first stage of the inquiry. Schedules of estates from the geld
survey probably informed the process by providing the salient details of estates:
assessment to the geld, TRE holder, and possibly values. Ploughlands were
an additional item of information but, as a measure of the fiscal capacity of
the warland, they seem to have had an equal bearing on the geld. Moreover,
close attention was probably paid to the distinction between demesne and
enfeoffed land. The extent of the warland held by the lord, as measured by
assessment to the geld, is consistently noted in Exon and intermittently in
ICC, and within their internal hundredal divisions both take pains to distinguish tenants by a careful use of toponyms or other identifying by-names.
Above all, the data were presented in a geographical form. Details of estate
resources and management were undoubtedly provided by the tenant-in-chief.
But only in the counties of Circuit II and in Gloucestershire, Worcestershire,
and Herefordshire in Circuit V was a seigneurial form retained. There, for
whatever reason, the survey did not proceed beyond inbreviation. In the remaining twenty counties of Domesday England circuit commissioners went on to
draw up a record of the proceedings hundred by hundred.

At this stage the emphasis of the survey was still the community. Seigneurial
aspects were, however, beginning to appear. If the summaries were produced
at the same time as the circuit reports, then the holdings of individuals had
clearly become an interest of the inquest. The number of manors, ploughs,
and inhabitants for each fee seem to have been totalled, and a value given.

---

[11] GDB 154c–d: *DB Oxon.*, 1,1–11.

Nevertheless, the underlying motif of geld payment underlies the record. Separate statistics are given for the demesne and enfeoffed lands, and a special priority is accorded to the ploughland figures. The summaries are undoubtedly the seigneurial counterpart to the geographically arranged circuit reports, but they were produced with similar concerns in mind.

Legal actions arising from the survey proceeded in parallel with these activities, and, indeed, were to continue after the completion of the Domesday inquest. The process was largely demand-led. The survey had thrown disputed title into relief and provision had to be made to satisfy the claims that had come to light. The crown, however, was not interested in the determination of title *per se*. Entries in the *clamores*, *invasiones*, and *terre occupate* appear to have been a record of the income that the crown might expect from the actions through the processes of the law.

The focus of the first two stages of the inquest, then, and the record of the legal proceedings that they engendered was the geld and the resources of estates within a communal context. The focus of GDB and LDB was otherwise. For the first time the tenant-in-chief comes to centre-stage. With the exception of a handful of anomalous passages, the geographical arrangement gives way to an unremitting seigneurial form. Demesne and tenanted lands are duly noticed, but no attempt is made systematically to record the assessment of each. Furthermore, the compiler felt it unnecessary always to distinguish one tenant from another: where the commissioners' reports carefully identify individuals, GDB omits all clues and, on occasion, even fails to record the fact of tenancy at all. Ploughlands are duly recorded, but there is a sense that they had ceased to be an essential item of information. The compilers of LDB saw little need to refer explicitly to arable potential at all, while in GDB the scribe failed to find the data or forgot to enter them in many counties and, moreover, seemed to be little fussed by the fact. Manors also ceased to be a matter of interest. LDB is little more than a simple seigneurial rearrangement of the circuit report. But with the commencement of work on GDB with the account of the northern counties an attempt was made to represent the structure of the manor in the fullest way possible. Thereafter, interest in manorial structure waned and from Circuit I onwards no deliberate cognizance was taken of it. The scribe's account of the Circuit IV counties, the last to be abbreviated, probably represents the bare minimum that was considered essential. Details of pre-Conquest landholding were confined to those that bore directly on tenure in 1086, disputes were disregarded, the structure of estates was ignored. There remains the economical account of the lands of each tenant-in-chief in terms of location, assessment, stocking, and value. The focus of GDB is the tenant-in-chief and the identity of his lands and their resources.

All of these activities formed a unity in the sense that they impinged on the same materials. Geld survey and related processes produced the evidence from which the tenant-in-chief made his presentment, and LDB and GDB were abbreviated from the reports that the commissioners made thereof. However, the relationship between each was essentially contingent. At every stage there was a specific and distinctive focus. The preoccupations of LDB and GDB are so different from those of the geld survey that it is clear that the one was not prefigured in the other. One process led on to another, but there was no unifying programme. The context of each stage and its relationship to the next is the subject of the remainder of this chapter.

The Royal Fisc and the Income of the Crown

The writer of the 1085 annal of the Anglo-Saxon Chronicle graphically describes the context of the Domesday inquest as William's 'deep speech with his council at Gloucester about England, how it was occupied or with what sort of people'.[12] No doubt with this passage in mind, some historians have argued that the Domesday inquest was in its broadest context a function of William's curiosity about his new realm.[13] This, however, is redolent of nineteenth- and twentieth-century notions of social monitoring as exemplified by the census. Disinterested curiosity—or indeed the social conscience that it might suggest—of this kind is not a very medieval notion. The chronicler was fully aware of the realities of eleventh-century government. He was in no doubt that the king sought to review the resources of his lands, the issues of the geld, that is, 'how many hundred hides there were in the shire', and his regular income from the shire.

The royal fisc and taxation were central concerns of every medieval king who had to 'live of his own'. In the twelfth and thirteenth centuries the king's demesne lands were administered by the sheriff or specially designated farmers or keepers. Throughout the period their activities were monitored on a regular basis through the Exchequer in its annual audit of shire accounts. A more searching examination was undertaken by justices in eyre, and there were periodic inquests as the need arose.[14] In the eleventh century and before, the mechanisms of oversight were not as sophisticated, but were probably of essentially the same kind. The sheriff or king's reeve appear to have compounded for the dues of the estates and rendered their account at the Exchequer. The farms, renders, and values that are appended to the accounts of royal manors were the sums that they paid.[15]

Since the Conquest the renders had generally appreciated. Almost every estate that had been held by Edward the Confessor in 1066 was worth more in 1086. Likewise, other estates that had come into the king's hands experienced

[12] ASC 161.

[13] Loyn, 'Introduction to Domesday Book', 15. Loyn cites Stenton (Stenton, Anglo-Saxon England, 657) for this view, but he emphasizes the imperatives which drove the king to find out more about England—'how it was peopled and with what sort of men'.

[14] Warren, Governance of Norman and Angevin England, 151–5.

[15] In many counties the fact is made explicit by the use of reddidit and reddit instead of valuit and valet in the accounts of the terra regis.

an increase in value.[16] William clearly demanded a high return from his estates, and often the demand was more than could be borne. In Winfarthing in Norfolk the free men and the soke rendered £7, 'but cannot render so much any more',[17] while Brook in the Isle of Wight seems to have paid £14 although its value was assessed at £7.[18] But by the nature of the relationship most renders were probably out of kilter with the actual issues of estates. GDB notices several instances of undervaluation or failure to demand as much as was possible. Leominster, for example, was at farm for £60, but the county estimated that it would yield £120 if correctly assessed, and the value of Lower Slaughter in Gloucestershire in 1066 was unknown because the sheriff had rendered what he wished and in 1086 paid £27.[19] The grant of farms was as much an exercise in patronage as estate management, and the degree to which returns were audited was often a measure of political favour. Inevitably, there was always room to squeeze out more if the need be, and the inquest provided the necessary data.[20] As in Oxfordshire, the issues of individual resources may have been widely listed. But, above all, the ploughland figures gave some indication of the extent of land available.[21]

The king's estates were the bedrock of the crown's regular income.[22] It was supplemented by, in the words of the Chronicler, '[the] dues he ought to have in twelve months from the shire'. These are not very well recorded in the Domesday corpus, but were evidently various. A partial list is given in the Oxfordshire folios of GDB:

The county of Oxford pays a farm of three nights, that is £150; from an increment £25 by weight; from the borough £20 by weight; from the mint £20 of pennies at 20 to the *ora*; for arms 4s; from the 'gersum' of the queen 100s by number; for a hawk £10; for a pack horse 20s; for the dogs £23 of pennies at 20 to the *ora*; 6 sesters of honey, and 15d from custom.[23]

Sundry other dues are recorded throughout the text. Often the most conspicuous were the issues of hundred courts, the king's two pennies, which are sometimes noticed in the value of royal estates or boroughs. In Lincolnshire, the customs of the king and earl recorded at the end of the account of Lincoln probably refer to these dues; south Lincolnshire rendered £28, the North Riding of Lindsey £24, the West Riding £12, and the South Riding £15.[24] Elsewhere

---

[16] Harvey, 'Domesday England', 86.

[17] LDB 130a: *DB Norfolk*, 1,174. *Liberi cum soca* is better translated thus than the 'free with soke' of the Phillimore edition.

[18] GDB 52b: *DB Hants*, IoW1. This entry may be garbled, for the implications are not clear.

[19] GDB 180a, 162d–163a: *DB Hereford.*, 1,10b; *DB Gloucs.*, 1,10.

[20] For the most detailed account of the issues of royal estates, see GDB 154c–d: *DB Oxon.*, 1,1–11 where almost every resource is separately valued.

[21] The intention here cannot have been to extend the geld over exempt demesne since the concept was inapplicable to the king's own lands.

[22] Hoyt, *Royal Demesne*, 1–8; Harvey, 'Domesday England', 92–5.

[23] GDB 154d: *DB Oxon.*, 1,12.   [24] See e.g. GDB 336c: *DB Lincs.*, C28–31.

the dues are omitted or hidden in other figures. The large discrepancies between the renders of the king's Oxfordshire manors and the issues of each
of its separate components, for example, are probably accounted for by the
pleas of the hundreds attached to them that were otherwise unvalued.[25] The
profits of courts were probably among the most substantial of the dues that
accrued to the king as sovereign. The value of the various aids, rents, and customs that were rendered to the king by free men and sokemen is largely unknown.
In Circuit III there are references to customs and rents, but only escort and
cartage duties are regularly noticed. The former is not valued and the latter
was occasionally rated at 3d to 6d per person.[26] In Circuit I escort was either
valued at 12d or in kind.[27] There are, however, no totals, nor, indeed, anything
like a systematic account, for, as with the royal demesne, the sheriff compounded
for the sums. Here was yet another source of income that could be more
efficiently exploited. The dues themselves were customary and therefore not
subject to revision. But the amount that the sheriff returned could be increased;
the increment in the county renders of Oxfordshire is probably an example,
as is the £60 which Edward the sheriff of Wiltshire paid *de cremento*.[28]

The issues of the king's demesne and the 'customs' of the shire were
regular sources of income. Others were, theoretically at least, by their nature
occasional. First, there were personal services, renders, and dues of those who
were 'nigh to the king'. King's thegns were in the soke of the king and as a
result their heriots or reliefs, forfeitures, and the like were made directly to
the crown.[29] In Nottinghamshire and Derbyshire local peculiarities resulted
in a full record of the relationship:

A thegn who has more than six manors does not pay relief on his land, save only to
the king, £8. If he has only six or less, he pays relief to the sheriff, three silver marks,
wherever he may live, within the borough or outside.

If a thegn who has sake and soke should forfeit his land, the king and the earl
between them have half of the land and of his stock; his lawful wife, and his lawful
heirs, if any, have the other half.[30]

The wife and heirs' portion was probably not generally recognized, but otherwise similar customs obtained throughout the country.[31] Likewise, those king's
thegns who held ministerial tenements (the *taini regis* of the Domesday texts)
rendered their dues and services directly to the crown in much the same way
as their successors, the king's sergeants, were to do in the twelfth and thirteenth

[25] GDB 154c–d: *DB Oxon.*, 1,1–11.
[26] GDB 133c, 137b, 141a–b, 141c: *DB Herts.*, 4,1.17,4.36,8;9;11.37,1.
[27] GDB 1b: *DB Kent*, D24.
[28] GDB 154d, 64c: *DB Oxon.*, 1,12; *DB Wilts.*, B4. For the later history of increments on the farm
of the county and the means by which they were calculated, see Carpenter, 'The Decline of the Curial
Sheriff in England 1194–1258', 1–32; Roffe, 'Hundred Rolls of 1255', 207.
[29] Roffe, 'Thegnage to Barony,' 158.   [30] GDB 280c: *DB Notts.*, S3–4.
[31] GDB 56c, 1b, 337a, 298d: *DB Berks.*, B10; *DB Kent*, D17; *DB Lincs.*, S5; *DB Yorks.*, C40.

centuries. All of these incidents and services were probably rendered in the shire and were evidently still of some importance in 1086. To what extent they applied to the Norman tenants-in-chief is not clear. Tenure by what subsequently became known as barony was informed by Old English law in this respect, but Domesday is silent on the arrangements for the collection of their reliefs.[32] Nevertheless, there were still many thegns, free men, and burgesses who were subject to the same provisions in 1086. Periodic audit of their dues was always a necessity. Despite the systematic management of feudal incidents, at first through the sheriff and then through specially commissioned officers like the escheator, sergeancy was regularly the subject of oversight in inquests and eyres up to the late thirteenth century.[33] The potential for uncovering unpaid dues in 1086 must have been considerable.

The significance of these dues to the royal finances is impossible to determine. It was clearly dwarfed, however, by the second occasional source of income, the Danegeld. In the early years of the eleventh century the capacity of the tax had been considerable, raising, the Anglo-Saxon Chronicler alleges, no less than £87,500 in 1018 at its height.[34] This may well be an exaggeration,[35] and certainly by 1086 successive concessions had transferred capacity from the king to the tenant-in-chief. The assessment of vills in some areas had been slashed, as had individual estates in others, and demesne had probably been exempted throughout the kingdom.[36] Nevertheless, the Danegeld was still the greatest single source of income that the king enjoyed.[37] William the Conqueror had reintroduced the tax after its suspension in the reign of Edward the Confessor, and by the 1080s it had probably become an almost annual impost.[38]

---

[32] The compilation of GDB and LDB by tenant-in-chief within counties may suggest that many dues that they owed were mediated through the shire. Military service would seem to be one such. A possibly authentic writ addressed to Abbot Æthelwig of Evesham between 1066 and 1078 ordered him to assemble all the knights within his bailiwick, as well as the five knights that he himself owed, at Clarendon on the octave of Pentecost (*Regesta Regum: Acta*, no. 131); and he would seem to have been in charge of the seven counties of Worcestershire, Gloucestershire, Oxfordshire, Shropshire, Staffordshire, Herefordshire, and Warwickshire (Darlington, 'Abbot Aethelwig', 10–14). Royal castle guard may have been another, for it seems to have been generally performed in the king's castle within the shire where the *caput* of the honour was situated. For a notable exception, see GDB 151c–d: *DB Bucks.*, 40,1.

[33] Cam, *Studies in the Hundred Rolls*, 92–3; *Book of Fees*, 1163–6.   [34] *ASC* 97.

[35] For the debate on the meaning of the figures, see Lawson, 'The Collection of Danegeld and Heregeld in the Reigns of Aethelred II and Cnut', 721–38; Lawson, 'Those Stories Look True: Levels of Taxation in the Reigns of Aethelred II and Cnut', 385–406; Gillingham, 'The Most Precious Jewel in the English Crown', 373–84.

[36] Green, 'Last Century of Danegeld', 242–6; Hart, *Hidation of Northamptonshire*; Hart, *Hidation of Cambridgeshire*.

[37] On the Domesday hidage and carucage of 68,734 hides and carucates, a geld of 2 shillings would raise £6,873. In Wiltshire as much as one-third was demesne, but elsewhere less was exempt.

[38] *Hi omnes habent sacham et socham; rex habet de omnibus geldum per annum* (GDB 246a: *DB Staffs.*, B11). The referent is to the non-customary tenants in Stafford. As they were holders of sake and soke, *geldum* in this context almost certainly refers to Danegeld, one of the few imposts that was generally reserved to the king.

The capacity of the system was a matter of pressing concern. There is no compelling evidence to indicate that the purpose of the *inquisitio geldi* was a reassessment of liability. The TRE assessments of Domesday were extensively used in the twelfth and thirteenth centuries, and the schedules that pre-date LDB and GDB exhibit no hint of a movement to a different taxation base.[39] On the contrary, the geld accounts of Exon indicate that the existing assessments were widely accepted. Much of the effort of the inquest was evidently put into the identification of exempt demesne and of unassessed lands to the end of enforcing the payment of the geld already due. A six-shilling geld had been imposed in 1084, but the geld inquest seems to have been concerned with a subsequent imposition. According to the Berkshire Domesday, Christmas and Whitsun were the traditional dates for payment.[40] Elsewhere autumn and Easter may have been preferred, but two instalments were probably the norm.[41] An inquest in early 1086, then, would have audited the returns from a first instalment of a tax in 1085 and determined what was due from the second.

The activities that can be identified with the earliest stage of the Domesday inquest and the documentation that they appear to have produced are consistent with the annalist's perception of the process as an audit of the royal fisc. Each of its elements can have been far from unprecedented. Central government had continually to monitor its resources and the officers who administered them. Domesday Book itself attests the oversight of the sheriff's management of the *terra regis* in the increases in the farms since 1066. Similar reviews of the shire customs and geld renders must also have been undertaken periodically.[42] The coincidence of all three processes, however, hints at extraordinary circumstances. No more extraordinary were those of 1085. The mercenaries that William had hired in Normandy and Brittany to counter the imminent invasion from Denmark must have required vast resources in coin. The army was, according to the annalist, the largest that had ever been brought into England, and its servicing must have posed a considerable challenge to the king's finances. Current expenses were borne by the tenants-in-chief and, no doubt, their men, but the king had to pay their wages. The Domesday inquest appears to have started with an effort to maximize the king's income from every possible source to meet his commitments in the emergency.

The Lord's Demesne and the Geld

The impact of the geld inquest on the tenant-in-chief was probably minimal. With his inland unassessed and his demesne exempt, the burden of taxation

---

[39] See above, pp. 106–12, 162.   [40] GDB 56c: *DB Berks.*, B10.

[41] Welldon Finn, *Liber Exoniensis*, 100–1, citing various passages from Exon.

[42] The Northamptonshire Geld Roll is one of the few survivals.

fell largely upon his tenants. In the north the sokeman seems to have acquitted his land himself, and elsewhere the equation of one villein to the virgate suggests similar arrangements. But exemptions had probably already begun to erode the direct relationship between free man and king that the payment of geld suggested. Beneficial hidation has usually been seen as a device that benefited the tenant-in-chief by relieving him of the necessity to pay geld.[43] In reality, however, his warland demesne was already quit (if not created by such exemption), and the effect of beneficial hidation was to transfer the geld of his tenants to himself. As for the abbot of Burton in the early twelfth century, the levy put money into the tenant-in-chief's pocket. It must often have been a small step to declaring that the land was inland and its occupiers unfree. Not the least of the advantages of the geld inquest to the tenant was the implicit recognition that his land was geldable, and thus that he was free, even if it was declared to be demesne. It was the lucrative source of income that was geld exemption that was the subject of the second stage of the inquiry.

Both the annalist and Bishop Robert of Hereford were impressed by the inquest's intrusion into the minutiae of estate management. And yet the context in which they placed the inquest, either implicitly or explicitly, was taxation. What can be reconstructed of the commissioners' reports substantiates the perception. Various types of document found their way back from circuit sessions, but the majority were considered compilations in a geographical arrangement. Now, although the form of commissioners' reports does not necessarily reflect the purpose of an inquiry, much less the use to which it was put, here is evidence of a widespread *perception* of what was required. The community rather than the individual overwhelmingly remained the focus of the commissioners' concerns.

Within that framework it was the lord, whether tenant-in-chief or his tenant, and his demesne that were of interest. Historians have long recognized the bias. Commodities and resources were recorded because they impinged upon the profits of the lord's demesne rather than from any desire comprehensively to represent the society and economy of an estate or settlement. Numerous studies have demonstrated the so-called 'deficiencies' of Domesday in this respect, and the inference is commonly drawn from the fact that the primary interest of the commissioners was thus in the total resources and income of the tenant-in-chief. That inference can now be seen to be unwarranted. It was the extent and value of the demesne *within the vill* that were the focus of attention. Detailed statistics of livestock and infrastructure were drawn up vill by vill because they were of relevance to the vill itself. Within this context it can only have been the exemption of the demesne to the geld that was of interest. The ploughland figures indicate to what end. As the summaries illustrate, the government took

---

[43] For the use of exemption as an instrument of patronage in the post-Conquest period, see Green, 'Last Century of Danegeld', 252.

an especial interest in the statistics (where assessment to the geld, ploughs, manorial infrastructure and population, and value were all separately enumerated for the demesne and enfeoffed lands, a single total was given for ploughlands). As a measure of the capacity of the warland, including the exempt demesne, to render the geld assessed upon it, they were an indicator of the amount of geld that was diverted to the lord's pocket. The enumeration of ploughlands within the vill suggests an intention to extend the geld to the formerly exempt demesne.

Whether the ploughlands were intended to amount to a formal reassessment is at best a moot point. If assessment was to be anything more than symbolic, the determination of the burden of taxation can never have been an entirely arbitrary process, and was thus to a greater or lesser degree based upon measurement. The line between that and assessment was often a fine one, but it was nevertheless real. Measurement was the basis on which negotiations could take place, and assessment or settlement subsequently followed. So it is that the pre-Conquest hidation and carucation were equitably distributed at a local level, but rates varied from area to area. As in much else, the processes of assessment was a mutual one far removed from the bureaucratic procedures of modern government. So must be viewed the determination of the number of ploughlands. The unit was undoubtedly perceived as a real measure of land, but did not necessarily constitute an assessment.

The absence of the ploughland from later records, then, is no objection to its fiscal referents. There is no indication that a reassessment was introduced after the Domesday inquest, but the information collected was clearly effective, for the government's apparent determination to tap surplus geld capacity was subsequently implemented. Neither the Lindsey, Leicestershire, nor Northamptonshire surveys take any special notice of demesne; in entry after entry the full Domesday assessments are given. By the early twelfth century geld was apparently paid on the whole of the warland. Thus, in the Pipe Roll of 1129/30 it was levied from land that was assessed at totals closely approximating to the Domesday hidage of demesne and non-demesne lands in county after county. In Rutland, for example, Danegeld was charged on 116 hides and carucates where Domesday Book records 112, while in Buckinghamshire there were 2,047 as against 2,074.[44] Not all figures are quite so close, but they are considerably greater than the Domesday totals less the assessment of the demesne where that can be determined. In Wiltshire, for example, 3,896 hides paid in the twelfth century where there where 4,050 hides in Domesday, of which at least 1,365 were in demesne.[45] In some counties even the geld reductions of the Conqueror's reign had been reversed by 1129/30. Berkshire,

[44] Maitland, *Domesday Book and Beyond*, 464–5. For the aberrant Yorkshire and Leicestershire figures, see Green, 'Last Century of Danegeld', 244.

[45] Darlington, 'Wiltshire Geld Rolls', *passim*.

Hampshire, Surrey, and possibly Cambridgeshire geld was paid on more hides than in 1086, and it would seem that pre-Conquest assessments had been reimposed.[46]

The issue was a vexed one in the early twelfth century. Henry I granted numerous charters exempting individuals, and many of these pardons are recorded on the Pipe Roll. He himself had reimposed the charge, for in clause eleven of the charter of liberties that he issued at his coronation in 1100 he had exempted all demesnes in unequivocal terms: 'I grant by my own gift that the demesne ploughs of those knights who hold by knight service should be free from all gelds, so that, being relieved of such a great burden, they may furnish themselves so well with horses and arms that they may be properly equipped and prepared to discharge my service and to defend my kingdom.'[47] The cancellation of exemptions was clearly a late-eleventh-century initiative and one that can almost certainly be associated with the Domesday inquest. According to the *Leges Edwardi Confessoris*, the demesnes of the church had been first taxed in 1096 by William Rufus to finance his brother Robert's participation in the first crusade.[48] But the Domesday corpus indicates that it was already prefigured in 1086. By the time that GDB came to be written, the extent of demesne appears already to have been of little moment; the scribe recorded the statistic early on in his work, but subsequently consistently omitted it. Demesne was no longer an issue, and it is therefore likely that William the Conqueror had already enacted the proposal (at least as far as lay lands were concerned).

The immediate purpose of the second stage of the Domesday inquest, then, was probably the evaluation of demesne to the end of taxing it. The annalist was in no doubt that William's greed lay behind the whole enterprise, and he leaves the impression of a realm cowed into submission by an all-powerful king who brooked no opposition to his will. But even William had to recognize political realities. Demesne was an especially contentious issue in 1086. By its nature the lord's inland had probably always been quit of communal dues, for the holder of bookland, the king's thegn, rendered service personally to the king for his franchise. Thus it was that his men were in his surety rather than a tithing.[49] Domesday demesne was largely warland that had been exempt from payment, and as a common expectation was probably a post-Conquest phenomenon. If the statement that estates had gelded TRE for the whole assessment charged against them cannot be taken literally, then widespread reductions in assessment had at least greatly increased in extent in the reign

[46] Green, 'Last Century of Danegeld', 244; Hart, *Hidation of Cambridgeshire*, 14.

[47] Stubbs, *Select Charters*, 119. Translation from Green, 'Last Century of Danegeld', 246. Hoyt saw this as an extension of the privilege to all knights (Hoyt, *Royal Demesne*, 53).

[48] *Die Gesetze*, i. 634–7. For the impact of this impost, see *Chronicon Monasterii de Abingdon*, ii. 38.

[49] Robertson, II Cnut, 31. For the most recent discussion of the origins of inland, see Faith, *English Peasantry and the Growth of Lordship*, 15–55.

of William the Conqueror. The limiting of the inquiry to 'the day on which King Edward was alive and dead' at least indicates that the king was only interested in this period. The implication must be, nevertheless, that the newly exempted demesne was likewise held by personal service, and at the time of the inquest that service was specific and onerous. William had billeted his mercenaries in the crisis of 1085 on his tenants-in-chief, and they had undoubtedly pressed their tenants to defray the cost. But despite the aid that the imposition of a geld afforded, the burden of supplying food and equipment must have fallen squarely on demesne.[50] Any attempt to extend the geld might be expected to lead to cries of foul or worse.

The geld apparently was extended, and there is no record of violent dissent. At Salisbury in August 1086 William received the homage of all of his tenants-in-chief and of their honourial barons. As has been rightly divined,[51] here was surely an agreement consequent to negotiation that provided a *quid pro quo*. The nature of that agreement can only be a matter for speculation. There are, however, indications that taxation was part of the equation. The passage in the Anglo-Saxon Chronicle which retells the events has been widely quoted. That which follows has, however, been little noticed. It states that from Salisbury the king went into the Isle of Wight because he meant to go to Normandy: 'and so he did later. But all the same he first acted according to his custom, that is to say he obtained a very great amount of money from his men where he had any pretext for it either just or otherwise.'[52] This has every appearance of being a commentary on what had happened immediately before, and probably expresses some disillusionment or bitterness after the striking of a hard bargain. In the context of 1086 the terms of that bargain can be outlined. What might be expected as a consideration for the reimposition of geld on the demesne was the lifting of the requirement to billet mercenaries.[53] There would have been attractions for this course of action on both sides. The duty had probably always been an unpopular one, and in living memory in 1086 had been the immediate cause of a political crisis. In 1051 Eustace of Boulogne and his men had demanded billets in Dover, and the resistance of one of the townsmen led to a riot and several deaths on both sides. Eustace repaired to King Edward the Confessor to seek redress and he ordered Earl Godwin to carry war into Kent and Dover. The earl's refusal to despoil his own people and province led to his exile and that of his family,

---

[50] Higham ('Domesday Survey: Context and Purpose', 14–15), argues that the burden of billeting must have been distributed on the basis of geld assessment since the Anglo-Saxon Chronicle states that the yardstick was 'the extent of their lands'. However, if this had been the case, then it might be expected that the annalist would have referred to billeting on the shire.

[51] Holt, '1066'.   [52] *ASC* 162.

[53] Billeting in pre-Conquest England has not been studied, but presumably its origins are to be found in the free man's duty to entertain the king and all those on his business (Stenton, *Anglo-Saxon England*, 288–9).

in one of the defining moments of late Anglo-Saxon England.[54] Billeting was the occasion of great expense for the tenant and a source of potential civil discord for the crown.

In the event, billeting is not known to have been demanded of tenants-in-chief after 1085, and in the twelfth century it was apparently not an obligation of military tenures. It may well have been abolished at Salisbury in 1086. If so, it was not the only change in the relationship between the king and his tenants-in-chief. It was probably accompanied by a redefinition of personal service. The distinctive feature of clause eleven of Henry I's coronation charter is the linking of demesne, taxation, and military obligation; the point of the concession is not exemption but the release of resources for the defence of the realm. An echo of a similar linkage at Salisbury may been found in clause two of the text known as 'The Laws of William the Conqueror': 'We decree also that every free man shall affirm by oath and compact that he will be loyal to King William both within and without England, that he will preserve with him his lands and honour with all fidelity and defend him against all his enemies.'[55] This text is not without its difficulties,[56] but, since it refers to the recognition of liege lordship, it would seem to embody a memory of events in 1086. What is striking, then, is the insistence on the free men's duty to defend the realm, where in 1085 it had been entrusted to mercenaries. The implication seems to be that there was at the same time a redefinition of the *servitium debitum*, the duty to fight in defence of the king and his realm.

This is indeed a theme that was central to Orderic Vitalis's understanding of the Domesday inquest. In a passage that is otherwise unparalleled he writes: 'King William carefully surveyed his whole kingdom, and had an exact description made of all the dues in the time of King Edward. Also he allocated land to knights and arranged their contingents in such a way that the kingdom of England should always have 60,000 knights, ready to be mustered at a moment's notice in the king's service whenever necessary.'[57] The figure of 60,000 knights is clearly an exaggeration, but there can be no doubt that Orderic viewed the Domesday inquest as a decisive point in the definition of military service in England. In that context, the seigneurial summaries begin to take on a palpable significance. The juxtaposition therein of the number of manors held by the lord and his tenants, the resources available to him therefrom and their value, and finally a measure of the fiscal capacity of the whole fee, is pointed. The number of manors was clearly understood as a yardstick of service. In the northern counties thegns who held six or less manors paid reliefs to the sheriff and those with more than six to the king.[58] The use of the Anglo-Norman term *relevium* here rather than the Old English *heriot*

[54] *ASC* 116–22.   [55] *Die Gesetze*, i. 486; *EHD* ii. 399.
[56] Holt, '1086', 63–4.   [57] *Orderic Vitalis*, ii. 267.
[58] GDB 280c, 298d: *DB Notts.*, S3; *DB Yorks.*, C40.

suggests that the referent is the post-Conquest period, and the subject the tenant-in-chief. Elsewhere there are references to the number of manors that had been granted to a lord, suggesting an appropriate service owed in return. Orsett in Essex was held by Count Eustace, but it 'was not [part] of his hundred manors';[59] one manor in Feering, likewise in Essex, was delivered to Hugh de Montfort 'in the number of his manors';[60] lands in Egmere, Dersingham, and Alburgh in Norfolk were granted to Frederic, Eudo son of Spirewic, and Herfrith respectively 'to make up [their] manors [ad perficienda sua maneria]'.[61] The numbers of manors given in the summaries were apparently derived from a rule of thumb, but the usual datum of a TRE tenant merely emphasizes the connection with service. Since the manor was a point of interception of regalian dues, the identification of a soke lord in 1066 was a fair indication of the dues that might be expected therefor.

The separate enumeration of the manors of the tenant-in-chief and of his tenants was presumably intended to indicate the distribution of resources and manpower and possibly liability to service. Many, if not most, of the tenants noticed in the inquest were probably honourial barons holding in hereditary fee. One outcome of the meeting at Salisbury was the recognition of their acquisition of what was effectively a franchise and their subjection to the crown for the privilege.[62] Tenants took an active and often leading part in the Domesday inquest, and as a class were clearly emerging as a force to reckon with. In the summaries, however, the record of the number of manors held by them seems to be a measure of the tenant-in-chief's capacity to render service.

The summary of ploughs, labour force, and value provides a measure of the resources underpinning the fee from which service was demanded. Throughout the Domesday corpus there are scattered indications of an appropriate size and value for the manor. The bishop of Lincoln's estate outside of the West Gate of Lincoln is called 'a little manor [maneriolum]', and land assessed at one-and-a-half virgates in 1066 and one virgate in 1086 in Over Wallop in Hampshire was held by Hugh de Port 'as half a manor'.[63] Adjustments to an acceptable level were probably common. Land and men in Sidestrand and Knapton in Norfolk were delivered to William de Warenne 'to make up his manor of Gimingham [ad perficiendum manerium Gimingeham]'.[64] Several other examples are to be found in LDB,[65] and elsewhere the numerous references to the adding of small parcels of land to manors may attest the same process.

[59] LDB 9b, 26b: DB Essex, 3,2.20,4. For this reading of the passage, see Welldon Finn, Domesday Inquest, 10 n. His renewed doubts, in Eastern Counties, 16 n, seem unwarranted.
[60] LDB 100a: DB Essex, 90,17.
[61] LDB 170b, 245b, 246a: DB Norfolk, 8,117.29,4;7. See also LDB 173b: DB Norfolk, 9,8.
[62] Roffe, 'Thegnage to Barony', 174–5.
[63] GDB 336a, 45d: DB Lincs., C11. DB Hants., 23,41.
[64] LDB 170b–171a: DB Norfolk, 8,120–1.
[65] LDB 206b, 242b, 257b, 258a, 336a: DB Norfolk, 13,10.25,24.34,13;18–19; DB Suffolk, 7,55.

No pattern emerges from the extant summaries, and therefore no 'going rate' can be suggested. It was probably only in aggregate that these figures were used.

Finally, the ploughland figures provide a measure of the fiscal capacity of the fee as a whole. They were perceived as a key statistic and a number of calculations could have been made from them. Correlation with the assessment to the geld would have indicated the amount of geld that was diverted to the lord's use, whereas comparison with the number of working ploughs might have given some idea of the extent of unassessed resources. More complex multivariate analyses are perhaps unlikely to have been undertaken, but such rough calculations would have been enough to assess the balance between taxation, services, and value. As the common form and language of the documents indicate, the summaries were compiled under the supervision of central government and as such were probably the basis on which negotiations between king and lord took place.

There is, of course, no record of services due, and hitherto the notion that the Domesday inquiry was concerned with the *servitium debitum* has thus been roundly dismissed. The criticism, however, is misconceived. The surviving records from the process were the products of the inquest and, as evidentiary documents, clearly would not prejudice the settlement. No record survives of the discussions at the Salisbury meeting, and the absence of references to services is therefore not surprising. The dichotomy between communal and personal service is an anachronism. The Domesday process was grounded in the payment of the geld, and the collection of evidence was predicated on that objective. But in reality the matter could never be separated from wider questions of service. The corollary of exemption from communal dues was personal service, and any tampering with the one necessarily affected the other. Ultimately, then, it is probably the seigneurial summaries that epitomize the whole business of the inquiry.

Whether service was increased or decreased was presumably a matter of negotiation between the king and his tenants-in-chief. The former might be suspected in the light of the comments of both the annalist and Bishop Robert of Hereford. The deal as here reconstructed looks as if it is very much in the favour of the king: an increase in service and the loss of demesne exemption in return for the possible withdrawal of demands for billeting. But this is to forget the common threat in 1085/6. Every baron recognized his own obligation to defend the commonweal as much as the king's. The burden may have been heavy, but the definition of duty brought with it the recognition of rights. The performance of homage at Salisbury cannot have confirmed the tenant-in-chief in all his lands, since title had not as yet been determined in many cases. But it was the outward sign of a new compact between the king and his man that recognized his intrinsic right to land, his honour in the widest sense, in return for the service that he owed.

The second stage of the Domesday inquiry, then, saw a move away from an audit of revenues to a review of tax capacity and a redefinition of services that that implied. This course of action may well have been suggested by the verdicts of the initial geld inquest. The actual sums in tax collected after allowances for demesne cannot have compared very well with the total assessment recorded, and may well have suggested a review of what more could be recovered. Equally, the initiative could have been prompted by a general feeling among the aristocracy that 'something had to be done' during or in the aftermath of the crisis of 1085 to distribute more equitably the burdens that defence of the realm demanded. In this scenario the deep speech at Gloucester must have resulted in an agreement by which the king undertook to review the issues of his own fisc in return for a similar undertaking from the tenants-in-chief to reassess the fiscal capacity of their own estates. This process would, of course, suggest that something like the Salisbury meeting was prefigured to resolve the problem at issue. But the terms of the settlement that was negotiated there, dependent as they were on the results of the inquest, cannot have been foreseen.

The Making of Domesday Book

There would be a pleasing symmetry to the inquest if Domesday Book were the record that embodies that settlement. But it cannot be so. The compilers of LDB and GDB took no especial interest in the extent of demesne and they adopted a form that would have been singularly inappropriate for the levy of Danegeld, which continued to be collected hundred by hundred.[66] Above all, there is no indication of service owed to the king for each lord. Neither LDB nor GDB lends itself to use as a geld book or directory of service. The survival of documentation in private archives from the inquest itself emphasizes the fact. Some of the official documents may have found their way into ecclesiastical records because of the participation of clerics in the Domesday process. But the more extensive ones, like ICC, covering all the fees in one county, and IE, all the lands of a church in three separate circuits, suggest that they were copied for their own interest and importance. It may often have been to documents of this type that appeal was made in the late eleventh and early twelfth century when Domesday evidence was invoked. In 1111, for example, the abbot of Abingdon demonstrated that its manor of Lewknor owed suit to Lewknor Hundred rather than Pyrton by reference to a *librum de thesauro*.[67] The work cited was presumably GDB, but the claim was apparently based on a different source, since neither hundred nor suit to it

---

[66] The early-twelfth-century surveys are all geographically arranged by vill and hundred or wapentake. The Lindsey Survey is seigneurially arranged within wapentakes, but the MS is a fair copy that was probably produced for references purposes. See above, pp. 52n., 187n.

[67] *Chronicon Monasterii de Abingdon*, ii. 116.

is mentioned in the Oxfordshire folios. It would seem that it was widely felt that the earlier documents represented something that GDB did not.

Domesday Book was perceived as having a significance other than that of the documentation from which it was produced, and it was one that also prompted widespread copying, although probably at a later date.[68] To state the obvious, LDB and GDB are simple records of landholding with a decided focus on the lord. Baldly put thus, the content can have been of little intrinsic interest to tenants-in-chief. Each, it must be supposed, managed his estates in a more or less efficient way and needed no Domesday Book to tell him what lands he held and how much he received from them. The imperative to copy entries was clearly otherwise. It must have ultimately been founded in the knowledge that the account was what the king knew about his lands. GDB and LDB were the king's books and, like later abbreviations of inquest records of a similar kind, they were evidently compiled for his purposes.

Those purposes are, of course, contingent to the record, but the uses to which it could be put in an eleventh-century context are limited. That the work was a record of tenure is axiomatic—it constituted no register of title— and there is the distinct possibility that it functioned as a feodary, that is as a work of reference in the administration of feudal incidents like relief, wardship, forfeiture, and the like. As has been aptly pointed out,[69] GDB is laid out to facilitate reference. The numbered list of tenants-in-chief directs the inquirer to the relevant chapter, and capital letters and rubrication direct the eye to the salient details of each estate. There can be no doubt that Domesday Book was widely used in the routine business of government. However, it must be suspected that neither volume was drawn up specifically for that purpose. In the later Middle Ages the royal demesne was generally omitted from works that were primarily concerned with feudal incidents, for by their nature they were not subject to such customs. And yet the *terra regis* is an integral element in the Domesday schema. It is both royal and baronial lands that are the subject of the work. It is this juxtaposition that ultimately characterizes the volumes. The chronology of the texts suggests a context.

The date of composition of LDB is seemingly fixed by the colophon at the end of the volume, which states that 'this survey was made in the 1086th year of the incarnation of the lord'. As has been seen, however, this was a postscriptal comment by the scribe who rubricated the volume, apparently with the intention of bringing it into conformity with GDB.[70] He may well have been ignorant of the exact nature of LDB but, more likely, he probably understood *ista descriptio* as referring less to the volume than to its source. At any event, he was almost certainly writing some time in the reign of William Rufus. That work on GDB extended into at least 1088 is demonstrated by

[68] See above, p. 8.   [69] Holt, '1086', 50–4.
[70] Rumble, 'Domesday Manuscripts', 80.

the two postscriptal Staffordshire entries written after the forfeiture of Thorkill of Arden in that year.[71] Initial drafting was equally late. The current references to William de Warenne as earl of Surrey in the Huntingdonshire and Surrey folios indicate that work on the Sussex and Huntingdonshire folios cannot have been completed before William's preferment to the earldom by William Rufus between late 1087 and mid-1088.[72] It is now clear from the chronology of composition presented above that the scribe was only some hundred folios at most into his work when he wrote the Huntingdonshire reference, and it is thus unlikely that he had made a start before the death of William the Conqueror in September 1087. A *terminus ante quem* for the process is provided by an authentic writ, probably dating from 1099–1100, which refers to the *liber regius*.[73] If this is to be taken literally, it must refer to Domesday *Book* and is thus the first notice of the volume. A date-range of late 1087 to 1100 is therefore suggested for the writing of GDB. No textual evidence has come to light to suggest that LDB was worked on at such a late date. But it has been argued that the volume is unlikely to have been the Circuit VII report brought to the king at Salisbury, and as an element, integral or otherwise, in the programme that produced GDB, it was probably written after 1086. LDB is earlier than GDB, but probably within the same range.

Further research may fix the date of composition more precisely, but at present an earlier date within the period indicated might be expected. The tenurial pattern of 1086 continued to be of interest and use to later generations because Domesday Book was there, and such was its repute that the very fact commanded attention. But it must have been the pattern itself that prompted composition in the first place, and this can have been of less and less relevance with the passage of time. In particular, the early years of William Rufus's reign saw a tenurial upheaval during and after the revolt against the king of 1088. The rebels numbered some of the greatest landholders in the kingdom. Bishop Odo of Bayeux, the leader, was the biggest, and he seems to have carried with him many of the tenants-in-chief of the south-east. Roger Bigod rose in East Anglia; Bishop Geoffrey of Coutances, Robert de Mowbray, and William de Eu in the south-west; Roger of Montgomery and Roger de Lacy, with numerous vassals and allies, in the Welsh Marches; Hugh de Grandmesnil in the Midlands; and famously, William de St Calais, the bishop of Durham, in the north.[74] William of Malmesbury's statement that 'nearly all the Normans' were involved is clearly an exaggeration,[75] but the suppression of the revolt and subsequent forfeitures saw a widespread and often permanent distribution of lands. The writing of LDB and GDB much after these events would seem unlikely.

---

[71] GDB 250b: *DB Staffs.*, 12,31; Gullick, 'Manuscripts', 106.
[72] See above, p. 88.   [73] Galbraith, 'Royal Charters to Winchester', 389.
[74] Barlow, *William Rufus*, 53–98.   [75] *Willelmi Malmesbiriensis de Gestis Regum*, ii. 361.

Curiously it is precisely at this time that a reference is found to work on Domesday. In his chapter devoted to the events of 1089 in his Ecclesiastical History, Orderic Vitalis provides a sketch of the character and activities of William Rufus's chaplain Rannulf Flambard. He paints an unattractive picture of a rapacious, amoral, and scheming minister who led his master astray to the detriment of the realm, and as proof of his assertions he writes:

This man unsettled the young king with his fraudulent suggestions, inciting him to revise the survey of all England [*incitans ut totius Angliae reuiseret descriptionem*], and convincing him that he should make a new division of the land of England and confiscate from his subjects, invaders and natives alike, whatever was found above a certain quantity. With the king's consent he measured all the ploughlands, which in English are called hides, with a rope, and made a record of them; setting aside the measures which the open-handed English freely apportioned by command of King Edward, he reduced their size and cut back the fields of the peasants to increase the royal taxes. So by reducing the land which had long been held in peace and increasing the burden of the new taxation he brutally oppressed the king's helpless and faithful subjects, impoverished them by confiscations, and reduced them from comfortable prosperity to the verge of starvation.[76]

The passage has long been viewed as a garbled account of the Domesday inquest.[77] Harvey, however, has drawn attention to its seemingly accurate assumption that the ploughland lay at the centre of the Domesday enterprise.[78] Orderic clearly had some accurate information on the conduct and subject matter of the inquest. But more resounding in the present context is the assertion that Rannulf made a revision.

Is there here, then, an authentic memory of the making of Domesday Book? Rannulf Flambard is not known to have had the connections that the northern affinities of the GDB scribe's hand would suggest in the author of GDB in the late 1080s. He became bishop of Durham in 1099, but it is possible that he had administrative responsibility for the bishopric during the three-year vacancy following the death of William de St Calais in 1096. However, the chronology here suggested would require that he was in charge at Durham during the exile of William between early 1089 and 1091. A miracle story in Symeon of Durham's *Libellus* mentions a certain Rannulfus whom King William (whether father or son is not clear) sent to Durham to compel the people of the saint 'to pay tax [*solvere tributum*]',[79] but there is no explicit notice of a connection before 1099. There is, nevertheless, no reason to question Orderic's chronology at this point in his narrative. It is, moreover, a time when Rannulf might be expected to have busied himself with ecclesiastical affairs.

---

[76] *Orderic Vitalis*, iv. 172.   [77] Southern, 'Rannulf Flambard', 107, 109; *Orderic Vitalis*, iv. 172 n.

[78] Harvey, 'Domesday Book and Anglo-Norman Governance', 191–3; Harvey, 'Taxation and the Ploughland in Domesday Book', 100–1.

[79] *Symeonis Monachi Opera Omnia*, i, Lib. III, cap. XX, p. 107. I am grateful to Dr William Aird for this reference and for discussion of the point.

By 1088 he had become what Barlow has termed 'a specialist' in the administration of vacant sees and abbeys. In that year he was administering Ely,
Ramsey, and Winchester on the king's behalf, and in the following year added
Canterbury to his portfolio.[80] It is not at all unlikely, then, that he had a
finger in the rich Durham pie.[81]

The aftermath of the 1088 rebellion that Orderic suggests as the time for
the revision of 'the *descriptio* of the whole of England' does indeed make some
sort of sense of the form of LDB and GDB. The Anglo-Saxon Chronicle reports
that the rebels pillaged the king's demesnes, seized royal castles, and attacked
boroughs.[82] Royal estates were naturally a target, and many throughout the
country were probably seized. Likewise, the lands of tenants-in-chief were
vulnerable to invasion. The rebels, again according to the Anglo-Saxon
Chronicle, ruined the lands of the men who remained loyal to the king, and
they in their turn probably despoiled the estates of the rebels. A Durham source
called the *De injusta vexatione Willelmi episcopi* asserts that the bishop of Durham's
Yorkshire estates were seized at the order of the king.[83] The widespread disruption of both royal and seigneurial estates may well have suggested the need
to compile a detailed account of the lands of the king and the tenants-in-
chief. As a snapshot of the *status quo ante*, both LDB and GDB were well suited
as the basis of a settlement. Orderic insists that the king was generous in vic-
tory and forgave many of his opponents.[84] But the composition of a register
of tenure would have aided the restitution of land and, more generally, have
functioned as a constant reminder of the power that the king exercised over
the lands of his subjects.

The identification of Rannulf Flambard as 'the man behind the Domesday
Book' (as opposed to 'the man behind the survey') has much to recommend
it. The re-dating of GDB makes it clear that the author of the project cannot
have been William de St Calais. As an influential cleric he must have had an
important role in the Domesday inquest; the reference to him enrolling a grant
in brevibus in Exon probably indicates that he was a commissioner in the south-
western circuit.[85] But he was in exile when the bulk of GDB was probably
written. Rannulf, by contrast, was at the centre of government throughout the period, becoming in the reign of William Rufus the king's principal

[80] Barlow, *William Rufus*, 200.

[81] There is no record of the provisions made for the administration of the bishopric at this time.
Early-twelfth-century tradition as embodied in a series of *miracula* seems to indicate that Prior Turgot
acted as William de St Calais's deputy for much of his episcopate (Aird, *St Cuthbert and the Normans*,
152–5). Nevertheless, it seems unlikely that he remained unsupervised during the period of William's
exile.

[82] *ASC* 166.   [83] 'De Vexatione Willelmi Episcopi', 74.   [84] *Orderic Vitalis*, iv. 135.

[85] Exon, 175ᵛ. The passage occurs in a hand, with Durham affinities, that is otherwise not found
in the manuscript. Chaplais therefore thought it unlikely that William de St Calais worked as a commissioner in the south west ('William of Saint-Calais and the Domesday Survey', 75). Chaplais himself, however, acknowledges that the passage is a fair copy and postscriptal, and so the hand can
reveal little of the involvement of William in the production of Exon itself.

administrator. He too must have been closely involved in the Domesday inquest, and must also have been well versed in the documentation that it produced. Whether he had a central role in its organization is impossible to determine. There are hints, however, that his presence was a constant in the mind of the main scribe as he composed GDB. Flambard's name is recorded a number of times in its folios. He appears as a tenant-in-chief in Hampshire, but is otherwise found as a tenant, of the bishop of Salisbury, the bishop of London, the church of Bath, the king, the church of Malmesbury, and, as a canon, of St Frideswide, Oxford, in Berkshire, Middlesex, Oxfordshire, Somerset, Surrey, and Wiltshire.[86] The two Hampshire entries (he held in the New Forest as well as the shire) are probably postscriptal, but are otherwise in the form that might be expected of the land of a tenant-in-chief. The tenanted entries, by contrast, are anomalous. In every case he is positively identified either by interlining Flambard above Rannulf or, in Wiltshire, by writing his name in full. Although annotation of this kind is used of other individuals, it is rare to find a tenant so consistently identified. The scribe may therefore have paid especial attention to his lands.

This, of course, does not necessarily imply that Rannulf was looking over the scribe's shoulder. Galbraith's argument for Samson as 'the man behind the survey' was based on the special treatment of the account of his manor of Templecombe in Exon and GDB, and there the evidence is hardly conclusive.[87] But the repeated identification of Rannulf Flambard does indicate a proper and perhaps prudent respect for a powerful figure in the administration. One further reference to Rannulf may be of relevance. In the Chronicle of John of Peterborough Rannulf is said to have compiled a book on the laws of England.[88] No such volume is known, but the reference is an interesting testimony to a belief in the Middle Ages that Rannulf was a compiler of books. Curiously, it was Rannulf as bishop of Durham who attested the writ in which the witness of the *liber regius* was first invoked;[89] GDB may well be a memorial to his abilities as a consummate administrator.

The conclusion that Domesday Book was compiled by an administrator for administrative purposes brings the argument full circle. The Domesday inquest was no bureaucratic process, but the production of Domesday Book apparently was. All the extant abbreviations of medieval surveys were compiled for references purposes and were preserved in the relevant department for ease of use. In the Exchequer, for example, were kept the Red Book and the Testa de Neville. As composite sources these were self-evidently not the

---

[86] GDB 58b, 49b, 51b, 127b–c, 154a, 157a, 89d, 30d, 67a–b: *DB Berks.*, 3,3; *DB Hants.*, 66.NF8; *DB Middlesex*, 3,4; *DB Oxon.*, B9, 14,6; *DB Somerset*, 7,12; *DB Surrey*, 1,14–15; *DB Wilts.*, 8,6;9.

[87] A fact that Galbraith admits ('Notes on the Career of Samson', 86; *Domesday Book*, 50).

[88] *Chronicon Angliae Petroburgense*, 53.

[89] Galbraith, 'Royal Charters to Winchester', 389.

purpose of any inquisitorial process. Nor was Domesday Book. The work is often cited as the earliest public record, but in origin it was no such thing. Unlike the inquest verdicts, it was not available for copying at an early date and references to it emphasize that it was the king's record. Domesday Book was the bumf of late-eleventh-century English government.

10

Afterword

THE AVOWED AIM of this study has been to examine afresh the relationship between the Domesday inquest and Domesday Book. Its assertion that the aims and objectives of the survey were manifold, on the one hand, and executed within a different context from that which produced LDB and GDB, on the other, are at variance with the consensus embodied in recent historiography. Following the publication of Galbraith's article on the making of Domesday Book in 1942, and with increasing confidence after his more lengthy study of 1961, a generation of historians have argued that Domesday Book was the aim of the Domesday inquest. The argument was originally formulated as a radical reaction to what was seen as an earlier generation's preoccupation with the geld. Round, it seems, was never entirely clear what Domesday Book was for. But he was in no doubt that the 'original returns' of the inquest were hundred rolls and that the aim of the survey was connected with the collection of the geld. It is ironic that the current consensus is largely founded on these, the terms of debate formulated by Round in 1895.

Galbraith's rejection of the geld hypothesis is, of course, predicated on the essential unity of the Domesday process. He chose Exon (as has been seen, erroneously) and GDB as the key to the process as opposed to Round's choice of ICC. But he shared a key concept with his protagonist that prejudiced his analysis. Round introduced, and Galbraith accepted, the term 'return', with all its common law overtones, into the debate. The word, redolent of the increasingly bureaucratic procedures of the late twelfth and early thirteenth centuries, insinuated an anachronism into an understanding of eleventh-century government and misrepresented the business of the inquest as a tool of government generally. Within its common law context, the return marked the end of a process over which the crown maintained a supervision, and in so far as it entailed a verdict, would suggest a recognition. The implications of the use of this seemingly innocent term for an understanding of the Domesday inquest have been far-reaching. First and foremost, it introduces the notion of a single process, and from that perception it follows that the 'returns' must embody the business of the inquiry. So was born a preoccupation with, on the one hand, the taxonomy of the Domesday sources, and the hunt for 'satellites' and the real key to Domesday on the other, that have dominated the modern debate.

A single process presupposes a single purpose, and so Galbraith's analysis is but the distaff of Round's: geld book gives way to feudal book. In neither case has a totally convincing picture emerged; the lameness of his explanation of the hundredal survey is as resounding as Round's silence on Exon. Although Galbraith's analysis has now been broadly accepted, modifications have been proposed to account for the many different concerns evidenced by the Domesday corpus and bring them within the compass of the single process. In particular, Harvey's attempt to explain the diversity of sources as a function of existing administrative records dragooned into use in the survey, and to unite evident interest in taxation with the seigneurial form by hypothesizing a reassessment of the geld on the basis of the fee, has been widely welcomed. The scope for such ingenuity, however, is limited, and in reality it has done little to resolve the fundamental problems. The assumption of a single process and purpose has still required the historian to make stark choices: the geographical must be opposed to the seigneurial, geld to service, public to private. Above all, the concept of a single process has given birth to the certainty that the Domesday corpus contains the purpose. It has seemed inconceivable that either the Domesday inquest or even Domesday Book itself could have been about knight service, since quotas are not given and the matter is rarely if at all mentioned. Just as the return to a writ of novel disseisin is about seisin, so must Domesday contain the whole business of the process.

So much has hinged on the word 'return'. Given the manifold problems that it has created for the historian, it is perhaps surprising that it has not been rejected before with all of its baggage. The present analysis has eschewed the word and its connotations. The normal outcome of the inquest was not a recognition, but a verdict that informed future action. It was an open-ended process in which, by definition, the end was not predicated on the beginning. The immediate implication of this formulation is an unsettling one for the historian. Verdicts inform but do not determine decisions. They are only contingently related to the purpose of an inquest and its outcome, and Domesday Book can therefore no more embody the whole business of the inquiry than any other document drawn up in the Domesday process.

This realization is both a boon and an insurmountable barrier to interpretation. It is immediately apparent that the activities of the Domesday inquest find their purpose in themselves rather than being means to an end. Within that context it is possible to perceive what the participants understood by their engagement at various stages. Thus, compilation of reports by vill, for example, was no whim; it embodied a perception of what was required to further the matter in hand. By the same token, the purpose of the Domesday inquest cannot be demonstrated from the extant corpus since no record of the negotiations to which it gave rise have survived. The problem that William and his advisers set out to examine in the Domesday inquest was formulated on Christmas Day at Gloucester, and a resolution was reached on 1 August 1086 at Salisbury, and in both cases nothing more than the fact of the meetings is known.

Short of additional documentation coming to light, the problem is ultimately incapable of resolution beyond all doubt. But the possibilities are limited by the activities of the participants in the inquest and subsequent changes in the matters to which they paid attention. Audit against a background of financial embarrassment is an underlying theme of all of the processes that have been identified. But the principal area of interest seems to have been the extent of exempt demesne. Ploughlands, however calculated, were a measure of the resources diverted to the tenant-in-chief's pocket and were never intended as a reassessment of the geld. The figures spoke for themselves in making a case for the reimposition of the geld, and so was it enacted. The *quid pro quo* was probably a redefinition of personal services of one sort or another.

So it is that the orthodoxies of Domesday studies dissolve. Geld and service were not mutually exclusive opposites but complementary quantities. Exemption from the geld presupposed personal service, and any adjustment to the one necessitated an adjustment to the other. The Domesday inquest collected evidence that informed a process of negotiation that impinged upon both. It was, then, no bureaucratic process. Only in the compilation of Domesday Book itself is seen the workings of executive government, and then only to produce a reference book. Underlying the hard-edged image of *Normanitas* is a perennial reality of politics: ultimately, governments rule by consent. The Domesday inquest is an eloquent testimony to the process of consultation.

In 1086 England could look back to a long tradition in this respect. English kingship had probably been grounded in the inquest from as early as the reign of Alfred, certainly from that of his son, Edward the Elder. The Norman Conquest changed no more than the constituency. The device was at once the most powerful instrument in the armoury of kingship and a limitation on its untrammelled use. As such, it was to have a long history in Angevin and Plantagenet England until it was superseded by parliament in the late thirteenth century. But that is another story.

Bibliography

Primary Sources

Anglo-Saxon Charters, ed. A. J. Robertson, 2nd edn. (Cambridge, 1956).

The Anglo-Saxon Chronicle: A Revised Translation, ed. D. Whitelock, D. C. Douglas and S. I. Tucker, 2nd edn. (London, 1963).

Anglo-Saxon Writs, ed. F. E. Harmer (Manchester, 1952).

Annales Monastici, ed. H. R. Luard, Rolls Series, 36, 5 vols. (1864–9).

The Book of Fees, PRO, 2 vols. in 3 (1920–31).

Bracton De Legibus et Consuetudines Angliae, ed. and trans. G. E. Woodbine and S. E. Thorne, 4 vols. (Cambridge, Mass., 1968–77).

Calendar of Documents Preserved in France, 918–1206, ed. J. H. Round, PRO (1899).

Calendar of Inquisitions Miscellaneous (Chancery) Preserved in the Public Record Office, PRO, 7 vols. (1916–68).

Calendar of Inquisitions Post Mortem and Other Analoguous Documents Preserved in the Public Record Office, PRO (1904 and in progress).

Cambridge, University Library, MS 3021, the Red Book of Thorney.

Cartularium Monasterii de Rameseia, ed. W. H. Hart and P. A. Lyons, Rolls Series, 79, 3 vols. (1884–9).

Cartularium Saxonicum, ed. W. de Gray Birch, 3 vols. (London, 1885–93).

The Cartulary of Worcester Cathedral Priory (Register I), ed. R. R. Darlington, Pipe Roll Society, NS, 38 (1968).

The Charters of Burton Abbey, ed. P. H. Sawyer (Oxford, 1979).

Charters of the Honour of Mowbray 1107–1191, ed. D. E. Greenway, Records of Social and Economic History, NS, 1, British Academy (1972).

Chronica Rogeri de Houedene, ed. W. Stubbs, 4 vols., Rolls Series, 51 (1868–71).

The Chronicle of Battle Abbey, ed. E. Searle (Oxford, 1980).

Chronicon Angliae Petroburgense, ed. J. A. Giles, Caxton Society (1845).

Chronicon Petroburgense, ed. T. Stapleton, Camden Society, OS, 47 (1849).

Chronicon Monasterii de Abingdon, ed. J. Stevenson, Rolls Series, 2, 2 vols. (1858).

'De Injusta Vexatione Willelmi Episcopi Primi per Willelmum Regem Filium Willelmi Magni Regis', ed. H. S. Offler, in *Chronology, Conquest and Conflict in Medieval England*, Camden Miscellany 34, Camden Society, 5th series, 10 (1997), 49–104.

Dialogus de Scaccario, the Course of the Exchequer, and Constitutio Domus Regis, the King's Household, ed. C. Johnson (London, 1950).

Die Gesetze der Angelsachsen, ed. F. Liebermann, 3 vols. (Halle, 1903–26).

Documents Illustrative of the Social and Economic History of the Danelaw from Various Collections, ed. F. M. Stenton, British Academy Records of Social and Economic History, 5 (1920).

Documents Relating to the Manor and Soke of Newark-on-Trent, ed. M. W. Barley, Thoroton Society, Record Series, 16 (1956).

Domesday Book; seu Liber Censualis Willelmi Primi Regis Angliae inter Archivos Regni in Domo Capitulari Westmonasterii Asservatus, ed. A. Farley, 2 vols. (London, 1783).

—— *Bedfordshire*, ed. J. Morris (Chichester, 1977).

—— *Berkshire*, ed. P. Morgan (Chichester, 1979).

—— *Buckinghamshire*, ed. J. Morris (Chichester, 1978).

—— *Cambridgeshire*, ed. A. Rumble (Chichester, 1981).

—— *Cheshire*, ed. P. Morgan (Chichester, 1978).

—— *Cornwall*, ed. C. Thorn and F. Thorn (Chichester, 1979).

—— *Derbyshire*, ed. P. Morgan (Chichester, 1978).

—— *Devon*, ed. C. Thorn and F. Thorn (Chichester, 1985).

—— *Dorset*, ed. C. Thorn and F. Thorn (Chichester, 1983).

—— *Essex*, ed. A. Rumble (Chichester, 1983).

—— *Gloucestershire*, ed. J. S. Moore (Chichester, 1982).

—— *Hampshire*, ed. J. Mumby (Chichester, 1982).

—— *Herefordshire*, ed. F. Thorn and C. Thorn (Chichester, 1983).

—— *Hertfordshire*, ed. J. Morris (Chichester, 1976).

—— *Huntingdonshire*, ed. S. Harvey (Chichester, 1975).

—— *Kent*, ed. P. Morgan (Chichester, 1983).

—— *Leicestershire*, ed. P. Morgan (Chichester, 1979).

—— *Lincolnshire*, ed. P. Morgan and C. Thorn (Chichester, 1986).

—— *Middlesex*, ed. J. Morris (Chichester, 1975).

—— *Norfolk*, ed. P. Brown (Chichester, 1984).

—— *Northamptonshire*, ed. F. Thorn and C. Thorn (Chichester, 1979).

—— *Nottinghamshire*, ed. J. Morris (Chichester, 1977).

—— *Oxfordshire*, ed. J. Morris (Chichester, 1978).

—— *Rutland*, ed. F. Thorn (Chichester, 1980).

—— *Shropshire*, ed. F. Thorn and C. Thorn (Chichester, 1986).

—— *Somerset*, ed. C. Thorn and F. Thorn (Chichester, 1980).

—— *Staffordshire*, ed. J. Morris (Chichester, 1976).

—— *Suffolk*, ed. A. Rumble (Chichester, 1986).

—— *Surrey*, ed. J. Morris (Chichester, 1975).

—— *Sussex*, ed. J. Morris (Chichester, 1976).

—— *Warwickshire*, ed. J. Morris (Chichester, 1976).

—— *Wiltshire*, ed. C. Thorn and F. Thorn (Chichester, 1979).

—— *Worcestershire*, ed. F. Thorn and C. Thorn (Chichester, 1982).

—— *Yorkshire*, ed. M. L. Faull and M. Stinson (Chichester, 1986).

The Domesday Monachorum of Christ Church, Canterbury, ed. D. C. Douglas, Royal Historical Society (1944).

The Earliest Lincolnshire Assize Rolls A.D. 1202–1209, ed. D. M. Stenton, Lincoln Record Society, 22 (1926).

Early Yorkshire Charters, ed. C. T. Clay, Yorkshire Archaeological Society, Record Series, Extra Series, vols. 4–10 (1935–55).

Early Yorkshire Charters, ed. W. Farrer, 3 vols. (Edinburgh, 1914–16).

The Ecclesiastical History of Orderic Vitalis, ed. M. Chibnall, 6 vols. (Oxford, 1969–80).

An Eleventh Century Inquisition of St Augustine's, Canterbury, ed. A. Ballard, Records of the Social and Economic History of England, 4 (London, 1920).

The English Register of Oseney Abbey, ed. A. Clark, Early English Text Society (1907).

Facsimiles of English Royal Writs to A.D. 1100 Presented to Vivian Hunter Galbraith, ed. T. A. M. Bishop and P. Chaplais (Oxford, 1957).

Feudal Documents from the Abbey of Bury St Edmund's, ed. D. C. Douglas, Records of the Social and Economic History of England and Wales, 8, British Academy (1932).

Glanville, ed. G. D. G. Hall (London, 1965).

The Great Chartulary of Glastonbury, ed. A. Watkin, 3 vols., Somerset Record Society, 59, 63, 64 (1947–56).

Great Domesday, ed. R. W. H. Erskine (London, 1986).

The Great Roll of the Pipe for the Sixth Year of the Reign of King Richard the First, Michaelmas 1194, ed. D. M. Stenton, Pipe Roll Society, 43 (1928).

Hemingi Chartularium Ecclesiae Wigorniensis, ed. T. Hearne, 2 vols. (Oxford, 1723).

Henrici Archdiaconi Huntendunensis Historia Anglorum, ed. T. Arnold, Rolls Series, 74 (1879).

Henry de Bracton: On the Laws and Customs of England, 4 vols. (Cambridge, Mass., 1968–77).

Inquisitio Comitatus Cantabrigiensis . . . Subjicitur Inquisitio Eliensis, ed. N. E. S. A. Hamilton (London, 1876).

Inquisitions and Assessments Relating to Feudal Aids; With Other Analogous Documents Preserved in the Public Record Office AD 1284–1431, PRO, 6 vols. (1899–1920).

The Kalendar of Abbot Samson of Bury St Edmund's and Related Documents, ed. R. H. C. Davis, Camden Society, 3rd series, 84 (1954).

The Laws of the Earliest English Kings, ed. F. L. Attenborough (Cambridge, 1922).

The Laws of the Kings of England from Edmund to Henry I, ed. A. J. Robertson (Cambridge, 1925).

Leges Henrici Primi, ed. L. J. Downer (Oxford, 1972).

The Letters of Lanfranc Archbishop of Canterbury, ed. and trans. H. Glover and M. Gibson (Oxford, 1979).

Liber Eliensis, ed. E. O. Blake, Camden Society, 3rd series, 92 (1962).

Libri Censualis, vocati Domesday Book, Additamenta ex Codic. Antiquiss. Exon Domesday; Inquisitio Eliensis; Liber Winton; Boldon Book, ed. H. Ellis (London, 1816).

Lincoln Archives Office, Longley 7.

The Lincolnshire Domesday and Lindsey Survey, ed. C. W. Foster and T. Longley, Lincoln Record Society, 19 (1921).

The Lincolnshire Survey Temp. Henry I, ed. J. Greenstreet (London, 1884).

London, British Library, Arundel 178.

London, British Library, Cotton MS Vespasian E.

London, British Library, Cotton, Claudius C.5.

London, British Library, Harleian MS Y 6.

London, PRO SC5 Extract Rolls.

London, PRO SC5/Cambs/Chapter House/4.

London, PRO SC5/Devon/Chapter House/1.

London, PRO SC5/Kent/Chapter House/1

London, PRO SC5/Wilts/Chapter House/1a;

London, PRO, SC5.

London, Society of Antiquaries, MS 60, the Black Book of Peterborough.

London University Library, Fuller MSS.

Matthei Parisienis, Monachi Sancti Albani, Historia Anglorum, ed. F. Madden, 3 vols., Rolls Series, 44 (1866–8).

Memorials of St Guthlac of Crowland, ed. W. de Gray Birch (Wisbech, 1881).

Monasticon Anglicanum, ed. J. Caley, H. Ellis and B. Bandinel, 6 vols. in 8 (London, 1817–30).

North Yorkshire Record Office, Outfac 125.

Northampton, Northampton Record Office, ZB 347.

Papsurkunden in England, ed. W. Holtzmann, 3 vols. (Berlin and Göttingen, 1930–52).

The Peterborough Chronicle 1070–1154, ed. C. Clark, 2nd edn. (Oxford, 1970).

Peterborough, Peterborough Dean and Chapter MS 1, The Book of Robert of Swaffham.

Radulphi de Coggeshall Chronicon Anglicanum, ed. J. Stevenson, Rolls Series, 66 (1875).

The Red Book of the Exchequer, ed. H. Hall, 3 vols., Rolls Series, 99 (1896).

The Red Book of Worcester, ed., M. Hollings, 4 vols., Worcester Historical Society (1934–50).

Regesta Regum Anglo-Normanorum 1066–1154, ed. H. W. C. Davis, C. Johnson, H. A. Cronne, and R. H. C. Davis, 4 vols. (Oxford, 1913–69).

Regesta Regum Anglo-Normanorum: The Acta of William I 1066–1087, ed. D. Bates (Oxford, 1998).

The Registrum Antiquissimum, ed. C. W. Foster and K. Major, Lincoln Record Society, 27–9, 32, 34, 41, 42, 46, 51, 62, 67, 68 (1931–73).

Rerum Anglicarum Scriptores Post Bedam, ed. H. Savile (Frankfurt, 1601).

Rerum Anglicarum Scriptores Veteres, i, ed. W. Fulman (Oxford, 1684).

Rotuli de Dominabus et Pueris et Puellis de XII Comitatibus, ed. J. H. Round, Pipe Roll Society, 35 (1913).

Rotuli Hundredorum, ed. W. Illingworth, 2 vols., Record Commission (1812, 1818).

Rotuli Parliamentorum, 6 vols., Record Commission (1783).

Select Charters, ed. W. Stubbs, 9th edn., revised by H. W. C. Davis (Oxford, 1913).

Some Sessions of the Peace in Lincolnshire 1360–1374, ed. R. Sillem, Lincoln Record Society, 30 (1937).

Southwell, Minster Library, MS 1, The White Book of Southwell.

The Statutes of the Realm, ed. A. Luders *et al.*, 11 vols. in 12, Record Commission (1810–28).

Symeonis Monachi Opera Omnia, ed. T. Arnold, Rolls Series, 75, 2 vols. (1882–5).

Tractatus de Legibus et Consuetudinibus Anglie qui Glanvilla Vocatur, ed. G. D. G. Hall (London, 1965).

The Valuation of Norwich, ed. W. E. Lunt (Oxford, 1926).

Visitations and Memorials of Southwell Minster, ed. A. F. Leach (London, 1891).

Westminster Abbey Charters 1066–c.1214, ed. E. Mason, London Record Society, 25 (1988).

Willelmi Monachi Malmesbiriensis de Gestis Regum Anglorum Libri Quinque; Historiae Novellae Libri Tres, ed. W. Stubbs, Rolls Series, 90, 2 vols. (1887–9).

York, Minster Library, MS. L2(1), part 1, f. 61;

Yorkshire Hundred and Quo Warranto Rolls, ed. B. English, Yorkshire Archaeological Society, Record Series, 151 (1996).

Secondary Sources

ABELS, R. P., 'Bookland and Fyrd Service', *Anglo-Norman Studies*, 7 (1984), 1–25.

—— *Lordship and Military Obligation in Anglo-Saxon England* (London, 1988).

—— 'Sheriffs, Lord Seeking, and the Norman Settlement of the South-East Midlands', *Anglo-Norman Studies*, 19 (1996), 19–50.

AIRD, W. M., *St Cuthbert and the Normans: The Church of Durham, 1071–1153* (Woodbridge, 1998).

ANDERSON, O. S., *The English Hundred Names*, 3 vols. (Lund, 1934–9).

BALLARD, A., *The Domesday Inquest* (London, 1906).

BARING, F. H., *Domesday Tables for the Counties of Surrey, Berkshire, Middlesex, Hertford, Buckingham and Bedford and the New Forest* (London, 1909).

—— 'The Exeter Domesday', *EHR* 27 (1912), 309–18.

BARLOW, F., 'Domesday Book: A Letter of Lanfranc', *EHR* 78 (1963), 284–9.

—— *William Rufus* (London, 1983).

BATES, D., *Normandy Before 1066* (London, 1982).

—— 'Two Ramsey Writs and the Domesday Survey', *Historical Research*, 63 (1990), 337–9.

—— 'The Conqueror's Charters', in *England in the Eleventh Century*, ed. C. Hicks, Harlaxton Medieval Studies, 2 (1992), 1–15.

BOLLAND, W. C., *The General Eyre* (Cambridge, 1922).

BRADBURY, J., 'Introduction to the Buckinghamshire Domesday', in *The Buckinghamshire Domesday*, ed. A. Williams and R. W. H. Erskine (London, 1988), 1–36.

BRIDGEMAN, C. G. O. (ed.), 'The Burton Abbey Twelfth Century Surveys', *Collections of the History of Staffordshire*, William Salt Archaeological Society (1916), 20–47.

CAIN, T., 'Introduction to the Rutland Domesday', in *The Northamptonshire and Rutland Domesday*, ed. A. Williams and R. W. H. Erskine (London, 1987), 18–34.

—— 'An Introduction to the Leicestershire Domesday', in *The Leicestershire Domesday*, ed. A. Williams and G. H. Martin (London, 1991), 1–21.

CAM, H. M., *Studies in the Hundred Rolls* (Oxford, 1921).

—— *The Hundred and the Hundred Rolls* (London, 1930).

CAMPBELL, J., 'Observations on English Government C10–C12', in *Transactions of the Royal Historical Society*, 25 (1975), 39–54.

—— 'Some Agents and Agencies of the Late Anglo-Saxon State', in *Domesday Studies*, ed. J. Holt (Woodbridge, 1987), 201–18.

CARPENTER, D. A., 'The Decline of the Curial Sheriff in England 1194–1258', *EHR* 91 (1976), 1–32.

CARRINGTON, W. A., 'Illustrations of Ancient Place-Names in Bakewell and the Vicinity from Original Archives Preserved in Haddon Hall, and Other sources', *Journal of the Derbyshire Archaeological and Natural History Society*, 15 (1893), 31–64.

CHAPLAIS, P., 'William of Saint-Calais and the Domesday Survey', in *Domesday Studies*, ed. J. Holt (Woodbridge, 1987), 65–78.

CHIBNALL, M., *Anglo-Norman England 1066–1166* (Oxford, 1986).

CLANCHY, M. T., *From Memory to Written Record* (London, 1979).

CLARK, C., 'Domesday Book—a Great Red-herring: Thoughts on Some Eleventh-Century Orthographies', in *England in the Eleventh Century*, ed. C. Hicks, Harlaxton Medieval Studies, 2 (1992), 317–31.

CLARKE, H. B., 'The Early Surveys of Evesham Abbey: An Investigation into the Problem of Continuity in Anglo-Norman England', unpublished Ph.D thesis, Birmingham University, 1977.

—— 'The Domesday Satellites', in *Domesday Book: A Reassessment*, ed. P. H. Sawyer (London, 1985), 50–70.

CLEMENTI, D., 'Notes on Norman Sicilian Surveys', in Galbraith, *The Making of Domesday Book*, 55–8.

CROOK, D., *Records of the General Eyre* (London, 1982).

DARBY, H. C., *Domesday England* (Cambridge, 1977).

—— 'Domesday Book and the Geographer', in *Domesday Studies*, ed. J. Holt (Woodbridge, 1987), 101–19.

—— and MAXWELL, I. S., *The Domesday Geography of Northern England* (Cambridge, 1962).

DARLINGTON, R. R., 'Aethelwig, Abbot of Evesham,' *EHR* 48 (1933), 1–22, 177–98.

—— 'Wiltshire Geld Rolls', *VCH Wiltshire* (1955) ii. 169–221.

DAVIS, R. H. C., 'Domesday Book: Continental Parallels', *Domesday Studies*, ed. J. Holt (Woodbridge, 1987), 15–39.

DEMAREST, E. B., 'The *Firma Unius Noctis*', *EHR* 35 (1920), 78–89.

—— 'The *Consuetudo Regis* in Essex, Norfolk and Suffolk', *EHR* 42 (1927), 161–79.

DENTON, J. H., *English Royal Free Chapels 1100–1300* (Manchester, 1970).

DODGSON, J. McN., 'Domesday Book: Place-names and Personal Names', in *Domesday Studies*, ed. J. Holt (Woodbridge, 1987), 121–38.

DODWELL, B., 'The Making of the Domesday Survey in Norfolk: The Hundred and a Half of Clacklose', *EHR* 84 (1969), 79–84.

DOUGLAS, D. C., 'Some Early Surveys from the Abbey of Abingdon', *EHR* 44 (1929), 618–25.

EALES, R., 'An Introduction to the Kent Domesday', in *The Kent Domesday*, ed. A. Williams and G. H. Martin (London, 1992), 1–49.

ENGLISH, B., *The Lords of Holderness 1086–1200* (Oxford, 1979).

—— 'The Government of Thirteenth-Century Yorkshire', in *Government, Religion and Society in Northern England 1000–1700*, ed. J. C. Appleby and P. Dalton (Gloucester, 1997), 90–103.

EYTON, R.W., *A Key to Domesday: The Dorset Survey* (Dorchester, 1878).

—— *Domesday Studies: An Analysis and Digest of the Somerset Survey and of the Somerset Gheld Inquest of AD 1084*, 2 vols. (London, 1880).

—— *Domesday Studies: An Analysis and Digest of the Staffordshire Survey* (London, 1881).

FAITH, R., *The English Peasantry and the Growth of Lordship* (London and Washington, 1997).

FAULL, M. F., MOORHOUSE, S. A. and MICHELMORE, D., *West Yorkshire: An Archaeological Survey to A.D. 1500* (Wakefield, 1981).

FEILTZEN, O. VON, *Pre-Conquest Personal Names of Domesday Book* (Uppsala, 1937).

FLEMING, R., 'Domesday Book and the Tenurial Revolution', *Anglo-Norman Studies*, 9 (1986), 87–102.

—— *Kings and Lords in Conquest England* (Cambridge, 1991).

—— 'Oral Testimony and the Domesday Inquest', *Anglo-Norman Studies*, 17 (1994), 101–22.

—— *Domesday Book and the Law: Society and Legal Custom in Early Medieval England* (Cambridge, 1998).

FOARD, G., 'The Great Replanning?', *The Origins of the Midland Village*, Department of English Local History (Leicester, 1992), 1–10.

FOWLER, G. H., 'An Early Cambridgeshire Feodary', EHR 46 (1931), 422–3.

GALBRAITH, V. H., 'Royal Charters to Winchester', *EHR* 35 (1920), 383–400.

—— 'An Episcopal Land-Grant of 1085', *EHR* 44 (1929), 353–72.

GALBRAITH, V. H., 'Making of Domesday Book', *EHR* 57 (1942), 161–77.
—— *The Making of Domesday Book* (London, 1961).
—— 'Notes on the Career of Samson, Bishop of Worcester (1096–1112)', *EHR* 82 (1967), 86–101.
—— *Domesday Book: Its Place in Administrative History* (Oxford, 1974).
GARNET, G., review of A. Williams, *The English and the Norman Conquest, EHR* 112 (1997), 1236–7.
GILLINGHAM, J., 'The Most Precious Jewel in the English Crown: Levels of Danegeld and Heregeld in the Early Eleventh Century', *EHR* 104 (1989), 373–84.
GLÉNISSON, J., 'Les Enquêtes administratives en Europe occidentale aux XIIIe et XIVe siècles', in *Histoire Comparée de l'Administration*, ed. W. Paravicini and K. F. Werner (Munich, 1980), 17–25.
GOLOB, P. E., 'The Ferrers Earls of Derby: A Study of the Honour of Tutbury 1066–1279', unpublished Ph.D. 7 thesis, University of Cambridge, 1985.
GOVER, J. E. B., *The Place-Names of Northamptonshire* (Cambridge, 1933).
GREEN, J. A., 'The Last Century of Danegeld', *EHR* 96 (1981), 241–58.
—— 'David I and Henry I', *Scottish Historical Review*, 75 (1996), 1–19.
GREENWAY, D. E., 'A Newly Discovered Fragment of the Hundred Rolls of 1279–80', *Journal of the Society of Archivists*, 7 (1982), 73–8.
GULLICK, M. and THORN, C., 'The Scribes of Great Domesday Book', *Journal of the Society of Archivists*, 8 (1986), 78–80.
GULLICK, M., 'The Great and Little Domesday Manuscripts', in *Domesday Book Studies*, ed. A. Williams and R. W. H. Erskine (London, 1987), 93–112.
HALL, D., 'Fieldwork and Field Books: Studies in Early Layout', in *Villages, Fields and Frontiers: Studies in European Rural Settlement in the Medieval and Early Modern Period*, ed. B. K. Roberts and R. E. Glasscock, British Archaeological Reports, International Series, 185 (Oxford, 1983), 115–32.
—— 'An Introduction to the Northamptionshire Domesday', in *The Northampton-shire and Rutland Domesday*, ed. A. Williams and R. W. H. Erskine (London, 1987), 1–17.
HALL, H., *Studies in English Official Historical Documents* (Oxford, 1908).
HALLAM, E. M., *Domesday Book Through Nine Centuries* (London, 1986).
HAMSHERE, J. D., 'The Structure and Exploitation of the Domesday Book Estate of the Church of Worcester', *Landscape History*, 7 (1985), 41–52.
HART, C. R., 'Hidation of Huntingdonshire', *Proceedings of the Cambridge Antiquarian Society*, 61 (1968), 55–66.
—— *The Hidation of Northamptonshire*, Department of English Local History (University of Leicester), Occasional Papers, 2nd series, 3 (1970).
—— *The Hidation of Cambridgeshire*, Department of English Local History (University of Leicester), Occasional Papers, 2nd series, 6 (1974).
HARVEY, P. D. A., 'Rectitudines Singularum Personarum and Gerefa', *EHR* 108 (1993), 1–22.
HARVEY, S. P. J., 'The Knight and the Knight's Fee in England', *Past and Present*, 49 (1970), 3–43.
—— 'Domesday Book and its Predecessors', *EHR* 86 (1971), 753–73.
—— 'Domesday Book and Anglo-Norman Governance', *Transactions of the Royal Historical Society*, 5th series, 25 (1975), 175–93.

—— 'Taxation and the Ploughland in Domesday Book', in *Domesday Book: A Reassessment*, ed. P. H. Sawyer (London, 1985), 86–103.

—— 'Taxation and the Economy', in *Domesday Studies*, ed. J. Holt (Woodbridge, 1987), 249–64.

—— 'Domesday England', in *The Agrarian History of England and Wales*, ed. J. Thirsk (Cambridge, 1991), 45–136.

HAŠEK, J., *The Good Soldier Švejk and his Fortunes in the World War*, trans C. Parrott (London, 1973).

HIGHAM, N., 'Settlement, Land Use and Domesday Ploughlands', *Landscape History*, 12 (1990), 33–44.

—— 'The Domesday Survey: Context and Purpose', *History*, 78 (1993), 7–21.

HIGHAM, N. J., 'Patterns of Patronage and Power: The Governance of Late Anglo-Saxon Cheshire', in *Government, Religion and Society in Northern England 1000–1700*, ed. J. C. Appleby and P. Dalton (Gloucester, 1997), 1–13.

HILL, D., 'The Nature of the Figures', in *The Defence of Wessex: The Burghal Hidage and Anglo-Saxon Fortification*, ed. D. Hill and A. R. Rumble (Manchester, 1996), 74–87.

HOLLISTER, C. W., *The Military Organization of Norman England* (Oxford, 1965).

HOLT, J. C., 'The Prehistory of Parliament', in *The English Parliament in the Middle Ages*, ed. R. G. Davies and J. H. Denton (Manchester, 1981), 1–28.

—— '1086', in *Domesday Studies*, ed. J. Holt (Woodbridge, 1987), 41–64.

HOYT, R. S., *The Royal Demesne in English Constitutional History, 1066–1272* (Cornell, 1950).

—— 'A Pre-Domesday Kentish Assessment List', in *A Medieval Miscellany for Doris Mary Stenton*, ed. P. M. Barnes and C. F. Slade, Pipe Roll Society, NS, 36 (1962).

HUDSON, J., 'Life Grants of Land and the Development of Inheritance', *Anglo-Norman Studies*, 5 (1983), 67–80.

—— *The Formation of the English Common Law: Law and Society in England from the Norman Conquest to Magna Carta* (London, 1996).

HYAMS, P., '"No Register of Title": The Domesday Inquest and Land Adjudication', *Anglo-Norman Studies*, 9 (1986), 127–41.

JACOB, E. F., *Studies in the Period of Baronial Reform and Rebellion, 1258–1267*, Oxford Studies in Social and Legal History, 8 (Oxford, 1925).

JOLLIFFE, J. E. A., 'Northumbrian Institutions', *EHR* 41 (1926), 1–42.

—— 'A Survey of Fiscal Tenements', *Economic History Review*, 1st series, 6 (1935–6), 157–71.

JOY, C. A., 'Sokeright', unpublished MA thesis, University of Leeds (1974).

KAPELLE, W. E., *The Norman Conquest of the North: The Region and its Transformation 1000–1135* (London, 1979).

—— 'Domesday Book: F. W. Maitland and his Successors', *Speculum*, 64 (1989), 620–40.

KEATS-ROHAN, K. S. B., *Domesday People: A Prosopography of Persons Occurring in English Documents, 1066–1166: 1. Domesday Book* (Woodbridge, 1998).

—— *Continental Origins of English Landholders Anglo-Norman Prosopography Database*, CD-ROM (forthcoming).

KER, N. R., 'The Beginnings of Salisbury Catheral Library', in *Medieval Learning and Literature: Essays Presented to Richard Hunt*, ed. J. J. G. Alexander and M. T. Gibson (Oxford, 1976).

KING, E., 'The Peterborough "Descriptio Militum" (Henry I)', *EHR* 84 (1969), 84–101.

KRISTENSEN, A. K. G., 'Danelaw Institutions and Danish Society in the Viking Age: *Sochemanni, Liberi Homines* and *Königsfreie*', *Medieval Scandinavia*, 8 (1975), 27–85.

LATHAM, R. E., *Revised Medieval Latin Word List from British and Irish Sources* (London, 1965).

LAWSON, M. K., 'The Collection of Danegeld and Heregeld in the Reigns of Aethelred II and Cnut', *EHR* 99 (1984), 721–38.

—— 'Those Stories Look True: Levels of Taxation in the Reigns of Aethelred II and Cnut', *EHR* 104 (1989), 385–406.

LEAVER, R. A., 'Five Hides in Ten Counties: A Contribution to the Domesday Regression Debate', *Economic History Review*, 41 (1988), 525–42.

LEES, B. A., 'The Statute of Winchester and the *Villa Integra*', *EHR* 41 (1926), 98–103.

LENNARD, R., 'A Neglected DB Satellite', *EHR* 58 (1943), 32–41.

—— *Rural England 1086–1135: A Study of Social and Agrarian Conditions* (Oxford, 1959).

LEWIS, C. P., 'An Introduction to the Herefordshire Domesday', in *The Herefordshire Domesday*, ed. A. Williams and R. W. H. Erskine (London, 1988), 1–22.

—— 'An Introduction to the Shropshire Domesday', in *The Shropshire Domesday*, ed. A. Williams and R. W. H. Erskine (London, 1990), 1–27.

—— 'The Earldom of Surrey and the Date of Domesday Book', *Historical Research*, 63 (1990), 327–36.

—— 'An Introduction to the Cheshire Domesday', in *The Cheshire Domesday*, ed. A. William and R. W. H. Erskine (London, 1991), 1–25.

—— 'An Introduction to the Lancashire Domesday', in *The Lancashire Domesday*, ed. A. Williams and R. W. H. Erskine (London, 1991), 1–41.

—— 'Domesday Jurors', *The Haskins Society Journal*, 5 (1993), 17–44.

LIEBERMANN, F. and PEACOCK, M. H., 'An English Document of About 1080', *Yorkshire Archaeological Journal*, 18 (1905), 412–6.

LOYN, H. R., *The Governance of Anglo-Saxon England 500–1087* (London, 1984).

—— 'A General Introduction to Domesday Book', in *Domesday Book Studies*, ed. A. Williams and R. W. H. Erskine (London, 1987), 1–21.

—— 'William's Bishops: Some Further Thoughts', *Anglo-Norman Studies*, 10 (1988), 223–35.

MACDONALD, J. and SNOOKS, G. D., *Domesday Economy: A New Approach to Anglo-Norman History* (Oxford, 1986).

MACK, K., 'Changing Thegns: Cnut's Conquest and the English Aristocracy', *Albion*, 16 (1984), 375–87.

MADDICOTT, J. R., 'Edward I and the Lessons of Baronial Reform: Local Government 1258–93', in *Thirteenth Century England i: Proceedings of the Newcastle upon Tyne Conference*, ed. P. R. Coss and S. D. Lloyd (Woodbridge, 1986), 1–30.

MAHANY, C. M. and ROFFE, D. R., 'Stamford: The Development of an Anglo-Scandinavian Borough', *Anglo-Norman Studies*, 5 (1983), 197–219.

MAITLAND, F. W., *Domesday Book and Beyond* (Cambridge, 1897).

MARTIN, G. H., 'Domesday Book and the Boroughs', in *Domesday Book: A Reassessment*, ed. P. H. Sawyer (London, 1985), 143–63.

—— 'An Introduction to the London Domesday', in *The Middlesex and London Domesday*, ed. A. Williams and G. H. Martin (London, 1991), 1–21.

MASON, J. F. A., 'The Date of the Geld Rolls', *EHR* 69 (1954), 283–9.

—— *William the First and the Sussex Rapes*, Historical Association (1966).

MAWER, A. and STENTON, F. M., *The Place-Names of Bedfordshire and Huntingdonshire* (Cambridge, 1926).

MILLER, E., *The Abbey and Bishopric of Ely* (Cambridge, 1951).

MOORE, J. S., 'The Domesday Teamland: A Reconsideration', *Transactions of the Royal Historical Society*, 5th series, 14 (1964), 109–30.

—— 'The Population of Domesday England', *Anglo-Norman Studies*, 19 (1996), 307–34.

O'BRIEN, B. R., 'From *Morðor* to *Murdrum*: The Pre-Conquest Origin and Norman Revival of the Murder Fine', *Speculum*, 71 (1996), 321–57.

PALLISER, D. M., *Domesday York* (York, 1990).

—— 'An Introduction to the Yorkshire Domesday', in *The Yorkshire Domesday*, ed. A. Williams and G. H. Martin (London, 1992), 1–38.

—— 'Domesday Book and the Harrying of the North', *Northern History*, 29 (1993), 1–23.

PALMER, J., The Domesday Manor', in *Domesday Studies*, ed. J. Holt (Woodbridge, 1987), 139–54.

PERCIVAL, J., 'The Precursors of Domesday: Roman and Carolingian Land Registers', in *Domesday Book: A Reassessment*, ed. P. H. Sawyer (London, 1985), 5–27.

PHYTHIAN-ADAMS, C., 'Rutland Reconsidered', in *Mercian Studies*, ed. A. Dornier (Leicester, 1977), 63–86.

—— 'The Emergence of Rutland', *Rutland Record*, 1 (1980), 5–12.

—— *The Norman Conquest of Leicestershire and Rutland: A Regional Introduction to Domesday Book* (Leicester, 1986).

POLLOCK, F. and MAITLAND, F. W., *The History of English Law*, 2nd edn., 2 vols. (Cambridge, 1923).

POOLE, A. L., *The Obligations of Society in the Twelfth and Thirteenth Centuries* (Oxford, 1946).

PRESTWICH, J. O., 'The Career of Ranulf Flambard', in *Anglo-Norman Durham, 1093–1193*, ed. D. Rollason, M. Harvey and M. Prestwich (Woodbridge, 1994).

Public Record Office, *Domesday Book Rebound* (London, 1954).

RABAN, S., 'The Making of the 1279–80 Hundred Rolls', *Historical Research*, 70 (1997), 123–145.

RAFTIS, J. A., *The Estates of Ramsey Abbey* (Toronto, 1957).

REID, R. R., 'Barony and Thanage', *EHR* 35 (1920), 161–99.

ROFFE, D. R., 'The Lincolnshire Hundred', *Landscape History*, 3 (1981), 27–36.

—— 'Norman Tenants-in-Chiefs and their Pre-Conquest Predecessors in Nottinghamshire', in *History in the Making*, ed. S. N. Mastoris (Nottingham, 1985), 3–7.

—— *The Derbyshire Domesday* (Darley Dale, 1986).

—— 'The Origins of Derbyshire', *The Derbyshire Archaeological Journal*, 106 (1986), 102–22.

—— 'Nottinghamshire and the North: A Domesday Study', unpublished Ph.D thesis, Nottingham University, 1987.

—— 'An Introduction to the Huntingdonshire Domesday', in *The Huntingdonshire Domesday*, ed. A. Williams and R. W. H. Erskine (London, 1989), 1–23;

—— 'Domesday Book and Northern Society: A Reassessment', *EHR* 105 (1990), 310–36.

—— 'An Introduction to the Derbyshire Domesday', in *The Derbyshire Domesday*, ed. A. Williams and R. H. W. Erskine (London, 1990), 1–27.

—— 'From Thegnage to Barony: Sake and Soke, Title, and Tenants-in-Chief', *Anglo-Norman Studies*, 12 (1990), 157–76.

—— 'Place-Naming in Domesday Book: Settlements, Estates, and Communities', *Nomina*, 14 (1990–1), 47–60.

—— 'The Yorkshire Summary: A Domesday Satellite', *Northern History*, 27 (1991), 242–60.

ROFFE, D. R., 'An Introduction to the Lincolnshire Domesday', in *The Lincolnshire Domesday*, ed. A. Williams and G. H. Martin (London, 1992), 1–31.

—— 'The Descriptio Terrarum of Peterborough Abbey', *Historical Research*, 65 (1992), 1–16.

—— 'Hundreds and Wapentakes', in *The Lincolnshire Domesday*, ed. A. Williams and G. H. Martin (London, 1992), 33–9.

—— '*On Middan Gyrwan Fenne*: Intercommoning Around the Island of Crowland', *Fenland Research*, 8 (1993), 80–6.

—— *Stamford in the Thirteenth Century: Two Inquisitions from the Reign of Edward I* (Stamford, 1994), 12–19.

—— 'The Making of Domesday Book Reconsidered', *The Haskins Society Journal*, 6 (1994), 153–66.

—— 'The Historia Croylandensis: A Plea for Reassessment', *EHR* 110 (1995), 93–108.

—— 'The Hundred Rolls and their Antecedents: Some Thoughts on the Inquisition in Thirteenth-Century England', *Haskins Society Journal*, 7 (1995), 179–87.

—— 'Great Bowden and its Soke', in *Anglo-Saxon Landscapes in the East Midlands*, ed. J. Bourne (Leicester, 1996), 107–20.

—— 'The Hundred Rolls of 1255', *Historical Research*, 69 (1996), 201–10.

—— 'The Anglo-Saxon Town and the Norman Conquest', in *Centenary History of Nottingham*, ed. J. V. Beckett (Manchester, 1997), 24–42.

—— 'An Introduction to the Norfolk Domesday', in *The Norfolk Domesday*, ed. A. Williams and G. H. Martin (forthcoming, 2000).

—— 'The Early History of Wharram Percy', in *A Study of Settlement on the Yorkshire Wolds 8: The South Manor Area*, ed. P. A. Stamper and R. A. Croft, York University Archaeological Publications (forthcoming).

—— and MAHANY, C. M., 'Stamford and the Norman Conquest', *Lincolnshire History and Archaeology*, 21 (1986) 5–9.

ROUND, J. H., 'The Great Carucage of 1198', *EHR* 3 (1888), 501–10.

—— *Geoffrey de Mandeville* (London, 1892).

—— *Feudal England* (London, 1895).

—— 'The Domesday Manor', *EHR* 15 (1900), 293–302.

—— 'The Hidation of Northamptonshire', *EHR*, 15 (1900), 78–86.

RUMBLE, A. R., 'The Palaeography of the Domesday Manuscripts', in *Domesday Book: A Reassessment*, ed. P. H. Sawyer (London, 1985), 28–49.

—— 'The Domesday Manuscripts: Scribes and *Scriptoria*', in *Domesday Studies*, ed. J. Holt (Woodbridge, 1987), 79–100.

—— An Edition and Translation of the Burghal Hidage', in *The Defence of Wessex: the Burghal Hidage and Anglo-Saxon Fortification*, ed. D. Hill and A. R. Rumble (Manchester, 1996), 14–35.

SANDERS, I. J., *Feudal Military Service in England: A Study of the Constitutional and Military Power of the Barons in Medieval England* (London, 1955).

SAWYER, P. H., 'The "Original Returns," and Domesday Book', *EHR* 70 (1955), 177–97.

—— 'The Place-Names of the Domesday Manuscripts', *Bulletin of the John Rylands Library*, 38 (1955–6), 483–506.

—— 'Evesham A, a Domesday Text', *Worcestershire Historical Society Miscellany*, 1 (Worcester and London, 1960), 3–36.

—— 'The Charters of Burton Abbey and the Unification of England', *Northern History*, 10 (1975), 28–39.

—— '1066–1086: A Tenurial Revolution?', in *Domesday Book: A Reassessment*, ed. P. H. Sawyer (London, 1985), 71–85.

SEARLE, E., 'Hides, Virgates and Settlement at Battle Abbey', *Economic History Review*, 2nd series, 16 (1963–4), 290–300.

SHEPPARD, J. A., 'Pre-Conquest Yorkshire: Fiscal Carucates as an Index of Land Exploitation', *Institute of British Geographers Transactions*, 65 (1975), 67–78.

SOUTHERN, R. W., 'Rannulf Flambard and Early Anglo-Norman Administration', *Transactions of the Royal Historical Society*, 4th ser., 16 (1933), 95–128.

STAFFORD, P., *The East Midlands in the Early Middle Ages* (Leicester, 1985).

STATHAM, S. P. H., 'The Brailsfords', *Journal of the Derbyshire Archaeological and Natural History Society*, 59 (1938), 53–65.

STENTON, D. M., *English Justice between the Norman Conquest and the Great Charter 1066–1215* (Philadelphia, 1964).

STENTON, F. M., 'Domesday Survey', in *Victoria History of the County of Derby*, I, ed. W. Page (London, 1905), 293–326.

—— 'Domesday Survey', in *Victoria History of the County of Nottingham*, I, ed. W. Page (London, 1906), 207–46.

—— *Types of Manorial Structure in the Northern Danelaw* (Oxford, 1910).

—— *The First Century of English Feudalism 1066–1166* (Oxford, 1932).

—— *The Free Peasantry of the Northern Danelaw* (Oxford, 1969).

—— 'The Danes in England', in *Preparatory to Anglo-Saxon England*, ed. D. M. Stenton (Oxford, 1970), 136–65.

—— *Anglo-Saxon England*, 3rd edn. (Oxford, 1971).

STEPHENSON, C., 'Commendation and Related Problems in Domesday Book', *EHR* 59 (1944), 289–310.

—— 'Notes on the Composition and Interpretation of Domesday', *Speculum*, 22 (1947), 1–15.

STEVENSON, W. H., 'Land Tenures in Nottinghamshire', in *Old Nottinghamshire*, 1st series, ed. S. P. Briscoe (Nottingham, 1881), 66–71.

—— 'A Contemporary Description of the Domesday Survey', *EHR* 22 (1907), 72–84.

SUGGETT, H., 'An Anglo-Norman Return of the Inquest of Sheriffs', *Bulletin of the John Rylands Library*, 27 (1942), 179–81.

TAIT, J., review of Maitland, *Domesday Book and Beyond*, *EHR* 12 (1897), 768–77.

—— 'A New Fragment of the Inquest of Sheriffs (1170)', *EHR* 39 (1924), 80–3.

TAYLOR, A. J., *Four Great Castles: Caernarfon, Conwy, Harlech, Beaumaris* (Newtown, 1983).

THACKER, A. and SAWYER, P. H., 'Domesday Survey', in *Victoria History of the County of Chester*, I ed. B. E. Harris (London, 1987), 293–341.

THORN, C., 'Marginal Notes and Signs in Domesday Book', in *Domesday Book Studies*, ed. A. Williams and R. W. H. Erskine (London, 1987), 113–35.

THORN, F., 'Hundreds and Wapentakes', in *The Buckinghamshire Domesday*, ed. A. Williams and R. W. H. Erskine (London, 1988), 37–41.

—— 'Hundreds and Wapentakes', in *The Sussex Domesday*, ed. A. Williams and R. W. H. Erskine (London, 1990), 26–42.

THORNE, S. E., 'English Feudalism and Estates in Land', *Cambridge Law Journal* (1959), 193–209.

TROLLOPE, A., *The Small House at Allington* (Ware, Wordsworth Editions, 1994).

VINOGRADOFF, P., *English Society in the Eleventh Century* (Oxford, 1908).

WALMSLEY, J. F. R., 'The "Censarii" of Burton Abbey and the Domesday Population', *North Staffordshire Journal of Field Studies*, 8 (1968), 73–80.

—— 'Another Domesday Text', *Medieval Studies*, 39 (1977), 109–20.

WARREN, W. L., *The Governance of Norman and Angevin England, 1086–1272* (London, 1987).

WELLDON FINN, R., 'The Evolution of Successive Version of Domesday Book', *EHR* 66 (1951), 561–4.

—— 'The Exeter Domesday and its Construction', *Bulletin of the John Rylands Library*, 41 (1958–9), 360–87.

—— 'The *Inqusitio Eliensis* Reconsidered', *EHR* 75 (1960), 385–409.

—— *The Domesday Inquest and the Making of Domesday Book* (London, 1961).

—— *Domesday Studies: The Liber Exoniensis* (London, 1964).

—— *Domesday Studies: The Eastern Counties* (London, 1967).

WHALLEY, P., *The History and Antiquities of Northamptonshire, Compiled from the Manuscript Collection of John Bridges* (Oxford, 1791).

WHITELOCK, D., 'Foreword', in *Liber Eliensis*, ed. E. O. Blake, Camden Society, 3rd series, 92 (1962), pp. ix–xviii.

WIGHTMAN, W. E., *The Lacy Family in England and Normandy, 1066–1194* (Oxford, 1966).

WILLIAMS, A., 'Apparent Repetitions in Domesday Book', in *Domesday Book Studies*, ed. A. Williams and R. W. H. Erskine (London, 1987), 90–2.

—— 'An Introduction to the Worcestershire Domesday', in *The Worcestershire Domesday*, ed. A. Williams and R. W. H. Erskine (London, 1988), 1–39.

—— 'An Introduction to the Gloucestershire Domesday', in *The Gloucestershire Domesday*, ed. A. Williams and R. W. H. Erskine (London, 1989), 1–39.

—— *The English and the Norman Conquest* (Woodbridge, 1995).

—— 'A West Country Magnate of the Eleventh Century: The Family, Estates and Patronage of Beorhtric son of Ælgar', in *Family Trees and the Roots of Politics*, ed. K. S. B. Keats-Rohan (Woodbridge, 1997), 41–68.

WORMALD, P., 'Ethelred the Lawmaker', in *Ethelred the Unready*, ed. D. Hill (Oxford, 1978), 47–80.

—— 'Domesday Lawsuits: A Provisional List and Preliminary Comments', in *England in the Eleventh Century*, Harlaxton Medieval Studies, 2, ed. C. Hicks (Stamford, 1992), 61–102.

Index

abbreviation:
of later records 186–7
in production of GDB 187–91
Abels, R. P. 35
Abingdon A 109, 110, 111, 140, 172, 227
Abingdon Abbey 65, 111
abbot of 242
lands in Berks. 140
monks of 122
Abington (Cambs.) 141 n., 217 n.
manor of 204
Adam, brother of Eudo the king's steward 144
commissioner 124
Adderbury (Oxon.) 132
Addington, Great (Northants.) 102, 104
Addlethorpe (Lincs.) 160
Adewelle (Lincs.):
manor of 145
Ælfeva, Countess 34
Ælfgeth 83
Ælfgifu, daughter of Leofwin 21
Ælfric 130
Ælfric Kemp 38
Ælmar of Bourn 190 n.
Ælmer 38
Æthelred the Unready, King:
fourth law code 64
Æthelsige, abbot of Ramsey 168
Æthelstan 34
predecessor of Guy de Craon 33
Æthelwig, abbot of Evesham 233 n.
Agbrigg Wapentake (Yorks.) 85
Agmundr son of Valhrafn, lawman of Lincoln 121
Ailmer Hogg of *Wellen* 64
Ainsty Wapentake (Yorks.) 72
Aki 34
Alan 157
Alan of Brittany, Count 19, 21, 27, 30, 34, 46,
65, 78, 89, 92, 99, 119, 167, 178, 181, 204
Cambs. breve 79
lands in Yorks Summary 76
Lincs. lands 75, 83
summary 86, 98, 183
tenants in Cambs. 190
Yorks. lands 85–6, 182, 180, 194
see also Ralph the staller, predecessor
Alburgh (Norf.) 240
Alconbury (Hunts.) 103, 214
royal manor of 214

Aldborough (Yorks.) 74 n.
Aldene 42
Aldgyth 213
Alditha, daughter of Wigod of Wallingford
21
Alfred of Lincoln 32, 36, 65
fee in Stamford (Lincs.) 132
Alfred of Spain 188
Alfred the carpenter 157
Alfred, King 57, 251
'survey of England' of 60, 105, 227
Alfwine, sheriff of Gloucestershire:
widow of 21
Alfwold:
lands of 36
Alfwold and his brothers 214
Algarkirk (Lincs.) 102
flood at 105
Alnodestou Hundred (Salop.):
measurement of woodland in 176
Alnoth 35
Alresford (Essex) 166
Alstoe Wapentake (Rutland) 128, 162
Alveston (Warks.) 127, 183
Alwardesley Hundred (Northants.) 104
Alwig 26
Alwine 213
Amounderness 45, 77, 85, 86, 119, 136, 163
ancient demesne 6
Anglo-Saxon Chronicle 1, 2, 4, 8, 9, 13, 67, 68,
69, 71, 151, 224, 230, 231, 233, 234, 235, 237,
238, 238 n., 241, 246
antecession 20, 22, 25, 27, 36
antecessor 25–6, 213
honour of 36
soke of 35
Appleby (Derby.) 154
Appleby (Lincs.) 160
Appleton Roebuck (Yorks.):
manor of 213
Appletree Wapentake (Derby.) 20, 28
Archenfield 119
Armingford Hundred (Cambs.) 79
Arnketill 26
Arnold (Notts.):
king's manor of 214
Arnulf of Hesdin 96
articles of inquest 114–17
see also IE prologue

Arundel (Sussex):
    rape of 21
Asgar the staller 19, 23, 36, 37
    see also Geoffrey de Mandeville, successor
Ashby, Cold (Northants) 81
Ashfield (Suff.) 166
Ashley (Cambs.) 218 n.
Asketill 35
Aswardhurn Wapentake (Lincs.) 21, 103
Aswulf 203
Athelstan, King 33
Atiscross Hundred (Flint.) 209
    ploughland in 153
    record of churches in 176
Atsurr son of Svala 34
    predecessor of Robert Malet 26
Atterton (Kent) 118
Aubrey de Vere 141 n.
Aubrey, Count 207 n.
Augi 29
Aust (Gloucs.) 138
Aveland Wapentake (Lincs.) 167
Avethorpe (Lincs.) 36
Axholme, Isle of (Lincs.) 174
Axminster (Devon):
    king's manor of 130

Badby (Northants.) 104
Badlingham (Cambs.) 99
Bakewell (Derby.) 215
    manor of 214 n.
Bampton (Oxon.) 132
Banham (Norf.) 164
Bardi, lord of Sleaford 21
Baring, F. H. 97, 217
Barley (Worcs.) 38
Barlington (Devon) 97
Barlow, F. 246
barones 123, 147, 166
    see also commissioners; legati
barony:
    tenure by 44-5
Barton Bendish (Norf.) 92
Barton on Humber (Lincs.) 214
Baschurch Hundred (Salop.):
    measurement of woodland in 176
Basford (Notts.) 203
Basset family 8
Bassetlaw Wapentake (Notts.) 28, 215 n.
Bates, D. 168
Bath A 72, 94 n., 142, 146, 151, 173
    Exon and 101, 172-3
    forms and content 101
    GDB and 101
    scribe 101
Bath Abbey 65, 247
    cartulary of 101

Bath B 109, 110
Bath Hundred (Somerset) 172
Battle Abbey 157
    Sussex breve 207 n.
Baumber (Lincs.) 214
Bayeux 113
Bayeux Tapestry 14
Beckering (Lincs.) 160
Bedfordshire:
    hidation of 61
Belchford (Lincs.):
    manor of 105
    soke of 104
Beltisloe Wapentake (Lincs.):
    warnode in 175
Belton (Lincs.):
    manor of 213 n.
Bempstone Hundred (Somerset) 134
Benson (Oxon.) 132
Beorhtric son of Ælfgar 35, 38
    estates of 38
Berengar 94
Berengar of Tosny 188 n.
Bergh Apton (Norf.) 101
Berkshire:
    assessment in C12 236
Beverley (Yorks.) 136
Bible 11, 49 n.
Bibury (Gloucs.):
    manor of 82
Bicker (Lincs.) 167
Bill of Rights 7
billeting 15, 69, 70, 238, 239, 241
Billing, Great (Northants.) 159
Billingborough (Lincs.) 34
Bircham, Great (Norf.) 136 n.
Birkby (Yorks.) 180 n.
Blackburn Hundred (Lancs.) 180
Blockley (Worcs.):
    manor of 219
Bloxham (Oxon.) 132
Bluntisham (Hunts.) 66, 152, 153
Blyth (Notts.) 37
Blyth Priory 37
    foundation charter of 31
Bochelau Hundred (Ches.):
    record of churches in 176
Boga of Hemingford:
    sons of 66
Bolesforde Wapentake (Yorks.) 85
Bolingbroke Wapentake (Lincs.):
    churches in 176
    priests in 176
Bondi the staller 20
book:
    tenure by 33-4
Book of Fees 186

bookland 22, 33–6, 40, 45, 63, 212, 237
Borough English 216
boroughs 78
  survey of 132–3
Borrowby (Yorks.) 180 n.
Botolph Bridge (Hunts.) 22
Bourn (Cambs.) 190 n.
Bradmore (Notts.) 26
Brailsford (Derby.) 36, 43
Bramber (Sussex):
  rape of 21
Bramcote (Notts.) 80
Brampton (Hunts.):
  king's manor of 215
Bramshott (Hants.) 47
Brand, abbot of Peterborough:
  family of 26
Brasted (Kent) 206 n.
Braybrooke Cartulary 109, 116
Bredestorp (Lincs.):
  12-carucate hundred of 145
Bredon (Worcs.):
  manor of 219
breves regis 131, 167, 172–3, 227
breviates 4
Brictwin 208 n.
Brington (Hunts.) 157 n.
Brittany 69, 234
Brixton Hundred (Surrey) 74
Bromley, King's (Staffs.) 156
Brook (IoW) 231
Broughton (Hunts.) 65, 157 n.
Broughton, Brant (Lincs.) 214
Broxtow Wapentake (Notts.) 28, 128
Brungar:
  man of Robert son of Wymarc 29
Brunner, H. 54
Buckingham (Bucks.) 132
Buckinghamshire:
  assessment in C12 236
Buckland Brewer (Devon) 155
Bucknall (Lincs.) 104, 105
Burghal Hidage 60, 171
Burghshire Wapentake (Yorks.) 85 n. .
Burnham, East (Bucks.) 31
Burrough Green (Cambs.) 218 n.
Burton Abbey 42, 44, 213 n.
  abbot of 162, 235
  estates of 152, 155, 157, 216
  inland of 154
  surveys 152, 215
Burton on Trent (Staffs.) 156
Burton Agnes (Yorks.) 213
Burton B 151
Burton by Lincoln (Lincs.) 21
Bury A 109, 123, 138, 139, 140
Bury B 109, 138, 139, 140

Bury C 41, 142
Bury St Edmund's (Suff.) 162 n.
Bury St Edmund's Abbey 138, 162 n.
  abbot of 19, 185
  free men of 41–2, 142
  manors of 109
  Suffolk liberty 41
Bushley (Worcs.) 38
Bychton (Flint) 153
Bytham, Little (Lincs.):
  12-carucate hundred of 145
Bythorn (Hunts.) 157 n.

Caldecote (Cambs.) 190 n.
Caldwell (Derby.) 157
Calvely (Norf.) 164 n.
Cambridge (Cambs.) 66
  lawmen of 121
  see also Picot, sheriff of
Cambridgeshire 1
  assessment of in C12 237
  ICC account of 98
  jurors of 121
  reduction in assessment of 110
Came Hundred (Worcs.) 143
Camois:
  barony of 23
Canterbury, archbishop of 137
  see also Lanfranc; Stigand
Canterbury, St Augustine's:
  men of 118
  monks of 122
Canterbury, Christchurch:
  monks of 137
Canterbury, diocese of 246
Careby (Lincs.) 145
Carlton (Cambs.) 218 n.
carriage 31, 41, 215
carte baronum 186
Cartuther (Cornwall) 134
carucage of 1198 52–3, 148
  see also inquest of 1198
carucation 62
castleries 21, 25, 37, 78, 86, 119, 181
  see also Dudley; Clifford Castle;
    Richmondshire; Tickhill; Tutbury
Catworth (Hunts.) 22
censarii 155
  services of 215
Chaplais, P. 113, 114
Charford (Hants):
  manor of 118
Charlemagne 55
Charlton (Devon) 130
Chedglow Hundred (Wilts.) 135
Chedworth (Gloucs.):
  manor of 171

Chertsey, St Peter of 74
  monks of 122
Cheshire 21, 22
  churches and priests in 176
  measurement of woodland in 125
  Ribble and Mersey in GDB account of 120
  status of TRE holders of land 22 n.
  Welsh lands in GDB account of 119
Chester (Ches.) 59
  judges of 121
  see also Peter, bishop of
Chesterton Hundred (Cambs.) 79
Cheveley Hundred (Cambs.) 79
Chilford Hundred (Cambs.) 79
churches:
  in Cheshire 176
  in Lincs. 176
circuits 124–8
Civil War 10
Clackclose Hundred (Norf.) 92, 146 n.
clamores 22, 67, 83, 84, 94, 98, 119, 122, 167, 184, 185, 222, 229
Clarborough (Notts.) 36
Clent (Worcs.) 44 n.
Clifford Castle (Hereford.) 153
Clifton (Notts.) 139
Cnut, King of England 28
  Laws of 33
Cnut, King of Denmark 69
Cola 134
Colchester (Essex) 132
Colle 42
  grandson of 42
Collingham (Notts.) 33 n.
Colne (Hunts.) 175 n.
Colston Basset (Notts.) 8
Colston, Car (Notts.) 8
commendation 23, 24, 27, 28–30, 32, 33, 34, 215, 217
commissioners 13, 123–4, 147, 149, 168, 180, 235
  see also 'S'; Adam, brother of Eudo the king's steward; Osmund, bishop of Salisbury; Remigius, bishop of Lincoln; Walter Giffard; William de St Calais, bishop of Durham
compurgation 50, 55
  inquest and 66–7
Conditre Hundred (Salop.):
  measurement of woodland in 176
Condover Hundred (Salop.):
  measurement of woodland in 176
Coningsby (Lincs.) 34
Conisbrough (Yorks.) 30
consuetudines 30
Coppingford (Hunts.) 156
Cornwall 21
Cossall (Notts.) 80

cottars 162 n.
Cottenham (Cambs.) 23
County Hidage 60–1, 171
Coventry Abbey 81
Cowley (Oxon.) 153 n.
Cowton, East (Yorks.) 180 n.
Craven 77, 85, 136, 163
Crediton (Devon):
  manor of 138
Cromwell (Derby.):
  Cromwell family of 42
Crowland (Lincs.) 102
  fens of 103 n.
Crowland Domesday 105, 111, 140, 172, 227
  content 102–3
  sources of 102–5
Crusade, First 237
Cullifordtree Hundred (Dorset) 96
Culvestan Hundred (Salop.):
  measurement of woodland in 176
Cumbria 220
Curry Rivel (Somerset) 59
Curry, North (Somerset):
  royal manor of 135

Danegeld 58, 59, 110, 233 and n., 242
Danelaw 57, 62, 150
  breach of the peace in 59
  12-carucate hundred in 56
  carucation of 58
  wapentake of 58
Danes 57
De injusta vexatione Willelmi episcopi 246
Deeping (Lincs.):
  lord of 103 n.
Deeping, East (Lincs.) 214
Deerhurst (Gloucs.):
  capital manor of 36
demesne:
  exemption from geld 154, 236–8
  geldable 153–4, 235
  personal service and 239
Denmark 69, 234
Derby (Derby.) 132, 191
  shire court of 127 n.
Derby Hundred, West (Lancs.) 131, 180
Derbyshire:
  Basset estates in 8
  carucation of 62
  sokes of 145
Dersingham (Norf.) 240
Descriptio Terrarum of Peterborough 110, 136, 137, 138, 145, 167 n.
Desning (Suff.):
  soke of 214
Dialogue of the Exchequer 5, 10
Dic Wapentake (Yorks.) 85

Dickleburgh (Norf.) 109 n.
dimensions of vills 190, 223 and n.
disputes 47, 165–8, 183–5, 229
  see also *clamores; invasiones; terre occupate*
Diss Hundred (Norf.) 179 n.
Ditton, Wood (Cambs.) 23
Docking Hundred (Norf.) 179
Doda 66
Dodwell, B. 177 n.
Domesday Book:
  copying of extracts from 4
  early references to 4, 5, 88, 110–11, 227, 242,
    244, 247
  facsimiles 72
  as feudal register 13
  as geld list 11–12
  'man behind' 113–14, 245–7
  meaning of name 5
  mystique of 4–7
  neo-fiscal view of 14–15, 18, 70
  'Norman order' view of 12–14, 18
  perception of purpose in Middle Ages
    8–10
  'satellites' 12, 13, 116, 163, 227, 249
  as start of history 8
  study of 10–16, 249–51
  symbolism of book form 5
  use of 4
  see also GDB; LDB
Domesday Book Rebound 192
Domesday inquest:
  circuits 124–8
  copying of records of 4, 8
  descriptio 2, 49, 68, 94, 243, 246
  endorsement of records by hundred 144
  evidence of landholders 141–4
  fiscal concerns 14, 132–40, 230–8
  juries and jurors 120–2
  local sessions 119, 128–36, 145
  number of participants 122–3
  organization of 117–20
  reception of 2–3, 9
  regional sessions 127, 140–6
  use of adminstrative documents 13
  use of schedules 146
  see also inquest; inquisitio geldi
Domesday Monachorum A 110, 136, 137,
  167 n.
Domesday Monachorum B 110, 124, 137, 139,
  140, 174 n., 206
Dorchester on Thames (Oxon) 20
Dorchester, bishop of 83, 162 n.
  diocese of 20
  see also Wulfwige
Dover (Kent) 238
  burgesses of 118
  GDB account of 113

Dover, St Martin's of:
  breve of 158, 206
  estates of 113
  master of 113
Doveridge (Derby.) 36
Dowdyke (Lincs.) 103
Down, East (Devon) 97
Dowsby (Lincs.):
  manor of 36
Drayton (Lincs.) 67, 83, 167
Drayton (Staffs.) 88 n.
drengage 40, 43, 213
drengs 40, 182, 189, 213, 214
Driffield (Yorks.) 213
Drogo de Beuvrière 21, 119, 167
  Yorks. lands of 85
Drogo son of Mauger 207
Dudestan Hundred (Ches.):
  record of churches in 176
Dudley (Worcs.):
  castlery of 25
Duntisbourne (Gloucs.) 136
Durand Malet 38
Durham (Dur) 245
Durham, bishop of 245
  diocese of 245
Durham, County 220
  omission from GDB 220–1
Durham, St Cuthbert's:
  MSS from 73
  scriptorium of 73, 113, 245
  see also Turgot, prior of

Eadgytha, widow of Hemming 21
Earsham Hundred (Norf.) 179 and n.
Easter, High (Essex) 23
Easton (Beds.) 29
Eastrey Lathe (Kent) 118
Edeva the Fair 27, 31, 131 n., 204
Edith, Queen 42, 128, 207 n.
  lands of 207
Edmer Ator 155
Ednaston (Derby.) 36
Edric 38, 152
Edward I, King 49, 54, 186, 225
Edward of Salisbury, Sheriff of Wiltshire 47,
  232
Edward the Confessor, King 64, 230, 238
Edward the Elder, King 66, 251
Edwin, Earl 22, 37
Eggardon Hundred (Dorset):
  geld collectors in 149
Egmere (Norf.) 240
Eirikr 30
Elborough (Somerset) 185
Elfin 43
Ellington (Hunts.) 157 n.

Elloe Wapentake (Lincs.) 147, 176 n.
  churches in 176
  entry forms of 82
Elmington (Northants.) 104
Elsworth (Cambs.) 152
Elton (Hunts.) 157 n., 215 n.
Ely (Cambs.) 167
  two hundreds of (Cambs.) 79
Ely A 112, 142
Ely Abbey 23, 31, 43, 46, 47, 106, 111, 142, 246
  abbot of 30, 106, 153, 162 n.
  breve abbatis of 111
  claims in Essex 167
  Essex lands 181
  Hunts. lands 190, 216, 174
  land pleas of 100
  thegnlands and sokelands of 32, 111
  see also Symeon, Thurstan, abbots of
Ely B 142
Ely C 111, 146
Ely D 106, 167, 167 n.
  lands in Essex 181
Emma, Queen 88
Erchenbald, *see* Rainald son of
Ernuin the Priest 214
Ertald 135
Esch Hundred (Worcs.) 143, 144, 163 n.
  manors in 163
Essex 2
  ploughland in 165
  sheriff of 171
Eu, Count of:
  Sussex breve 206
Eudo the steward 20, 38, 205
  Cambs. tenants of 108
  see also Adam brother of
Eudo son of Spirewic 240
Eustace of Boulogne 238
Eustace, Count 89, 240
Eustace, sheriff of Huntingdon 21, 47, 149, 168
Evesham A 117, 143, 144, 145
Evesham Abbey 111, 144
  abbot of 233 n.
  see also Æthelwig
Evesham F 110, 136
Evesham K 108, 146
Evesham M 108
Evesham P 111, 146, 227
Ewell (Surrey) 59
Excerpta of St Augustine's, Canterbury 139, 140, 174 n.
Exchequer 4, 230, 247
  Receipt of 6
Exestan Hundred (Ches.):
  record of churches in 176
Exeter, church of 1
  cathedral library 94
  see also Osbern, bishop of

Exning (Cambs.) 131
Exon 1, 12, 117
  Bath A and 172–3
  contents 95–6
  description of fees in 96–7
  GDB and 97
  GDB scribe writing in 113–14
  scribes of 95, 130
  summaries in 98, 181
  terre occupate in 97–8
Extract Rolls, *see* inquest of 1274/5
Eynesford Hundred (Norf.) 179
eyre 11, 51, 53, 186, 225, 230, 233
  justices in 147
  procedure of 11, 140–1
Eyton, R. W. 96

Fakenham (Norf.):
  manor of 92
Falsgrave (Yorks.) 214
  soke of 158
Farcet (Hunts.), *see* Thurulf the fisherman of
Farthegn 213
Fawsley Hundred (Northants.) 104
Feering (Essex) 240
Feltwell (Norf.) 30
Fenkel 35
Fenton (Notts.) 36
Fiacc 34
Finborough (Suff.) 94
Fincham (Norf.) 92
fiscal tenements 156–7
Fishborough Hundred (Worcs.) 111, 143
Fiskerton (Lincs.) 157
Fladbury (Worcs.) 58
  manor of 82, 219
Fleming, R. 14, 15, 27, 28, 30, 35
Flendish Hundred (Cambs.) 79
Flintshire 119
foddercorn 41
foldsoke 29 n.
Folkingham (Lincs.)
  soke of 214
food rents 32, 41, 57, 212
Fordingbridge Hundred (Hants)
    122
forest 54
forfeitures:
  after Hastings 19
Foulden (Norf.) 178
Fowlmere (Cambs.) 188
Foxton (Cambs.) 188
France 69
  inquest in 54
frankpledge 30, 44, 56
Frederic 240
Frome hundreds (Somerset) 172
Froxton (Cornwall) 134

Fulbourn (Cambs.) 31
Fulham (Middlesex) 156

Galbraith, V. H. 12, 13, 113, 114, 133, 135, 141,
    177, 179, 188, 192, 222, 224, 247, 249, 250
Gamlingay (Cambs.):
    manor of 205
Gartree Wapentake (Lincs.) 105
GDB:
    additions to 74–6
    author of 113, 114, 245–7
    binding sequence 73
    correcting scribe 73
    corrections 74
    date of 87–8, 243–4
    demesne livestock omitted 190
    diplomatic forms 80–1, 191–211
    duplication of entries 46–7
    entry formation 82, 145–6
    forms and content 72–89
    hundredal order 12, 79–80
    IE prologue and 116, 171
    LDB, diplomatic links with 221–3
    lists of tenants-in-chief 189
    main scribe 73, 113–14
    manor in 80–1, 211–20
    organization of text 76–82
    presentments in 83, 138
    ruling patterns 191–4
    subtenants in 78–9
    tenants in 189–90, 190, 229
    villar order 80
    see also Domesday Book
geld 156
    accounts 66, 228
    collectors of 149
    Danegeld and 218
    defines freedom 63
    extention to demesne 235–8
    scope of 58–9
    service and 242
geneat:
    services of 31 n.
Geoffrey Alselin 135
Geoffrey de la Guerche 21, 174, 219
Geoffrey de Mandeville 20, 36, 38, 166
    honour of 23
    lands of 19
    see also Asgar the staller, predecessor
Geoffrey, bishop of Coutances 130, 185, 207, 244
    breve in Devon 130
Gerbod the Fleming 21, 22
Gereburg Wapentake, (Yorks.) 85 n.
Germany:
    inquest in 54
Gidding (Hunts.) 22, 214
Gilbert 135
Gilbert de Clifton 147

Gilbert de Gant 37
Gildberg:
    Four Shires Stone in 127
Gilling Wapentake (Yorks.) 86
Gimingham (Norf.) 240
Glapthorn (Northants.) 102, 104
Glastonbury (Somerset) 143
Glastonbury Abbey 165 n., 185
    abbot of 181, 185, 185
    Somerset lands 143
    Worcs. and Somerset breves of 146
    see also Thurstan, Abbot of
Gloucester (Gloucs.) 1, 3, 12, 69, 108, 114, 132,
    224, 230, 242, 250
Gloucestershire:
    hidation of 61
    Monmouthshire in GDB account of 119
    ploughland in 163
    sheriff of 171
    terra regis of 131
Gocelin son of Lambert 121
Godbold 189
Godiva, Countess 33 n.
Godlamb 190
Godmanchester (Hunts.) 215
Godric 26, 203
Godric brother of Godwin 155
Godric the sheriff 20, 83
Godwin 157
Godwin, Earl 238
Godwine 25, 34
    see also Sighvatr, Fenkel, Alnoth, and Asketill,
        sons of
Gonalston (Notts.) 214
Good Soldier Švejk 17
Gos 162 n.
Gosberton (Lincs.) 33, 167
Goxhill (Lincs.) 160
Graffoe Wapentake (Lincs.) 176 n.
Grafham (Hunts.) 22
grand assize 51
Grantham (Lincs.):
    manor of 75, 213 n.
    soke of 215 n.
Graveley (Cambs.) 157 n.
Gravesend Hundred (Northants.) 104
Greenhoe Hundred, North (Norf.) 179
Greenhoe Hundred, South (Norf.) 179
    values in 179
Greetham (Lincs.) 33
Gullick, M. 191
Gurlyn (Cornwall) 66
Guthlac Roll 104
Guthrothr 135
Guy de Craon 33, 36, 167
    see also Æthelstan, predecessor
Guy de Reinbudcurt 108
    lands of 111

Gwynned 119
Gyrth:
    sokeman of 92

Haddon, West (Northants) 81
Haldane 37
Haldane, subdeacon 103 n.
Halfdan and his brothers 26
Hallikeld Wapentake (Yorks.) 86
Hallington (Lincs.) 104
Hamestan Hundred (Ches.) 176
    record of churches in 176
Hamfordshoe Hundred (Northants.) 103
Hampshire:
    assessment in C12 237
    Isle of Wight in GDB account of 120
    jurors of 45
    New Forest in GDB account of 120
Hang Wapentake (Yorks.) 86
Hankham (Sussex):
    manor of 141
Hardwin of Scales 23, 110, 155
    Cambs. breve 79
    lands of 111, 167
Hargrave (Hunts.) 22
Harold 34
Harold, Earl 30
Harrying of the North 158, 212, 214
Hart, C. R. 150
Hartley Mauditt (Hants.) 47
Harvey, S. P. J. 13, 14, 18, 65, 113, 114, 133, 150, 245, 250
Hastings (Sussex):
    battle of 19, 20
    omssion of Domesday account of 75
    rape of 21
Hatley St George (Cambs.) 190 n.
Haverstoe Wapentake (Lincs.) 105
Hayling Island (Hants) 88
Haythby (Lincs.) 217
Headington (Oxon.) 132
Heming's Cartulary 8 n.
Hemingford (Hunts.) 157 n.
    see also Boga of
Hemingr 26
Hemming 63
Hemming, monk of Worcester 143
Henry de Braybrooke 108
Henry de Ferrers 28, 36, 42, 139, 144
    lands of 20
Henry I, King 138, 237
    coronation charter 237, 239
Henry III, King 54
Henry of Huntingdon 9
Henry, bishop of Winchester 10
Henstead Hundred (Norf.) 179 and n.
Hepmangrove (Hunts.), see Wulfgeat the
    fisherman of

Hereford (Here) 219
Hereford, bishop of 44
    men of 141
    see also Robert Losinga, Walter
Hereford, church of
    canons of 209, 219 n.
Herefordshire 21
    ploughland in 163
    render of farm in 131
    Welsh lands in GDB account of 119
Hereward 157
Hereward (the Wake) 104 n.
Herfrith 240
heriot 239
Hertfordshire:
    jurors 121
Hervey of Bourges:
    manor of 178
Hickling (Notts.) 32
hidage 41–2
hidation 58–62
    assessment of 60, 64
    beneficial 15, 61–3, 235
    five-hide unit 61–2
    ploughland and 156–8
Higham, N. 15, 150
Highway (Wilts.) 81
Highworth Hundred (Wilts.) 134
Hildersham (Cambs.) 218 n.
Hinton, Cherry (Cambs.):
    manor of 31
Hinton, Piddle (Dorset) 96 n.
Historia Croylandensis 59, 101
hlaford 29, 30, 33
Hodnet Hundred (Salop.):
    measurement of woodland in 176
Holbeach (Lincs.) 46
Holderness (Yorks.) 21, 43, 85, 119
Holland (Lincs.) 62
    men of 65, 103 n.
    ploughland in 160
Holt, J. C. 13, 14, 15
Holywell (Hunts.) 157, 158
Honiton (Devon) 130
Hope (Derby.):
    manor of 214 n.
Houghton (Hunts.) 157 n.
Howden (Yorks.) 136
    soke of 195
Howdenshire (Yorks.) 213
Hugh Bigod 225
Hugh de Grandmesnil 244
Hugh de Montfort 240
Hugh de Port 122, 240
Hugh of Avranches, earl of Chester 21, 22, 33, 89, 104, 120, 135, 138, 141
Hugh son of Baldric 135
    lands of 85

Humphrey de Tilleul 21
hundred:
   12-carucate 56, 59, 62, 82, 122, 128, 138, 145,
      162, 174, 183, 187 n.
   functions of 58
Hundred Rolls Inquest, *see* inquest of 1279/80
Hunef 162 n.
Hunmanby (Yorks.):
   manor of 200 n.
Huntingdon (Hunts.) 66, 162 n.
Huntingdonshire:
   fen 64
   hidation of 61
   royal estates of 22
Hunworth (Norf.) 92
Hurstingstone Hundred (Hunts.) 65, 152, 153
Huttoft (Lincs.) 33
Hutton (Somerset) 185
Hyams, P. 13

ICC 1, 11, 13, 72, 108, 109
   circuit report 173
   diplomatic of 174–5
   form and content 98
   GDB and 99
IE 72, 117
   forms and content 100–1
   GDB and LDB and 100–1, 116
   ploughland in 165
   prologue 114–17, 171
   sources 100–1
   summaries in 181
Ilbert de Lacy 86
Impington (Cambs.) 23
inbreviation 142, 172–3, 181, 184, 228
Ingoldsby (Lincs.) 25
Ingulf, abbot of Crowland 59, 101, 105
inland 24, 154–5, 213 n., 235, 237 n.
   geld of tenants of 162 n.
   in Lincs. and Yorks. 154 and n.
   in the Northants. Geld Roll 154 and n.
   in Salop. 154 n.
   in Staffs. and Derby. 154 n.
inquest 49–70
   fiscal before Conquest 64
   in C12 and C13 49–50, 52, 54
   in Europe 54–5
   in pre-Conquest Danelaw 55–6
   procedure of 11, 117
   use in disputes over land before Conquest 64
   verdicts of 50–4, 169–70
   see also Domesday inquest
inquest *de Dominabus* of 1185 186
inquest of 1258 53, 147, 225
inquest of 1274–5 6, 53, 71, 121, 170, 186, 225–6
   articles of 148
   Cambs. records 170
   Devon records of 170

Essex records of 170
Extract Rolls of 225
inquest of 1279/80 71, 186, 225
   rolls of 53, 170
inquest of carucage of 1198 52–3, 148
inquest of regalia of 1255 53, 54
   articles of 148
   rolls of 170, 187
inquest of regalia of 1274 147
inquest of scutage of 1212 53, 54
   Lancashire roll 52
inquest of scutage of 1242/3 53–4, 187
inquest of sergeancies of 1250 53
inquest of sheriffs of 1170 52–3, 169
inquisitio geldi 69, 96, 96 n., 128, 133–9, 145,
   146, 151, 162, 167, 171, 172, 188, 228,
   234
   impact on tenant-in-chief 234, 235
   records of 136–40
   see also Domesday inquest
Instituta Cnuti 33
intermarriage 21, 24–5
invasiones 22, 89, 93–4, 98, 106, 167, 184, 185,
   222, 229
   of William de Partenay 185
   scale of 23–4
Ipswich (Suff.) 132
Ireland 9
Isham (Northants.) 22, 168
Isle of Wight 77, 120, 238
Isleham (Cambs.) 218 n.
Ivo Taillebois 105

Jaulfr, predecessor of Ralph de Brimou 104
John of Peterborough, chronicle of 247
John son of Waleran 112 and n.
Judael of Totnes 134
judges of Chester 121
Judith, Countess 135
juries and jurors 49–50, 120–2
   function of 11
   verdicts 50–4

Kalendar of Abbot Samson 41
Karli 34, 200 n.
Keisby (Lincs.):
   manor of 36
Kempsey (Worcs.):
   manor of 219
Kenilworth (Warks.) 81
Kent 21, 238
   ploughland in 158
Kentish Assessment List 108–10, 146, 180
Kesteven 36, 62
   clamores of 65
   ploughland in 160
Ketilbjorn 135, 189, 200 n.
   Lincs. lands of 189 n.

Keynsham (Somerset):
    king's manor of 130, 220
Keynsham Hundred (Somerset) 172
Kilsby (Northants) 81
king's thegn 34
    services of 34–5, 40–2
    tenure by book 34
Kingsdelf (Hunts.) 64
Kingston (Cambs.):
    manor of 99
Kinoulton (Notts.) 32
Kinver (Staffs) 44 n.
Kinwardstone Hundred (Wilts.):
    geld collectors in 149
Kirby Wiske (Yorks.) 180 n.
Kirkby La Thorpe (Lincs.) 102
Kirkby Underwood (Lincs.) 36
Kirtlington (Oxon.) 132
Knapton (Norf.) 240
Knaresborough (Yorks.) 74 n.
knight fee 42
    size of in north 43
    service of 70
    see also *servitium debitum*
knights of the shire 121
    see also *milites inquisitores*
knights, household 43–4
Kolgrimr 189

labour services 212
Lambert of Wheathill 134
Lancashire 77, 119, 163
Lancaster (Lancs.):
    honour of 45
landhlaford 29, 33
Landmoth (Yorks.) 180 n.
Laneham (Notts.):
    manor of 32
Lanfranc, archbishop of Canterbury 3, 71, 124, 142
Langbargh Wapentake (Yorks.) 85
Laughton (Sussex) 157
Laughton-en-le-Morthen (Yorks.) 37
Lavington, Little (Lincs.):
    manor of 36
lawmen 121
Laythorpe (Lincs.) 102
LDB:
    colophon 89, 94, 177, 221, 243
    date of 94, 243–4
    diplomatic forms 92
    entry formation 93
    GDB, diplomatic links with 222–3
    hundredal order in 91
    IE prologue and 100–1, 116
    organization of text 89–93
    ploughland in 163–5

scribes of 89, 177
sources of 177–9
villar order in 91
    see also Domesday Book
leases 23
Ledforda' (Somerset) 97
Lefsi Crevleta 64
Lefstan Herlepic of Whittlesey 64
legati 13, 123, 123 n., 147, 166
    see also commissioners; barones
Leges Edwardi Confessoris 44, 237
Leges Henrici 45
Leicestershire:
    king's thegns of 38
    ploughland in 149, 151, 158, 210
    terra regis 210
Leicestershire Survey 52, 151, 187, 236
Leighton Bromswold (Hunts.) 20
Leintwardine Hundred (Salop.):
    measurement of woodland 176
Leis Willelme 44, 239
Leofnoth 128
    predecessor of Ralph fitz Hubert 37
Leofric, predecessor of Ralph fitz Hubert 37
Leofric 26, 157
Leofric son of Leofwin 21
Leofwin 21, 162 n.
Leofwin le Savage 157
Leominster (Hereford.) 231
    manor of 218, 219 n.
Levellers 10
Leverton (Notts.) 32
Lewes (Sussex):
    rape of 21
    exchange of 91
Lewis, C. P. 180 n.
Lewknor Hundred (Oxon.):
    suit to 242
Leyland Hundred (Lancs.) 180
Liber Eliensis 31, 66
Limington (Somerset) 185
Lincoln (Lincs.), City of 20, 75, 195, 231
    church of St Laurence of 135
    geld account of 135
    inland in 154
    lawmen of 121
    little manor outside West Gate of 240
    see also Agmundr son of Valhrafn, lawman of
Lincoln, bishop of:
    lands 142
    see also Remigius
Lincoln, earl of:
    bailiffs of 147
Lincoln, St Mary of 135
Lincolnshire:
    carucation of 62
    customs of 231

ploughland in 160
Roteland entries in 127
sheriff of 20
Lindsey, South Riding
   clamores of 83
Lindsey 62
   clamores of 50, 83
   customs of 231
   North Riding 30, 105
   ploughland in 160
   South Riding 33, 50, 105
Lindsey Survey 52, 104, 105, 151, 187, 236, 242 n.
Lisois de Moutiers 38
loanland 23
local government:
   development of 57–8
Loddon Hundred (Norf.) 179 and n.
Lolworth (Cambs.) 23
London 64
   omission of Domesday account of 75
   reeve of 64
London, bishop of 64, 204, 247
London, St Paul's, *see* Sired, canon of
Longdendale (Derby.) 214 n.
Longley, T. 62 n.
Longstow Hundred (Cambs.) 79, 80, 190 n.
Longstowe (Cambs.) 190 n.
Longtree Hundred (Gloucs.) 141
lordship and land 26–7, 31–2
Losoard 135
Loveden Wapentake (Lincs.):
   churches and priests in 176
Loyn, H. R. 230 n.
Luddington (Hunts.) 22
Lythe Wapentake (Notts.) 28

Madingley (Cambs.) 23
Magna Carta 7
Maine 9
Maitland, F. W. 12, 15, 54, 55, 56, 149, 164, 218, 224
Malmesbury (Wilts.), church of 81, 247
Manasses the cook 96
Maneshou Wapentake (Yorks.) 85
manor:
   capital 36, 44
   court of 56–7
   and land in Cambs. 217–18, 218 n., 220 n.
   in north 195, 199, 211–16
   numbers of in summaries 182
   pro manerio formula 219–20
   and service 239–41
   and soke 213, 218
   in south and west 204–5, 208, 211, 216–20
Mareham-on-the-Hill (Lincs.) 34
Margaret 157 n.
Marham (Norf.) 92

Marianus Scotus, Universal History of 3 n., 9
Martinsley Wapentake (Rutland) 128, 162
Martley (Suff.) 178
Martley (Worcs.) 131
Mashbury (Essex) 166
Matilda, Queen 109, 127, 128, 138
Matthew Paris 10
measurement:
   vills 190 n.
   woodland 125, 176
Meldreth (Cambs.) 108 n.
Mellis (Suff.):
   manor of 92
Melton Mowbray (Leics.):
   manor of 219
Membury (Devon) 130
mercenaries 14, 15, 69, 70, 234, 238, 239
Mercia 57
Merton (Devon) 97
milites inquisitores 52, 117, 170
mill soke 140 n.
Molton, North (Devon) 97
Monmouthshire 119
Moore, J. S. 150
Morcar 215 n.
Morcar, Earl 167
   estates in Lincs. 40
Morden, Guilden (Cambs.) 127
Morden, Steeple (Cambs.) 110
Mortain, Count Robert of, *see* Robert of Mortain
Mortain, Notre-Dame of 96 n., 188 n.

Navisland Hundred (Northants.) 102
Ness Wapentake (Lincs.) 176 n.
New Forest 77, 120
Newark Wapentake (Notts.) 33 n.
Newton Hundred (Lancs.) 180
Nigel, servant of Count Robert of Mortain 141
Nigel Fossard 30
Nomina Villarum 123
Norfolk 2
   ploughland in 165
Norman Crassus 135
Norman settlement 19–28
Normancross Hundred (Hunts.) 61
Normandy 1, 9, 55, 69, 88, 234, 238
Normanitas ix, 251
Northallerton (Yorks.) 136
   manor of 180 n.
Northampton (Northants.) 159
   3,200 hides of 61
   32 hundreds of 61
   shire court at 168
Northamptonshire:
   ploughland in 159
   reduction of hidation of 61
   terra regis of 210

Northamptonshire Geld Roll 70, 103, 154
Northamptonshire Survey 52, 104, 110, 151, 187, 226, 236
Northorpe (Lincs.) 214
Northstow Hundred (Cambs.) 79, 98
Northumbria 57
  earl of 127
Northwick (Worcs.):
  capital manor of 36, 219
Norton, Blo (Norf.) 111
Norwich (Norf.) 132
Nottingham (Notts.) 161, 191
  comital estates around 40
  sheriff of 120, 127
  sheriffdom of 128
  shire court 127
Nottinghamshire:
  Basset estates in 8
  carucation of 62
  English undertenants in 43
  ploughland in 161–2
  Roteland appended to GDB account of 120
  sokes of 145
Nuneham Courtenay (Oxon.) 156
Nuthall (Notts.) 42
Nympton (Devon) 97

Oakham (Rutland) 128, 200 n.
Oakington (Cambs.) 23
Oakley (Bucks.) 83
Odger the Breton:
  Lincs. breve 102
Odin the chamberlain 96
Odo of Bayeux 21, 89, 109, 154, 244
  lands in Worcs. 111
Odo the arblaster 189
Oger the Breton 104
Okeover (Staffs.):
  ploughlands of 152
Onibury (Salop.) 44
Orderic Vitalis 113, 119, 239, 245, 246
Ordmer 99
'original returns' 171, 249
  see also return; seigneurial presentment
Orsett (Essex) 240
Orton (Hunts.) 22
Osbern de Arches 213
Osbern, bishop of Exeter 138
Osbournby (Lincs.) 32 n.
Osfram 36
Osmaston by Derby (Derby.) 42, 139
Osmondiston (Norf.) 164 n.
Osmund, bishop of Salisbury:
  Domesday commissioner 124
Oswaldbeck (Notts.):
  soke of 31, 37
Oswaldbeck Wapentake (Notts.) 28, 37, 215 n.

Oswaldslow Hundred (Worcs.) 32, 103 n., 163 n., 219
Outwell (Norf.) 92
Overbury (Worcs.):
  manor of 219
overlordship before the Conquest 26–7
Overs Hundred (Salop.):
  measurement of woodland in 176
'overstocking' 150–1, 155
Oxford (Oxon):
  borough renders 231
Oxford, St Frideswide of 247
Oxfordshire:
  hidation of 61
  increment of the farm of 232
  renders of 231
  terra regis in 210

Padstow (Cornwall) 162
Palmer, J. 217
Panfield (Essex) 163, 164
Papworth Hundred (Cambs.) 79
parage 26, 31 n., 35, 44
parliament 251
partible inheritance 31
Patton Hundred (Salop.):
  measurement of woodland in 176
Peakirk (Northants.) 102, 103, 104
Pendrim (Cornwall) 134
Percy:
  barony of 23
Pershore (Worcs.):
  manor of 81
  two hundreds of 143, 144
Peter de Valognes 135
Peter, bishop of Chester 96
Peterborough Abbey 33 n., 103 n., 142, 145, 157, 226 n.
  abbot of 135
  arrangement of lands in GDB 78
  Lincs. breve 26, 217
  Lincs. lands 137–8, 145
  see also Brand, abbot of
Pevensey (Sussex):
  rape of 21
Pickering (Yorks.) 155
Picot, sheriff of Cambridge 23, 118, 141 n., 149
  Cambs. tenants of 108
  lands 111, 165 n.
Pilsley (Hunts.) 215
Pinchbeck (Lincs.) 102
Pipe Roll of 1129/30 236
plogsland 60
ploughland 14, 18, 53, 60, 98, 106, 149–65, 182, 206, 228, 229, 231, 235, 236, 241, 245, 251
  in Burton surveys 152, 155 n.
  geld and 151, 236, 241

LDB and 163–5
  in Leicestershire 158–9, 210
  nominalist view of 149–50
  in north 160–3
  in Northants. 159–60
  'overstocking' 150–1, 155
  ploughs and 158–9, 163–5
  realist view of 149–50
  in Shropshire 163, 209
  summaries and 182–3, 236
  in Worcestershire 163, 208
ploughs 240
  ploughland and 158–9
  pre-Conquest 60, 149–50, 158–9
polyptych surveys 55
Provisions of Oxford 53, 225
Pyrford (Surrey):
  manor of 88
Pyrton Hundred (Oxon.) 242
Pytchley (Northants.) 110 n.

Quadring (Lincs.) 65
Quo Warranto proceedings 13
Quy (Cambs.) 218 n.

Radfield Hundred (Cambs.) 79
radknights 31 and n., 40
Ragman inquest, see inquest of 1274/5
Rainald son of Erchenbald 188
Rainer de Brimou:
  predecessor Jaulr 104
Ralph de Bapaume 135
Ralph fitz Hubert 37
  see also Leofnoth, Leofric, predecessors
Ralph Guader, Earl 65
Ralph of Pomeroy 130
Ralph Pagenel 33 n., 135
Ralph Taillebois 29
Ralph the staller 33–4
  predecessor of Count Alan 33
Rampton (Cambs.) 218 n.
Ramsey Abbey 22, 32, 64, 84, 152, 168, 246
  abbot of 64, 65, 67, 83, 162 n., 168
  demesnes 155
  estates 155, 157
  see also Æthelsige, abbot of
Rannulf Flambard 113, 245–7
Ranskill (Notts.) 203
Rawridge (Devon) 130
rebellion of 1088 246
recognition 11, 47, 50, 51, 52, 57, 66
Rectitudines Singularum Personarum 31 n., 60
Red Book of the Exchequer 186, 247
Reginald son of Orgar 157
Reid, R. R. 45
Reigate (Surrey) 59
Reinald son of Hagenilde 157

Reinbald 96, 97
relief 35, 35 n., 40, 44, 213, 229, 232, 233, 239,
  243
Remigius, bishop of Lincoln 67, 83, 135, 144
  Domesday commissioner 123
return 12, 67, 68, 134, 142 n., 169, 250
  see also 'original return'; seigneurial
    presentment
Reweset Hundred (Salop.):
  measurement of woodland in 176
Ribble and Mersey 40, 45, 77, 98, 120, 180, 182,
  209, 213
  six hundreds of 131
Richard fitz Neal 5, 10
Richard I, King 52
Richard Iuvenis 21
Richard son of Count Gilbert 38
Richard son of Thorolf 134
Richmond (Yorks.):
  castlery of 85, 86, 119, 180–1
Richmondshire (Yorks.) 21, 180
Rinlau Hundred (Salop.):
  measurement of woodland in 176
Ripon (Yorks.):
  soke of 195
Rippingale (Lincs.) 102, 104
Ripple (Worcs.):
  manor of 219
Ripton, Abbot's (Hunts.) 215 n.
Risby (Lincs.) 160
Riseton Hundred (Ches.):
  record of churches in 176
Robert 157
Robert Curthose 237
Robert d'Oilly 20, 21
Robert de Brus:
  GDB breve of 73, 195
Robert de Bucy 188
Robert de Mowbray 244
Robert Gernon 123, 136
Robert Losinga, bishop of Hereford 2, 3, 9, 69,
  71, 118, 123, 135, 145, 151, 235, 241
Robert Malet 25, 26, 38, 89, 142
  see also Atsurr son of Svala, predecessor
Robert of Flanders, Count 69
Robert of Mortain, Count 21, 66, 78, 89, 130,
  134, 135, 141, 155, 165 n., 194, 213
  summary of 182
  Yorks. breve of 26
  Yorks. fee of 85, 86
  see also Nigel, servant of
Robert son of Gerold:
  summary of 182 n., 183
Robert son of Wymarc 29
  see also Brungar, man of
Robert the bursar 34
  Leics. breve 210

Robert the knight 157 n.
Rochester, bishop of 137
Roelau Hundred (Ches.):
  record of church in 176
Roger Bigod 89, 244
  sokemen of 111
Roger de Bully 28, 37
  honour of 37
Roger de Courseulles 185
Roger de Lacy 44, 46, 244
Roger de Stanton 220
Roger of Auberville 94
Roger of Hoveden 52, 148
Roger of Montgomery 21, 244
  demesne in Salop. 176 n.
Roger son of Ralph 141
Roger the Poitevin 45, 88 n., 89, 180, 221
  Yorks. breve 87
  Yorks. lands 85
Roger, Earl 110
Romanby (Yorks.) 180 n.
Roteland 77, 120, 135, 140, 183
  assessment in C12 236
  GDB accounts of 125, 127, 128, 129, 174
  ploughland in 153, 161
  soke of 42, 128, 139
Rotuli de Dominabus 186
  see also inquest *de Dominabus*
Rouen:
  church of St Mary of 130
Round, J. H. 11–13, 18, 41, 60, 61, 114, 140, 144,
    150, 177 n., 186, 217, 222, 224, 249, 250
royal demesne, see *terra regis*
royal fisc:
  administration of 230–4
  sources of income 230–4
Rumble, A. R. 177
Rushall (Wilts.):
  royal manor of 134
Rushcliffe Wapentake (Notts.) 28
Ruskington (Lincs.):
  soke of 160
Rutland, see *Roteland*

'S', commissioner 3, 71
St Petroc, church of 162 n.
sake and soke 22, 26, 32–6, 38, 42, 44–6, 78,
    121, 133, 139, 162, 211, 212, 215, 215 n., 232,
    233
  in East Anglia 33 n.
  honours and 35–6
  render of 33 n.
Salford Hundred (Lancs.) 180
Salisbury (Wilts.) 238
  meeting at 13, 227, 238, 239, 240, 241, 242,
    244, 250
  Oath of 13

Salisbury, church of:
  scriptorium 94 n.
Salisbury, bishop of 247
  see also Osmund
Samson the chaplain, bishop of Worcester 247
  Domesday Book and 113
Sandlings (Kent) 206 n.
Sawcliffe (Lincs.) 160
Sawtry (Hunts.) 22
Sawyer, P. H. 27, 30, 37, 174, 177 n.
Saxon Street (Cambs.) 218 n.
Saxthorpe (Norf.) 92
schedule 228
  diplomatic forms of GDB derived from 219
  of disputes 165–6
  forms and content 106–12
  GDB and 108–12
  orthography of 106
Scotland 9
Scots, king of 220
Scrivelsby (Lincs.):
  manor of 34
scutage inquest, *see* inquest of scutage of 1212,
    1242/3
seigneurial presentment 140–6
  bishop of Worcester's 143, 208, 219
  see also Bath A
sergeancies 43, 186, 232
  see also inquest of sergeancies
Serlo de Buci 96
servitium debitum 42, 43, 239, 241
Shelfanger (Norf.) 19
Shellow Bowells (Essex) 164 n.
sheriff:
  acquisition of land by 21–2
  aid 41
  removal of before inquest 147–8
  role in inquest 117–18
ship soke 179 n.
Shipton-under-Wychwood (Oxon.) 132
shire court:
  forum of Domesday inquest 119, 128–36, 145
  functions of 57–8
Shropshire 21
  ploughland in 163, 209
Sicily 67
Sidestrand (Norf.) 240
Sighvatr 35
Sired, canon of St Paul's, London 205 n.
Siward 26, 34
Siward Barn 20
  under-tenants of 20 n.
Siward, Earl 162 n.
Skipton (Yorks.):
  honour of 23
Skirbeck Wapentake (Lincs.) 83, 147
  jurors of 67

Skyrack Wapentake (Yorks.) 85 n.
Slaughter, Lower (Gloucs.) 231
slaves 97, 98, 112, 114, 153, 163, 181, 182, 190,
    191, 216, 223
Sleaford (Lincs) 20
    hundred of 56
    see also Bardi, lord of
Small House at Allington 7
Smallridge (Devon) 130
Smeaton, Great (Yorks.) 180 n.
Smeaton, Little (Yorks.) 180 n.
Smethdon Hundred (Norf.) 179
Snailwell (Cambs.) 23
Snarehill, Little (Norf.) 164
socage tenure 43, 216 n.
Soham (Cambs.) 99
    royal manor of 99
soke 30–2, 34
    jurisdiction 30
    manor and 213, 218
    see also foldsoke; mill soke; *terra*
sokeland 40–1
    service of 33 n.
sokeman 191
    freedom of 32 n.
    services of 215 n.
    tenure of 31–2
Somersham (Hunts.):
    thegnland in 214
Southorpe (Lincs.) 36
Southwell (Notts.) 146
Sowerby under Cotcliffe (Yorks.) 180 n.
Spalding Priory 103 n.
Spaldwick (Hunts.) 153
Staffordshire:
    hidation of 61
    GDB account of 125
Staincliffe Wapentake (Yorks.), *see* Gilbert de
    Clifton, bailiff of
Staine Hundred (Cambs.) 79
Staines, church of 31
Stamford (Lincs.) 75, 132
    borough of 59, 195
    lawmen of 121
    Portland in 76
    West Field of 76
Stanton Drew (Somerset) 220
Stanton Harcourt (Oxon) 154
Stanton near Newhall (Derby.) 44, 213 n.
Stapleford (Cambs.) 218 n.
Staploe Hundred (Cambs.) 79
Statute of the Exchequer 53, 225
Statute of Westminster I 53, 225
Steinchete 152
Stenton, F. M. 25, 28, 150, 160, 213 n., 230 n.
Stepney (Middlesex):
    manor of 204

Stetchworth (Cambs.) 218 n.
Stevington (Beds.):
    manor of 205
Stigand, archbishop of Canterbury 23
Stockingham (Sussex) 157
Stoke Rochford (Lincs.):
    manor of 215 n.
Stoneleigh (Warks.):
    king's manor of 81
Stow Hundred (Suff.) 141
Stow St Mary (Lincs.):
    manor of 142
Strafforth Wapentake (Yorks.) 85
Stretton (in Burton on Trent) (Staffs.) 152
Suckley (Worcs.) 131
Suffolk 2
    ploughland in 165
sulung 60
summaries 165 n., 180–3, 228, 229, 240, 241
    Alan of Brittany's 86, 98, 183
    manors, number of 182
    ploughlands in 182–3, 236
    Robert of Mortain's 182
    Robert son of Gerold's 182 n., 183
surety 29, 34, 56, 237
    see also commendation 29
Surrey:
    assessment in C12 237
Surrey, earl of:
    creation of William de Warenne as 88,
    244
Sussex rapes 22
Sutterton (Lincs.):
    church of 103
Sutton Passeys (Notts.) 80
Svartbrandr 189
    Lincs. lands of 189 n.
Swallow (Lincs.) 160
Swanborough Hundred (Wilts.) 134
Swinehead Hundred (Gloucs.) 141
Swineshead (Hunts.) 22
Symeon of Durham, Libellus of 245
Symeon, abbot of Ely 165 n., 181

taini regis 40, 42, 75, 78, 121, 189, 232
Tait, J. 217
Tanshelf (Yorks.) 86
Tardebrigge (Worcs.) 44 n.
Tathwell (Lincs.):
    soke of 104
Taunton (Somerset) 7, 208
    manor of 227
Tavistock Abbey 166
    abbot of 166
    lands in Cornwall 189
Tealby (Lincs.) 30
Templecombe (Somerset) 113, 247

tenuit formula 34, 38, 93 n., 211, 218 n., 220
Teodbert 135
terra 30–4, 40, 213, 215, 220 n.
  manor and 217–18
  soke and 30–2
terra regis 15, 131, 151, 174, 180, 189, 234
  administration of 230–4
  Cambs. 179
  churches on 87 n.
  diplomatic forms of 131
  Domesday inquest and 128–40, 171–2,
    230–4, 243
  in Exon 130, 179
  farming of 231
  geld free 219 n.
  Herefordshire 208
  issues of 231 n.
  in LDB 179
  Leicestershire 210
  Northamptonshire 210
  northern shires 202 n.
  Oxfordshire 210
  south-west 172
  Yorkshire 222
terra tainorum regis 189
terre occupate 22, 97, 167, 184, 185, 229
Testa de Neville 247
Teversham (Cambs.) 31, 112
Tewkesbury (Gloucs.) 35
thegnage 28, 31, 37, 40, 43, 104, 121, 131, 188,
  213, 214, 232, 240
thegnland 111, 153, 166, 168, 214
  in the Northern Danelaw 213 n.
  Somersham (Hunts.) 214
thegns:
  jurors 121
  median 40 n.
Thetford (Norf.) 132
Thetford, bishop of 91
Thoraldr of Greetwell 135
Thorent (Somerset) 113 n.
Thorir 26
Thorkill of Arden 244
  forfeiture of 88
Thorn, C. and F. 97
Thorney, abbot of 64
Thornfalcon (Somerset):
  manor of 135
Thornton (Lincs.) 34
Thornton le Beans (Yorks.) 180 n.
Thriplow Hundred (Cambs.) 79
throughtoll 37
Thurgarton Wapentake (Notts.) 128
Thurleigh (Beds.) 20
Thurstable Hundred (Essex):
  king's salt houses in 171
Thurstan 66, 88 n.

Thurstan son of Rolf:
  fee in Somerset 36
Thurstan, abbot of Glastonbury 182
Thurstan, abbot of Ely 175
Thurulf the fisherman of Farcet 64
Tickhill (Notts.):
  castlery of 25
  free chapelry of 37
Ticknall (Derby.) 44, 213 n.
Tidenham (Gloucs.) 60
Tiscott (Herts.) 29
tithings 56
Toki 23
tolenea, see throughtoll
toll and team 26, 34, 36, 45, 121, 133, 212, 215 n.
Tonni 213
Tope 66
Tories 10
Torksey (Lincs.) 75
  borough of 195
Toseland Hundred (Hunts.) 153
Tosti, Earl:
  estates in Lincs. 40
Toton (Notts.) 42
Treasury 5, 10, 110, 111, 135, 140, 162, 172
Tredington (Worcs.):
  manor of 219
Trollope, A. 7
Trumpington (Cambs.) 23
Tunendune Hundred (Ches.):
  record of churches in 176
Turgot, prior of Durham 246 n.
Tutbury (Staffs.):
  castlery of 25

Uffculme (Devon) 21
Uggescombe Hundred (Dorset):
  geld collectors in 149
Uggeshall (Suff.) 94
Ulcombe (Kent) 206 n.
Ulf Fenisc 34, 37, 162 n., 200 n.
Ulnod 152
ultimogeniture 216 n.
Upton (Warks.) 81
Uptongreen Hundred (Northants.) 102
Upwell (Norf.) 92
Urse de Abitot 149
Urso 208 n.
Uttlesford Hundred (Essex):
  witness of 123 n.

value 41–2, 44, 139–40
  in Docking Hundred (Norf.) 179
  in Greenhoe Hundred, South (Norf.) 179
ville integre 56
Vinogradoff, P. 150
Vulgate 49 n.

Walcot in Alkborough (Lincs.) 217
Walcot near Threekingham (Lincs.) 217
Wales 2, 9, 77, 153, 209
    GDB account of lands in 77
Wallington Hundred (Surrey) 74
Wallop, Over (Hants.) 240
Walmsley, J. F. R. 155 n.
Walter 135
Walter de Aincurt 26, 37
Walter de Douai 21, 134
Walter de Lacy 46
Walter Giffard, Earl 144
    commissioner 124
Walter, bishop of Hereford 219
Waltheof, Earl 127
Wantage Code 55, 56, 121
wapentake:
    functions of 58
wardpenny 41
Waresley (Hunts.) 22
Warin de Chaucombe 147
warland 152–8, 162, 228, 235–7
    demesne as 153–4, 235
Warminster (Wilts.) 96
Warmundestrou Hundred (Ches.):
    record of church in 176
Warrington Hundred (Lancs.) 180
Warwickshire:
    hidation of 61
Washington (Sussex) 162 n.
Waterbeach (Cambs.) 23
Welbourn (Lincs.):
    manor of 25
Weldon (Northants):
    Basset family of 8
Welldon Finn, R. 38, 97
Wellen (Hunts.), see Ailmer Hogg of
Welsh Marches 21, 244
    ploughland in 152
Welton (Lincs.) 20, 21
Welton by Lincoln (Lincs.) 142
Werrington (Devon):
    manor of 166
Wessex 57
    boroughs of 59
Westbury (Gloucs.) 138
Westmancote (Worcs.) 208 n.
Westminster Abbey 81, 143
    estates in Surrey 88
Weston (Somerset) 101
Weston Colville (Cambs.) 23, 218 n.
Weston, Hail (Hunts.) 22
Weston, Old (Hunts.) 22, 157 n.
Wetherley Hundred (Cambs.) 79
Wetmore (Staffs.) 155
    men of 154
Whaplode (Lincs.) 46

Wharram Percy (Yorks.) 40
Whigs 10
Whitford (Flint.) 153
Whittlesey (Cambs.), see Lefstan Herlepic of
Whittlesford Hundred (Cambs.) 79
    Ragman roll 170
Wick Episcopi (Worcs.):
    manor of 219
Wigod of Wallingford 29
    see also Alditha, daughter
Wilaveston Hundred (Ches.):
    record of churches in 176
Wilbraham (Cambs.) 218 n.
Wilksby (Lincs.) 34
William Cheever 130
William de Braose 45
William de Chatterton, justice 147
William de Chenet 118, 122
William de Eu 244
William de Partenay:
    invasiones of 185
William de St Calais, bishop of Durham 135,
        168, 227, 244–6, 246 n.
    commissioner 124
    Domesday Book and 113
William de St Omer 147
William de Warenne 21, 45, 89, 178, 240, 244
    created earl of Surrey 88
    honour of 23
    lands of Lewes Exchange 91
William fitz Osbern 21
William I, King 1, 2, 10, 13, 19, 88, 227, 238,
        239, 250
    character 9
    lands in Yorks. 86
    reintroduction of Danegeld 233
William II, King 4, 18, 47, 88, 138, 168, 221,
        227, 237, 244
William Maudit 47
William of Cahagnes 168
William of Ecouis 89
William of Malmesbury 244
William Peverel 28, 40, 80
    Notts. estates 37
William Rufus, see William II, King
William son of Ansculf 88 n.
Willington (Derby.) 155, 157
Williton (Somerset):
    royal manor of 98
Willoughby in the Marsh (Lincs.) 36
Wiltshire:
    assessment in C12 236
    geld accounts of 96, 134
    increment of 232
    inquest of 1255 in 187
    jurors of 120
    see also Edward, sheriff of

Winchcombe (Gloucs.) 108, 132
Winchester (Hants.) 172
  omission of Domesday account of 75
Winchester, bishop of 110, 227
  diocese of 246
  Somerset lands 227
  see also Henry
Winchester, New Minster 88
Winchester, Old Minster:
  monks of 122
Winfarthing (Norf.) 231
Winnianton (Cornwall) 130
Winwick (Hunts.) 22
Winwick (Northants):
  manor of 81
Witchley Hundred (Northants.) 76, 128
Witham (Lincs.):
  12-carucate hundred of 145
Witham, South (Lincs.) 127 n.
Withgar 38
Wollaton (Notts.):
  manor of 80
women in GDB 78
Wooburn (Bucks.) 20
woodland:
  in Cheshire 176
Woodstock Code 56
Wootton (Oxon.) 132
Worcester (Worcs.):
  city of 9, 44
Worcester, bishop of 38, 144
  lands of 43, 219
  Worcs. breve of 143, 146, 190 n., 208, 219
  see also Samson; Wulfstan
Worcester, church of 82, 110, 163
  annalist of 4, 5
  cartulary of 8, 63
  demesne of monks of 82
  Gloucs. lands 138
  liberties 103
  men of 32
Worcester, sheriff of 44, 132
  see also Urse de Abitot
Worcester A 110, 136, 138, 167 n.
Worcester B 108

Worcestershire:
  commissioners in 124
  hidation of 61
  1,200 hides of 61
  12 hundreds of 61
  king's manors in 44
  ploughland in 163, 208
Wormald, P. 24, 47, 166, 183, 184
Wramplingham (Norf.) 92
Wrockwardine Hundred (Salop.):
  measurement of woodland in 176
Wulfbert 213
Wulfgeat 20
Wulfgeat the fisherman of Hepmangrove
  64
Wulfmer 130
Wulfmer of Eaton 20
Wulfnoth 66
Wulfric 166
Wulfric Spot 37
Wulfstan, bishop of Worcester 127, 144
Wulfward 130
Wulfwige, bishop of Dorchester 67, 83
Wyton (Hunts.) 157 n.

Yafforth (Yorks.) 180 n.
Yarmouth (Norf.):
  borough of 179 n.
Yatton (Hereford.) 166
York, abbot of 188
York, archbishop of 32, 146, 203
York, church of 121
York (Yorks.), city of 62, 129, 130
  account of 76, 129, 194
  84 carucates of 85, 129, 135, 136, 161, 174,
    183, 194, 195, 223 n.
  lawmen of 121
Yorkshire:
  estates of bishop of Durham in 246
  ploughland in 160–1
Yorkshire Summary 84–6, 119 and n., 136, 180,
    188, 189, 222, 223
  Count Alan's lands in 76
  summary in 86, 98, 180
Youlgreave (Derby.) 42

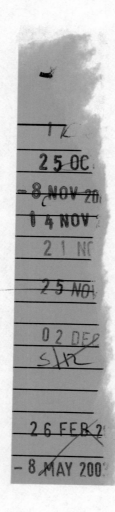